LORD READING AND HIS CASES

THE MACMILLAN COMPANY
NEW YORK · BOSTON · CHICAGO · DALLAS
ATLANTA · SAN FRANCISCO

LORD READING

Reproduced by courtesy of the London
" Evening News."

LORD READING AND HIS CASES: the Study of a Great Career ❦ By DEREK WALKER-SMITH

NEW YORK
THE MACMILLAN COMPANY
1934

AUTHOR'S NOTE

I wish to make it clear that, although I informed Lord Reading of my intentions with regard to this book and have by his courtesy seen him from time to time in the course of its preparation, the book is in no way " inspired " by him; it follows that he does not take responsibility for its contents. The book is primarily an account of the principal cases in which Lord Reading figured prominently as counsel or judge in what is perhaps the most interesting period of his brilliant career. It aims to present a balanced and impartial estimate of the career of a man happily still living, and it would on that account have been clearly impossible to exercise the independent judgment necessary to such a task, if my responsibility for the book had been less complete.

" The life of a great advocate
is a social document "—p. 117.

CONTENTS

xi

CONTENTS

LORD READING AND HIS CASES

CHAPTER I

RUFUS ISAACS, THE MAN

RUFUS DANIEL ISAACS was born on October 10th, 1860. A foreigner, unacquainted with our national habit of cloaking the identity of our distinguished citizens, might perhaps be pardoned for not at once recognizing him in the Marquess of Reading, P.C., G.C.B., G.C.V.O., G.C.S.I., G.C.I.E. And even those, whom a knowledge of our peculiar application of the principle *ars est celare artem* has prepared for these transfigurations, might stand in amazement at the contemplation of the vast and varied fields of achievement which stretch between that cradle and the present day. For the most cursory glance at Rufus Isaac's career reveals two striking characteristics; the magnitude of his successes and the extended front along which they have been achieved. His has been no ordinary ascent, no steady plodding up the careful stages of success, with eyes fixed, eager yet anxious, on the final goal; it has been rather a series of frontal assaults on the heights of attainment, and an easy passage from peak to peak, the conquest of any one of which might be the life ambition of a skilled and daring mountaineer.

"The world still holds glittering prizes for those whose courage is high and whose swords are sharp," said the late Lord Birkenhead in a famous Rectorial address. Attorney-General; Lord Chief Justice; Special Envoy; Ambassador; Viceroy; Secretary of State for Foreign Affairs; all these glittering prizes were gained by one who at fifteen was a cabin-boy and at twenty-five a failure in his chosen profession. It is a very notable illustration of the truth of Lord Birkenhead's virile doctrine. Yet it is not easy to fit Lord Reading to the rôle of apostle of glittering prizes. That his courage is high and his sword is sharp has been

I

proved on various occasions; but he has drawn his sword only when he has had need of it, and, save to draw it, his hand has never been on the hilt. His stamina, too, is of a calm, self-reliant quality, which has not sought expression in words; but it is tempered like true steel, keen and strong and unbreakable. His slim figure, upright and taut still in the seventies, his handsome, chiselled features, his keen eye and lofty forehead, are the embodiment of distinction and intellectual prowess; they are their own passport and need no advertisement. He has, too, a charm of manner which is famous, a charm which consists not so much in a boisterous hail-fellow-well-met camaraderie, as in a quieter and more insinuating form. It won him considerable and instantaneous popularity among those who came into contact with him at the Bar or in politics, in America or in India, which was yielded to him almost without reluctance even by those to whom his political principles and his race were alike anathema. The possessor of such qualities found that he did not need to assess his qualities or his services in terms of glittering prizes; he merely smiled his way unscathed through life, to be crowned with one of the most richly jewelled diadems of attainment that have adorned the brow of any Englishman of this generation. He did not need to make claims for himself; he was promoted to high office because he was a man of ability, who had succeeded. Success breeds success, and, what is just as important, a universal recognition of ability. So it has been with Lord Reading. *Omnium consensu capax imperii.*

It would be wrong to assume from this that Lord Reading achieved his career without the prick of ambition. For ambition, in one sense, is merely the spur which gives directive energy to a man's abilities, and the curb which keeps him to the steady pursuit of things significant and saves him from that dissipation of energies which is the mark of the dilettante. With this sort of ambition Lord Reading was well endowed. Lady Oxford, whose opinion is entitled to respect as one who for half-a-century has had an intimate knowledge of men and affairs, has placed it on record that Lord Reading is one of the four most ambitious men of her acquaintance. If she uses the word in the rather colourless sense indicated above, then the view is clearly unexceptionable; but if she uses the word in any more technical sense her opinion challenges analysis and question. What of ambition in this, the vulgar, sense? It is fairly clear that Rufus Isaacs never pursued a single goal of attainment, to which he directed all effort and subordinated all activity. He was rather, in a sense, an opportunist, determined to develop and to exploit his abilities, and anxious to find the best field for their exercise. This involved experiment and empiricism, and as such was agreeable to an adventurous nature, which loved variety and liked better to operate in a wide and generous sphere than to follow the straitened path of a single ambition. Every phase of his life illustrates the truth of this. As a boy he ran away to sea, instead of winning the scholarships which are the more conventional prelude to the Woolsack; the law itself, the practice of which was to bring him much wealth and distinction, was adopted as a second choice at the age of twenty-seven. At the age of forty-nine, by becoming a law officer of the Crown, he cut himself off from the immensely lucrative practice of his profession, and less than four years later, after being in politics for scarcely ten years, he denied himself the opportunity of further political advancement by accepting the office of Lord Chief Justice. In the prime of active life, that is to say, with the spirit of adventurous ambition still strong within him, he condemned himself to all appearances to a lifetime in the honourable, useful and quiet detachment of the Bench.

These things require explanation; and in the explanation will be found the keynote to Rufus Isaacs' career and an indication of the strength, the quality and the limitations of his equipment. In the first place it will be noticed that the bulk of the offices held by him are associated with politics; yet Rufus Isaacs was never primarily a politician, at least in our accustomed sense of the word. He did not fight an election campaign till he was forty, and he was nearing his forty-fourth birthday before he obtained a seat in Parliament. He sat for five and a half years as a private member in that House of Commons which calls out the greatest efforts of ambitious men, and made comparatively few speeches; he always had the attention of the House, but never attempted to make any great impression there. He was in fact never a " House of Commons man." The reason for this was twofold, arising partly from equipment and partly from inclination. His style of speaking was forensic; lucid, subtle and persuasive, he was adept at picking out the features in a case which were at once significant and favourable, and driving them home with great force of argument. It was these qualities which made him so supremely successful both as an advocate before a jury and in arguments directed to the consideration of the Bench; for the jury want instruction and guidance in performing their duty, while the Bench is concerned solely to hear the case argued and is not interested in language or in emotional considerations. In the House of Commons, especially in the stormy period in which Rufus Isaacs sat, it is widely different; every member embodies his own personal principles, passions and prejudices, and, in addition, officially as it were, the principles, passions and prejudices of his constituents and of his party. The atmosphere, therefore, is widely different from that of the Law Courts, and members expect, in the ordinary default of original thought, either a certain warmth and passion to be introduced, or that a dry theme be adorned with eloquence. (Of late years there has been a strong tendency to create in the House of Commons the dry businesslike, detached atmosphere of the Courts, with what measure of success those who are familiar with the House may judge for themselves; Rufus Isaacs, however, left the House of Commons in 1913.) With neither of these two requirements did Rufus Isaacs comply; he had always a great belief in the efficacy of argument between reasonable men, and the introduction of strong feeling could only debase argument and make men less reasonable. " I think," he said in one of his Viceregal speeches, when referring to a personal interview with Mr Gandhi, " two men cannot exchange ideas and discuss problems without deriving some benefit to either side." The passage is revealing, for it illustrates that belief in negotiation which has been a lifetime characteristic; but it is an attitude which, unless enforced by the robuster quality of whole-hearted advocacy, must often carry less weight than perhaps it deserves in a democratically elected assembly. Nor were Rufus Isaacs' speeches eloquent in respect of verbal felicity; they relied for their effect on their lucidity of argument, their command of the facts, and the personality of the speaker. Of verbal adornment and literary quality there is little trace; they are speeches to hear rather than to read, a vehicle for argument, rather than a medium of literary expression. He had neither the tempestuous imagery of a Bright or a Lloyd George, with its literary inspiration in the Bible, nor the perfect classical periods of a Burke or an Asquith, moulded on the orators of Greece and Rome.

Now if these things are detrimental to the chances of success in the House of Commons, they are clearly far more so in respect of the public platform; and since to be a leading politician it is essential to have a good platform style, here is another reason why Rufus Isaacs was not equipped to be primarily a politician. But this brings us to the other, and deeper, question of inclination and temperament; for, though it is possible to imagine Rufus Isaacs wishing to be a " House of Commons man," he was temperamentally no more inclined to platform oratory than to the rôle of belligerent apostle of glittering prizes. In a democratic community, the politician must be, amongst other things, a platform speaker, who can establish emotional contact with his audience; to do this he may employ either the eloquence of the Gladstonian period, or the verbose taciturnity of a later day, which consists in long speeches, calculated to assure the audience that the speaker is a proper representative of a tongue-tied nation. One or other of these methods he must adopt, and neither were methods suited to the temperament and equipment of Rufus Isaacs.

Now we have been so long a democratic community that we virtually take it for granted that a man ambitious of serving the State in public affairs must, except in the case of a small and favoured minority, follow the well-worn tracks of political advancement. In point of fact this is far from being of universal application; we are not like the Athenians, governed direct from the assembly, nor do we attempt to administer an empire from the market place. It is still possible to rise high in the State without being a leader of the people. And this is what Lord Reading has done; he is by temperament, and has been in fact, a ruler, not a leader, of men. A leader of men is associated with causes, with those causes in which he has believed so strongly and so profoundly that he has exerted his powers of leadership to the full to rally men to them; such a man is Lord Carson, Rufus Isaacs' great contemporary and forensic rival, whose name is immortally coupled with the great struggle on behalf of Ulster. The ruler of men on the other hand is connected with administration or reform; and the name of Lord Reading suggests the tenure of legal office, the despatch of delicate diplomatic negotiations, and the administration of a province, which is unrivalled alike in the magnitude of its extent and in the complexity of its problems.

It follows from this that Lord Reading is not altogether a democrat. He believes in government in the interest of the people, and even in government delegated from the people. But the exercise of his talents has not depended on the accident of his having been born into a democratic community. In the Middle Ages, Rufus Isaacs would (putting aside the question of race) have been a counsellor of kings and a governor of provinces, whereas the bulk of democratic leaders might never in such conditions have emerged from obscurity. His rarest abilities have lain in negotiation and conciliation, in putting a case and winning the hearts of small groups of men, and these are qualities which the eye of the responsible individual is quicker to detect than the instinct of the democracy; and he is possessed neither of the platform nor of that identification with the aspirations, characteristics and even shortcomings of the people, which is the real sense in which democratic leaders are representative of the electorate. Subtlety of mind, charm of address, calmness of outlook and firmness, not advertised by bluster but cloaked by courtesy; these are pre-eminently the qualities of Lord Reading. From the time when his office disjoined him from party, successive governments have recognised his gift for negotiation and have utilised it by sending him on important diplomatic missions for which a party politician would have been less suitable. It is indeed quite possible that, had he been born within the charmed circle, Rufus Isaacs would have followed a career of diplomacy. But, had he done that, the law would have been immeasurably the loser, while, owing to this country's habit of entrusting important diplomatic missions to people outside the ranks of professional diplomacy, the country would not have been greatly the gainer.

Lord Reading is, as has been said, in some sense of the word, an opportunist; therefore he has throughout his career recognised the importance of the work in hand for its own sake. This does not necessarily mean that principles and causes have made no appeal to him; but it does mean that constitutionally he is better adapted to finding the best means to arrive at an end that is not in dispute than to devise the end itself. Consequently, although he has been a Liberal all his political life, he has always been detached in controversy; he is no partisan, and suspects the effects of the passions of partisans on the chances of reasonable settlement. This detachment, which appears remarkable in view of the whole-hearted vigour, amounting sometimes to lack of restraint, practised by politicians in the decade before the Great War, is a result partly of temperament, but also the effect of his race.

Lord Reading is a Jew; a Jew by birth, temperament, and preference. Throughout his life he has been devotedly proud of the race from which he springs, and unswervingly loyal to it. His qualities, too, are those of his race; and no account of him can be complete, or even comprehensible, which does not take into consideration the racial factor. The Jew inevitably surveys national problems in greater detachment, for he sees them against a different background; a Jew, for instance, whose people had been without a national home for centuries, could not feel the burning passion on the question of Irish Home Rule, which has consumed generations of Englishmen and Irishmen. A Jew, too, whose people had preserved their religion for centuries amid fierce persecution, might be forgiven for thinking that in the eye of History, Welsh Disestablishment would loom considerably less large than it did to excited partisans in 1912. It is this quality of balanced perspective that Lord Reading has always had in a superlative degree; it was clear to him, as being emotionally further from the scene than the other actors, that some of the dramas which were being played out with such intensity of feeling were of more transitory interest than appeared, and that the final working out would gain infinitely if there were more calmness and less feeling. That this attitude was correct is in many cases apparent after the lapse of years; but it would perhaps be demanding too much of those who were near to events to expect of them the retrospective calm of the historian, or the detached reasonableness of the spectator. It is perhaps due as much as anything to the fact that he did not altogether share the emotional outlook of his countrymen that Lord Reading has been a ruler rather than a leader, for he is not close enough in temperament to the ordinary man to be representative of him in the sense in which, for instance, Mr Baldwin is held to be at the present day, or Lord Palmerston was in the nineteenth century. Here again this is partly due to race, for it is not natural for Jews to be quite representative of the national characteristics and aspirations of any people; rulers and administrators they often are, and are to be found, too, generally among the first in the arts, the sciences and the professions, but not as leaders and inspirers of a great national, democratic community. The obvious exception to this rule is more apparent than real. For Disraeli was not only a Jew, but an Oriental, and it was the Oriental in him which captured the popular imagination; the philosophy, too, which he gave to the British people was one which clothed fundamentally British ideas with the more gorgeous garment of an exotic inspiration. But Lord Reading is an Occidental, and a lawyer; a man of affairs, romantic in his achievement rather than in his ideas. So to him it has been given less to inspire and to lead, than to advise, to administer and to rule.

So there we have him; a ruler rather than a leader, a diplomat rather than a politician. Incisive in reasoning, lucid in exposition, sagacious in counsel, fertile in resource, he has united in himself many of the great qualities of the Bench and Bar. Lofty but not aloof, detached but not distant, the flavour of his personality seems rare and delightful; his charm of manner has won for him many friends and much admiration. In private life his devotion to his family is considerable, and he has had two ideally happy marriages, one in youth and one in age; to the Jewish race his loyalty has been conspicuous. In public life he brought to the affairs of State those qualities of mind and character which, united with self-discipline, tireless devotion, and enthusiastic assiduity, had served his clients so well in the Courts; over twenty years of public life have scarcely dulled that enthusiasm nor blunted his abilities. Set-backs and disappointments there inevitably have been, but remarkably few; and they have been the fewer because he has always contemplated his private fortunes with that sense of perspective which has served him in public affairs, and encountered reverses and recovered from them with that supple and resilient strength which is foremost in the arsenal of his equipment. Honours there have been and high office in ever-increasing abundance; high office has provided a field for the exercise of his abilities, and honours are the sign and symbol that those abilities have wrought not unsuccessfully in varied fields. Truly, a man whom the gods have loved; but he has borne himself with a modesty that has not challenged the nemesis which the gods too often visit on their favourites.

CHAPTER II

RUFUS ISAACS, THE BOY

THE well-known story of Rufus Isaacs as cabin-boy has given rise to a very widely-spread belief that he was born in humble circumstances. In fact this is not so; his going to sea was an early manifestation of adventurousness of spirit, and not due to economic pressure. He was born in London in October, 1860, of Jewish parents in a substantial way of business. His father, Joseph Isaacs, had a family business of fruit-broking in the City, which still flourishes under the direction of Rufus' brother, Harry Isaacs. His father's brother, Henry Isaacs, who was also in the City, subsequently attained the ultimate goal of civic ambition by becoming Lord Mayor of London. His mother, Sara Woolf, was also the daughter of a Jewish merchant in the City; consequently Rufus Isaacs came of pure Jewish stock. and inherited on both sides the commercial tradition of his race.

Rufus was one of three sons. Of his brothers, Godfrey, the younger, who became a financier, is since dead, but the elder, Harry, who resembles his brother in his youthful and vigorous appearance, though in the seventies, is still a familiar figure in the City and in the Reform Club. His sister married the late Mr Sutro, the famous dramatist. The affection between the children was great, for Rufus had and retained to a highly developed extent the racial characteristic of strong family affection. We shall see how his mother's influence and affectionate insistence served him at a turning-point of his life.

At an early age Rufus was sent with Harry to a Jewish preparatory school. But he made no effort to emulate the childish precocity of Macaulay, of whom the story is told how, on being asked at the age of three by a lady visitor whether his toothache was better, replied with dignity, " I thank you, madam; the agony is abated." The young Rufus, on the contrary, did not lisp very effectively in numbers; for all that he was obviously quick-witted, the child steadily refused to be father of the Lord Chief Justice. He had, however, as a compensation to his pastors and masters, great vitality and an inexhaustible taste for mischief. This is a combination with which schoolmasters are traditionally expected to cope, but Rufus' efforts were so ably seconded by Harry that the unusual result ensued of the headmaster finding himself forced to confess that the boys were unmanageable. He wrote, therefore, to their father to ask that they should be withdrawn, and the two brothers were locked in a room to await the arrival of their parents to remove them in disgrace. So unimpressed, however, were the two little boys by the solemn character of the occasion that they improved upon it by throwing all the furniture out of the window. And so it was into a bare room, sparsely but effectively inhabited by two flushed, wide-eyed little boys, that the headmaster ushered Mr and Mrs Isaacs as a prelude to their withdrawing their unsatisfactory offspring from his charge.

When he had thus stamped the impress of his personality on English education, it was decided to give Rufus a wider field for his activities, and he was sent to school in Brussels. Here a welcome improvement was early indicated by his winning of the *prix de mémoire* in his first term, an almost incredible feat for a small English child in his first term at a foreign school; it turned out to be, however, only the first instance of that astonishing power of memory which was to be among Rufus Isaacs' chief assets at the Bar. It may be assumed that the inevitable loneliness and shyness of that first term away not only from his parents but from his country and his language, made work appear for the first time in the new light of a solace and a distraction. The improvement was to some extent maintained, though it may be assumed that his liveliness soon reasserted itself when the strangeness of his new surroundings had worn off. He continued abroad for a time, but it was his parents' intention that he should have his secondary education in England, and consequently his name was entered for the University College School in London.

The school, which was then and is now a day-school, had not in 1873 when Rufus Isaacs went there, moved to its present extensive premises in Frognal. It was then concentrated in a smaller space in Gower Street near to the buildings of University College, with which at the time the school maintained a very close connection. Rufus was thirteen when he entered the school, and though there is no suggestion that he was the ideal schoolboy (a circumstance which there is no need to regret) he had already shown that he was possessed of an acute and ready mind. It would have been a legitimate assumption to suppose that from the age of thirteen onwards Rufus would have been increasingly attracted to his books; and had this been the case, so intelligent a boy must certainly have scored considerable academic success. Towards the end of his school career, the authorities would have advised his parents to let him compete for a scholarship at Oxford, and Rufus might easily have found himself an undergraduate in the late 'seventies. How he would have liked Oxford is conjectural, but it is certain that a community which acknowledges social and intellectual qualities all the more readily because they are neglected somewhat during school life, would have accorded a ready welcome to the charm of manner and intellectual possibilities of the youthful Rufus Isaacs. And from Oxford his path would have lain, clearly and smoothly, to the career of the Bar and politics, which he ultimately followed.

So it might well have been. And so indeed might a boy, who was one day to be Lord Chief Justice and Viceroy, have planned it to be. But Rufus Isaacs was a boy who followed his own bent, and he put the youthful gods of adventure on a higher plane than the more settled and sombre deities of adult distinction. His career at University College School was short and, scholastically speaking, undistinguished. The records contain no proud reference to glittering prizes, but the memory of his contemporaries at the school is of a lively boy, not very unlike an older edition of the child who had thrown the furniture out of the window. But Rufus was now old enough to know that throwing one's headmaster's furniture out of the window is scarcely discreet, however diverting an occupation it may be, and his early departure from the University College School was in no way compulsory. It is commonly supposed that Rufus Isaacs ran away from school to go to sea; this is not quite accurate. In point of fact, he was withdrawn from the University College School in order to pursue his education abroad, and it was after he had spent some time at Hanover studying languages that he returned to England and formed the resolution, conventional in a certain type of exciting fiction, but unusual in future Lord Chief Justices, of going to sea.

Going to sea to serve on a small ship is one of the things that is still practically as exciting as it used to be. Rufus Isaacs found on the ship in which he was signed on as cabin-boy, that there was much hardship and some danger to stimulate an excitement that might otherwise have flagged. The captain of the *Blair Atholl* was a mariner of the old school, hard, tyrannical, unsympathetic, a believer in the divine right of constituted authority and commendably free from modern notions of sentiment. The crew, and the cabin-boy amongst them, suffered considerably in words, blows, and hard treatment at the hands of this martinet; but it did have the effect of making the crew a trade-union of fellow-sufferers, and it is possible that the sympathy thus engendered saved Rufus from a certain amount of rough usage from potential disciplinarians lower down in the maritime hierarchy. It also happened that when the crew, sore beset and greatly daring, decided to send a deputation to the captain, they appointed Rufus Isaacs as their spokesman. The somewhat unnatural selection of the cabin-boy to fill this important rôle requires explanation; but it must remain a matter for conjecture whether Rufus was chosen because nobody else dared risk the captain's wrath and he was not in a position to refuse the proffered honour, or because they thought that Rufus' youthful charm of manner might melt the captain's heart or whether it was that instinct had supplemented the expert knowledge, which they were not in a position to possess, and had whispered that their cabin-boy was to be the foremost advocate of his generation. However that may be, Rufus addressed the captain at length on behalf of the crew; marshalling facts and arguments, he adroitly mingled exposition, persuasion and appeal in a manner that was to become famous in the High Court. The upshot was that the captain relented, and Rufus Isaacs had won his first important case, for it is not recorded that he addressed the Court on his own behalf on the occasion when the furniture was thrown out of the window.

After this signal triumph, Rufus not unnaturally became of more consequence in the eyes of the crew, though his status still lacked distinction, and the captain, being of the old school, had his own view on forensic cabin-boys. The *Blair Atholl* was bound for South America, where it found a cargo awaiting transport to India. The arrival of the ship in India bespoke romance of a different sort, romance that lay in the future, beckoning him to a destiny hidden as yet and unsuspected. For as the ship came slowly up the Hoogly, the cabin-boy saw from the deck for the first time the shores of that great, mysterious land which years later he returned to govern. There were no intervening visits, and in his viceregal speech on landing Lord Reading commemorated this first and other visit, and with it the fact that the age of romantic achievement is not entirely past.

It had been a gay adventure, but Rufus Isaacs was not to spend his life at sea; and it was time now to turn his thoughts to the quieter, but more sustained and no less enthralling adventure of life.

For a short time he went to Magdeburg to look after the interests of the family business in Germany. Continuance in the family business would have spelt security, a chance of substantial prosperity, and comparative freedom from anxiety. But Harry was already destined for the family business, and Rufus' zest for adventure was still strong, demanding more exciting possibilities than that of security. The Stock Exchange seemed a more attractive proposition than business, and Rufus' keen intelligence and quick wits held forth promise that he might well make a success of that profession; consequently he became a clerk to a firm of stockbrokers with a view to himself becoming a member of the Stock Exchange when he should come of age.

And so Rufus Isaacs spent that time when had he remained at school he would no doubt have been at Oxford, working in his firm of stockbrokers in London. He was more industrious now, for he was beginning to be ambitious, and the chain of causation between work and success was forged more clearly in his mind. It seemed indeed highly probable that in time he would make a conspicuous success of his profession; on coming of age, he was admitted to membership of the Stock Exchange, and for a while prospered there. The course of his life seemed clear; he would make an early and enduring success on the Stock Exchange, and follow without deviation the path of prosperity that appeared to lie open before him. So it might well have been, and so in the early 'eighties it appeared that it would be; in which case the world would never have heard of Rufus Isaacs. But, just as he had been switched off his apparent course when he went abroad and again when he went to sea, so now his destiny did not let him follow the easy path; he was reserved for greater things and the passage to them seldom lies exclusively by still waters.

He had chosen his profession in part because of its uncertainty and its excitement. In 1884 he had experience of the less pleasant manifestations of these qualities; in a crisis on the Stock Exchange he found himself unable to meet his obligations, and this, of course, meant disaster. It is well-known that defaulting, through no fault of one's own, on the Stock Exchange implies no moral censure (and it should perhaps be stated here at once that, when his earnings at the Bar made it possible, Rufus Isaacs paid his creditors in full). But we may legitimately be surprised that a person of the acumen of which Rufus Isaacs showed himself to be possessed, should have fared so badly; such a circumstance does not, however, of necessity cast a slight upon his acumen. For success on the Stock Exchange is not exactly analogous to success at the Bar, which is a fairly accurate index to industry and ability; success on the Stock Exchange, on the other hand, involves not only doing the right thing but doing it at the right time. It is not enough, that is to say, to know what is going to happen; one must know, in addition, the precise moment when it is going to happen, and that unfortunately depends on a knowledge of when the other stockbrokers will realise what is going to happen. The danger, in short, is that a man of superior intellect and quick perception will fail in his " timing " because he will give credit to the mass, on the working of whose minds the movement depends, for as sharp an insight as his own; and while a certain anticipation is good, to be too far-sighted is as fatal as an inability to keep up. That wise man of affairs, Mr E. S. P. Haynes, whose shrewd knowledge of the world is seldom at fault, has summed up the situation when he says: " Many an intelligent man has been hammered on the Stock Exchange because he relied on other brokers being as quick-witted as himself."

These considerations are perhaps apparent on reflection, but they would be poor consolation to a young man of twenty-four, who is faced with the disturbing realisation that he has failed in his chosen calling, even if moments of sudden and crushing adversity were notoriously not conducive to calm and logical reflection. To Rufus Isaacs the blow was heavy and unexpected. It came, too, with a finality that was new in his life. Hitherto, life had been a gay adventure; the Stock Exchange, no doubt, was on a lower plane of pure adventure than the sea, but it had shared with it moments of excitement, risk and triumph. Set-backs there had been, but they had been ephemeral, and had acted as a spur to further efforts and a spice to future triumphs. But this reverse was serious, and had a new, disturbing possibility of permanence; it revealed adventure and uncertainty, hitherto seen as more light-hearted things, in a cruel, unrelenting and rather frightening aspect. The outlook for Rufus was bleak and forbidding. " Oh to be twenty-two! " said the late Charles Masterman on one occasion, " no-one's a failure at twenty-two." But it looked perilously as if Rufus Isaacs might be a failure at twenty-four. To live on in England under the shadow of failure was not a prospect to attract an ambitious young man. In retrospect two or three years in failure and adversity may seem no very great thing; but at the time the feeling of humiliation and despair may be strong and insistent, and there is no guarantee that it will be temporary. But there was an alternative to staying in England; through the ages adventurous spirits, whom Fortune has treated none too kindly, have felt the call of the New World. Rufus Isaacs had previously been adventurous, and now Fortune had turned her back on him. He would go to America, where at least he could start anew. Thither the finger of fortune seemed to beckon; and it was not his custom to neglect its signal.

Once again we are tempted to speculate on what would have happened if Rufus Isaacs had followed the course which seemed to lie before him. That he would have been successful in America is very probable; indeed it is unlikely that he would have failed ultimately to make a success of anything to which he turned his hand, for he is built of the very stuff of achievement. But that success must almost certainly have lain in business; he would not have practised at the American Bar nor could he very well have played any part in public life. His life then might well have been successful, but it must have been widely different from what it has been, and greatly inferior to it in distinction; once again the world might never have heard of Rufus Isaacs. But Destiny had a greater future in store for him than that of being a successful business man in a strange land, and to that end brought pressure to bear on him of a sort that he could scarcely resist. For, when his decision to go was already taken, his mother came to him and pleaded with him not to cut himself off from his family, his country and his friends; she was convinced that if his desire was to go to the Bar, then that was the proper field for his talents, and she told him that his parents would assist him to that end. The appeal was not to be refused, and perhaps his mother's faith helped to kindle the glow of enthusiasm for the Bar in his own heart. Maternal judgments about their sons' futures are notoriously fond and optimistic; but in this case the prophecy erred on the side of understatement. For not even the eye of maternal faith could envisage the glorious future which the success of her prayer was opening out to her son.

The passage to the Bar, not difficult to-day, was considerably easier in the 'eighties. There were examinations to pass, and these he passed; but he was too untrained in the academic tradition to distinguish himself in the acquisition of honours or prizes. Terms, however, had to be kept too, and this was done by partaking in the ancient rite of dining in mess in Hall, popularly known as " eating dinners." Rufus had joined the Middle Temple, and so he dined in the lovely old Middle Temple Hall with its gallery, its coats-of-arms around the wall, and its magnificent Van Dyck hanging on the far wall over the high table; here, too, he would stand up and watch the stately procession of Masters of the Bench, veterans of Bench and Bar, proceeding to and from the dais on which the high table is placed. Not twenty years later he too became a member of that procession and dined in the seats of the mighty.

But this lay in the future. For the moment he was occupied with the humble task of qualifying for the Bar, to which he was called in 1887. In 1887, therefore, he stood on the threshold of his new life; he could not expect that the struggle would be short or the victory easy, for he was challenging the competition of rare intellects and great talents. But he no longer stood alone, for in this year he married Alice Cohen, third daughter of Albert Cohen, who was connected with the Welsbach Lighter Company. It so happened that their journey through life together was attended by a success that swelled into the more resounding notes of triumph. But that, one feels, was immaterial, for their union was as much independent of material greatness as it was potent in producing it. The great felicity and perfect sympathy of their marriage lasted for over forty years, until dissipated only at last by her death in 1930.

CHAPTER III

THE practice of the law attracts to itself a large and varied congregation of acolytes. Men of ambition and ability turn to it with their eyes on the prizes of the profession; the dilettante anchors to it his somewhat fluttering pursuit of literature or the arts. The man of education follows it because his education has fitted him for it; the man of no education aspires to it in the hope of being educated in the process. And yet among the varied types who throng its halls there exists the camaraderie of a great self-confident trade-union, whose laws are mainly the inherited tradition of etiquette and not formal rules in black and white. As becomes it, old and new are curiously mingled. There is great reverence for ancient precedent, but the authority of the greatest judgment may be overturned in the tag-end of any weary night at Westminster; the mingling extends even to legal architecture, for the profession is pursued partly in grand, sombre old buildings, which have stood the test of time, and partly in the neo-Gothic erections of the later Victorian period. But there is in the gardens and courts of the Temple an almost collegiate atmosphere which breathes the corporate spirit of an institution, that evokes loyalty rather than demands it; and that loyalty is no small thing, for in the honourable and efficient conduct of the law lies the very basis and foundation stone of the structure of a civilised society.

It is a profession where many are called and few indeed are chosen; necessarily so, for the prizes are limited, and the competition of rare talents is strenuous and unrelenting. In entering late for so arduous a race, Rufus Isaacs was undeniably acting boldly, nor were his qualifications exactly those that are normally looked for in one who is a potential success at the Bar. He had not had the conventional schooling and academic training which is the normal prelude to such success; and a casual observer, anxious to gauge the future chances of the initiates of the 'eighties might have been pardoned for overlooking Rufus Isaacs in favour of those younger men, supported by money and legal connections and with the backing behind them of youthful triumphs at the Union or in the Schools. But there is an education other than that of the Universities and a training other than that in scholarship; Rufus Isaacs had not the intensive training of classical culture, but his training had ranged over a wide and varied field of experience. Indeed the dictum, used by a speaker in addressing an Oxford Society might perhaps be applied to Rufus Isaacs: " You have graduated in this great university of Oxford: I have graduated in the still greater university of Life." He had followed the path of adventure, and emerged with a keen mind, strong courage, and a muscular intensity of purpose. He had, too, as a result of the Stock Exchange, a specialised knowledge of business which his competitors lacked; he was at home in the intricacies of commerce, and could unravel the complicated mysteries of statistics. And so the observer, on looking closer, would have prophesied for him an almost certain success in commercial cases, and possible triumphs in a larger arena.

A barrister's years as a junior are normally of immense interest to himself, but a little tedious in the narration; (though it might incidentally be mentioned that the conversation of many young barristers reveals a pre-occupation with the former fact, to the entire exclusion of the latter). On being called to the Bar, a man will spend twelve months as a pupil in chambers. During this probationary period, he will be employed in devilling cases and looking up points for the man whose pupil he is and probably for other barristers in the chambers in addition. At the end of his time as a pupil, he may, if he is lucky, remain where he is, but more probably he sets up in chambers on his own somewhere else. His position is then equal to that of the other occupants of the Chambers, for he pays his share of the rent for the Chambers and for the clerk instead of his former fee as a pupil; but in all probability he will for a time find himself considerably less occupied than he was as a pupil, for the arrival of briefs in a young barrister's chambers is a slow and an occasional process. The briefs, when they do come, are generally for the County Court or the Police Court, and concern small debts, petty crime, poor persons' divorce, maintenance cases and running-down cases. This class of work may perhaps be varied by cases in the High Court, but in these " silk " will generally be briefed and the junior's duties will be more in the preliminary work of preparing the pleadings and making applications than in the actual conduct of the case in Court. A junior's practice may be varied, interesting and remunerative, but the exciting part of a great advocate's career comes in the main after he has exchanged the stuff gown of the junior for the silk one of a King's Counsel.

Rufus Isaacs went as a pupil into the chambers of the veteran Sir Harry Poland, who laid down the rule for him: " Never come to the Temple later than 10 a.m., and never leave it before 6 p.m." In later life Lord Reading assured Sir Harry that he had always acted on the rule. He made, too, an early association with Mr (afterwards Sir John) Lawson Walton. Lawson Walton was the son of a Nonconformist minister and had the somewhat narrow vision of his training, but he united to it the assiduity and tenacity of purpose which are equally characteristic of his stock. He was, too, a humane man, and his relations with Rufus Isaacs, both as mentor and later as competitor and antagonist, were always friendly. Like Rufus Isaacs he was a Liberal, and, after the long Liberal exile from office, he became Attorney-General in Campbell-Bannerman's administration in 1906. It was Lawson Walton who said of Rufus Isaacs: " He is the only man I know who has not had to go through the grind of Quarter-Sessions and the County Court like the rest of us."

throughout the racing season for the constant and inexplicable in-and-out running of its horses . . .   But the darkest part of the matter is this—that the owners or nominal owners of the horses to which I am alluding win large stakes when their horses are successful, but do not lose much when they are beaten.   If you wish to purify the Turf you must go to the fountain head."

The speech created a great sensation in racing circles, and there was a stampede to identify the people referred to, and to pin down the allusions.   This was no very great task, however, for opinion was general that the speech applied primarily to Sir George Chetwynd and that the stables referred to were Chetwynd House, where one Sherrard was trainer.   Now Sir George Chetwynd was known as the ablest man on the Turf; though a young baronet of good family he was not possessed of large means and subsisted primarily on his winnings on the Turf.   There is no reason why a clever man, well versed in the ways of the Turf, should not make a reasonable income out of racing by the employment only of the most scrupulous methods, though admittedly it is not an easy thing to do; but the fact that he was so dependent made the charge—if indeed it was directed against him—doubly serious, for it not only reflected on his honour but imperilled his means of livelihood as well.   Any doubts as to whether it was Sir George who was aimed at were resolved by the action of Lord Durham himself, after Sir George had instituted legal proceedings, for, in order to facilitate their hearing, Lord Durham wrote to the Stewards of the Jockey Club, offering to give them a copy of his speech at York and promising to raise no other issue at the trial than that of the truth or falsehood of his statement; the letter ended: " I now state that the substance of my speech at the Gimcrack Dinner at York was to the effect that the horses in Sherrard's stables have shown constant and inexplicable changes of form, and that Wood, the jockey in that stable, has been in the habit of pulling them.   I also accuse Sir George Chetwynd of having connived at serious malpractices which are contrary to the rules of racing."

The issue was now joined. Chetwynd claimed £20,000 damages, alleging that the speech was a libel on himself, and Durham, by this letter and in his pleadings, admitted speaking the words but said that they were true in substance and fact. The case aroused immense interest, both because of the personalities involved and the nature of the charges; for racing in those days had an even greater grip on the popular imagination than it has to-day. Indeed it would not be too much to say that politics and racing were the chief preoccupation of every class of Englishman of the time, and the Chetwynd-Durham case strongly challenged the Parnell Commission itself in its claims on national attention. The importance to the parties concerned was fully equal to the measure of popular attention. The consequences to Sir George Chetwynd if he lost his case were apparent and disastrous; and Lord Durham, though to him the personal effect was not perhaps so immediate, would not improbably, if he failed to establish the truth of his charges, be held to have acted in a dangerously impetuous manner, while holding a responsible position, and thus calling unnecessarily in question another gentleman's honour.

In this case, as in so many libel actions, the plaintiff was really on the defence; for, though if the verdict went against Lord Durham he would be mulcted in heavy damages, failure on the part of Sir George Chetwynd to establish his case meant the loss of something more important than money. He would be compelled to pay in a currency in which there is no liquidation. The charge which Lord Durham had made against Chetwynd, and for the disproving and punishing of which the action was brought, was really two-fold. The more serious one was that Chetwynd had employed Charles Wood to " pull " horses belonging to Sherrard's stables so as to obtain more favourable handicaps and longer odds in those races in which they were really being ridden to win. The other charge was that he was guilty of various malpractices contrary to the rules of racing; the principal allegation in this connection was that he helped Wood to evade the recent rule of the Jockey Club, by which jockeys were not allowed to own race-horses, by being himself the nominal owner of Wood's horses.

It was on the refutation of these charges that Rufus Isaacs spent many anxious hours of preparation before the case finally came into Court. It was not an ordinary High Court case, for, though the action would normally have been tried in the Queen's Bench, it was referred instead, owing to the technical aspects of the case, to the arbitration of the Stewards of the Jockey Club, who were at that time, James Lowther, M.P., the Earl of March and Prince Soltykoff. The hearing was begun on June 10th, 1888, in Court V of the Queen's Bench Division; this was during the Whitsun vacation, for both leading counsel were engaged in the Parnell case, which was still in progress. The case, however, extended into the new law term, for it lasted twelve days and the Court did not sit in Ascot week, which considering the tastes of the various protagonists is perhaps not surprising. Sir Charles Russell led Mr Charles Matthews, subsequently Public Prosecutor, and Mr Magniac for Lord Durham, while Sir Henry James had as his juniors Mr Pollard, Mr A. T. Lawrence and Rufus Isaacs. It is interesting to remember that Mr Lawrence, as Lord Trevethin, succeeded Lord Reading as Lord Chief Justice in 1921; it must be very rarely indeed that two future Lord Chief Justices are found together as juniors on the same side in one case.

The first few days of the case were remarkable chiefly for Sir Charles Russell's strenuous cross-examination of Sir George Chetwynd and for the distinguished persons who successively occupied the witness box, some of whose names would have seemed more in place in the pages of Froissart's Chronicles than in the list of witnesses for a court of law. Sir Henry James opened his case with an address to the jury, outlining the facts, and then put Sir George into the box, who maintained a stout front under Russell's expert handling of the cross-examination. Sherrard, the trainer, then gave evidence, and was followed by Wood, who had had previous experience of legal proceedings and proved rather taciturn under Russell's cross-examination, possibly on that account.

Sir Charles Russell did not open the defence with a speech. Instead he put Lord Marcus Beresford, Lord Arthur Somerset, Major Egerton, the official handicapper, and the Hon. George Lambton into the box. Most of their evidence was not of great importance, but James secured corroboration of an important point in Chetwynd's evidence in his cross-examination of Egerton. This was in respect of the allegation of " pulling " horses in order to secure a more favourable handicap in subsequent races, which in the year 1886 was concerned principally with the horse Fullerton. Major Egerton confirmed Chetwynd's statement that he had informed him, as official handicapper, that Fullerton was not fit at the time of these races, so that the horse's running could not be taken as an exact index of his proper form; this action Major Egerton described as a " very proper one." Lord Durham and the Duchess of Montrose also gave evidence and Lord Durham in his cross-examination by Sir Henry James had some of those sharp passages with counsel which are so frequent in courts of law when people accustomed to having their own way find themselves subject to the rules of evidence and confined to the points raised by clever and hostile counsel. But from the point of view of the plaintiff the most important evidence was that of Sydney Howard, the stable-lad and jockey who had had instructions from Wood and Sherrard not to exert himself in certain races; for it became clear in his cross-examination by Sir Henry James that he had not had these instructions from Chetwynd, nor had he communicated them to him. The establishing of this fact went a long way to exonerating Chetwynd from the more serious charge of tampering with the form of his horses in order to secure an unfair advantage in other races.

At the conclusion of the evidence for the defence, Sir Charles Russell addressed the jury. He did not neglect the charges of " pulling," but his speech was more directed to establishing the second charge of " malpractices contrary to the rules of racing." He urged, however, that in 1886 Fullerton was not run to win, but to obtain good handicaps for 1887, and maintained that Sherrard must have been acting on the implied wish of Chetwynd when he instructed the lad Howard " not to exert himself " in certain races; why otherwise, in the face of such suspicious circumstances, did Sir George make no inquiry? In respect of the second charge, Sir Charles pressed the point that Chetwynd's position was very different from that of the other owners, whose horses were trained at Chetwynd House; he alone was the man who made racing pay, to the tune of £5,000 or £6,000 a year in bets, and he too was so involved with Wood and Sherrard that he could not disclaim their conduct. It was Wood, according to Russell, who was the real owner and occupier of Chetwynd House, Sherrard being really only his servant; and Chetwynd must have known, since Wood was a rich man and Sherrard a poor man, that Wood was the real owner of the horses belonging to Sherrard. Then, too, in support of this there was Chetwynd's letter to Wood, marked " Private," which said: " I am quite sensible of your wish that I should lose nothing if I take the horses. If they turn out badly we shall arrange between us and Sherrard in a friendly way what shall be done. Nothing of this need be known . . . " This letter, said Russell, showed that Chetwynd was only lending his name to Wood's proprietorship of the horses; and his letter to the official handicapper in which he stated that he had bought the horses outright, was clearly an effort to conceal the true fact, which was that he was holding the horses for Wood. Russell finally summed up his view of the situation in the words: " He (Sir George) had got into such complications with his trainer and his jockey that he was led into transactions from which in happier circumstances he would fairly have recoiled."

Sir Charles had presented a fairly strong case, but it had one clear weakness; it depended too much on assertions that Chetwynd must have known certain things, because there were circumstances which might reasonably have led him to

suspect them.   This, however, is not the same thing as proving that he actually did know them, and it was on this
element of weakness that Sir Henry James concentrated
the main force of his criticism.   Speaking at considerable
length and with great force, Sir Henry conducted a difficult
case with great skill and address; and Rufus Isaacs, sitting
behind him, was fascinated to hear the expert handling, in
a way in which only a master could, of the case which he
had assisted so laboriously and so assiduously to prepare.

On the first charge, Sir Henry relied principally on what
he had elicited from Howard and Major Egerton in cross-
examination; and in support of his contention that the
stable's running of Fullerton had been impeccable, he
showed that in 1887 Chetwynd had persistently backed him
and had lost £1,077 in doing so, while Wood had also lost
£100 on him.   As to the general question of his relations
with Wood, many distinguished owners had also employed
Wood; why had not Lord Durham said to them too: " you
ought to have known about these things, because I knew " ?
In point of fact Lord Durham had proceeded on suspicion;
he knew very little when he made his speech at York.   And
in this connection, Sir Henry quoted very effectively Bacon's
saying that there is nothing which makes a man suspect much
more than knowing little.   In the trial of Cox *v.* Wood,
Wood had been acquitted of the charge of pulling
" Success; " should Sir George have gone up to him after
that verdict and said that he had lost confidence in him?
Similarly at what precise moment ought he to have withdrawn his horses from Sherrard's stables?   He had done the
chivalrous thing and stuck up for Wood, and it was because
of this that Lord Durham had acted as he had.   There was
no evidence that Chetwynd had employed Wood because
he could square other jockeys, and there was no trace of
Wood having been the owner of the horses after the date
of the transfer.   As to the horses that were owned by
Sherrard and Wood, Sir Charles Russell's whole case was
simply that he ought to have known the true state of
affairs because Wood was rich and Sherrard was poor.   But

this was at best a flimsy structure on which to base a conclusive argument; and further, if it was to apply to Chetwynd, why should it not apply to all the other owners who had horses in the stables? The speech concluded with an eloquent appeal on the twelfth day of the case, for James had resumed in the morning after speaking for five hours on the previous day till near the point of exhaustion.

The public, which had followed the case through its proceedings with a very lively interest, waited with growing excitement for the decision of the arbitrators. The decision was given on June 30th; as the trial was conducted by arbitrators and was not an ordinary High Court case, there had been no summing up, and when the decision was given, it was delivered as a bare announcement, the reasons for it remaining locked in the breasts of Mr Lowther, Lord March and Prince Soltykoff. The decision was a draw, the arbitrators finding for Sir George Chetwynd on the more serious charge of " pulling " of horses, but finding the charge of lesser malpractices proved. But, though the decision was thus in a sense a draw, Sir George was really the loser, for he was awarded on the first charge a farthing damages, a contemptuous sum, which suggested that his reputation was not of a sort to entitle him to any more substantial compensation for an unfounded slight upon it. This, coupled with the fact that the other part of the decision, even though it was on a less serious point, had gone against him, was enough to finish his career on the Turf and to embarrass his position; while Lord Durham, by proving half his case, had shown that at least he had had reason to be dissatisfied with the state of affairs and some justification for taking his strong line in calling attention to it.

The case did something to clear the air in the world of racing, and to this extent it need not be regretted. But while the case itself might be welcomed, the circumstances that had given rise to it could not but be deprecated. They alone could justify a case which in its details, like the famous Tranby Croft baccarat case of two years later, could give satisfaction to none but the moralists, to whom it supplied a grateful illustration that pitch and defilement cannot be far separated. From the aspect of those interested in the law and drama of the Courts, however, the case has considerably more to commend it, and to Rufus Isaacs it had especial importance, because it was the first great case with which he had been personally concerned. It had given him, too, the chance of studying Sir Henry James' conduct of the case in Court from within. Edifying and instructing as it is to hear great counsel in Court, his performance can only really be appreciated by one who knows the brief in advance and has an intimate knowledge of where lie the strength and weakness of the case. This was exactly Rufus Isaacs' position in this case, and from it he was able to learn much. And it inspired him, too, with the great possibilities of the Bar at a time when he could see about him only the lean harvest of the County Court.

CHAPTER IV

AFTER the Chetwynd-Durham suit Sir Charles Russell
and Sir Henry James returned to the intricate proceedings of the Parnell Commission, while Rufus
Isaacs betook himself once again to the obscurer labours
which are the lot of a young junior. The County Court
still had its place in his activities, but he was rapidly qualifying for the proud, if rather intermediate, designation of a
" rising junior." There was a period in those early years,
when he nearly became disheartened; work did not come as
rapidly as he had hoped, and he feared that perhaps after
all he would not be able to outstrip those who had come to
the Bar by more regular channels. It began to look as if
perhaps it might once again be as it had been in the City—
failure after a fair start. But in spite of a momentary dis-
couragement he was not easily to be daunted or deflected;
he was now, too, a family man, for Gerald Isaacs, the present
Lord Erleigh, had been born in 1889, and so to his own
personal determination was added the tenacity of purpose
of a husband and father. This time the determination
brought its reward, and from the early 'nineties Rufus
Isaacs' career at the Bar was one of vaulting and unbroken
success.

His practice, both in his earlier days and later when he
appeared more frequently in the High Court, was principally in London. He had joined the Northern Circuit but,
although he fought two great cases in Liverpool in the heyday of his triumphs as King's Counsel, he rarely at any
time practised in the provinces. It is true to say that from
about five years after the date of his call to the Bar, Rufus
Isaacs' practice lay almost exclusively in the High Court.
The principal field of his activities lay in commercial cases,

33

and for one whose bent was in this direction, Isaacs was very fortunate in the period in which he was practising, for the later years of his career as a junior coincided with the successful establishment of the Commercial Court.

In the early 'nineties the relations between the Courts of Law and the City were strained. The gravamen of the complaints of the business men was of a sort that has echoed through the history of the administration of justice. It was alleged that the judges were frequently ignorant of mercantile matters and had to be instructed in their business before the proceedings could start; litigation was said to be unnecessarily costly; and the sterile interlocutory applications added to the protraction and complication of the proceedings, which were already long and costly enough. Such complaints against the law's delays are traditional; but in this instance there was sufficient substance in them to impress Mr Justice Mathew, who formerly as counsel had had a great and unrivalled practice in commercial cases and was later to become a Lord Justice of Appeal. He realised that the business community had reasonable grounds of complaint, and that the difficulty must be met if the Courts of Law were to retain their jurisdiction over mercantile matters. The consequence was the creation of the Commercial Court to provide a better and speedier hearing for such cases. The effort was crowned with success, for it was not spoilt by ambitious rearrangement. No new rules were made, for it was intended that the Court should work within the existing rules, but in an original way and with a new spirit. Thus, for instance, procedure from first to last was controlled by the judge who tried the case out; a definite day was to be fixed for trial, with only a short interval between the issue of the writ and the trial; secondary evidence, too, was to be admissible when strict proof would involve exorbitant cost. These improvements implied a tightening-up of the system, which was evidence of a desire to get behind the technicalities and down to business which restored the confidence of the City and increased commercial business into the Courts.

It was in this Court that a great deal of Rufus Isaacs'

practice, by now lucrative and extensive, lay from 1895. It was realised that here was a barrister whose profound knowledge of commercial matters was equal to his skill in the law, and whose conduct of a case in Court, with his grasp of the essentials of a situation, his destructive cross-examination and his subdued yet penetrative eloquence, was inferior to neither. They were interesting years, busy years, and successful years; but the detailed narration of commercial cases, however absorbing to the few, could not be of general interest. We must be content, therefore, with a bird's-eye view of these years, and refrain from challenging Nemesis by following exactly in the footsteps of our subject.

Not all his cases, however, were, of course, commercial actions, and there was one which was not which demands and deserves our closer attention. The case of Allen *v.* Flood is not a *cause célèbre* in the sense that it was dramatic in its incident, or that it involved conspicuous personalities or great financial interests; but it is a leading case in that it fixes and establishes a great point of law, and is cited as a leading authority in our Courts. It belongs, in fact, to that select class of case, the name of which trips readily to the tongue of any lawyer, and the principle of which must be familiar to anyone desirous of possessing the most general knowledge of our law. Further it gave rise to a long and well-matched legal battle, and evoked some of the greatest judgments in the history of the Courts. It is also, from our more immediate standpoint, the greatest of the cases fought by the partnership, frequent and familiar in those years, of Lawson Walton as leader and Rufus Isaacs as junior.

The case of Allen *v.* Flood went the whole distance of our civil procedure; that is to say, it was argued first before judge and jury in the Queen's Bench Division, then before the Court of Appeal, and finally before the House of Lords, which is, under Parliament, the supreme Court in the land. It might perhaps here be explained, as the matter will recur, that in civil cases, the party losing the action in the court of instance (that is to say, the court first hearing the case) may, if there are grounds of appeal, argue them before the Court of Appeal, which consists normally of three Lord Justices of Appeal, sitting without a jury; if still dissatisfied, a further appeal lies to the House of Lords, which for judicial purposes consists of the Lords of Appeal in Ordinary, commonly known as the Law Lords. In criminal cases, the position is rather different. At the period under discussion, there was, properly speaking, no appeal as of right from the Court of first instance at all; the Judge could, if a difficult point of law arose, state a case for the consideration of the Court of Crown Cases Reserved, but there was no appeal from a decision on a question of fact. The position was amended in 1907 by an Act of Parliament creating the Court of Criminal Appeal; the existence of this Court clearly recognises the principle of appeal in criminal cases, and the appeal on questions of law is absolute, though on questions of fact the certificate of the judge trying the case or of the Court of Criminal Appeal is necessary. The Court of Criminal Appeal generally consists of the Lord Chief Justice, supported by two High Court Judges, sitting of course without a jury; its decision is usually final, but not always, for if the Attorney-General certifies that the point raised is one of public importance, then the case may go a stage further to the Lords. This practice has obvious drawbacks, for in an important prosecution the Crown's case may well be conducted by the Attorney-General, who may thus be called upon to play a dual rôle, of which the two elements might seem incompatible to some. In the Casement trial, Lord Birkenhead had to exercise this dual rôle, for he prosecuted Casement both before Lord Reading and in the Court of Criminal Appeal; and then in a judicial capacity he decided after consideration to refuse the application for a hearing in the House of Lords. The case of Allen v. Flood was not, of course, a criminal trial, but it is convenient to make clear at once the position with regard to appeals, as the question will from time to time recur in the course of this book.

[Those readers who, while interested in the drama of the Courts, find less appeal in strictly legal problems, are advised to omit pages 37 to 46: they can do so without losing the continuity of the narrative.]

Allen *v.* Flood, although intricate in its argument and complicated in the extensive variety of cases cited, is in general principle not difficult to understand. It is concerned with the important question of breach of contract. Now it had been laid down as far back as 1853 in the case of Lumley *v.* Gye, which concerned Miss Wagner, a well-known singer of the period, that it is a wrong actionable at Common Law knowingly to induce a person to commit a breach of contract. The point at issue in Allen *v.* Flood was really a refinement of this question. Put simply it was this: if a person induces a party, by means which are not unlawful, lawfully to terminate a contract with another, and is actuated by malice, does it give that other cause of action? The point is clearly of immense importance, in consideration of the frequency with which Trade Unions persuade their members to terminate their contracts or, in other words, call them out on strike. Allen *v.* Flood decided that in such a case no action will lie, for in Lord Watson's words, " the existence of a bad motive in the case of an act which is not in itself illegal will not convert that act into a civil wrong for which no reparation is due." This opinion he based on the theory, which he had already enunciated in another very important case, the Mayor of Bradford *v.* Pickles, that " the law of England does not, according to my apprehension, take into account motive as constituting an element of civil wrong." This view ultimately carried the day and is now indisputably the law of England. But it became so only after a fierce struggle in three Courts, which evoked and exhausted the finesse in argument of the leading counsel of the day, and against the opinion of the court of first instance, the Court of Appeal, and a minority of Law Lords in the supreme tribunal.

The events leading up to the bringing of the action can scarcely be considered commensurate in importance with the points of law which it decided; indeed, as in the case of the Great War, its origin lay in a local squabble, which might have passed off unnoticed, but in fact gave rise to a conflict whose vastness was ill-proportioned to its immediate cause.

In April of 1894, the good ship *Sam Weller* lay in Regent's Dock undergoing repairs at the hands of the Glengall Iron Company. Among the men working on her were two shipwrights, Flood and Taylor; they were honest men and good craftsmen, whose thoughts while at work can be conjectured only. But whatever they were, it is certain that no flights of fantasy induced them to imagine that their names would be commemorated in a great civil law-suit. They had cause for uneasiness, however, if they let their minds dwell upon it, for, although they were employed only on the woodwork of the *Sam Weller*, they had come to their work straight from the yard of Messrs. Mills & Knight, where they had worked on the ironwork in addition; and the ironworkers of the Boilermakers' Union, as good Trade Unionists, took fierce exception to the practice of shipwrights working on iron. The story of the iniquity of Flood and Taylor became known, and, while affecting to go unconcernedly about their work, the two shipwrights could not but be uneasily aware of the black looks cast in their direction. Nor was Nemesis far behind them; for one of the boilermakers, by name Elliott, telephoned the awful news to Allen, who was the London delegate of the Boilermakers' Union. Allen went at once to Regent's Dock, unaware that he was about to make legal history, but with the agreeable consciousness of doing his duty. On arrival he behaved as an impeccable Trade Union leader should. He first told Elliott that the men must remain at work till the matter was settled, and warned him that if the men left work without the sanction of the Union, he would use his influence to have them deprived of their benefit. This done, he went to Mr Halkett, the managing director of the Glengall Iron Company, and told him that if Flood and Taylor continued at work, the ironworkers would " knock off." Faced with this possibility, Halkett discharged Flood and Taylor " for peace and quietness' sake," as he put it.

If this was what he desired, Mr Halkett had hardly gone the right way to ensue it. However, it was impossible for the aggrieved shipwrights to bring an action against him, for they had only been working on piece work, and were therefore liable to dismissal at the end of any day; normally, it is true, they might expect to retain their employment until the end of the job, but certainly no breach of contract had been committed by their dismissal. However, although no action would lie against Halkett, it appeared that an action would lie against Allen for the part which he had played. Accordingly an action for damages was brought against Allen, and Jackson, the chairman, and Knight, the secretary, were joined with him as co-defendants. In point of fact, there was little chance of pinning any of the responsibility for the transaction on to Jackson and Knight, who had not even heard of the transaction. The jury found that they had not authorised Allen in his action, which was one that lay within the scope of his authority. Lawson Walton and Rufus Isaacs argued that it was a case of co-agency, in which every member is responsible for the actions of every other; but it was decided, both by Mr Justice Kennedy and the Master of the Rolls, Lord Esher, in the Court of Appeal, that neither the relationship of master and servant, nor that of principal and agent, existed between Allen and any member of the Union. The case against them was accordingly dismissed.

The main issue, that against Allen, was fought as a question of principle, for both sides had the financial support of their Unions. Consequently counsel were briefed who could do justice to the intricate legal argument involved, Lawson Walton, Q.C., and Rufus Isaacs appearing for the plaintiffs, Flood and Taylor, Mr Murphy, Q.C., and Mr Pike for Knight and Jackson, while Mr Robson, Q.C., who as Sir William Robson was successively Solicitor and Attorney-General in the Liberal Government of 1906 and then became a Law Lord, led Mr Morten for the defendant Allen. The plaintiffs' statement of claim contained references to conspiracy amongst the defendants and to intimidation and coercion; but these could not be sustained, for Mr Justice Kennedy said " there is no evidence here, of course, of anything amounting to intimidation or coercion in

any legal sense of the term." The struggle, therefore, con-
verged on the central issue: did Allen maliciously induce
the Company to discharge the plaintiffs, and, if so, was he
liable in law?

The trial opened before Mr Justice Kennedy and a
Common Jury. Flood and Taylor gave evidence of a non-
descript sort, and were followed by John Edmunds, foreman
to the Glengall Company, who said that he had told Allen
that his action was " very arbitrary." The phrase was clearly
chosen with care by one who had a sense of the responsibility
of his position as foreman, but the standard of repartee was
somewhat lowered, if invigorated, by the evidence of
Richard Moseley, master mariner, who, with the blunt
enthusiasm of the sea, had told Allen that it would give him
great pleasure to " chuck him into the dock." Allen, however, had escaped this fate, and appeared instead in the
witness-box where he provoked great laughter by saying
that " while he came down with the olive-branch in his
mouth, Mr Edmunds not only kindled a fire but poured oil
upon it." At the conclusion of the evidence Mr Justice
Kennedy asked the jury whether Allen had maliciously
induced the Company to discharge the plaintiffs. The jury
found that he had, and that each plaintiff had thereby
suffered damage to the extent of £20. The facts being thus
decided upon, the case was reserved for argument and judgment on the legal aspect.

It might have been expected that where a leader of the
eminence of Lawson Walton was engaged that he alone
would argue the point of law in Court; but Lawson Walton
knew his junior, and the experience of their association had
given him great confidence in him. Consequently they
shared the burden of the case in Court. Rufus Isaacs
opened. He argued that there was no material difference
between inducement to break a contract and inducement not
to enter into a contract, and that where the inducer was
actuated by malice he was liable. In support of this latter
contention, he quoted the cases of Tarleton v. M'Gawley
and Keeble v. Hickeringill where it is laid down that " he

that hinders another in his trade or livelihood is liable to an action for so hindering him." Similarly the plaintiffs had a lawful right to work on iron, and it was gross tyranny to prevent them from doing so. Lawson Walton followed on the same lines, claiming that there had been a wrongful interference with the plaintiffs' lawful rights and with their freedom of action; Baron Bramwell had laid down in the famous Trade Union case of Regina v. Druitt that, under the common law, liberty of thought and freedom of will were part of the inalienable liberty of the subject.

On March 5th, 1895, Mr Justice Kennedy gave judgment in favour of the plaintiffs with damages of £40. The size of the damages was, of course, virtually immaterial as both sides were contending for a principle, which would govern future relationships. Allen appealed against the decision, and applied for a new trial on the ground of misdirection of the jury. The appeal was heard on April 3rd before the Master of the Rolls, Lord Esher, and Lord Justices Lopes and Rigby. After hearing counsel for the appellant, Lawson Walton and Isaacs were only called upon to argue their own cross-appeal against the finding of the lower court in favour of Knight and Jackson. The Court unanimously found that the fact of Allen having acted " maliciously " gave a cause of action against him. It may be remarked, however, that Lord Justice Rigby hinted, in his judgment, that if the matter were *res integra* his decision might be for Allen; but he conceived that they were bound by precedent.

With this shred of encouragement Allen took his appeal one step further, and the case went to the House of Lords. So, after eight years at the Bar, Rufus Isaacs enjoyed the rare honour of addressing the highest Court in the land. He was destined to appear in the Lords many times and it is a Court to which he always found his talents well suited; indeed he was always extremely effective in any class of appeal case. In this he differed from a great many successful jury advocates, but this arose perhaps from a difference of method before the jury. The advocate, who sweeps the jury off their feet with his torrential eloquence, is rarely able to adapt his style to the colder and more judicial atmosphere of the Appeal Courts. But this was never Rufus Isaacs' way; he realised that the jury normally wants to be instructed rather than impressed, and so, instead of trying to sweep them off their feet—for which indeed his style of speaking is unsuited—he stretched out a guiding hand to lead them through the intricacies and difficulties of the case. This quieter method of exposition is considerably easier to adapt to arguments directed to the Bench alone, and Rufus Isaacs never had to employ the conscious rearrangement of style for appeal cases, which is necessitated in the case of some advocates.

Allen v. Flood, having reached the last stage provided by civil procedure, dallied there considerably longer than is customary, for it was accorded the unusual honour of two hearings in the Lords. (It may be noticed that the case did not start as Allen v. Flood. It started as Flood and Taylor v. Jackson, Knight and Allen; but in the Court of Appeal and the House of Lords, Allen was the appellant, and by the time the case reached the House of Lords, Jackson and Knight had dropped out. So the case became Allen v. Flood, and under that name it continues as one of our greatest leading cases). The case was first argued before the House of Lords in December, 1895, but it was then decided that there were certain preliminary questions to be disposed of before their Lordships could deliver judgment. Consequently they took the unusual course of summoning eight High Court Judges to hear the arguments of counsel and decide the question whether, assuming the evidence given by the plaintiffs' witnesses to be correct, there was any evidence of a cause of action fit to be left to the jury. It was some time before so many judges could be spared from their ordinary routine simultaneously, and it was March 25, 1897, fifteen months after the first hearing in the House of Lords, that the final round of this long and extraordinary contest began.

It was, therefore, before a Court consisting of eight High

Court Judges and nine Law Lords, presided over by the Lord Chancellor, that Lawson Walton and Rufus Isaacs prepared to defend their victory in the two lower Courts. They based their case on two main arguments. In the first place, Allen had obstructed and interfered with the trade and means of livelihood of the plaintiffs; this in itself was an unlawful act. Secondly, even if the act had been lawful, any desire on the part of Allen to punish the plaintiffs or any " malice " in his action would render it unlawful. There was a third argument, imported for the first time into the case by Rufus Isaacs in the first hearing before the Lords and adopted by Lawson Walton in the second, namely that Allen had been guilty of misrepresentation in securing the termination of the contract. But since this point was not in the statement of claim or pleadings, and had not been advanced in the lower Courts, it could not be admissible at this stage. The Lord Chancellor thought that it was; but the Court adopted the view of Lord Davey: " It is not the practice of your Lordships, where there has been a trial by jury, to allow a new issue or question to be raised at the Bar which might or ought to have been, but was not, submitted to the jury for their consideration on the evidence. To do so would be to usurp the functions of the jury." The new argument, therefore, was disallowed and the case rested on the two main contentions.

The decision of the Judges, which was given after consideration on June 3rd, marked yet another victory for Lawson Walton and Rufus Isaacs. For the Judges decided by a majority of six to two that there was evidence of a cause of action fit to be left to the jury. The words of Mr Justice Hawkins may be taken as summarising the view of the majority: " Being satisfied that that right of the plaintiffs is established by law, I think there is an abundance of evidence fit to be left to the jury that, without excuse or justification, and not in the exercise of any privilege or in defence of any right either of his own or the boilermakers, the defendant has wilfully, unlawfully, unjustly and tyranically invaded and violated the plaintiffs' right by in-

timidating and coercing their employers to deprive them of
their present and future employment to their injury; and
the plaintiffs, therefore, are entitled to maintain their
injury."

Lawson Walton and Rufus Isaacs had reached the last
stage of a long struggle, leading strongly, for they had
won in every encounter.   But their victories were to
avail them nothing, for the Law Lords, representing the
final Court of Appeal, found that no action would lie
against Allen.   The decision was not unanimous, and
the view of Lawson Walton and Rufus Isaacs was
endorsed by the Lord Chancellor, Lord Halsbury, in an
extremely interesting and eloquent judgment.   This judgment and the monumental judgment of Lord Watson
express the two divergent points of view.   It is impossible
to summarise them here, but anybody interested in the
principles of law or in the brilliant reasoning of trained
minds, should read them verbatim.

It is possible, however, without going into the question
of legal precedents, to see the two attitudes of mind reflected
in the judgments.   Lord Halsbury took his stand on the
liberty of the subject to pursue his legitimate avocation unimpeded.   The point is put very well in Sir William Erle's
Memorandum on Trade Unions in which he wrote: " Every
person has a right under the law, as between himself and his
fellow subjects, to full freedom in disposing of his own
labour or his own capital according to his own will.   It
follows that every other person is subject to the correlative
duty arising therefrom, and is prohibited from any obstruction to the fullest exercise of this right which can be made
compatible with the exercise of similar rights by others."
This right had been violated, and this duty neglected; there
had been malice and there had been damage; so Lord Halsbury expressed his belief that " in denying these plaintiffs a
remedy we are departing from the principles which have
hitherto guided our Courts in the preservation of individual
liberty to all."

Lord Watson also took his stand on a fundamental right,

but it was a different aspect of the same liberty of action. " It is," he said, " in my opinion, the absolute right of every workman to exercise his own option with regard to the persons in whose society he will agree or continue to work." Allen's action had been no more than the delegated exercise, so to speak, of this right on behalf of the boilermakers, and for this he could not be made liable. It was admitted that the person, actually committing the act of dismissal, was not liable, and consequently the person inducing the act could not be liable either, since motive is not taken into account as constituting an element in civil wrong.

Lord Watson's view prevailed, and it is now undoubtedly the law that a bad motive does not create civil liability, where without it there is no cause of action, and that people in the position of Flood and Taylor have no legal remedy. Where two such Titans of the law as Lord Halsbury and Lord Watson were in disagreement, it would perhaps be impertinent to venture an opinion. But apart from the legal aspect, the question has great sociological interest and importance. And here perhaps the decision may fairly be regretted; for it must seem to the ordinary man or woman that the right of the individual to work unimpeded is a thing of greater ethical and social importance than the right of a worker to exercise an option as to whom he will work with. For in practice this latter right can only be exercised by strongly organised bodies of men, and it seems hardly in accordance with the English tradition of liberty and equality before the law that a man's employment should be at the mercy of the majority decision of a body, to which he may not belong and at whose deliberations he will not be represented. Lord Herschell who gave judgment on the same side as Lord Watson evidently saw some of the difficulty, and endeavoured to meet it. " I am not behind my noble and learned friend (Lord Halsbury)," he said, " in the desire to preserve individual liberty. But I think it is never in greater danger than when a tribunal is urged to restrict liberty of action because the manner in which it has been exercised in a particular instance may be distasteful."

The argument is plausible; but in point of fact, what else is the repression by the Courts of crime than the restriction of liberty of action because in particular instances the exercise of it is distasteful?   Liberty of action must, in the interests of the community, be restricted when that liberty of action infringes on the rights of others; and it seems to me that Allen *v.* Flood was just such a case and that, apart from the strictly legal issue, the decision may fairly be regretted, since it is desirable for courts and legislature alike to afford all possible legitimate protection to the individual whose liberty or livelihood is threatened by the arbitrary action of mass organisation.

Though we may regret that their point of view in this long and technical struggle was not sustained at the end, no blame for the ultimate failure attached to Rufus Isaacs or his leader. For they had displayed considerable fertility of resource and subtlety of reasoning during the protracted proceedings; and Rufus Isaacs could congratulate himself that at an early age he had been actively and prominently engaged in one of the longest and most hardly contested battles at the Bar, out of which there emerged a decision which is a leading authority on a most important principle of law.

CHAPTER V

IN 1898 Rufus Isaacs took silk; that is to say he made
application to the Lord Chancellor, Lord Halsbury, who
granted him permission to exchange his stuff gown for
the silk one, which is the distinguishing sartorial feature of a
King's Counsel. It is a step that is never taken without
anxious consideration, and not seldom with considerable
misgiving; for it involves participation in the narrower and
more select competition of those who have already distinguished themselves in the pursuit of their profession, and
it may not altogether inaptly be compared to the entry into
the finals of those who have done well in the heats. The
work of a King's Counsel (it was, of course, Queen's Counsel when Rufus Isaacs took silk) is different from that of a
junior and more restricted in scope; it is confined mainly
to " leading " in considerable cases in the High Court, and
therefore comparatively successful juniors, part of whose
incomes depend on work in lower courts, hesitate before
taking a step which will involve the sacrifice of an assured
source of income. Neither are qualities, which make a
successful junior, necessarily those which fit a man to be a
good King's Counsel, for skill in the preparation of cases
does not always go with the flair for the handling of the
case in Court, which is indispensable in a leader. Consequently many a good junior with a substantial income has
suffered a severe reverse in his fortunes on taking silk, and
even those who ultimately make a reputation as King's
Counsel, often undergo a temporary eclipse.

Rufus Isaacs was in a fortunate and special position. He
was extremely successful as a junior, and had in addition the
qualities that pointed to a potential success as a leader. By
the time he took silk his practice had grown so extensive,

especially in the lucrative sphere of commercial cases, that he was earning an income of £7,000 a year, then as now a very considerable income indeed for a junior to make at the Bar. The size of his income would, on the " bird in hand " principle, have been a legitimate inducement to stay at the junior Bar, though he need have had no qualms as to his chances as a " leader." Nevertheless he had only been at the Bar just over ten years, and in normal circumstances might well have postponed taking silk for a few years. What finally decided him, however, was not so much the glamorous possibilities of a career as a leader as the great burden of work which his large practice at the junior Bar imposed upon him. He has always been an industrious man, and through the greater part of his legal career it was his practice to rise in the very early morning and to put in several hours' work on his briefs before the consultation with his clerk, which preceded a day's work in the Courts, often involving participation in two cases which were going on simultaneously. Such a life involved a considerable physical strain, and in time his Parliamentary duties levied an additional toll on his time and energies.

It is a matter of mystification to some how it is possible to lead so crowded a life. One of the factors which helped Rufus Isaacs, as it has so many men of distinguished and varied achievement, is his capacity to do with little sleep, and to regulate his need for it according to the time which could be spared for it. This also spared him time for social life, of which he has always been fond. He has, however, always lived abstemiously and was at no time one of those whom the stimulus of heavy potations enabled to be as witty and entertaining in society in the evenings, as they have been brilliantly effective in affairs in the daytime. This Rabelaisian school of public men, of whom Charles James Fox is the most famous English example, is fascinating to observe in action; but even the strongest constitution must normally succumb to it before reaching old age. Lord Reading has not employed these adventitious aids either in business or in society; he has taken the quieter and wiser course of husbanding his resources with the result that in the seventies he retains his skill in the one, equally with his aptitude for the other.

Another faculty of which he is possessed, and without which great achievement in a varied and extensive field is virtually impossible, is the ability to turn his attention completely to the matter in hand to the exclusion of other preoccupations, no matter how important they may be. It is this capacity of, so to speak, departmentalising the mind, which alone enables it to carry the weight of varied interests, and which alone allows of that terrific concentration, which must normally precede great achievement. It was this quality which enabled Napoleon to lie on the floor for hours on end, sticking pins into a map, and to beat Blucher as a result. It is a quality, too, possessed by a contemporary advocate and statesman of great distinction, who recently gave a young advocate his first lesson in the necessity of departmentalisation of the mind. The great man was leading the young barrister in an important case, and the young man, remembering no doubt all that he had been told about the invariable accessibility of leaders to be consulted on equal terms by their juniors, called on his leader to ask him to elucidate a knotty point in the brief. He was unlucky enough to find him engaged in his rôle of statesman, in preparing a speech on India, and the interview was short and one-sided. The great man merely raised his head slightly and said, " Are you aware that there are three hundred million people in India? " and, like jesting Pilate, on the occasion of another rhetorical question, stayed not for an answer.

The combination of these qualities allowed Rufus Isaacs to get the maximum of result from the expenditure of his energies; but even with their assistance, he found that the work of his later period as a junior was imposing a strain upon him, which it would be unwise to continue indefinitely. It is true that his practice as a silk soon caught up and over-took his previous practice, but the work of a leader is less exacting than that of a succesful junior; for, though he has a great deal to do in Court and must always be keyed up to his best form when he appears there, he is nevertheless spared the drudgery of preparation which precedes the presentation of a case in Court. And so it was not only with high hopes but with a sense of the inevitability of his action that he made his application to Lord Halsbury; and in due course he went down to the House of Lords to receive his patent and went through the ancient ritual of being called " within the Bar," by the judges in their various Courts. Of the six other juniors who were called with him, the most interesting was Edward Marshall Hall, who was two years older than Rufus Isaacs and had been at the Bar a few years longer. Fate threw them occasionally, though not frequently, into opposition, and the Seddon trial many years later provided a splendid background for their very divergent types of advocacy.

Rufus Isaacs' first year or two as a silk were, not unnaturally, not marked by the great cases with which in later days his name became almost automatically associated; but they were years of steady advance, in which he rapidly acquired a growing practice as a silk, consisting largely at first of commercial cases, in which his proficiency was already well proved. Among these were his appearance in the lengthy bankruptcy proceedings of Ernest Terence Hooley, the financier, and his defence of Beall, the ex-solicitor company promoter, on charges of making and publishing a false prospectus and of obtaining money by false pretences.

Beall's trial came on at the Old Bailey on October 31st, 1899, and lasted for fifteen days. Three other men—Lambert, Singleton and Wain—were indicted with him on the same charges, which were concerned with the floating of the London and Scottish Banking and Discount Corporation. This company, which had been registered on August 18th, 1892, went into liquidation in 1895 after having obtained £30,000 in subscriptions from the public. It was, therefore, rather ancient history when it came before the Court, but the reason why no prosecution had been instigated before was that the Company had been registered in Scotland, to which the stringent provisions of the Act of 1890, requiring investigation after liquidation, did not apply. The company was formed as a discount bank, especially for small tradesmen, but very little by way of business was ever done. However, it was decided to increase the capital, which at the date of registering had been stated to be £102,000 to £1,000,000 and to this end, in March, 1893, it was resolved to issue 100,000 ordinary shares of £10 each. With the aid of 124,000 copies of the prospectus, which had been sent out, and a loyal and vigorous boosting in Beall's paper, the *Financial Gazette*, £20,000 was subscribed by the public. A new prospectus was then issued, of which 50,000 copies were sent out, inviting subscriptions for £50,000 4¾ per cent. Debenture Stock; but this time the public made a less flattering response, the sole tangible sign of approval coming from an invalid lady in Gloucestershire, who sent £189, 6s. 2d. for £200 of Debenture Stock. On the strength of this, however, they declared an interim dividend of 7 per cent. for the half-year, ending September, 1893, and sent out a new prospectus with a letter stating that a 7 per cent. dividend had been declared and inviting subscriptions for ordinary shares at a 10/- premium. When the order for winding up the company was made in Scotland in January, 1895, the total assets were found to be £336.

Rufus Isaacs had the difficult task of defending Beall, who was, in the words of Mr Justice Channell, who tried the case, the " brains of the undertaking " and clearly a man of ability; he was, however, in spite of the " dash " which he invariably cut in the City (something after the manner of Whittaker Wright) an undischarged bankrupt in 1892, just before the company was launched. The defence of Lambert was entrusted to Mr Marshall Hall, while the Solicitor-General, Sir Robert Finlay, led Mr Sutton, Mr Avory, now a famous High Court Judge, and Mr Archibald Bodkin, lately Public Prosecutor, for the Crown. The evidence for the prosecution occupied seven rather tedious days, and at the conclusion of it Rufus Isaacs at once put Beall into the box without addressing the jury. To-day this practice is

not exceptional in criminal trials, but at the time of Beall's
case the Criminal Evidence Act which first made it possible
for prisoners to give evidence on their own behalf, was only
a year old, and Rufus Isaacs' action made a considerable
impression on the jury; it was at once a gesture of confidence
and of defiance, which considerably enhanced the prospects
of his client. These, however, were slender enough. Rufus
Isaacs made a spirited effort in his behalf and in his address
to the jury urged that the Company was bona fide and was a
concern which might have had a considerable success if things
had gone more smoothly; for there was a good opening in
England, and more especially in Scotland, for a half-way
house between the ordinary banking establishment and
usurious concerns, which could give facilities to traders. The
reason why Beall's company had been unable to meet this
want was to be found in the hostility with which it had
been treated by the old-established and conservative banks

Rufus Isaacs' persuasiveness was, however, on this occasion
of no avail, and Beall was found guilty and sentenced to
four years' penal servitude. Singleton and Wain, who were
also found guilty, were held to be less culpable and received
respectively eighteen months and twelve months in the
second division. Lambert alone, who had not been privy to,
or even aware of, many of the Company's transactions, was
found not guilty. It is interesting to observe that counsel
for two of the other prisoners followed Rufus Isaacs'
example and put their clients into the witness-box, only
Singleton refraining from submitting himself to cross-
examination. This shows how widespread the practice,
authorised by the Act, instantly became, and for many years
now it has been almost obligatory for counsel to put his
client into the box; or at any rate it is a very grave responsibility not to do so, for it is apt to be taken as a confession of
guilt. This is clearly not what was intended by the Act,
which was intended to confer a boon upon prisoners by
removing a disability from them, of which their counsel had
often eloquently, if perhaps a trifle insincerely, complained;
and, in so far as a virtually compulsory element has been

introduced, the workings of the Act have to a certain extent justified the forebodings of its critics. Prominent among these was Lord Carson, who said in the House of Commons in the debate on the Bill: " We are putting an end to a great safeguard the citizens of this country have enjoyed for centuries, namely, that the Crown must prove its case." He also declared that in his experience he could recall no case of any suggested miscarriage of justice by reason of the inability of the prisoner to give evidence, and said " I think counsel will look upon such obligations as are thus thrown upon them with horror." That this latter prophecy was not unfounded can be seen from the fact that Mr Marjoribanks tells us that Sir Edward Marshall Hall would not accept the responsibility in capital cases, but gave the prisoner an alternative form to sign, the one reading " I intend to give evidence in this case," the other " I do not intend to give evidence in this case." But while admitting the strength of these arguments and the great authority of Lord Carson's, it must be remembered that an Act of Parliament, passed to remove a disability from a prisoner on trial, is only incidentally passed in the interests of the prisoner; it aims primarily at furthering and facilitating the course of justice. And this is just what the practice would appear to do, for justice can only be attained with certainty if the whole truth can be arrived at, and this is clearly more feasible if no avenues of approach are barred. If the prisoner is innocent he will almost certainly be the gainer by giving evidence, for even if he is flustered and gives contradictory evidence, his counsel can assist him to put it right in re-examination; while if he is guilty, then the interests of justice demand that his own words should not be excluded as a possible pathway to truth. Years later it fell to the lot of Rufus Isaacs to show, in one of the most famous murder trials of the century, that a clever man, who has covered up his tracks, may be exposed in cross-examination; and it is possible that if it had done nothing else but indicate the interests of justice in that case, the Act would not have failed entirely of its higher purpose.

The period of his early days as a " silk " marked, too,

Rufus Isaacs' first incursus into politics. In politics he was
a Liberal; this perhaps was natural, for Liberalism at that
time was the normal political faith of his race and exercised
a great attraction for young lawyers. It was then possible
to be a radical without being a revolutionary, and a pro-
gressive without ceasing to be a patriot. And whatever may
be said of the Liberal Party's philosophy in those days it
could not be said to lack a policy; and a party which included
Asquith, Rosebery, Morley and Haldane could not be fairly
accused of that narrowness of vision and interest which is
sometimes associated with Liberalism. The Tory Party,
too, presented fewer attractions to the young man of zeal
and vision than it does to-day; for although it had long
been rescued by Disraeli from the reactionary class-
consciousness which Croker had striven to elevate into a
political philosophy, it was still undergoing, at the hands of
Mr Chamberlain, its education in the reflection and representation of democratic interests and aspirations. To the
Liberal Party, Rufus Isaacs accordingly adhered; but,
though he was a convinced Free Trader and social reformer,
he was not a revolutionary nor a " Little Englander."
Consequently his membership of the House of Lords and
his tenure of the Viceroyalty have not been incongruous;
we have been spared in his case the nauseating and pathetic
spectacle presented by ex-revolutionaries who end up by
sitting in a Chamber, which they have spent their political
lives in abusing, or by holding a post in the administration
of an Empire to which their only claim is an abundance of
effort directed to its disintegration. It is a category in which
it would be unfair to place Lord Reading; for though in the
long Liberal campaign to limit the powers of the House of
Lords, he stated that he would prefer an elective chamber,
he was careful not to degenerate into the abuse which was all
too prevalent at the time. And his first entry into politics
as a Liberal Imperialist was not an unfitting prelude to the
Viceroyalty.

Nevertheless all could not be said to be well with the
Liberal Party in the late 1890's. The general election of

1895 had brought a disaster which was aggravated by the disagreement, in the very course and conduct of the election, of some of the leaders of the party; in the new Parliament the opposition numbered 259, of whom 82 were Irish Nationalists, while the Unionist had 411. But the position of the party was worse even than the figures indicated; for it was becoming, in the words of Sir William Harcourt, " a party rent by sectional disputes and personal interests," and as such it was increasingly difficult to maintain it in a semblance of unity. Lord Rosebery for a time kept his uneasy crown as leader of the party, but was in constant conflict with Sir William Harcourt; for in the case of these two there was added to the difference of principle between the Liberal Imperialist and the " Little Englander " the strained relationship of two antagonistic personalities. It was not a position which he relished or desired to keep for long, and he took the first opportunity of relinquishing it; this occurred as a result of Mr Gladstone's final public oration, in which he made his famous appeal for British intervention in the matter of the Armenian massacres. A large section of the party responded to his call, but neither Rosebery nor Harcourt favoured intervention in the manner suggested. That there might be a certain amount of dissension on the question was clear, but nobody expected extreme measures. It was, therefore, a matter of considerable astonishment to his followers when on October 8th, 1896, Rosebery renounced his leadership of the party. According to Harcourt he " funked the future which he saw before him "; however this may be, his resignation certainly left Harcourt the most commanding personality in the Liberal Party.

It might have been supposed that this retirement would at least have given internal tranquillity to the councils of the Liberal Party. In point of fact, however, it did not, for Sir William Harcourt took advantage of the Fashoda incident to resign his leadership of the party in the House of Commons in December 1898; and his action was endorsed and his retirement shared by Mr John Morley. The depleted ranks of the Liberal Party then elected Sir Henry Campbell-Bannerman, " a person of a pretty tolerant and easy-going disposition "—the description is his own—as leader of the Party. The choice was a good one, for Campbell-Bannerman, though a man of obvious limitations, served his Party loyally and well. But the impact of public events came to reinforce the personal elements of discord within the Party, for in 1899 war broke out in South Africa against the Boers. It is always difficult for a party in opposition to decide on its attitude at the advent of war; for it usually maintains that the war is the direct outcome of the policy of the Government, which it has been active in criticising, but at the same time, when the war has actually begun, a certain support is usually accorded to the Government in its prosecution of it. The Liberal Party was caught in these difficulties to an unusual extent, and the Party was split again. They were united in their opposition to the attitude and tactics of Mr Chamberlain, but even this was really a retrospective point. On the question of the war itself Lord Rosebery and the Liberal Imperialists, supported by Mr Asquith and his group, were emphatic; it must be waged and it must be won. Campbell-Bannerman on the other hand, although in his own words he was " anti-Joe but never pro-Kruger," laid so much more stress on his criticisms of the Government and the legitimate grievances of the Boers than on the necessity of winning the war, that his attitude was generally termed " pro-Boer." It was in these circumstances and in this condition that the Liberal Party were called upon to fight the General Election of 1900.

The Conservative Government decided to appeal to the country in the autumn of 1900 in the belief that the war was over; the belief turned out to be premature, but the election was held all the same. Thus it was through the rather unsatisfactory medium of a wartime election that Rufus Isaacs made his political début, for he had been adopted as Liberal candidate for North Kensington. It was not a particularly good seat from a Liberal point of view, for, though it had been won in the election of 1892 by 210 votes, it had been solidly Unionist in the elections of 1885, 1886 and 1895. In 1895 the Conservative majority had been 916, which was considerable in the small electorates and narrow margins of those days; and, as his Conservative opponent, Mr Thompson Sharpe, though not a distinguished politician, was competent enough, his task would have been formidable at any time. But the circumstances of the war-time election made it doubly difficult. For, although Rufus Isaacs was a Liberal Imperialist and shared Lord Rosebery's views as to the proper attitude of the Liberal Party to the war, the Conservative Party made no distinction between the different sorts of Liberalism in their electorial onslaught; the contemporary slogan " every vote given to the Liberals is a vote given to the Boers " made its appearance in North Kensington as elsewhere, and its effect was potent in a " khaki election." It was no doubt true, in view of his attitude, that to place Campbell-Bannerman in charge of the conduct of the war would have been a dangerous thing; and it was felt that the Liberal Imperialists merely served to complicate the issue. In point of fact, however, neither of the two first general elections of the twentieth century afford much subject for congratulation, for the Conservative slogan at this election was not greatly more reputable than the Liberal cry of " Chinese slavery " at the 1906 election—a cry, it may be noted, never echoed by Rufus Isaacs in his campaign.

In 1900, however, the tide, at anyrate in England, was set against the Liberals, and Rufus Isaacs went down with his party. He made great efforts, aided by a concourse of carriages on polling day larger than his Conservative opponent could muster, and a poster, headed by the Union Jack and Royal Standard with the letters V.R.I. underneath, which stood, rather unexpectedly, for " Vote for Rufus Isaacs." But Mr Chamberlain wrote a letter to the elector-ate, exhorting them to vote for Thompson Sharpe; and Mr Chamberlain was all-powerful in those days. On October 5th the result was announced:

W. E. T. Sharpe (C.)	...	3257
Rufus Isaacs (L.) ...	...	2527
Conservative Majority	...	730

Rufus Isaacs, therefore, had succeeded in lowering the Conservative majority by 186, and that in a "khaki election" was no mean feat; and as it turned out, his chance of entering Parliament was not to be delayed till the next General Election.

CHAPTER VI

A " POLITICAL " LIBEL ACTION AND A BOER WAR
PROSECUTION

RUFUS ISAACS' failure to get into Parliament in the
1900 election was scarcely a matter for surprise; nor,
from a point of view of his private career, was it a
matter for regret. For his practice as a silk was rapidly
expanding, and he was about to enter into his great phase
as an advocate; in the years 1900-1904 are to be found some
of the most memorable cases with which his name is associated. An active attention to Parliamentary duties could not
but have affected, even if only in a small degree, the
enormous growth of his practice, for the people who talk
glibly about ambitious lawyers going into politics for their
own ends, tend to forget that they often do so at the cost
of a decline in their legal practice. The Boer War, therefore, did not do him a complete disservice in keeping him
out of Parliament, and it compensated him, too, for dashing
his first political hopes by providing him indirectly with two
or three great cases in the Courts.

The first of these was the celebrated libel action of
Chamberlain *v. The Star,* which arose out of certain articles
in *The Star,* alleging the use of political pressure in the
securing of Government contracts for cordite. Now at the
time of the Boer War there were constant rumours of corruption and allegations of incompetence in the supply of the
materials of warfare—and perhaps it was no exception to
the general run of wars in that respect—especially in the
matter of hay, out of which arose Colonel Morgan's action
in which Rufus Isaacs appeared three years later, and of
cordite. The rumours in respect of cordite were so emphatic
and the dissatisfaction so widespread that a select committee
of the House of Commons was appointed to investigate the

subject of the cordite contracts; this committee accepted the official view that it was necessary in the public interest to keep Kynoch's going as producers of cordite in order that the available supply might be readily increased in time of war. Kynoch's was a considerable Midland firm of cordite manufacturers, in which the Chamberlain family had an interest; and the *Star*, which of course was strongly opposed to Joseph Chamberlain's imperial policy, holding it to be the cause of the war, was not content with the findings of the select committee and proceeded, in articles appearing between August 2nd and October 12th, 1900, to attack a system which allowed contracts to be made at an apparently uneconomic figure.

The facts were as follows. The firm of Kynoch's was turned into a company in 1884, and thereupon went through a bad financial period, showing a loss of £18,000 in 1887. Then Mr Arthur Chamberlain, " Joe's " brother, was made chairman, and an immediate change for the better took place, a dividend of 10% being paid in 1889. In 1894 the Government—it was Lord Rosebery's—decided that contracts for cordite should be given to private firms, and accordingly in 1894, 1898 and 1900 tenders were invited and orders placed. In 1894, Kynoch's secured half the contract, although they were not at the time properly equipped for the manufacture of cordite. In 1898, Kynoch's tendered at 2/4½d, which was sixpence more than the tender of the National Explosives Company; Kynoch's, however, were given the opportunity of revising their tender so as to bring it into line with that of the National Explosives Company, and ultimately secured a contract for 380 tons. On the third occasion, in 1900, seven firms tendered, and Kynoch's tender at 2/6d was the highest. The Admiralty, however, proposed to allocate to them an order for 880,000 lbs. out of the whole, at the same time giving them an opportunity to revise their tender down to 2/3d; eventually the allocation was done, this time not by the Admiralty, but by the War Office, which gave Kynoch's an order for 330,000 lbs. at their original tender. The official explanation of this preferential treatment, and that of the select committee, was, as we have seen, that it was justified, and necessary, in the public interest; to the *Star*, on the other hand, it appeared that, since Arthur Chamberlain was chairman of Kynoch's while "Joe" Chamberlain was Secretary of State for the Colonies and Austen Chamberlain Civil Lord of the Admiralty, political pressure had been brought to bear in the interests of Kynoch's. There, however, the matter might possibly have rested but for "Joe" Chamberlain's statement in answer to a question in the House of Commons on August 8th, 1900: "I have no interest, direct or indirect, in Kynoch's or in any other firm manufacturing ammunition or war materials." The statement was in the main accurate, and, as far as he was aware, of course, entirely true; but the *Star* discovered at Somerset House that the Birmingham Trust Company, in which he had shares, had invested ten per cent. of its capital in Kynoch's. Mr Joseph Chamberlain, therefore, had an interest in Kynoch's, even if only indirectly, and Kynoch's had undoubtedly received preferential treatment. The *Star* decided that such manifestations of a bad system must be attacked; the attack was duly launched in a series of articles, which gave strong vent to the *Star's* criticisms and lost nothing in vigour from the circumstance that the General Election made it a time of considerable political rancour.

Mr Joseph Chamberlain himself contemplated bringing an action for libel, but was advised that it would not lie, and the Chamberlain of Chamberlain *v. The Star* was his brother Arthur, chairman of Kynoch's. He maintained, as plaintiff, that the articles, alleging that he brought family influence to bear to obtain Government contracts for cordite on advantageous terms, were a libel upon himself. The *Star's* case was that, in so far as the remarks complained of were statements of fact, they were not defamatory; and in all other respects the articles were fair comment on matters of public interest. The case came on in the King's Bench Division before the Lord Chief Justice, Lord Alverstone, and a special jury, on March 21st, 1901, and lasted for five days. Sir Edward Clarke, K.C., led Dr. Blake Odgers, K.C., and Mr Whitmore Richards for the plaintiff, while Rufus Isaacs led Mr Eldon Bankes, K.C., for the *Star*. Thus at the age of forty, Rufus Isaacs found himself matched with the acknowledged leader of the Bar, for as such Sir Edward Clarke, who had been Solicitor-General in the Salisbury administration of 1886-90 was generally regarded after the elevation to the Bench of Sir Charles Russell, with whom he had crossed swords in the famous Tranby Croft case. To be chosen by a leading London newspaper to carry their colours against such a champion in a case of great importance and public interest was a considerable honour; the opposition, too, was all the stronger as Sir Edward had the assistance of the monumental legal learning of Dr. Blake Odgers, who was a distinguished ornament of what may be termed the academic side of the profession. Rufus Isaacs also had distinguished assistance, for Mr Eldon Bankes, who was descended from Lord Chancellor Eldon, was an extremely sound lawyer, although not a great orator. He subsequently became Lord Justice Bankes, and on the Bench he displayed, in addition to his great command of law, a charm of manner and a kindliness of disposition which impressed all who came into contact with him. In this case his position was peculiar, for when the case was entered he was a junior and as such prepared the defence; but by the time the case came into Court, however, he had taken silk—thereby becoming one of the youngest of the K.C.s. The case of Chamberlain *v. The Star*, therefore, presented the unusual spectacle of two young K.C.s appearing for the defence without the assistance of any member of the junior Bar.

The defence had a very difficult task, for they had to show, in order to establish the fairness of their comment, that Arthur Chamberlain had made an unfair use of his connections for the advantage of his private firm. In point of fact, the *Star* had really been concerned to attack the system, under which Government contracts were administered, but by citing the Kynoch contracts as an example, they were inevitably attacking a private firm in addition; and it is safe to say that, if newspapers extended the methods of criticism which they employ in respect of public men and public affairs, to commercial and private undertakings, they would very soon be involved in some very costly litigation. It would be judicious, therefore, to conduct the case with the soft pedal down. Nothing could be gained by aggressiveness, for the essential honesty of Mr Chamberlain was not in question; and, if the verdict was to be hostile, the damages would be greatly increased by any aggravation of the offence. This is a type of case—and they are far from uncommon—for which his command of himself, his restraint, and his exact discrimination especially fitted Rufus Isaacs. It is a type of case, too, in which he always excelled; for, where a stormier advocate might well be carried away by his eloquence or the force of the case which he was presenting, Rufus Isaacs never for a moment lost sight of the main issue. And that is perhaps the most fundamental, as it is probably the least showy, of the qualities of a great advocate.

It follows that the most interesting part of the case was Rufus Isaacs' address to the jury. But before this he subjected Arthur Chamberlain to a lengthy cross-examination. Mr Chamberlain said that in his opinion it would not be legitimate to use political influence to get contracts for Kynoch's, but admitted that one of his subordinates, Cullen, had written to the Agent-General to the Australian colonies to inform them that the secretary of Kynoch's was going to visit Australia, and that the chairman of the company was the brother of the Secretary of State for the Colonies; this, however, had been without his knowledge. In truth there was little headway to be made against Mr Arthur Chamberlain. For he was the very type and symbol of the Victorian successful man of business, with all the virtues and all the limitations of his class; and as such he impressed the jury very favourably. His attitude is well exemplified by a passage in his cross-examination. He had been asked by Rufus Isaacs whether Kynoch's had made any arrangements to " maintain prices " with other firms. On his replying in the negative, Rufus Isaacs asked:

" Do you say you would be acting properly if you made such an arrangement? "

" That kind of thing," came the reply, " does not have my approval. I do not think it pays."

Later on in his cross-examination, when questioned as to political pressure, he said that he had written to the manager of the works at Arklow, telling him to show Mr Field, M.P. over the works and had instructed him: " Don't say anything which is not true, but what you say must be illustrative of the advantages we have brought to Ireland." Such remarks might have been invaluable to Mr Lytton Strachey for a portrait in miniature, but they did no harm to the plaintiff's case. For what is material for the satirist is not always material for counsel, and certain limitations have always been considered conducive to good business.

Rufus Isaacs, therefore, opened his address to the jury by saying that he accepted Mr Arthur Chamberlain's evidence, and it was on the strength of that evidence that he would ask the jury to say that the articles were justified. No action was necessary to vindicate Mr Arthur Chamberlain's character because no imputation had been made on his private character, the articles having their inception in Joseph Chamberlain's statement in the House of Commons on August 8th, which had turned out to be incorrect. Nor was it, Isaacs insisted, Arthur Chamberlain who was really concerned with the case, for the *Star* had not imputed cor͘ ruption but had attacked the system as wrong; and the question in respect of that was not whether their views were right, but whether they were entitled to put them forward. The whole of the *Star's* campaign had been directed against Mr Joseph Chamberlain and Mr Austen Chamberlain, who were ministers of the Crown. But they had been advised that there were no statements on which they could found an action for libel and " therefore it is," said Rufus Isaacs, " that Mr Arthur Chamberlain, who is quite a minor person in these matters, comes forward and brings an action for

libel with two little pegs to hang his case on—Tubes and
Kynoch's—and alleging that he is charged in these articles
with corruption." He then outlined the history of the
allocation of the contracts, showing how on each occasion
Kynoch's had received preferential treatment. The plaintiff had said in cross-examination that it was the allegations
of "Government favouritism" to which he took exception;
but surely this continued preferential treatment was proof
of Government favouritism. The matter was one of great
public importance and the *Star*, which did not for a moment
impute corruption, but felt the finding of the Select Committee to be "kind," was doing its duty in drawing attention
to the facts. The kernel of the matter was Mr Joseph
Chamberlain's statement in the House of Commons, for it
was a public statement, inviting contradiction or refutation;
and "it is a thousand times to be regretted," said Rufus
Isaacs, his voice taking on an added note of sternness, " for
the sake of the purity and honour of our national life that
the statement which was made on August 8th was never
contradicted." He then concluded, not with an appeal, but
with a challenge, almost a command: " You must deal with
the whole question broadly and in a public spirit, and I look
to you to vindicate the position the defendants have taken
up in fearlessly commenting on matters of great public
importance."

Rufus Isaacs had handled a difficult case with considerable
tact, for he had maintained it firmly, but never aggressively;
and he had lost no chance of insisting that there was an
unreality in the whole proceedings, since the criticism was
directed at Mr Joseph Chamberlain and public administration, while the action was brought by Mr Arthur Chamberlain, chairman of a private company. But Sir Edward
Clarke was too wary and tried an advocate not to see where
the danger lay, and he insisted from the beginning of his
speech that they were concerned with the reputation of a
private individual and not with questions of public policy.
" The suggestion is," he said, " that the assault was intended
to be directed against Mr Joseph Chamberlain and Mr

Austen Chamberlain, and that if Mr Arthur Chamberlain
was hit in the attack that was because he enjoys the privilege
of being Mr Joseph Chamberlain's brother, and he must
always remember as a consolation that his brother is in the
Cabinet." Equally striking and effective was his method of
dealing with another of Rufus Isaacs' contentions, namely
that the attack had done Arthur Chamberlain no harm, as
his commercial reputation was so firmly established; in
reference to this Sir Edward said: " According to the
defendants' theory the only people who could ever get
damages for libel are shady financiers and ladies with a past,
and they are entitled to recover damages in order to set up
a somewhat damaged reputation."

Lord Alverstone then proceeded to a careful and fair
summing up; it left, however, little doubt as to what the
verdict would be, and after forty-five minutes' retirement
the jury duly found for the plaintiff. The verdict, however, which was on the whole to be expected was hardly as
important a consideration as the damages, which were
assessed at only £200. To keep the damages, awarded
against a great newspaper in a case of such importance, down
to the trifling sum of £200, may not unfairly be considered
a triumph on the part of Rufus Isaacs. This view, at any
rate, was taken by the *Star*, which was far from dissatisfied
with the verdict. In the course of a leading article on the
subject, it was stated that " no charge reflecting upon the
personal integrity of any member of his family was at any
time contemplated. If he (Arthur Chamberlain) is now
willing to take the view of our criticisms which we intended
them to present, he will be able to regard the verdict of the
jury with satisfaction equal to ours. Their verdict," the
article continued, " was given after a prolonged and arduous
intellectual battle between eminent counsel in which the
consummate ability of Mr Rufus Isaacs was pitted against
the eloquence of the greatest advocate now living." Elsewhere in the paper further complimentary reference was
made: " We more than anyone have reason to appreciate
the vast skill and the perfect discretion with which the

defence in the Chamberlain case was conducted by the counsel to whom it was confided. The youthfulness of both Mr Rufus Isaacs, K.C., and Mr Eldon Bankes, K.C., and the fact that in the face of even adverse circumstance and against such redoubtable opponents as Sir Edward Clarke—the unquestioned head of his profession—and Dr Blake Odgers, K.C., they kept the verdict down to the inconsiderable sum of £200 is the greatest feat of advocacy since Mr C. F. Gill, as an almost unknown junior, beat Sir Charles Russell in their forensic duel in the Marks and Butterfield case." In this sweeping assertion the *Star* was perhaps carried away by the enthusiasm of the moment; but it is pleasant to have so grateful a client.

Immediately on the conclusion of the case of Chamberlain v. *The Star*, a second came on for hearing, namely, Neville Chamberlain v. *The Star*. The facts of this case had no connection with the former case, for *The Star* had here drawn information from another paper, which they had believed to be true and which had turned out to be false. *The Star*, therefore, expressed in Court their desire to make full apology and withdrawal; they also paid £1500 to the plaintiff as full indemnity in respect of his claim. So ended the Chamberlain litigation against *The Star*. It is a curious incidental fact that Sir Edward Clarke, who was leading counsel for the Chamberlains, found himself forced to withdraw from active Conservative politics because of his disagreement with Mr Joseph Chamberlain's policy of Protection, while thirty years later Rufus Isaacs, who was counsel on the opposite side, was a fellow member with Mr Neville Chamberlain of the first National Government.

The other case in which Rufus Isaacs appeared, arose more directly out of the Boer War; for, whereas Chamberlain v. *The Star* had been concerned with what is sometimes called—though exclusively by non-combatants—the Home Front, Dr Krause had taken an active and leading part in South Africa. It was some months after the Chamberlain case, in January of 1902, that Rufus Isaacs appeared at the Old Bailey for the defence of the strange and talented Dr

Krause. This case, which excited great interest at the time on account of its connection with the Boer War, is chiefly remarkable as an illustration of how much an able and resourceful advocate can do, when the facts are for the most part not in dispute and are hostile to his client.

The case was in many ways very unusual, on account both of the personalities involved and of the circumstances attending it. Dr Krause was a young South African of Dutch extraction, who showed such marked abilities from the first, that after his schooling in South Africa was completed, he was sent over to study law at the University of Amsterdam. From there he came to England, and in 1893 joined the Middle Temple, from which he was called to the Bar. He then returned to South Africa to practise and so rapid was his rise that a few years found him risen to be State Prosecutor and acting Attorney-General for Witwatersrand under the Republican Government.

Like most young lawyers he was actively interested in politics, in which he was a determined anti-Uitlander, and it was his political views which brought him into conflict with another young lawyer called Forster, who was an extremely zealous Unionist. Forster was not so high in his profession as Krause, nor was he quite the " model " young man that the earnest, industrious young Attorney was; but he had founded a league for the defence of the Union and, as politics assumed an ever-growing significance in South Africa, so did Forster's importance—at any rate in the eyes of Krause—grow larger. And Krause felt against Forster the bitter animosity which at times of intense political and national feeling men entertain for their opponents.

All continued, however, to go well with Krause for a time. The outbreak of the Boer War, which he personally deplored, brought him into greater prominence as Special Commandant and Military Governor of Johannesburg. This position he continued to hold until May, 1900, when on the approach of Lord Roberts he surrendered the town without a struggle; in consideration of this, Lord Roberts sent him a letter, which was afterwards read by Rufus Isaacs

in the trial. It ran: "I desire to express to you how fully
I appreciate the valuable assistance you have afforded me in
connection with the entry into this town of the force under
my command . . . Thanks to your energy and vigilance,
order and tranquillity have been preserved, and I congratulate you heartily on the result of your labours. Permit me
also to tender to you my personal thanks for the great
courtesy you have shown me since I first had the pleasure
of meeting you." No doubt the easy surrender of Johannesburg was mainly due to the plan of the Boers to keep their
capital safe from the damage necessarily attendant on a siege.
But nevertheless Krause was undoubtedly anxious to reduce
to a minimum the bloodshed and suffering consequent on a
war, the very existence of which he regretted.

Krause had given his parole to the British that he would
not leave Johannesburg without leave. Accordingly he
applied for permission, which was granted, and he came to
London by way of Paris. In London he resumed his legal
practice, apparently without difficulty or comment; which in
one who had taken a leading part on the side of the enemy
in a war still raging, seems surprising enough, and affords
proof, incidentally, that British anti-Boer feeling was not as
ferocious as it is sometimes portrayed. He appeared in one
case for Mr Markham, M.P., in the action brought against
him by Krause's old enemy, Forster. And indeed his mind
was becoming more and more preoccupied with thoughts of
Forster; far away now himself from the scene of action,
and impatient perhaps at his enforced inactivity in the
struggle, Krause began to brood over the affairs of his
country, and became convinced that Forster was his country's
arch-enemy, and that it was his duty to draw the attention
of his countrymen on the spot to the menace in their midst.
Consequently he wrote letters to a friend, Broeksma, in the
summer of 1901, asking for information against Forster of
a derogatory nature which would discredit him, or suggesting, as an alternative, more drastic measures for his removal.
These letters never reached Broeksma, who was court-
martialled and shot on August 24th; but their discovery

led to the arrest of Krause on the charge of incitement to murder.

The Boer War was still in being—for though the worst of the fighting was over, peace was not signed until nearly six months later—when Krause came up for trial before the Lord Chief Justice in January, 1902. Public interest in the proceedings was, therefore, considerable, but it was to be a case more famous for refinement of argument employed by counsel than for the general circumstances surrounding it. Krause was charged on an indictment containing thirty counts, the gist of which was a charge of incitement to murder, under the Offences against the Persons Act of 1861; Rufus Isaacs led for the defence, while Sir Edward Carson, the Solicitor-General, led for the prosecution.

The task of the prosecution was comparatively simple. All that Carson had to do—at least to start with—was to outline the events, narrated above, and to read the letters, whose authorship was undisputed, and submit that the offence was made out. The letter of August 6th contained the most damning passage: " F—— is greatly the cause of this, and therefore I wrote to you the previous week that our people should be made aware of this, so that he can be shot dead in some lawful manner, or otherwise put out of the way." And in a letter of August 30th he wrote: " Of course I only wish to know this (this refers to his request to Broeksma to find out information derogatory to Forster) if the other matters concerning Forster have not reached their consummation. I would, of course, prefer the latter." Evidence was given by Forster and Colonel Davies of the Intelligence Department, who said that, as far as he knew, Krause had never taken the oath of allegiance or of neutrality. Forster, when cross-examined by Isaacs, was compelled to admit that a letter of his had appeared in the *Pall Mall Gazette* of June 17th, 1901, in which he had urged that all the enemy forces in the field should be treated not as belligerents, but as robbers and bandits—meaning, as he now alleged, as British subjects in rebellion.

Rufus Isaacs opened his case by reading the letter from

Lord Roberts and a letter written by Krause to Broeksma from Holloway on September 6th (the admissibility of which was admitted after discussion) which expressed astonishment at the charge brought against him, and ended with the postcript, " I have never in my life done or asked anybody to do an illegal or wrong act."

Isaacs then proceeded to his argument on the point of law. Briefly, his contention was that on a number of counts there was no evidence to support the charge. And as there was no evidence that Broeksma, who, it will be remembered, was executed on August 24th, had ever received the letters, there could not be a statutory offence under the Offences against the Persons Act. For the statute punished " soliciting," " persuading," " endeavouring to persuade," and to constitute these offences it was necessary that the mind of the person solicited should be reached. Thus " solicit " imported actual incitation, and " encourage " and " persuade " implied argument addressed to and reaching a mind; the only difficulty was with " endeavour to persuade " but even here the statute meant actual argument addressed to a person. But in this case what mind had been reached and what person addressed? There was no evidence that Broeksma, who had been executed so soon after the writing of the letters, had ever received them; and there was no justification in a criminal case for the presumption of due delivery of a letter.

To this ingenious and resourceful argument, Carson replied with a submission that solicitation imputed no such actual reaching of the mind. If Mr Isaacs' contention was correct, what would happen if a man received a letter and did not read it? Or if the letter were in a foreign language, which was incomprehensible to the addressee? Was there then no offence committed by the man who wrote the letter? But Rufus Isaacs answered these quandaries with the proposition that mere intention was no offence under the statute, and that intention plus an act was not sufficient to convict, when the person to be affected was not reached. It is, of course, a principle of English criminal law that mere intention of itself is not criminal; there must always be an overt act in addition to the *mens rea*, or criminal intention. An attempt to commit a crime demands overt acts just as much as the crime itself, since an attempt is an act, or series of acts, which if not interrupted would lead to the committing of the full offence; but what may be an overt act for the purposes of an attempt may not constitute an overt act in the commission of the full offence. Thus in the Krause case the crime with which he was charged was incitement to commit murder; and the only overt act was the writing and posting of the letters. The gist of Isaacs' argument, therefore, was that the overt act was not sufficient to support the crime; there must be somebody incited, and in this case there was nobody, who had been in the least affected by the letters. At the most, therefore, the offence would be an attempt to incite.

Isaacs' point of view prevailed with Lord Alverstone who, in giving judgment on the point, said: " In my opinion, the objection raised by Mr Isaacs with regards to the counts founded on the statute is an important objection and must prevail." The preliminary contest, therefore, had been won by Isaacs. And in truth it was the preliminary contest that was of most importance; for instead of being tried on the grave charge of incitement to murder, under the statute, the prisoner was now only faced with the much less serious common law offence of attempting to incite, with its maximum punishment of two years.

Isaacs made great play in opening his address to the jury —he called no witnesses, and indeed there was nothing for witnesses to prove—with the dwindling of the charges against his client. Originally, he had been arrested on a charge of high treason, the gravest charge known to the law; and that had been abandoned. Then there had been the statutory charge of incitement to murder; now that was gone too. There remained only a shadow of the former charges; the charge of attempting to persuade.

He urged Krause's high character and reputation, and pleaded for just treatment for an open and avowed enemy.

"However greatly," he said, "you may dissent from Dr Krause's observations you must remember that he is entitled to justice, and is an avowed enemy who has resolutely refused to take the oath of allegiance or neutrality ... Dr Krause has given a parole, which he has not broken." His enmity with Forster was purely a political one, and the steps to be taken to get rid of him were of a political nature. And then Isaacs put forward the hypothesis on which the defence rested. Krause clearly regarded Forster as his country's arch-enemy, and for that reason he felt that the Boers should proceed against him; but he wanted them to proceed, in the words of the letter of August 6th, "in some lawful manner." These words were clearly incompatible with a desire to incite Broeksma to murder Forster; so far from that being his intention, Krause's aim was to get Broeksma, who was a lawyer, to bring Forster's case before the Boers and have him court-martialled. And that, in Krause's view, Forster had earned such treatment is clear; for he regarded Forster's suggestion that the Boers should be treated as robbers and bandits as tantamount to incitement to wholesale murder, while Forster had in addition made allegations against the Boers of vile cruelty, which had been contradicted by Lord Kitchener himself.

After developing this argument, Isaacs put in a plea for his client. "He is an enemy—an honourable enemy who has kept his engagements—who held that his interests and those of this country were diametrically opposed to each other. Remember this man's past career, and Lord Roberts' emphatic testimony; and remember the extreme difficulty we all feel to rid ourselves of bias, and especially patriotic bias. ... You will, I am convinced, rid your minds of all such prepossessions, and if there is the slightest doubt of the prisoner's guilt, he is entitled to acquittal."

Rufus Isaacs had put up a strong case, and his interpretation of Krause's intentions was by no means improbable. But unfortunately there were circumstances which militated against the chance of the jury accepting it; and these circumstances were pointed by Carson in his reply, with an irony

and restraint which made the presentment all the more
effective.   The violence of the views expressed in the *Pall
Mall Gazette* could not justify the infliction of death on its
contributors; and as for the contention that Krause intended
Broeksma to proceed by court-martial, this would be difficult
in view of the fact that Johannesburg was at the time under
British jurisdiction.   Carson was especially good in dealing
with Isaacs' contention that the phrase " in some lawful
manner " was incompatible with the idea of murder.   " The
word lawful is said to acquit.   When a man writes to
suggest a crime it is usually in veiled, or even ironical,
language, as in the old story, ' Don't nail his ears to the
pump.' "

Lord Alverstone's summing-up was hostile to Krause,
and after only ten minutes the jury returned with a verdict
of " Guilty."   Unlike another and much more famous foe
to this country, who during a future and greater war made a
great speech to the Court after his conviction in a trial presided over by Rufus Isaacs, then Lord Reading, Doctor
Krause attempted no flights of oratory when asked if he had
anything to say.   " I only desire, my Lord," he said in a
firm and respectful tone, " to say that I deny that I ever
attempted to incite anyone to murder, or that the thought
of murder ever entered my mind. . . . I have only to thank
the Court for the fairness of my trial.   I have scrupulously
adhered to the terms of my parole.   I consider Mr Forster
is one of the persons whose conduct is in a great measure
responsible for this deplorable war."

The prisoner finished his brief statement in a firm voice,
and the Lord Chief Justice proceeded to pass sentence.   It
was clear from the words of Lord Alverstone—not ordinarily
perhaps the most imaginative of judges—that he realised
how exceptional was the case.   " This is to me," he said, " a
most painful case, and no ordinary case.   You are a barrister
of the Middle Temple, a member of my own profession,
and I doubt not a very able and energetic young man.   You
have been most ably defended.   Nothing that could be said
in your favour has been omitted. . . . The jury have found

you guilty, and in my opinion they could have found no other verdict. . . ."

It is true that no other verdict could have been expected on the facts, for the consideration that Johannesburg was under British jurisdiction, and a court-martial by the Boers therefore impossible, was no doubt conclusive in deciding the jury against Isaacs' hypothesis. But is it so impossible that this was the real meaning of the prisoner? He had known Johannesburg at a time when such a court-martial would have been very far from impossible; and then, when he was far from the scene, preyed upon by his inactivity, obsessed by his hatred of Forster, not as a person but as the embodiment of the spirit that caused " this deplorable war," is it not likely that he forgot the changed circumstances and felt that there must be some legal method of stopping the activities of such a man? At any rate it is gratifying to note that this early indiscretion did not ruin the career of this able and energetic young man, nor deprive South Africa of his services, for he was to live to rise high in the service of the Union of South Africa, a State as then unborn.

But where we can agree with Lord Alverstone is in his reference to the defence, for Isaacs had fought a difficult case with unflagging resourcefulness. Despite the ingenuity of his final argument, the verdict had gone against him on the final count; but this was perhaps inevitable, and it is for the arguing of the point of law, where he was brilliantly successful, that the case will be best, and deservedly, remembered.

CHAPTER VII

THE year 1902, so auspiciously inaugurated by the resourceful advocacy of the Krause case, was to be an annus mirabilis for Rufus Isaacs. For this year set the stamp upon his success as a silk with a number of famous cases, the diverse variety of which was as great a tribute to his versatility as his handling of them was to his skill. It was cases like the Hartopp divorce case and the Taff Vale case, one of great popular interest and the other of supreme social importance, which gave him a fame among the general public equal to that which he already enjoyed in the profession. He had for a considerable time been an established financial success in his profession, and the career which had begun, bravely and obscurely, in the small house off the Finchley Road was now conducted from the splendour of a Georgian mansion in Park Lane; for he had for some time been established in 32 Park Lane. Nevertheless he still had to continue his habits of early rising and tremendous assiduity in the preparation of his work; but this caused little difficulty to one whose complete self-discipline has been a great factor in success. Neither now nor at any time, however, did he cut himself off from society or other interests; for like all great workers, he never found it necessary or desirable to deny himself leisure. In the long summer vacation, he was able to get away with his family to the sea or the country, and here riding, tennis and golf—at the last of these he is said to have been a cheerful but incompetent performer—had recuperative qualities which helped him to face the rigours of a long and arduous session. In London he found time for intellectual relaxation; unlike Asquith and Haldane he was not a great reader, for his mind has always been of a practical, rather than a philosophic or

76

reflective, bent. Music and the drama, however, have always attracted him—a love of music again is a racial trait; and he was, too, a family man and a sociable man. Like most of the greatest members of the Bar, whose names have become public property, he has avoided the entire absorption in his profession which is often believed to be essential to success in it.

A few weeks after the Krause case Rufus Isaacs again appeared at the Old Bailey in a case, which was the culmination of one of the strangest tales of successful roguery and inexhaustible credulity that the annals even of that Court can furnish. The case was that of Rex v. Goudie and Others, popularly known as the Liverpool Bank Case. Goudie was a young Scot, who had come from the Shetlands to Liverpool, where he was employed as a clerk in the Bank. Unfortunately he had none of the hard-headed shrewdness of his countrymen; indeed, although he was an industrious and capable young man, his distinguishing characteristics were a child-like readiness to believe all that he was told and a capacity for making the most undesirable friends. These qualities, united to a taste for betting, were fairly certain to get him into trouble. The trouble duly came, but it was on a scale that nobody could have anticipated.

The first harbingers of trouble were a disreputable pair of Turf hangers-on, called Kelly and Stiles, who were men of no occupation and little means. Goudie met them in a train going from Newmarket to London on October 26th, 1900, and their practised eye told them that here was an acquaintanceship to be followed up. Consequently it was arranged that all three should meet at Hurst Park on the following day, where Stiles was introduced as a man of great wealth, who often had £5,000 or £10,000 on a race, and Kelly as his commission-agent, who betted for him and had a most important clientèle. Goudie was naturally delighted at the turn of events, and the keen edge of his pleasure was not at all blunted when he was informed at the end of the day that Kelly had been betting for Stiles and for him, with the result that Stiles had lost a great deal of money, while he, although winning on the first race, had lost £230 in all; Goudie cheerfully paid up the £230 and sent a further £1000 for "investment." So the game continued, Kelly "making bets" for Goudie, and Goudie always losing; but Goudie—although he never had the gratification of winning money—had the consolation of knowing that his friend Stiles was losing twice as much as he did, because whenever Goudie lost £5,000 Stiles was said to have lost £10,000. The system continued for a year, with the result, to cut a long story short, that Kelly got £29,615 and Stiles £35,332 from the credulous Goudie.

After about a year of this, however, new and larger vultures appeared, attracted by this unusually profitable prey, and Kelly and Stiles were driven off. The newcomers were three in number, Burge a former light-weight boxer*, Marks, a Starting-Price bookmaker doing a small business in Adelphi Terrace, and Mances, a card-sharper. Burge had formerly been a successful pugilist, and ten years earlier had been described by the *Sportsman* as a "bright, modest, well-spoken young fellow, fit to battle for his life . . . with an appetite quite unbeatable." The years, however, had coarsened the "modest young fellow," and the appetite had increased for other things than food; by 1900 he was at the end of his financial resources and in bad company. In October, 1901, he heard of Goudie, and without loss of time he and Mances travelled up to Liverpool, where they came upon Goudie in the bureau waiting for letters addressed to Scott—the name which he had assumed for racing purposes. Mances at once went up to Goudie and told him that he knew that he had been betting and losing; "You are a clerk in the Bank of Liverpool, in a position where you can command money," he said, and the manner was so threatening that Goudie was afraid and started to make feeble denials. But Mances reassured him and said that he could introduce him to a bookmaker who was so good that he would let him have £5,000 on a horse up to

---

* I notice that Lord Birkenhead refers to him as "the big boxer"; he was in point of fact, of course, quite a small man.

one hour of the start of the race, and also to a jockey called Ballard, who would give him good information. That Goudie believed this supplies almost unbelievable evidence of the extent of his credulity, for one would have supposed that his great interest in racing would at anyrate have made him realise that in the smaller races such a bet made at such a time would revolutionise the odds. But Goudie had an invincible capacity for belief, and he believed Mances, just as he had believed Kelly and Stiles. The bookmaker, of course, was Marks, and with him from this time on Goudie did his betting; Kelly and Stiles were dropped, for Goudie was afraid that, if he did not bet with Marks, Mances would give him away to the Bank authorities. The same procedure, however, was adopted; Goudie sent vast sums for " investment," which were pocketed by the trio, and Goudie was informed that they had been lost in betting. One winner he did back with Marks, Sansome, on November 11th, at 5-2, and as he had " invested " £10,000, he should have won £25,000; Marks, however, wired back to say that he was ill, and had been unable to get the money on, and that in consequence Goudie had not won his £25,000. One notable difference there was, however, between the method of Kelly and Stiles and that of their succesors. Kelly and Stiles had made their £60,000 odd out of Goudie in twelve months; the new trio played their fish so hard that as a result of three days' racing Goudie lost £25,000, and within three weeks they had made £91,000 out of him. Burge got £38,500 and opened an account with the Credit Lyonnais besides loading Mrs Burge with jewellery; Marks made £15,000; and Mances, who made £36,750, with commendable prudence invested £33,000 of it in Consols.

The question will naturally be asked: how was it possible to make such vast sums out of Goudie, who after all was only a bank-clerk? The answer is that he devised a system of swindling the bank, admirable in its simplicity and effectiveness, the devising and conduct of which on the part of Goudie is hard to reconcile with his crass stupidity in other directions. Goudie was in charge of the accounts of customers, whose names began with the initials H, I, J, K, thus including Mr Hudson, the millionaire soap-manufacturer. He opened an account of his own, so that he could get cheques, and to these he forged Mr Hudson's signature. After the cheques had been uttered they came to the bank for payment, where they were given to a clerk in the clearing department, who would enter them in a journal and then hand them over to Goudie for the purpose of making an entry in the ledger. Goudie, however, did not enter them into the ledger, but simply ticked the journal as if he had; then, instead of placing the forged cheques upon the file, he destroyed them. The scheme, therefore, was simplicity itself, but there were, of course, further obstacles to overcome. There was, for instance, the weekly bank sheet, but this he coped with by entering false debits. The auditings presented greater difficulties, for here he had to supply details for the inspection of the auditors. He dealt with this too, however, by entering a false debit to the account a few days before the audit; this entry appeared for the space of the audit, and he then rectified it by making a false credit entry so that attention was not called to the account. So successful was his scheme of fraud, in fact, that at the conclusion of the case, Mr Justice Bigham, who was a high authority on commercial matters—Rufus Isaacs was to plead before him two years later in the Whittaker-Wright case— said: " I am quite satisfied that no blame is to be imputed to the Bank of Liverpool for the very serious losses they have sustained. I think that no care could have prevented these frauds from being practised." And, however disquieting that statement might have been to honest citizens, accustomed to deposit their savings in the Bank, it was at all events high tribute to the ingenuity of the ingenious Goudie.

But such a dance, played to such a rollicking measure, could not go on for ever. On November 21st, Goudie was called up to explain the absence of a certain cheque from the file. He saw that discovery was inevitable, but he did not lose his head; he merely said that the porter must have

mislaid it, and, while the porter was being sent for, Goudie
left the room, picked up his hat and umbrella, and unostentatiously decided there and then to resign from the service
of the Bank, from which he had taken £160,000. On
December 2nd he was found in a cheap lodging-house,
living in abject penury, and was arrested. Meanwhile
Burge had been arrested, but Mances had made good his
escape, while Marks had gone from Liverpool to Brighton
and then across the Channel by way of Newhaven; he then
wired to Inspector Frost that he was returning, and the
Inspector met the boat at Newhaven. There a search soon
revealed Marks' bag, but there was no sign of him; he was
therefore assumed, " on not entirely convincing evidence,"
as the *Times* remarked, to have jumped overboard and committed suicide. As for Kelly and Stiles, Stiles absconded
when it was known that the frauds were discovered, but
Kelly came forward in Manchester, and said that his dealings
with Goudie were ordinary betting transactions. Colour
was given to this contention by the fact that some of the
earlier cheques given by Goudie to Kelly were bona fide
documents, but unfortunately for Kelly, in supplying evidence for his point of view, he handed over by mistake two
incriminating letters, which revealed the conspiracy between
him and Stiles. Consequently charges were preferred against
Goudie, the dupe, and all five rogues, who had taken
advantage in their own interest of that rare combination
in him of a capacity to believe them and to deceive others.
The charge contained a great variety of counts, for forgery,
conspiracy to obtain by false pretences, and unlawful receiving were all represented. Goudie took the prudent course
of detaching himself from his associates and pleading guilty
on all counts, while all of them—except Marks and Mances
who were not available—pleaded not guilty. Their position,
however, was rendered all the more difficult, since, owing
to Goudie's plea of guilty, he was now available as a witness
for the Crown.

This representative, if not entirely distinguished, collection
of sharpers brought to the Court an array of counsel which

was at once representative and distinguished. Mr Charles Gill, K.C., led Mr Charles Matthews for the Crown, Burge's defence being entrusted to Mr Horace Avory, K.C., and that of Kelly and Stiles respectively to Rufus Isaacs and Mr Marshall Hall, while Goudie was represented by a rising young junior from Liverpool, whose performance in this case first brought him prominently before the London public, and whose name was F. E. Smith. The case came on at the Old Bailey on February 17th, 1902, and was tried by Mr Justice Bigham, equally famous under that designation and subsequently as Lord Mersey.

The trial of Burge, Goudie, Marks and Mances was proceeded with first; as Goudie had pleaded guilty and Marks and Mances were not in Court, this meant the trial of Burge. Kelly and Stiles were not directly interested in these proceedings, as their transactions with Goudie were distinct from Burge's, but there was a close enough analogy to make the conduct and decision of this case of the utmost importnce to Kelly and Stiles, and consequently it was closely watched by Rufus Isaacs and Marshall Hall. Charles Gill opened the case for the Crown with a lengthy exposition of the facts of the case. He then put Goudie into the box, who told his extraordinary story in a frank manner; and indeed the very strangeness of the story made it most unlikely that he was lying. He remained unshaken, too, under Mr Avory's long and penetrating cross-examination, and at the conclusion of the Crown's case, the prospect looked very black for Burge. Mr Avory put him in the witness-box, where he maintained that he had had no idea that " Scott " was a clerk in the Bank of Liverpool. He thought that he was a rich man, indulging in bona fide betting transactions, and that he (Burge) was to take half Marks' proceeds. But when Mr Gill cross-examined him, closely and mercilessly, about his financial difficulties, his connection with Mances, and the telegrams which Marks had dictated to him, he did very badly, and finally the ex-pugilist burst into tears. In his speech to the jury, Mr Avory tried to redeem the situation by attacking the tendency of the Criminal Evidence

Act—it was still only four years old—to treat a case of suspicion as a case of proof, unless the prisoner made a good appearance in the witness-box. He also strongly attacked Goudie's credibility as a witness, and said that the whole question in the case really was whether Burge knew that " Scott " was really Goudie, a clerk in the Bank of Liverpool; if it was not made out by the evidence that he did—and he contended that it was not—then Burge's conduct was quite consistent with the evidence which he had given. In spite, however, of Mr Avory's skilful dialectics, the jury only required five minutes to find Burge guilty.

The conviction of Burge presented a difficult problem to Rufus Isaacs and Marshall Hall in respect of their defence of Kelly and Stiles, for the result of Burge's case made it clear that Goudie's evidence would be believed. Burge, too, had had one great advantage which Kelly and Stiles had not; for, curiously enough, Goudie had never set eyes on Burge until he saw him in Court—it was Mances who had spoken to Goudie in Liverpool. In spite of this, Burge had been unanimously found guilty in five minutes, and in face of this verdict there was clearly very little hope for Kelly and Stiles. Was there nothing to be done, except to fight the case, knowing it to be hopeless? Most men would probably have assumed that there was not, and have made vigorous, eloquent, and quite useless speeches on behalf of their clients. But the prisoners had the advantage of being defended by no ordinary counsel. It was perceived that there were differences between this case and Burge's; a practical difference, since technical difficulties with regard to evidence and jurisdiction were likely to arise, if the case were pressed, and an ethical difference since Stiles and Kelly had used no threats. In view of these facts, counsel came to the conclusion that the best policy for Kelly and Stiles would be to withdraw their plea of not guilty on the first count, that of conspiracy, for which the maximum sentence was two years' hard labour, in the hope that the Crown would accept a conviction on this one count, and not proceed further with the prosecution. Accordingly, when their case came up on February 20th, Kelly and Stiles, acting under the advice of Rufus Isaacs and Marshall Hall, followed this course. The tactics were entirely successful, for Charles Gill, on behalf of the Crown, accepted the plea and did not pursue the case, for the reasons given above.

Rufus Isaacs then addressed the Court on behalf of Kelly, stressing the absence of intimidation, and pointing out that Kelly did actually make bets with bookmakers on Goudie's behalf, and that, except on the first instance when a discretion was left him, Goudie had selected the horses for himself. After Marshall Hall had followed on the same lines for Stiles, the Court adjourned until the 22nd, when the question of restitution was to be discussed.

On the 22nd after Chartres Biron—lately retired from his London Police-Court magistracy at Bow Street—had addressed the Court in mitigation for Burge, F. E. Smith spoke in mitigation for Goudie. It is curious that a man, whose reputation rested primarily on clarity of reasoning, and power of invective, should have made his first notable appearance in London with a speech in mitigation; but his speech on this occasion displayed those powers of eloquence and versatility of application which were so characteristic of the late Lord Birkenhead. He contended that Goudie had embarked on a career of fraud to try and make restitution to the Bank for the first £100 which he had forged. "His object," he went on, "in the betting transactions he made was to replace the money in the bank. It was not to enjoy the proceeds of robbery. In the whole history of crime, there is not a case in which a man has enjoyed himself so little as the result of his crime as Goudie has. It is not on record that he had spent a farthing of the money on personal indulgence; on the contrary there is the strongest reason for believing he did not do so, as the expenses of his board and lodging only amounted to £1 a week." Rufus Isaacs then spoke again on behalf of Kelly, pointing out that he was anxious to make full restitution, had in fact restored £18,000, and had been in custody for three months already, awaiting trial. Marshall Hall then rose to make a further appeal on behalf of Stiles, but this constant procession of counsel was too much for Mr Justice Bigham's patience.

" How many more speeches am I to hear? " he said. " I heard you on Thursday."

The remark was not very fair, as Rufus Isaacs had addressed the Court twice without comment. A soft answer would, however, no doubt have turned away wrath, but soft answers did not spring very readily to Marshall Hall's lips and, in spite of all that Rufus Isaacs could do, he replied:

" I don't think your lordship did hear me; your lordship did not wish to hear me."

The scene which followed and the ultimate reconciliation are described in Mr Marjoribanks' *Life of Marshall Hall*.

After Marshall Hall had spoken, Goudie was asked if he had anything to say, and, on his replying " No," Mr Justice Bigham proceeded to sentence the prisoners. Goudie and Burge received ten years penal servitude each, while Kelly and Stiles escaped with two years hard labour, the maximum penalty for the charge, on which they had been convicted. Mr Justice Bigham remarked in sentencing them that he would have been glad to inflict a heavier sentence, and that comment is perhaps the best commendation of the tactics pursued by defending counsel on behalf of their clients.

So ended this strange case.* It may fairly be doubted whether in the whole course of his professional life—and a comprehensive practice at the Bar brings a wide range of clients of every sort—Rufus Isaacs ever had a more disreputable client than Kelly. But even he was the instrument in evoking a notable instance of Rufus Isaacs' flair for the tactical conduct of a case, a branch of his profession in which he was peculiarly at home. But, apart from this, no one could fairly regret his participation in a case which in many of its aspects was unique to the point of incredibility, and not least in the character of its principal figure, Goudie, of whom Mr Justice Bigham said: " I do not know whether

* Burge made good again on coming out of prison, resumed his boxing career and fought in the War.

to marvel more at the wickedness of his folly or the folly of his wickedness."

Very different was the case of Suffield *v.* Labouchère, in which Rufus Isaacs appeared two months later. For Suffield was Lord Suffield, soldier, courtier, administrator, and Master of Fox-hounds, while Labouchère, known to all as "Labby," was the Right Honourable H. H. Labouchère, M.P., lately a Minister of the Crown. The action was one for libel brought by Lord Suffield in respect of certain articles which had appeared during 1900 in *Truth*, of which Labouchère was proprietor. Now *Truth*, under the able administration of Mr Labouchère and his editor, Mr Vowles, had established a formidable reputation as the fearless exposer of "bogus" companies and commercial "ramps." Libel actions were brought against them by promoters and financiers, stung into action by the provocative directness of *Truth*, but they always failed, and Messrs. Labouchère and Vowles went on their way rejoicing.

In 1900, they decided that a commercial club known as the Article Club was a ramp. The club had been founded in connection with a paper called *Commerce*, which was owned by a Jewish gentleman named Cowen, and contained articles on leading business firms. The club was founded for the purpose of giving leading commercial people an opportunity of meeting and discussing matters of commercial interest together, but a condition of membership was that an article about the firm (only one firm being admitted for each industry) should appear in *Commerce* and that £300 should be paid the first year as a subscription. *Truth*, however, took the view that all this was only an elaborate façade to conceal a ramp for enlarging Cowen's advertising connection. Consequently when the Chinese Minister, anxious to visit British industrial centres with a view to facilitating the founding of industries in Shanghai and Peking, put himself under the auspices of the Article Club for the purpose of a tour, *Truth* published an article called " The Celestial Pilgrim's Progress "; in the article occurred a passage which ran: " a finer dodge for enlarging an advertising connection no newspaper has ever invented. . . . How much longer will these distinguished persons (*i.e.* the members of the council) continue to patronise such a piece of impudent and transparent humbug? " Now the Council of the Club, which was in a supervisory capacity, the committee being the executive, contained many distinguished names, and Lord Suffield, the President of the Club since 1898, held an office which had previously been successively held by Lord Winchelsea, Lord Jersey, and Lord Strathcona. Another article made direct reference to Lord Suffield and ran: " the consultative council is, I presume, a more or less ornamental body. It must be pointed out, however . . . that if the whole concern is, as many of the members consider it, a ramp, they are, whether ornamental or active members, personally participating in that ramp . . . they serve in fact . . . the purposes of decoys by means of which the smaller birds are lured into the snare. . . . This remark applies more particularly to Lord Suffield, the President of the Club."

This was plain speaking; but it was positively mincing words when compared with the references to Cowen. One of these ran: " Eight years ago Lawrence Cohen and his brother were a pair of bankrupt Hatton Garden Hebrews unable to offer a shilling in the pound to the creditors whom they had swindled. The cuter of the two, concealing his identity under an imposing pseudonym, manages somehow to start, or to obtain the control of, a commercial newspaper. He forms the magnificent idea of forming those who advertise in his paper into a club. . . . From every commercial member of his ' club ' he obtains for himself upwards of £300 in hard cash. . . . He launches wild-cat companies for them to subscribe to, and thereby gets sums out of them in hard cash to the tune of over £60,000 for himself, his relatives, and friends. He works the trick so well that at the end of three years, having remained all this time an undischarged bankrupt, he is able to pay off all his creditors and still remain a man of considerable means. . . . If he is the clever Hebrew that his history suggests, he will lose no time in securing whatever there is left of the swag and returning to the obscurity of Hatton Garden or elsewhere, for he may rely on it that, so far as *Commerce* and the Article Club are concerned, the game is up." This appeared on March 22nd, and on April 26th, it was followed up with a further article, which said: " In fairness to him (the Chinese Minister) it ought, I think, to be assumed, until he has an opportunity of vindicating himself that he has been in this case the dupe of a crafty and unscrupulous adventurer, who has grossly abused his confidence." The result of the campaign was that Lord Suffield and Cowen both brought actions for libel.

The two actions, although arising from the same set of facts were quite distinct; Mr Labouchère and Mr Vowles were joined as co-defendants, but Lord Suffield and Mr Cowen were plaintiffs in separate proceedings. In the first action, which was Lord Suffield's, Rufus Isaacs, who led for Lord Suffield, again crossed swords with Sir Edward Clarke, who appeared for Labouchère. In opening the case, Rufus Isaacs outlined the facts and said that the suggestion was that Lord Suffield had been paid to allow his name to appear as President, and that the Club was a swindle and he knew it. The whole gravamen of the attack really was that, because Cowen had previously failed in business, and was making money out of his paper *Commerce*, which was quite a legitimate thing to do, the Club was necessarily a swindle. The defence set great store by the complaint of Messrs. Milner that, although by the rules only one firm was admitted for each industry and they already represented safes, Sir George Chubb was allowed in as representing locks. This they said showed that the Club had no bona fides; " but then," said Rufus Isaacs, " if Messrs. Whiteley were admitted as ' universal providers,' no one else could have been admitted at all." He concluded by pointing out that there were two real questions for the jury: whether the Article Club was a swindle; and whether Lord Suffield as President had done anything dishonourable. He then put Lord Suffield into the box, who had several passages with Sir Edward Clarke in cross-examination. Sir Edward asked:

" Are you a member of the Committee of the Club? "

" I am not quite certain whether I am, but I think I am an *ex officio* member. I have attended the meeting."

" What had the Committee to do? "

" I do not wish to be rude to you, but if you do not know what the committee of a club does, I am afraid I cannot teach you."

Sir Edward then, having read at length from the issue of *Truth* of February 1st, 1900, asked if there were any statements of fact in it.

" Very few," broke in Lord Suffield.

" Which are untrue? " continued Sir Edward quietly.

" I should take a long time pointing them out," retorted Lord Suffield. But it is only fair to Sir Edward Clarke to say that the witness showed commendable restraint in the amount of time which he actually used in pointing them out.

Later Sir Edward asked him what meaning he attached to the word " ramp."

" I have looked the word out in all dictionaries," came the answer, " and in most of them it is defined as a ' discreditable undertaking,' and in one—I think Webster's—a ' gathering of dishonourable men.' I anticipated that question and so looked it up."

Sir Edward then cross-examined him as to some of the companies of which he had been chairman. In reference to one, he asked why it had been wound up.

" I think I can tell you," replied Lord Suffield amid laughter. " I was chairman."

But the quips were by now concealing a very real annoyance, and Lord Suffield burst out with an angry inquiry as to by what right counsel was going into these matters. At this Rufus Isaacs rose and said that if Sir Edward was cross-examining as to credit, he could not of course object; but if not, he was not entitled to go into questions which were not raised in the particulars of justification. Sir Edward replied that he was not cross-examining as to credit, but was entitled to ask questions about the companies with which Lord Suffield had been connected, and he was allowed to continue.

At the conclusion of his cross-examination, however, Lord Suffield gave vent to his feelings, and indignantly denounced the attempts to discredit him. " They don't originate with counsel," he shouted, " but with that gentleman there, who chooses to pose as a high moral character," and he pointed accusingly at " Labby," who stood unmoved at the back of the Court.

Evidence was then given by Sir John Heron-Maxwell, Sir Horace Tozer, Agent-General for Queensland, Dr Farquharson, M.P., who regarded the money which he had invested in the Doherty Casting Process as " not lost but gone before," and the Servian Minister, who had " invited himself to the dinner of the Club." Finally there was Mr. John Dixon, who had escorted the Chinese Minister to Southampton and shown him a Japanese warship; the Chinese Minister, however, had refused to go aboard, and when Mr Dixon told him that it was the " finest ship afloat, he had hardly seemed to appreciate the fact." But Rufus Isaacs and Sir Edward Clarke had already been in consultation, and, at the conclusion of Dixon's cross-examination, Rufus Isaacs rose and said that Sir Edward had intimated to him that the defendants made no imputation on Lord Suffield's honour, integrity, or veracity. In the circumstances he did not ask for damages, being much more satisfied with Sir Edward's statement. After a statement by Sir Edward, a juror was withdrawn, that being the procedure in a civil case, when it is settled during the hearing and before a verdict has been arrived at.

The case of Cowen v. Labouchère then came up, but in this Rufus Isaacs played a smaller part, since he was led by Lawson Walton and did not address the jury. After an extended hearing and a summing-up not unfavourable to Cowen, the jury at the end of an hour and twenty-five minutes announced that there was no prospect of their coming to an agreement. The case, therefore, was heard again some months later, but this time Cowen conducted his own case, which he did with astonishing skill; and his final speech to the jury was given with a rapid, passionate, and sometimes tearful eloquence, which was most moving. In spite of all, however, the verdict went against him, and " Labby " had triumphed again. It was somewhat of a Pyrrhic victory, however, for his costs in the three cases were enormous, and he had received a check, though scarcely a defeat, in the first at the hands of Rufus Isaacs.

But by the time these proceedings reached their conclusion, Rufus Isaacs had long passed to fresh fields, and was engaged simultaneously in two cases, one of enormous popular interest, and the other of great sociological importance, which brought him more prominently into the public eye than ever before.

CHAPTER VIII

HARTOPP DIVORCE CASE AND TAFF VALE

THE end of a century of prosperity brings leisure and litigation; and this is peculiarly true of the nineteenth century in England. The famous Tranby Croft baccarat case, Rufus Isaacs' own early Turf case, the Chetwynd-Durham suit, Sievier's subsequent action against Sir James Duke; all these cases reflect a way of life that is gone. They speak of the " spacious " lives of the leisured classes, of that decorative aristocracy which showed its adaptability by absorbing the wealthy of all classes and creeds, and its affability by mixing with the Bohemian world—at the right times and places. Sometimes the even tenor of this unruffled existence would be broken by internal factions; a magnate might slander a lord, or a Bohemian might intrude too far into a magnate's domestic life. And then the public, to its great delight—for those were the days when a Turf personality was more powerful than a Trades Union leader—would find in the sombre atmosphere of the Courts the curtain lifted on those remote and fascinating lives, and would glimpse for a moment the world of country houses, of County stands, of Romano's and of the Café Royal; of that existence which was all the more glamorous because the daily Press had not yet cast on it the disenchantment of publicity.

It is to this category that the Hartopp divorce case belongs; and indeed, curiously enough, the case has a link with the Baccarat case, for Lady Hartopp was the daughter of Charles Wilson, M.P., the wealthy shipowner who later became Lord Nunburnholme, and a connection of Mrs Arthur Wilson, owner of Tranby Croft. She was also on her mother's side descended from the great Duke of

Wellington, and was one of several sisters and cousins, daughters of Charles Wilson and of Mrs Arthur Wilson, who as débutantes had been the reigning beauties of the day. In June, 1895, at the age of twenty-two she married an easy-going baronet of thirty-seven, Sir Charles Cradock-Hartopp, and the couple went to live first in Mount Street and then in Seymour Street. Sir Charles was a short, stoutly-built man, with a " sporting " complexion—his wife called him " Bundle " because of his figure, as she explained —whose good nature was his best quality. He was not rich—he had £1400 a year, while Lady Hartopp had £1800 —and his financial position was such that he had put his property into the hands of trustees, Mr Ingoldsby and Mr Charles Wilson, who paid him the £1400; but in spite of this he had had to make frequent applications to Charles Wilson for financial assistance. But there were other difficulties besides his financial embarrassment. His tastes differed from Lady Hartopp's; but only, let it at once be added, within the sphere of interests then considered proper to their station. That is to say, Sir Charles liked racing and living in London, while his wife liked hunting and the country. And when, in addition to this, he started objecting to her friendship with Sir John Willoughby, of Jameson Raid fame, it seemed to Lady Hartopp that he was losing even his good-nature, so in August, 1900, she left him.

In the autumn of 1900, Lady Hartopp took Gaddesby Cottage, near Melton Mowbray, for the hunting. Now the cottage was only two and a half miles from Baggrave Hall, which was owned by Lord Cowley, who had been divorced by his former wife, Lady Violet Nevill, daughter of the Marquess of Abergavenny, in 1897, and had since then seen a year's service in the South African War. The two met out hunting a great deal, and soon were on very friendly terms, Lord Cowley being a frequent caller at the cottage. But her country pursuits did not make Lady Hartopp forget the problem of her husband, and in the following spring she suggested that she should give Sir Charles £20,000 if he would allow her to divorce him. Finding, however, that this proposition was illegal, she resolved on an effort at reconciliation, and wrote to him: " I can't let Easter pass without writing to say that I do wish we could start afresh once more. Let us put the past behind us, and try and begin all over again." The result was an interview, with Lord Gerard acting as mediator, and Lady Hartopp outlined her conditions, which were: that the past should not be referred to; that they should have no London house, but that the cottage should be kept; and that they should embark on a six months' trial, and, in the event of failure, separate. The conditions did not meet with Sir Charles' approval, and negotiations broke down. Lady Hartopp returned to Gaddesby Cottage, and in due course was served with Sir Charles' petition for divorce, on the ground of her adultery with Lord Cowley. Lady Hartopp and Lord Cowley filed an answer denying the charge, and subsequently on November 15th, 1902, eleven days before the trial Lady Hartopp amended her answer and put in a cross-petition, alleging that Sir Charles had been guilty of cruelty and of adultery with Mrs Sands, a beautiful actress living apart from her husband.

The case had all the ingredients of a *cause célèbre*. The principal parties were a Society beauty, a hunting earl, a racing baronet, and a lovely Edwardian enchantress. It was one of those cases in which all Debrett and his staff gave evidence, and the witnesses ranged from the Duke of Devonshire to parlour-maids and stable lads. There were concealed identities, too, and whispers of great names in unsavoury connections, while delightfully spirited passages occurred between leaders of Society and leaders of the Bar; for Debrett had decided to brief and had spared no expense. Sir Charles had Mr Lawson Walton, K.C., Mr Henry Duke, K.C., the great divorce lawyer, subsequently famous as Lord Merrivale, and Mr Barnard; Lady Hartopp countered with Mr Inderwick, K.C., Sir Edward Clarke, K.C., Mr Priestly and Mr Wontner, and in half alliance with these was Lord Cowley's team, consisting of Mr Bargrave Deane, K.C., later a Divorce Court Judge, Mr Charles Gill, K.C., and

Mr Pritchard; while the intervention of Mrs Sands was championed by Rufus Isaacs, supported by Mr Kisch. In all these circumstances enormous public interest was to be expected, and people who had never been near the Courts before vied with those to whom it was an habitual entertainment. Lovers of sensation, connoisseurs of legal argument, snobs, and devotees of forensic oratory mingled outside the tiny Court in their efforts to get places, and simultaneously devoured, if unsuccessful, the daily reports of proceedings in the Press; while every day fashionably-dressed women, lorgnette in hand and smelling-salts in reserve, were to be seen in the corridors shrilly demanding entry with all the imperious insistence of pampered femininity, and soundly rating the unfortunate ushers for the preference they gave to the wig and stuff gown of apprentice counsel. *Vox et praeterea nihil;* through the clamour of crowds and the hysteria of popular excitement the majesty of the Law took its stately course, unheeding.

On the day of the opening of the trial before Mr Justice Gorrell Barnes, there was a goodly muster of the leading dramatis personæ. Lady Hartopp arrived with her father in a smart brougham, and sat in Court, a tall, youthful figure with light brown hair, listening to Mr Lawson Walton open the case for Sir Charles, who sat, short, stocky, scant of hair, nervously smiling at his unaccustomed situation. Lord Cowley was there too, sitting rather apart, until he was joined by Sir John Willoughby, who had come to Court to answer any charges that might be made against him. The only notable absentee was Mrs Sands, who was not yet a protagonist; for at this stage of the case she was only a witness, and it was not till the fourth day of the trial that Mr Kisch announced that she desired independent representation. Rufus Isaacs' part in the opening of the case, therefore, was merely that of a careful spectator.

After Mr Lawson Walton had opened the case, he put Sir Charles Hartopp in the box to tell the story of his married life. Sir Charles did not make a very good witness, and was considerably harried in cross-examination by Mr

Inderwick on the subject of his finances, and in the course of cross-examination he had to admit in addition, applying to his father-in-law to pay off a discarded mistress. On the second day, therefore, he went back into the witness-box to " smooth off, with the tactful aid of Mr Lawson Walton, K.C., the ragged edges left by Mr Inderwick's cross-examination." His place in the box was then taken by a succession of Lady Hartopp's maids, who had been subpoenaed on behalf of the petitioner. There was Alice Blythe, the housemaid, who said that Lord Cowley used the bathroom at Gaddesby Cottage after hunting, and also used to change there. He used to do odd jobs, too, like hanging pictures, and on one occasion, when she went up to the boudoir to give him a telegram, she found him buttoning up his waistcoat. Edith Mason disagreed with Alice about the boudoir not being used in the evenings; but then her memory appeared to play tricks with her, for she spoke of having seen Lord Cowley in a pink coat at a time during the cubbing season, when pink coats are not worn except by the Master. Ethel Freestone gave evidence that sounded more significant, but when pressed for details, she became bashful. She said that, in consequence of what was taking place, she had written to her mother, who thereupon took her away; but beyond saying that she did not consider that Lady Hartopp and Lord Cowley were behaving properly, she was uncommunicative. Mr Justice Gorrell Barnes asked her what she had seen to make her say this, but, though he repeated his question two or three times, she refused to answer. Later in the trial she was recalled at the request of the jury, for it was clear that she might have something to say of vital importance. All she would say, however, was:

" I saw nothing, no more than I have said."

" What do you mean by not behaving properly? " the foreman insisted.

" I know no more than I have said."

" Are you speaking the truth when you say you saw nothing improper? "

" I saw nothing wrong," came back the obdurate answer; and in face of this even the foreman desisted.

It was not a particularly strong case that the petitioner had built up. It had been established, it is true, that Lord Cowley was a frequent caller at the cottage, and that he used it to bath and change in; but adultery cannot be inferred from friendliness or hygiene, nor can it depend on an unbuttoned waistcoat on a gentleman who is hanging pictures. Definite evidence of adultery in a disputed case is, for obvious reasons, rare; and where there is no such evidence, the jury must be satisfied that there was a guilty desire on the part of the persons concerned and an opportunity of gratifying it, before they may infer an act of adultery. In this case, the opportunity amounted to no more than the " opportunity " which any two people have, who are alone at any time of day—Lord Cowley never stayed the night at Gaddesby Cottage; as for the guilty desire, the case for the petitioner had been to graft this on to an obvious affection and the alleged use of endearing names. Sir Edward Clarke, on rising to address the Court for Lady Hartopp, took full advantage of the somewhat flimsy structure of the edifice, which he was called upon to destroy, and said at once that, had it been an ordinary case of civil liability, he would have submitted that there was no case to go to the jury; but since reputation was at stake, he preferred to have the matter thoroughly thrashed out. He pointed out that there was no evidence of any specific act of impropriety, and claimed that much of the case was mere servants' tittle-tattle, which could not be depended upon, since there did not exist " a household in which domestic servants do not find fault with the behaviour of their masters and mistresses." He then took the offensive and trained the massed artillery of his eloquence upon Sir Charles. He referred to the facts that, when Sir Charles proposed to marry, he was £8000 in debt; " this," he said with scornful emphasis, " was the state of affairs, when this girl of twenty-two was committed to the guardianship of this experienced man of the world." He then came on to the cross-petition:

" This English gentleman has not only treated his wife with violence, but had himself been guilty of matrimonial infidelity during a great part of his married life; for it has recently been discovered that he has been in the habit of visiting a very beautiful woman, who is living apart from her husband and is known to be accessible to gentlemen who are prepared to pay somewhat heavily for her favours."

Here was a frontal attack on Sir Charles and Mrs Sands, and on the fourth day of the trial all public attention was focussed on Mrs Sands, a beautiful, statuesque figure in ermine, as she listened to Mr Kisch make formal application for leave to intervene in the suit and to file an answer denying the charges against her; as soon as the application was made and granted, Mrs Sands rose and left the Court. Attention was then transferred to another lovely lady, for Lady Hartopp, whose examination had begun on the previous day, re-entered the box. She presented a striking appearance, which would have compelled attention anywhere, with her tall graceful figure, her well-poised head, and the confident beauty of her person; and those whose interest in the case was not primarily legal—and perhaps some, too, whose interest was primarily legal—noted with appraising glances the rich sables, crowned with a hat of sables and chiffon. But she was not only a lovely lady; she was spirited, too, in the witness-box, as in the hunting-field, as her clashes with Mr Lawson Walton showed. It was perhaps inevitable that Lady Hartopp should come into conflict with the counsel who cross-examined her. For he was the very embodiment of Liberal nonconformity; a lawyer, a man of serious preoccupations and ideas, who did not know a horse from a handsaw, while she was the spoilt darling of Fortune, leading her glittering, rather empty life with scarcely a realisation that any other existed. It is a bold and generally unwise thing to throw down the gauge of battle to opposing counsel; for, apart from the fact that he is generally a person of superior ability, he is necessarily fighting on his own ground and knows exactly which points of tactical advantage are really contributory to victory, and which are only a flashy exhibition of strength. Thus Oscar Wilde, with all his dialectical brilliance, won Pyrrhic victories over Carson in repartee, only to lose his case, his liberty, and his reputation. But Lady Hartopp had certain exceptional advantages; in the first place, the petitioner had not been able to present a very strong case, which meant that Mr Lawson Walton would have to strain points of minor importance. Further she had the inestimable advantage of being a woman, for a clever woman can use tactics which are not available to men and can make subtle appeals to the jury, which it is difficult to discount; Lady Hartopp, therefore, could at least claim a drawn battle.

The first bout came early. Mr Lawson Walton was cross-examining her about her friends.

" Do you not know that the choice of your friends has been brought to the notice of your husband?—It may have been."

" Do you not know that your mother had given advice to Sir Charles on the subject?—No, I do not."

" And did not your mother write to him on the subject? Just look at that letter. Don't be afraid of it."

" I am not a coward." The retort was thrown back with spirit.

" Just look at it; we shall see about that," was the dry comment.

Lady Hartopp disclaimed all knowledge of her mother's disapproval, and Mr Lawson Walton proceeded to cross-examine her about a friend whose name he did not wish to mention. The judge told him to write it down, and Mr Lawson Walton was continuing: " If, madam, you know to whom I refer," when Lady Hartopp broke in: " You heard what his lordship said; write it down."

" You are welcome to take every advantage you can," said Mr Lawson Walton, flushing at this unexpected and imperious command; and added with a hint of menace, " you may want it."

On the question of her offer of £20,000 to her husband,

on condition that he would let her divorce him, Mr Lawson
Walton again scored heavily.

" You thought you could play on his poverty? "

" I knew he was in debt."

" Do you not think it was a most dishonourable thing for
you to ask him to allow you to divorce him? "

" I now see that it was wrong. I know more about the
law."

" Which law, madam? "

" The law of England."

" You think more about the law of England than Divine
law. Was it morally right, do you think? "

" I don't think it was very wrong."

Here, in massing the ponderous artillery of ethical argument, Mr Lawson Walton was on his own ground; but there
were other passages where, in fencing with more delicate
instruments, he was worsted. For instance, there was
mention of a married man who had given Lady Hartopp a
diamond heart, and when Mr Lawson Walton pressed her
for his identity, she seemed to hesitate, until finally, amid
the sudden laughter of the Court, she confessed that it was
her brother-in-law, Mr Fairfax. A little later the Judge
asked her why she had not mentioned earlier the chain
bracelet which Sir John Willoughby had given her before
going to South Africa. "I am sorry, my Lord," she
answered, " but Mr Lawson Walton talks so much and tries
to muddle me! " Mr Lawson Walton also referred to a
telephone message of Lord Cowley's to Gaddesby Cottage,
saying: " Don't bother to send hare; have one in the
house," and suggested that this meant that she was dining
with him, which she denied.

" It is one of the many hares my friend is hunting in this
case," observed Mr Bargrave Deane drily.

But, although Mr Lawson Walton was apparently fond
of coursing, his knowledge of horse-racing was not extensive.
He was questioning Lady Hartopp about her stay in Paris.

" In Paris," he said, " you went to the French Derby.
Did you also go to Chantilly? "

" Why that is where the French Derby is run."

Mr Lawson Walton was ruffled at the laughter, which greeted this lapse, and to make it good, said: " Very well, that was the occasion on which Holocaust broke his leg? "

This time the Judge joined in the general laughter before explaining to the perplexed Mr Lawson Walton that this misadventure had occurred in the English Derby. Fortunately for Mr Lawson Walton, however, an intimate knowledge of the Turf has never been considered indispensable to success in the Liberal Party.

Despite their long conflict, however, when the Court met the following day, Lady Hartopp at once went over to Mr Lawson Walton, and stayed talking charmingly to him for a few moments. This graceful action left everybody the more unprepared for her father's amazing outburst; for Mr Charles Wilson rose in the well of the Court, and addressing the Judge in a voice shaken with anger, said: " I demand protection for my daughter from the studied insolence of yesterday's cross-examination," adding: " It is sufficient degradation for her to be tied to that lying scoundrel." The Court was astonished at this exhibition, but Mr Justice Gorrell Barnes, gentlest of judges, quietly repressed him. He came in for considerable criticism at the time for not taking firmer action, since the reference to Sir Charles Hartopp, who was a party to the case, was a most flagrant contempt of Court. Mr Justice Gorrell Barnes, however, took the view—not always unjustified—that it was better not to proceed to strong measures in order to punish an offence committed on the impulse of injured feelings.

The case, therefore, continued, and Lord Cowley, who had recently been injured in the hunting-field, limped into the box. He did not make such a good witness as Lady Hartopp, and his previous matrimonial difficulties were raked with the fire of Lawson Walton's rigorous cross-examination. The following day, when, according to contemporary account, " quite the most striking figure in Court was Mrs Sands, who wore a striking costume of violet, trimmed with sable," was occupied chiefly in the evidence of

servants and of friends. Among the latter who were called
to say that on visits they had never noticed the slightest
impropriety or familiarity of manner between Lady Hartopp
and Lord Cowley, were Viscount Acheson, Charles Wilson,
junior, the Earl of Essex, the Marquess of Cholmondely,
and the Hon. Francis Lambton. At the conclusion of this
evidence, Sir Edward Clarke said: " Mrs Fairfax would
probably have been our only other witness on this part of
the case, but her absence is explained by an announcement
which appears this morning in the first column of the
Times." For Mrs Fairfax had been the victim of a happy
event.

This closed the evidence on the petition, and Lady
Hartopp's team now moved to the counter-attack in their
effort to prove that Sir Charles had committed adultery
with Mrs Sands. The case for the petition had not presented
a very formidable appearance, resting as it did mainly on
Lord Cowley's visits to Gaddesby Cottage and various
trifling incidents which could quite well be explained without
presuming adultery. But here at least it was admitted that
there existed a degree of intimacy between the parties; in
the case of the cross-petition on the other hand, Sir Charles
and Mrs Sands denied having more than a nodding acquaintance. There was, however, this advantage in arguing the
cross-petition, that if evidence of visits and intimacy could
be established, there was a stronger and more immediate
presumption of adultery. The task of collecting such
evidence had been assigned to an ex-Scotland Yard detective,
Inspector Conquest, who, assisted by a Mrs Stevenson and
a Mrs Taylor, a former servant of Mrs Sands, had in a
short space of time built up a case on the information of ex-
servants and cabmen. The rebutting of this case in the
interests of their clients was the joint task of Rufus Isaacs
and Lawson Walton, and so the two of them, who had
constituted so famous a team as leader and junior, were now
as leaders linked in an unofficial alliance.

The evidence for the cross-petition was opened by Mrs
Alice Taylor, an elderly woman who was in the service of

Mrs Sands, who said that she had seen Sir Charles six times at South Street, and had taken a telegram, signed " Charlie," to Mrs Sands at the Café Royal.   Her cross-examination by Lawson Walton provided a dramatic incident.   She had admitted that she had been taken by Inspector Conquest to identify Sir Charles, and that she had tried to get a photograph from Mrs Butler, a former servant of Mrs Sands—" to increase your art collection, I suppose," said Mr Lawson Walton—showing that Mrs Sands and Sir Charles went to the Derby together.   Mr Lawson Walton then produced a letter, which he said she had written to Miss Wilson, another former servant.   The letter is worth reproducing for its individuality of style, rather than for literary quality.   It ran:

Dear Miss Wilson,

Trusting this will find you all well.   Miss W. will you kindly let me know by return of post if Sir Charles Hartopp went to the Derby with Mrs S. and Miss Clare from Gloster Terres the time Mrs S. was so ill that time or if you can tell me if he went anywhere with them and all you know about him, Sir Charles Hartopp I mean if you will be so kind I will make it well worth your wile nothing to do with Mrs Sands watever I have not seen her for a long time trusting to hear from you by return of post I remain in haste yours sincerely A. S. Taylor.   Will write all next time.

Mrs Taylor modestly denied authorship of this master-piece; Mr Lawson Walton insisted.   Fortunately there was an easy test, and the old lady stepped from the witness-box to the solicitors' table, where she was provided with pen and paper.   Slowly, peeringly, she formed the reluctant letters, while the Court hung breathless on the scratching of her pen.   At last she was done, and the paper was handed back to Mr Lawson Walton; he inspected it, and gave it to Rufus Isaacs, sitting next him, who read it and nodded.   It was then given to Mr Inderwick who did the same, while the junior counsel craned forward from behind, and Sir George Lewis leant back from the seat in front to try and see it. Mr Lawson Walton then announced with quiet triumph that the comparison left no doubt. The eccentric vagaries of spelling were reproduced; the writer of the two documents was clearly the same. This was too much for old Mrs Taylor; she was seen to sway, and was carried half-fainting from the Court.

On her return in the afternoon, she was cross-examined by Rufus Isaacs; he elicited from her the admission that her memory was not good, though she had relied on it entirely in fixing the dates of the events which she narrated. But there was little to be got out of her, for the old woman was still dazed, frightened and obstinate. Rufus Isaacs dealt gently with her and did not press her; indeed it was unnecessary, for she was already a thoroughly discredited witness. Indeed the bullying of witnesses, apart from the decencies involved, has no part in great advocacy; good counsel never find it necessary or desirable to bully a witness. Thus Carson's cross-examination of Wilde cannot in any way be said to have been a bullying one, while Rufus Isaacs' cross-examinations of Whittaker Wright, of Seddon, and of J. B. Joel in the Sievier case, though in each he had to be persistent and relentless, are equally free from any taint of bullying; in the Seddon case, it is significant that Rufus Isaacs always addressed the prisoner as " Mr Seddon." It is left to inferior counsel to try and mask their own inadequacy by bluster and discourtesy; but it is a device that rarely impresses a jury, and never deceives the Bench.

The eighth day of the trial was occupied largely with the evidence of cabmen, shop assistants and so on, who had for the most part been very recently imported into the case by the efforts of Inspector Conquest and his satellites. There was Herbert Law, a sturdy, elderly cabdriver, who professed to have driven Sir Charles with Mrs Sands and to be able to identify him; there was Robert Colebourne, who said the same, and there was Henry Summerfield, who went so far as to specify the places to which he had driven them— the Café Royal, Romano's, Prince's, the Empire and so on. Summerfield, who said that he had called on Charles Wilson, when he read Mrs Sands' name in the reports of the case, was cross-examined by Rufus Isaacs.

"How came you to call on Mr Wilson?" he was asked.

"I don't know. I found his name in the directory."

"No thought of money ever entered your head, eh?"

"No, never," said the disinterested fellow stoutly.

Mr Lawson Walton then recalled Sir Charles to the box to give his evidence on the cross-petition. This time he made a very good impression, bluntly maintaining that the whole story of his visits to Mrs Sands was a lie. He had never been to her house, either in Graham Street, or South Street, and had never taken her to restaurants. He had met her in 1897 at the Savoy, and subsequently seen her at race-meetings and so on; once he had made a bet for her. That was the extent of their acquaintance. The good impression lasted through his cross-examination by Sir Edward Clarke, for he remained quite unshaken in his story of the facts. The next day the Duke of Devonshire gave evidence, but, as so often happens in these cases, the importance of the evidence was in inverse ratio to that of the individual giving it. More important was the evidence of Edward Sargent, who amused the Court by saying that in the course of 1890 he was valet to Mr Justice Hawkins, and was then familiar with gentlemen who moved in sporting circles. He said that his wife had been told by Conquest that it was worth £100 to her if she could identify Sir Charles; he also knew of a man called "Sir Charles" who visited Mrs Sands, but he thought he was neither a knight nor a baronet, as "Mrs Sands was fond of conferring courtesy titles on her friends." Mrs Butler, also formerly in Mrs Sands' service, said that neither Mrs Stevenson nor Mrs Taylor had seemed familiar with Sir Charles' photograph.

Rufus Isaacs then called Mrs Sands. He realised that the cross-petition had been unable to present a strong case, and that he and Lawson Walton had wrought havoc among the hastily and professionally collected evidence; Sir Charles, too, had done well. But Mrs Sands' interest must depend mainly on her bearing in the box, and on his skill and eloquence; fortunately there was no need to doubt of either. A great, swelling rustle of expectation ran round the Court as Mrs Sands walked towards the box; before she had reached it, however, Lady Hartopp and her mother rose in their places and swept from the Court. But few had eyes for this diversion; their attention was given to the central figures of the drama. Some, however, perhaps may have cast curious glances at a silver-haired old lady sitting in a corner of the Court, and wondered what she was thinking; for it was Mrs Sands' mother, soon at a hint from the Judge to be joined by her husband. To them, whatever the result of the case, their daughter's evidence must be supremely and pathetically tragic, since it would reveal facts that would make many approve the demonstrative protest of Lady Hartopp and her mother; for the trial took place in 1902. But the crowded Court left Mrs Sands' parents to their thoughts and turned to the box, where Mrs Sands had thrown open her fur-lined jacket and, hands resting on the rail and head thrown back, gave her answers in a clear, sweet voice with the faultless articulation of a trained actress. And alternately, as question was given and answered, they turned from the handsome, erect, youthful figure of Rufus Isaacs to the beautiful woman in the box, as he guided her tactfully through the story of her life, her marriage, her separation, and her acquaintance—scarcely more than a nodding acquaintance—with Sir Charles Hartopp. Then, carefully led up to, but supremely effective in its apparent suddenness, came the crucial question, sounding almost indecent in its bluntness:

" Have you ever been guilty of any impropriety with Sir Charles Hartopp? "

And the answer, equally effective and spoken in a clear, musical tone:

" Absolutely, on my solemn oath, never."

She had perhaps considerable reason to fear cross-examination, but her courage was equal to it, and when Mr Inderwick said, " Do you say you have been leading a quiet and respectable life? " her answer, quiet, firm, and decisive, " No, I don't say that," robbed the question of its sting.

It fell to Rufus Isaacs, as counsel for the respondent in the cross-petition, to address the jury first. It was the tenth day of the trial when he spoke, and at first, of the principals in the case, only Sir Charles and Mrs Sands were present; Mrs Sands left the Court, however, on the conclusion of her counsel's speech and then Lady Hartopp and her mother, who had clearly determined to play at a species of Box and Cox with Mrs Sands, re-entered the Court. Rufus Isaacs' speech was a triumph of its sort. The case did not call for technical argument, but he analysed its features with that rapid precision which was customary with him. He spoke without a note, and without hesitation—a feat that is the more remarkable when it is remembered that his mind was loaded at the time with the intricate details of the great Taff Vale argument which he was contemporaneously conducting.

Right from the start of his speech he emphasised his client's favourable position in the case; she had taken only a small part in the controversy, and had come voluntarily into the witness-box, though she did not pose as a woman of irreproachable character. " Do not forget," he reminded them, " that every attempt has been made, as far as possible, to deter her from taking any part in the proceedings. Consider what sort of case it is that this lady had to meet. The charges that have been made against her were not put on the record until November 15th, or just eleven days before the first day of the trial." The charges had always been of the vaguest, as was natural when the evidence was procured by Conquest and his satellites, and by others whose names were not even revealed; it was a " professional " case, built up on lavish expenditure. " All that money could do in searching every nook and corner has been done; and what has all the investigation brought to light? Nothing except the vaguest evidence." Mrs Taylor stood clearly revealed as guilty of wilful and deliberate perjury; as to the other witnesses, " I will say that the workings of their minds has been lubricated, for even the scent of money in the air renders some people's consciences more elastic." He then proceeded to give a critical analysis of individual portions of the evidence. The cabmen, for instance; there was no doubt that Law had been paid, although he denied it. But in any case what was the value of their identification? " Is there anybody in Court, who after the lapse of two or three years, could have identified, as the cabmen say they could identify Sir Charles, having driven him but once or twice at most. And yet may we not hope that we are all as intelligent as they? " Mrs Taylor knew well enough that she was a convicted liar; and what of Mrs Stevenson, Conquest's chief assistant? How comes it that Mrs Stevenson has not ventured into the box? She is, forsooth, the captain of the band arrayed against Sir Charles—a ragged band enough, in truth; but perhaps it is enough for her to have seen Mrs Taylor there." But when he came to Mrs Sands' part, irony and criticism were abandoned, and he paid tribute to her conduct as a witness, for she had given her " evidence as truthfully as witness ever did." He ended, his voice strong with feeling, on a note of challenge, almost of triumph: " A history and a past are great deterrents for keeping persons from the witness-box, because they fear the raking-up. She has a history and a past but it has not kept her from the box. Every effort was made to prevent her from going into the box, but she went, hard as it must have been to her, with the knowledge of the sins she has committed, and she has given her denial of her guilt with Sir Charles."

There was a burst of generous and spontaneous applause in Court, when Rufus Isaacs concluded his appeal; and by the end of his speech it was tolerably certain, whatever the finding of the jury on the entire case, that Mrs Sands would get her verdict. For, as Mr Lawson Walton remarked in the course of a five hours' speech, whose sustained animation and not infrequent eloquence won him the congratulation of the profession and the applause of the public, " the charge of adultery between Sir Charles and Mrs Sands was started by an ex-inspector of Scotland Yard, and upon it the hall-mark of Scotland Yard is stamped." It had arisen merely because Lady Hartopp and Lord Cowley had " started looking about to see if they could not find out whether Sir Charles had ever been guilty of any infidelity towards his wife," and as such was scarcely worthy of consideration. Mr Lawson Walton's speech followed Mr Inderwick's for Lady Hartopp, Sir Edward Clarke having fallen ill in the course of the case. The audience had dwindled for Mr Inderwick's speech, for he spoke in a quick, soft voice which often dropped so low that he was scarcely audible even to the jury; his manner, too, with his arms tucked under his gown behind him and his eye-glasses aslant his nose, was rather like the layman's caricature of a typical lawyer. The Court was full, however, when Mr Justice Gorrell Barnes summed up on the thirteenth and last day of the trial. It was apparent that he did not really think the evidence amounted to very much, and was anxious for the jury to understand the social atmosphere in which the litigants moved; consequently he invited them, " who are probably mostly business men to step into the hunting-field " where " in a jolly state of sporting good fellowship Christian names and nicknames were flying about like brickbats among both peers and commoners." This complicated exercise took the jury—perhaps pardonably—three hours and a quarter, at the end of which time they returned a verdict that neither Lady Hartopp and Lord Cowley nor Mrs Sands and Sir Charles had committed adultery, nor had Sir Charles been guilty of cruelty. This complete retention of the matrimonial status quo was greeted with laughter, for it was not thought that the verdict was one for cheers.

Parturiunt montes: nascetur ridiculus mus. Debrett had gone to law, and commerce had scorned the allegations; the result was " as you were," but the costs were huge. The case cost in the neighbourhood of £15,000. Rufus Isaacs had secured an award of the costs of the cross-petition against Lady Hartopp. Sir Edward Clarke, as an ex-Solicitor-General, leading the way in fees with a retainer of 500 guineas, and a refresher of 100 guineas a day, while the other silks had retainers of 150 guineas and substantial refreshers. For the moment the result of all this outlay to the parties concerned was nothing. But the Hartopp marriage was not destined to last, whatever twelve jurors might say, and in 1905 it was formally dissolved. Lady Hartopp then married Lord Cowley, but unfortunately he exhibited the matrimonial instability not unusual among the less serious of the leisured classes, and he appeared as co-respondent in an undefended divorce petition brought by Major Buxton in January, 1913. As a consequence, Lady Hartopp divorced Lord Cowley in March, 1913, and subsequently married Major Duberly who was killed in action in the War, while Lord Cowley married Mrs Buxton. It is interesting to record that the counsel in Lady Hartopp's petition for the restitution of conjugal rights against Lord Cowley were Mr Barnard, K.C., who had been junior counsel to Mr Lawson Walton for Sir Charles Hartopp in the Hartopp divorce case, and Rufus Isaacs. But this Rufus Isaacs was Gerald Rufus Isaacs, then a young man of twenty-three starting his career at the Bar; for Sir Rufus Isaacs by that time was Attorney-General and leader of his profession, and could appear only for the Crown.

Many comments may easily, and some legitimately, be made about the Hartopp divorce case. The most obvious is the platitude, freely repeated at the time by commentators on the case, that " useless " lives lead to this particular sort of frustration. There is no need to discuss this point here except to say that, generally speaking, the platitude, unlike so many, is true, and that an abundance of leisure, without depth of interest, may very easily promote restlessness and craving for variety. To desert, however, the lofty plane of generalisation, it would seem most regrettable that Mrs Sands had to be dragged into other peoples' matrimonial squabbles, with which she had nothing whatever to do. Her position made her peculiarly vulnerable in such a case, and, therefore, as Rufus Isaacs pointed out, her action in coming forward and subjecting herself to cross-examination mainly in the interests of Sir Charles and of justice—for she was bound to be harmed herself by her appearance—was one of high courage. Whatever else may be said about her, she was a woman whose bravery equalled her beauty; and her conduct and demeanour during a trial that must have been hateful to her, were worthy of both. It may safely be said that if every counsel could enter the Divorce Court in as good a cause as that in which Rufus Isaacs went to champion Mrs Sands, that Court would be free from the sordid elements with which it is so frequently associated.

The other case with which Rufus Isaacs was contemporaneously concerned, was of a very different order; for there were no sables or chiffon in Court to hear the great Taff Vale case, though its proceedings were watched with anxious interest by organised labour over the whole country. For it was this case which signalised the end of the " long practical immunity " from being sued which the Trade Unions had enjoyed since the Act of 1871, and which led up to the highly controversial Trades Disputes Act of 1906. The case arose from the Taff Vale strike of August, 1900, which was a strike of railwaymen against the Taff Vale Railway Company; in consequence of it, the Company brought an action against the Amalgamated Society of Railway Servants, and asked for an injunction to restrain the Society from besetting the Great Western Railway. The Society, however, relying on the prevalent belief that a Trade Union could not be sued in law, took out a summons, asking that they should be dismissed from the action. There are, therefore, two parts of the Taff Vale case; first, there was the preliminary legal argument to decide whether the action would lie in law (Rufus Isaacs did not appear in this), and then, when after consideration by three Courts it had been decided that it did, the case had to be argued on the facts. In this part of the case, Rufus Isaacs led for the Society, its trustees, and its general secretary, Richard Bell, M.P. for Derby.

The argument of the Trade Unions on the point of law was briefly this. The only entities known to the Common Law of England, as being capable of suing or being sued, are individuals and corporations; a Trade Union is neither a corporation nor an individual, nor yet is it a partnership between a number of individuals. The contention was, therefore, that there was no capacity in which a Trade Union could be sued. This argument, however, overlooked the fact that in spite of this, the legislature can give to an association of individuals, which is neither a corporation nor a partnership, nor an individual, the capacity to own property and to act by agents; and that in such a case, in the absence of an express enactment to the contrary, there is necessarily a correlative liability, to the extent of the property, for the acts of the agents. Such a capacity to own property and to act by agents had been given to Trade Unions by the Acts of 1871 and 1876, and in the view of Mr Justice Farwell, who heard the case, there was nothing in those Acts to suggest that it was intended to exempt the Trade Unions from their proper correlative liability; for, in his own words, " it would require very clear and express words of enactment to induce me to hold that the Legislature had in fact legalised the existence of such irresponsible bodies with such wide capacities for evil." When the Society took the case to the Court of Appeal, however, the Master of the Rolls, A. L. Smith, took the opposite view: " when once one gets an entity, not known to the law," he said in his judgment, " and therefore incapable of being sued, in our judgment to enable such an entity to be sued an enactment must be found either express or implied enabling this to be done; and it is not correct to say that such an entity can be sued unless there be found an express enactment to the contrary." The judgment of Mr Justice Farwell was accordingly reversed, and the Company appealed; the case, therefore, like Allen v. Flood before it, went for hearing before the House of Lords. Here it was argued by Sir Edward Clarke and Mr Swinfen Eady for the Company, and a future Lord Chancellor and a future Solicitor-General, in the persons of Mr Haldane and Mr S. T. Evans, for the Society. The upshot was that the House of Lords reversed the judgment of the Court of Appeal, and restored the original judgment of

Mr Justice Farwell, taking the view that although a Trade Union was not a corporation, it could nevertheless, under the statutes, sue or be sued in its registered name. Or, as Lord Lindley put it, " the Act appears to me to indicate with sufficient clearness that the registered name is one which may be used to denote the Union as an unincorporated society in legal proceedings as well as for business and other purposes."

Thus it was decided—at any rate legally, for the decision brought an agitation which, as we shall see, was to lead to momentous conclusions—that a Trade Union could be sued, and that its funds were liable for the payment of damages given against it; and the Taff Vale case was accordingly remitted to the King's Bench to be argued on the facts. The hearing before Mr Justice Wills and a special jury began on December 3rd, 1902—the day following Mrs Sands' intervention in the Hartopp divorce case—and this time Rufus Isaacs led Mr Evans and Mr Clement Edwards, while the Company was also strongly represented by Sir Edward Clarke, Mr Francis Williams, K.C., and Mr Eldon Bankes, K.C. The statements of claim and of defence were lengthy documents but the crux of the case was this: the Company claimed damages for the violent and unlawful acts by which they had suffered during the eleven days' strike, and for which they alleged that the Society of Railway Servants was responsible. The Society denied the alleged unlawful acts and damage, saying that if there were any, they were unauthorised; further they denied taking any part in the dispute prior to the date of the strike (August 19th, 1900), and maintained that Bell had been sent down as a peacemaker, while on August 19th the executive committee had condemned the conduct of the men, who had taken action without their consent and contrary to the rules of the Society. There was a further defence that one of the terms of the final settlement of the dispute had been that the Company should discontinue all legal proceedings, and that this action was clearly a breach of that agreement. Now if this last point of defence could be established, there was an end of the case; consequently at the end of the plaintiffs' case, Rufus Isaacs rose and submitted that on the evidence there was clearly an agreement that no action for damages should be brought against the Society and Bell. The terms of the agreement, he said, obviously included the Society; and, in addition, as many of the men were members of the Society, the agreement not to sue them made it impossible to sue the Society. For the House of Lords' decision had not made a Trade Union an entity like a corporation; rather it was like a club or a firm, and since it is impossible to sue a firm consisting of A, B and C, if you had previously agreed not to sue B and C, it was clearly impossible to sue the Society, after an agreement had been made not to sue some of its members. The argument was ingenious and well sustained, but there was one definite flaw; the agreement had been made with the men, not with the Society, and, as the Society was not a party to the agreement, it could not in law take advantage of it. Mr Eldon Bankes seized upon this weak point, and it finally decided Mr Justice Wills, after listening to four hours' argument on the question, to overrule Rufus Isaacs' objection. But he had argued the point with a subtlety and persuasiveness, even though unsuccessfully, and his feat in sustaining such a technical argument is remarkable, when it is remembered that he came into Court to conduct it immediately on conclusion of his speech for Mrs Sands.

With the collapse of this objection the best hope of the defence was gone, for the Society had assumed control of the strike when once it was started, and it was undeniable that in the course of it the " imported men," who were under contract—" blacklegs," as the Trade Unionists called them—had suffered interference and intimidation. But it was not the first unpromising case that Rufus Isaacs had encountered, and he fought gamely. He pointed out that the dimensions of the plaintiffs' case had shrunk; it had at first been alleged that the events leading up to the strike had been the result of sham agitation, the men being goaded on by the officials of the Society for their own ends, and that, therefore, the strike, not being for the benefit of the

men, was illegal.   This case had fallen away, for it was
not difficult to show that the men had grievances, and had
themselves resolved to strike; indeed though the committee
in London had passed a resolution to support them, the men
had already declared a strike in ignorance of the fact.   Bell
had then been sent down to take charge until peace could
be secured, and found the system of picketing (which in
itself was legal) already in operation.   He had done his
best to prevent unlawful acts, and it was not right, Rufus
Isaacs concluded, to saddle Bell or the Society with responsibility for the acts of violence committed by pickets, whom
they had not nominated, or by persons who had acted
without instructions and outside their authority.

But Rufus Isaacs' plea was of no avail.   For after a long
summing up, in which Mr Justice Wills said that he considered the evidence of conspiracy to molest and injure the
plaintiffs by unlawful means to be absolutely overwhelming
—he also made the surprising but significant remark, " you
cannot make a strike effective without doing more than is
lawful "—the jury found for the plaintiffs on all counts.
The question of damages was reserved, and it was ultimately
settled by agreement between the parties that the defendants
should pay £23,000 as a complete composition for damages
and costs.

The rather dry facts of the Taff Vale case may make it
difficult at this distance of time, to realise the immense
interest which it attracted and the great importance which
attaches to it.   It was watched with an anxious interest by
all classes, that was sharply in contrast with the excitement
aroused by the drama of the Hartopp case.   The House of
Lords' decision and the subsequent verdict profoundly
stirred the whole community.   To Trade Unionists it
seemed that all the rights won by organised labour in long
and careful years of struggle were in jeopardy; to others
it seemed that a dangerous menace to the liberty of the
subject was removed.   For years political platforms echoed
and re-echoed with the rights and wrongs of Taff Vale;
and finally it was Taff Vale almost as much as Free Trade

and "Chinese Slavery" that swept the country in the General Election of 1906. At first sight it might seem absurd to compare a case of such palpable importance with the Hartopp case, which it is so easy to dismiss as a trivial and inelegant incident in the lives of the idle rich; but such criticism misses the point, for it is the wealth and position of the parties that is incidental. For cases like the Hartopp case are provoked by the tortuous complex of human emotions—love, hatred, jealousy, suspicion—that make up the inmost life of the individual; these things exist always, but it is only on such rare occasions that they are brought up for the gaze of the curious and the scrutiny of the theorist. It is good to be reminded of these things, for they are important; and it is in the Hartopp and similar cases that we are so reminded. For they are concerned with the very heartbeats of the individual, and Taff Vale with the nerves and sinews which bind and enforce the framework of society. To attempt to adjudicate further between them would be to trespass into the debating ground of the philosophers, and to try and resolve their doubts as to the comparative importance of the individual and of the community.

Here it is perhaps more appropriate to mark the versatility which allowed Rufus Isaacs to appear simultaneously and with such effect in two great cases, on such entirely different planes. There are some great advocates, among whom was Lord Carson, who will only appear in one case at a time (and it is a practice which has very much to recommend it); there are others, like Marshall Hall, who became so immersed in a great case that we cannot imagine them switching their minds daily from Mrs Sands to Taff Vale. Indeed, apart from the fact that there are very few advocates with an equipment that would secure them simultaneously briefs in a great Trade Union case and a sensational divorce case, there are still fewer who could achieve the necessary departmentalisation of mind to go from Court to Court, and achieve a success in both. But versatility of application, departmentalisation of mind, and economy of energy were, as we have seen, foremost among Lord Reading's qualities;

and the Hartopp case and the Taff Vale case even though
the facts were very favourable in the Hartopp case and he
lost the Taff Vale, provide an excellent instance.   Such
qualities bring a rich reward that is not merely financial;
for to Rufus Isaacs there fell in great degree that breadth
of scene and wide range of activity which to greater or less
extent are the lot of every barrister.   The life of a great
advocate is a social document, for he impinges in his work
on public affairs, commercial affairs, and the domestic affairs
of all classes of the community.   And these cases added
notable pages; for in one we can feel the throb of human
emotion and in the other we can lay our finger on the pulse
of national feeling.

CHAPTER IX

THE GORDON CUSTODY CASE

THE year 1902 had gone down in a blaze of forensic glory. 1903 was to contain cases of almost equal note, but one of the first cases in which Rufus Isaacs was engaged in the New Year struck a lighter vein. This was the case in which he appeared for " Lord " George Sanger, the veteran circus proprietor, in the action of Sanger *v.* Harmsworth; in this action " Lord " George claimed £35,000, which he alleged that Harmsworth had promised him in connection with the promotion of a company to take over the circus business. Harmsworth denied the promise, and said that, if he had made it, there was no consideration. At the start of the case, which was tried before Mr Justice Ridley and a special jury, Mr Justice Ridley inquired: " Is he Lord George Sanger? "

" Yes, my lord," replied Rufus Isaacs, " but I do not feel justified in conferring a peerage upon him."

Sanger was then put in the box, where he was thoroughly at ease, though perhaps not quite in place, and surprised the Court by the quaintness of his remarks. He gave accounts of various interviews with Harmsworth. At one of these when he broached the subject of £35,000, Harmsworth " called up a waitress and changed the subject, which he was very clever at doing. I never met a man who could do it so well, and I am a little bit of a trickster myself." This disarming confession was followed up by the account of an interview at Nantwich, where he had spoken to the unfortunate Harmsworth " so straight " that the gentleman " had to ask his landlady to bring him some tea directly." On a subsequent occasion at the solicitor's office his anger at Harmsworth's reticence reacted on himself for, he said, " I was so vexed that I threw my hat on the ground and trampled it, as you may say, out of shape." For all his tantrums, however, " Lord " George was a nice old man, who had a deep sense of reverent affection for the monarchy, as shown in his evidence, " I said I did not like taking gifts, although I had accepted one from the dear old Queen; " which displayed a nice sense of distinction. The case, however, only lasted two days, for Rufus Isaacs and Mr Shee, K.C., who led for Harmsworth, decided that, however amusing the continuance of the case might be to the Court, the interests of their clients would be better served by settling. Consequently, after a long consultation between counsel, an amicable settlement was arrived at, by which Harmsworth transferred to Sanger his shares in the Company and certain other shares in addition, while Rufus Isaacs, on behalf of the choleric but kind-hearted " lord " withdrew any imputations on Mr Harmsworth which Sanger might have made in the heat of the moment at their various meetings.

Very different from the light-hearted affairs of the circus " peer " was the Gordon custody case, which Rufus Isaacs argued in the Divorce Court the following month. The Gordon case, which chiefly centred round the relations of two cousins, members of a noble house, with the same woman, may fairly be termed an unpleasant case; but nevertheless it contained some most unusual features. It is part of the daily routine of the Divorce Court that two people should strenuously deny adultery; but it is a little unexpected to find two people just as strenuously insisting that they have committed adultery. Yet this is what happened in the case which is technically known as Gordon v. Gordon and Gordon.

It all arose through an American lady, Miss Margaret Humble, who had come to England and married a man named Close. She was left a widow by him, however, and subsequently meeting Lord Granville Gordon, who was the brother and heir presumptive of the eleventh Marquess of Huntly and at the time a well set up military-looking man in the thirties, she became, according to the evidence of the

parties at the trial, his mistress.   In course of time she met
Lord Granville's cousin, Christian Frederick Gordon (he
was always known as Eric), who was ten years younger than
his cousin and just starting his career on the Stock Exchange.
He was not too young, however, to fall in love with
Margaret Close, and he pressed his suit upon her.   He was
perhaps not so strong and positive a personality as his cousin,
but he too was tall, broad-shouldered and athletic in appearance; and he had one great advantage over his cousin in
that he was able to offer marriage to the lady, while Lord
Granville, who was already married, could not.   The lady,
however, was not too willing, and it was not until Eric had
proposed several times that she yielded and accepted him.
The chief ground of her reluctance was her relationship
with Lord Granville, which she was unwilling to give up.
Eric, however, saw no reason why she should not, after
marriage, be friendly with his cousin, and wrote to her,
" Please don't worry yourself at anything Granny (Lord
Granville) says, and don't make yourself unhappy about
him.   You shall see him as much as you like some day.   I
will come to tea to-morrow.   Sleep well, darling, to-night.
Yours always, Eric."   This letter was afterwards to be
variously interpreted.   Lord Granville and Margaret maintained that it showed that Eric was aware of their relationship and was prepared to connive at its continuance, while
Eric insisted that it showed no such thing, but was meant
to convey that there was no occasion for interrupting an
innocent friendship.

The marriage took place on August 29th, 1894, and the
married couple set up house.   They lived in various places
and stayed in still more, and always Lord Granville Gordon
was a very frequent visitor, staying often for several days
in mid-week, when Eric was away at the Stock Exchange
all day.   Such *ménages à trois* are not unknown, and are
very often entirely innocent, especially if the two men are
friends or relatives with tastes in common, as in this case;
for the two cousins shot together and had once been to
Norway for six weeks.   But rumour nevertheless generally

gets busy, and this case was no exception; in 1896 stories were in active circulation, but Eric, as he stated, decided that there could be no foundation in them, and that his wife and his cousin were above suspicion. Later, however, in 1899, when a daughter was born to Margaret, he was very annoyed when Lord Granville was admitted to her bedroom shortly after the event. But by this time all was clearly not well with the marriage, and when Lady Granville Gordon died in May, 1900, the position was simplified; for Lord Granville went on with Margaret, and Eric, who had previously refused a separation or divorce, obtained a decree nisi for the dissolution of his marriage on the ground of his wife's adultery with Lord Granville. This was on November 25th, 1901, and on June 2nd of the following year the decree was made absolute. On August 5th of the same year Lord Granville married Margaret at the British Consulate at Dieppe; and in this unromantic spot the matter might thus have ended, with no more serious consequences than an estrangement between the cousins and the addition of a courtesy title to the style of the former Miss Humble.

It might have; but in fact it did not. For, in granting the divorce, the Court gave Eric Gordon the custody of the child, and this did not suit the mother at all; consequently the child remained with the mother, who had every intention of keeping her, while Eric had every intention of enforcing his rights. Margaret Gordon's attitude can be seen from the letter which she wrote to Eric on July 17th, 1902, shortly before her marriage to Lord Granville, in which she said: " I swear baby is Granville's child and if this is not the truth, may she die to-day; it is absolutely the truth, and she is my whole world. If you take her, I shall not marry and it will probably soon kill me, which will be a good thing. For God's sake have a little mercy on me. If you insist, and I suppose you will, I will give her up, as unless I were married it would be so bad for her; but before you ruin two miserable lives, think well. I swear it was not your child; it was impossible." That these were her feelings on the subject is not surprising; but her expectation of keeping the child in face of the Court's decree requires explanation. In point of fact, she insisted that there was an understanding between the parties that the decree giving custody of the child to Eric should be treated as a mere formality, and the child should remain with her. And remain with her it did, at any rate long enough for her to get married to Lord Granville. In course of time, however, Eric made an application for the enforcement of the order of the Court, and the new Lady Granville Gordon encountered with an application to vary it.

Such an application would normally be heard in Chambers, but it was in this instance the desire of all the parties to have the case argued in open Court. Consequently the hearing came on in the Divorce Court before Sir Francis Jeune, President of the Division, in February of 1903. Mr Henry Duke, K.C., and Mr Priestly appeared for the petitioner, Eric Gordon, and were opposed, on behalf of the Granville Gordons by Mr Bargrave Deane, K.C., Rufus Isaacs and and Mr Barnard. It will be noticed that all these counsel had taken part in the Hartopp case two months previously; but the Gordon case, though similar to the Hartopp case in that aristocratic names were involved, did not attract the same enormous measure of popular attention. Partly, no doubt, this was because the appetite for this kind of case had been sated; but the chief reason lay in the difference between the two cases. The Hartopp case had been strongly fought, but it was fought in an atmosphere of chivalry and good nature; the Gordon case was a struggle à l'outrance, red in tooth and claw. There was all the difference between Queensbury rules and all-in wrestling, between a joust and a cock-fight; and, though a joust may be an attractive spectacle, there is something disgusting about the sight of a naked combat for possession. And the combat becomes no more edifying when its battle-ground is the adultery of persons no longer in the first flush of youth. But though the Gordon case was unpleasant, it was interesting and unusual. For the respondents could not rest their case solely on the alleged agreement not to ask for custody, since it could not be maintained that there was any definite agreement, which the Court must enforce. (It may be observed that there would be nothing improper in a petitioner for divorce not asking for the custody of a child, if he did not believe it to be his own, but if the wife agrees not to defend in return for a promise not to ask for custody, then that is collusion, and a divorce will not be granted.) Further, it is a rule of evidence that a parent may not give evidence which will bastardise her child. Consequently the respondents had to rely on yet another line of argument, which was that Eric Gordon had been aware of their adultery and connived at it, and was therefore a person unfit to have custody of the child. So it was that through a great part of the case the respondents were endeavouring to prove their own adultery to discredit not themselves, but the husband who—to use the Restoration term—had been cuckolded.

The case for Lady Granville Gordon was opened by Mr Bargrave Deane—for he was technically " leading "—who outlined the respondents' view of the case, alleging that Eric Gordon had been well aware of the relations between his wife and his cousin and urging that, if the agreement were reasonable and in the interests of the child, the Court ought to enforce it. The opening proceedings took up the whole of the first day of the trial, and it was the second day when Lady Granville Gordon entered the box to be examined by Rufus Isaacs. The Court turned curiously to see what manner of woman it was, who had captivated the two cousins and set a noble family by the ears; she turned out to be a handsome woman with a mature presence which indicated a decisive, if not a dominating, character. Her bearing in Court, both in Rufus Isaacs' examination-in-chief and subsequently under Mr Duke's severe cross-examination, was composed to a degree; nor was her composure affected in the slightest by the spectacle of her present husband and her former husband seated in the front row of seats, the one stroking his long fair moustache and rivalling his wife's composure, the other biting his nails in his nervousness and rarely raising his eyes from the ground. Rufus Isaacs found her a good witness, although her frank confessions of adultery could not be expected to make a good impression on the Court. After she had told how she and Eric Gordon had always had separate rooms, while Lord Granville, when he stayed with them at Maidenhead, had a room communicating with hers through a small sitting-room, which was known as " his Lordship's room," Rufus Isaacs put the question " Who is the father of the child? " The question, however, was disallowed. In cross-examination, of course, Lady Granville Gordon could not expect to escape lightly in view of her own admissions, and Henry Duke soon pressed home his advantage.

" Are you aware," he demanded, " that the marriage service contains certain vows entirely inconsistent with the continuance of your relations with Lord Granville Gordon?"

" Yes."

" Did you intend to observe those vows, madam? "

" No, I did not."

" Which oath has most weight with you—your oath in this Court or the oath you took before Almighty God on that occasion? "

The question was a clever one, rather of the " have you stopped beating your wife? " variety, for any answer would be damaging. However, only one reply was possible and she replied with firmness:

" The oath I have taken in this Court."

She stood up to the whole cross-examination with the same obstinate composure, but it could not but be damaging, especially as it was a case in which the impression made upon the Court was of enormous importance. Indeed her very composure in discussing her irregularity of conduct, which would seem sinful to some and selfish to all, was in a sense unfortunate; for nobody would give the custody of a child to a woman whom they considered hard and abandoned, even if she was the mother. That sort of impression is extremely difficult to efface, and Rufus Isaacs' re-examination of her, which did not sufficiently concentrate on this aspect, could not remove it, although it was conducted a week later at a time when Lady Granville Gordon was less composed and considerably less distinct owing to a heavy cold—circumstances not altogether disadvantageous. There was an added difficulty, too, by this time in that the President had heard the evidence of Lady Granville Gordon's sister, Mrs Graves, and had taken a definitely unfavourable view of the respondents' case. For Mrs Graves had said, in examination by Mr Barnard, that she knew that Eric Gordon was aware that his wife had committed adultery, and that he always accepted the situation. To which Mr Duke said:

" If you thought your sister was committing adultery, did you think it sisterly not to say anything about it? "

" I did not think it my place to say anything," she replied. " I was on friendly terms with Mr Gordon. I said I was awfully sorry."

This was too much for Sir Francis.

" Said you were awfully sorry, indeed! Was that all you said? "

" What else could I say? "

" Say, madam; I think I could tell you pretty clearly."

And no doubt he could have done; but what he would have said cannot be known, for he did not vouchsafe it to a curious Court.

The same bad effect was created, after Lady Granville Gordon's re-examination, by her friend Mrs Nias, and, to a much less degree, by her maid. Her maid said that she did not speak about what was going on because she thought Mr Gordon knew about it, and because she did not want to lose her situation. This was perhaps forgiveable, but Sir Francis took a very poor view of Mrs Nias' attitude in the matter. Mrs Nias, examined by Rufus Isaacs, told how she was staying with the Gordons shortly before the birth of the child, and how Eric Gordon would leave her and Lord Granville to keep his wife company. She said, in answer to Mr Duke, that she would not have gone to the house if she had known that they had committed adultery, but that she very soon came to that conclusion, when she was there, and also that Lord Granville was father of the child.

"And believing that, madam," said Duke, "you continued to sit at the table daily, morning and evening, with Mr Gordon."

"It was not for me to raise objections; I knew he knew."

"That makes it fifty times worse," put in Sir Francis sternly.

"Why," inquired Mr Duke, "did you not complain to the petitioner that decency must be observed in the house?"

"I thought it was," replied Mrs Nias ingenuously.

"What!" exclaimed the outraged President, and Mr Duke as a clever tactician knew any further questions must weaken the effect.

"I will not trouble you further, madam," he said coldly.

She was re-examined in the hopes of retrieving this disaster, and explained that the petitioner had told her, only a week before the birth of the child, that Lord Granville was the only person in whom his wife had any interest or affection. This, however, did not mollify Sir Francis.

"But why remain in the house at all?" he insisted.

"But, my Lord," she replied, "I live the other side of the Park."

"Well, well," said Sir Francis and fell silent; for even Divorce Court Judges can sometimes be bewildered in the inconsequences of feminine logic.

Mrs Nias was a bad witness; but even apart from that, it may legitimately be asked what purpose was served by calling these witnesses. The fact was that the respondents were in a dilemma. These people had to be called to say that in their belief Eric Gordon had known what was going on; but to do this, they had to admit that they, too, knew what was going on, and neither took action nor felt such conduct to be incompatible with the continuance of friendly relations with Eric Gordon or with the offenders. This difficulty ran through the whole case, and is apparent in the evidence of the Granville Gordons as well as in that of the lesser witnesses; it crystallised into this—that, in order to establish their case, the witnesses for the respondents had to give evidence of conduct of a sort that enabled Mr Duke to say that their evidence should be discredited. And ultimately they all succeeded in convincing the Court of their own wrongdoing, but not—which was the essential point—of Eric Gordon's knowledge of it. If there was to be any hope for the respondents therefore, it had to come from Rufus Isaacs' cross-examination of Eric Gordon, and he devoted himself with skill and patience to trying to make the witness admit knowledge of the love of his wife and his cousin. But Eric Gordon made a very good witness, especially in that he never tried to score off counsel and was not afraid of repeating his answers; for an attempt to make debating points in the box is always fatal, unless undertaken by a supremely able person, and even then, as in the case of Wilde, it is generally a mistake in tactics. And as for repetition, it may be monotonous but it often carries with it the conviction of truth. And so Rufus Isaacs, employing now the fast deliveries of shock tactics and now the slows of wily indirectness, met always the patient stonewalling defence which, unlike the cuts and drives of a more spirited performer, never exposed his citadel.

"Did it not occur to you," asked Rufus Isaacs, "that in the interests of your wife's reputation it was desirable that his visits should be less frequent?"

"No, I had such faith and trust in my wife and him that it did not."

"You might be satisfied, but a censorious world would not. You were anxious for your wife's reputation but you did not forbid him the house, although his own wife was quarrelling with him about your wife?"

"It never occurred to me, but I see now it would have been wiser if I had done so."

It is always good tactics to confess a mistake—as long as it is a miscalculation and not an ethical mistake—in the box, for nothing pleases a jury more than to reflect how much better they would have handled the situation themselves.

Later Rufus Isaacs asked:

"Would it have aroused any suspicion in your mind if he had come to live in your house?"

" Not if I had asked him to do so," was the reply.

" Would it not have seemed unnatural for you to ask him, after all the rumours you had heard? "

" No, I trusted him as a cousin and a friend."

" You say there was always another guest in the house when he visited you. Was this in order to play propriety? "

" Certainly not."

Rufus Isaacs extorted the admission that the witness was aware in 1896 that Lord Granville was not living with his wife, who was a jealous woman.

" Had she," he asked, " any other cause for jealousy apart from your wife? "

" No, not to my knowledge."

" Then, the sole cause of her jealousy being your wife, you did not consider it undesirable that he should visit at your house? "

As to the peculiar geographical arrangement of the *ménage à trois*, Rufus Isaacs said:

" If an intimacy were in progress unknown to you, were you not put to sleep in the room in which you were most unlikely to discover what was going on? "

" I do not think so."

" While the respondent and co-respondent occupied rooms most suitable for their purpose? Was not the room he occupied the one you, as the lady's husband, should have occupied instead of being given over to a stranger? "

" I did not consider him a stranger."

" I agree," said Rufus Isaacs drily, and there was one of the few laughs that this case provoked.

But Eric Gordon had emerged very well. He had taken his line and not deviated from it; it was a popular line, too, for he could always fall back on the great trust which he had placed in his wife and his cousin. And, since it was an age which had a great respect for property, the cuckold was not ridiculed, as in an earlier age, but was panoplied in the protective conscience of the community. Consequently it did not require the applause which greeted Henry Duke's speech—in which he maintained strongly that custody should be given to his client, who would hardly be anxious to maintain the child if he did not believe it to be his own, while it was almost unheard of to give custody to a guilty parent—to show which was the popular side.

The task of replying and saying the final word for Lady Granville Gordon was entrusted to Rufus Isaacs, whose dexterous eloquence was peculiarly fitted for putting a difficult and unpopular case in the best light. But before Rufus Isaacs made his speech there was a dramatic interlude, for the *Daily Mail* announced that Lady Granville Gordon had left for the Continent, taking the child with her; the report, which had been confirmed by Lord Granville Gordon under a misapprehension as to the bona fides of the *Daily Mail* representative, was erroneous—or, as it turned out, premature. Lady Granville Gordon's solicitors made inquiries and she replied from 26 Hereford Square, on March 2nd:

DEAR MR UPTON,

It is absolutely untrue that I have left town, or mean to until the case is over, and I think it most important that Mr Isaacs should make his speech, and it is also my intention to hear it.

Yours,

MARGARET GRANVILLE GORDON.

And so Margaret Gordon was in Court to hear Rufus Isaacs' speech, to which she listened with strained attention, and was visibly moved by the eloquence of his pleading. A much more important spectator, whose presence was noted with equal interest by the crowded Court which had come to hear the speech, was Israel Zangwill, the writer, who listened closely as Rufus Isaacs put his case. His main line of argument was that the practice by which the Courts had for some years been accustomed to deal with these cases in a penal light with regard to the guilty party was exploded doctrine; the true guiding principle was that there neither was nor could be any hard and fast rule in such cases, but that in all cases it was the interest of the children which must be looked to. The case of Witt *v.* Witt had given a precedent for the giving of custody by the Court to a guilty husband, and, though there was no case in which custody had gone to a guilty wife, there was no principle of law against it. In this case the child was in ailing health and should be with its mother, who indeed had had reason to believe that she was to have the custody. " I do not contend," he said, " that there was any agreement as to custody; but the respondent was undoubtedly under the impression that there was one, and she certainly understood that the asking for the custody at the trial was a mere formal demand." Further there was strong reason to believe that Eric Gordon had known of the relations between his wife and his cousin. How could it be supposed that he, a young man of twenty-eight and a man of the world, was ignorant? He knew that Lady Granville Gordon was complaining of her husband's attention to Margaret, and yet he allowed them to spend hours and days together alone in each other's company, while he, poor credulous man, was away on the Stock Exchange. If all these facts had come out at the divorce trial, the petitioner would never have been able to secure his divorce, and so could not have deprived the mother of her child.

It was a well-balanced and persuasive argument, the more so because he made no attempt to whitewash his client; but there was no reason, merely because her conduct had not been impeccable, why her evidence should be dismissed with a wave of the hand, as Mr Duke had been inclined to do. And if her evidence was right, and it was in the interest of the child, then there was a very fair case for granting the custody to her. But it could not be proved that Eric Gordon was away from his wife at the time of conception, nor could the respondent point to any one instance where he must have known of the relations between her and Lord Granville; and in law there is a presumption of legitimacy of a child born in wedlock, which can only be rebutted by conclusive evidence and not by the mere balance of probabilities.

Consequently Sir Francis in a three hour judgment—in the course of which he echoed Mr Duke's query: why should the petitioner want the custody of the child if he did not believe in his paternity?—said that, if he believed that Eric Gordon had connived at adultery, nothing would persuade him to give him custody, but that it was a long step from saying that he definitely did know; and he awarded the custody of the child to him.

There the matter might have been expected to end; but such calculation would leave out of account Lady Granville Gordon, who was a woman of determination. The order of the Court had stated that the child should be given into the father's custody at noon on Wednesday, March 11th, but when Colonel Gordon—this was Eric's father, for Eric had hurt himself when riding—and a nurse called at two o'clock, they found that the birds had flown. For Lady Granville Gordon had decided to leave nothing to chance, and forestalled the judgment of the Court by removing her child. On the Sunday which intervened between Rufus Isaacs' speech and judgment, the Empire Towing Company of Gravesend, in which Lady Granville Gordon had shares, received a telephone call from London booking a tug; the manager was informed that the " name did not matter," as the party would pay cash. Accordingly the steam-tug *Rescue* went from Gravesend to Tilbury and there received on board four women and two children; two of the women were landed at Southend, and the tug proceeded to Dunkirk. On landing at Dunkirk, one of the women said to the captain of the tug, " You may like to know that this is Lady Granville Gordon's child." In point of fact the captain was not very interested, for with the sturdy indifference of the busy man he had not even heard of the case. But, whatever the captain's feeling, there were people in London, more important than he, who were very interested, and Lord Granville who had stayed behind to " face the music "—" there'll be a row and I had better be here to see the whole thing through "—was powerless to prevent the law being set into operation. Mr Priestly made applica-

tion for a writ of attachment and committal against Lady
Granville Gordon, and it was granted; and determined
woman as she was, she had now conjured up forces too
strong for her. As she had been defeated in law, so she
was defeated in action.

It was perhaps appropriate that " one of the bitterest and
most unpleasant controversies in the annals of the Divorce
Courts " should thus have been fought to the last ditch.
That the case had an unpleasant flavour is undeniable; but
then the contemplation of human nature in the raw is rarely
aesthetically satisfactory, except perhaps to those with very
strong stomachs. In the struggle in the Courts the mask of
civilisation is apt to fall, and motives and actions are seen in
the crudity which ordinarily it is considered polite to camou-
flage. However this may be, the Courts do not choose, nor
do they create, the circumstances which lead people to seek
their intervention; the lawyer must take people as he finds
them; he cannot create his own raw material. Nevertheless
the case was extremely interesting, and not least significant
was Rufus Isaacs' appeal for the discontinuance of what was
virtually an automatic penal system in these cases, and for
the substitution of the higher criterion of the child's own
welfare.

CHAPTER X

RISE AND FALL OF WHITTAKER WRIGHT

THE Whittaker Wright case is perhaps the most famous of those trials, which provide a dramatic—and often a tragic—climax to a romantic career. There have been other cases not dissimilar, in which there has been enormous speculation and gigantic frauds alleged; there have been the cases of Jabez Balfour, of Horatio Bottomley and of Hatry. They have all been cases where a famous figure, looked up to with admiration and often with envy, has become almost overnight an object of the execration of those who lay the cause of their ruin at his door; but none has ever touched the popular imagination quite like Whittaker Wright. No one gave so huge and vivid an impression of rugged force and financial genius; no one was so completely the autocrat in the companies in which he was concerned; no one was so lavish in the ostentation which advertised his great position. These qualities place him in a unique position; and probably there are few indeed who have not heard of the rise and fall of Whittaker Wright. But though all know the circumstances of his career and the fact of his conviction, comparatively few know the nature of his offence and still fewer could understand the intricate manipulations of which it was composed. In point of fact he was one of that not uncommon type, which indulges in financial jugglery in order to tide over a bad period. Very few do succeed in tiding over their bad period; they are caught somewhere in mid-journey through the maelstrom, and when their tactics have been on the Napoleonic scale, the crash is immense. Whether men with financial genius could get through by these methods is open to doubt, but as the law at present operates they are bound to come into

133

conflict with those restrictions on the *laissez-faire* of finance, which have been imposed by society for the protection of those less talented. So it was with Whittaker Wright, for his tactics brought him to disaster, and like so many clever men he had to pay the penalty for his ambitious strategy; but though he paid the supreme penalty, he paid it as a voluntary sacrifice and had the satisfaction of cheating Fate at the last.

Whittaker Wright was by origin a Northcountryman, and to the end his voice retained its rough Northumbrian burr, and his personality its rugged North-country power. The age of twenty-one found him with no capital, save that of his abilities and his education, and like his great antagonist in the last struggle, his thoughts turned to America; unlike Rufus Isaacs, however, he went and prospered. He had an expert knowledge of mining chemistry, and in the United States became an assayer, and speculated on a small scale in mining shares. He saved and finally was able to buy a mining claim for £100 and to sell it at a profit, which allowed him to go on repeating the operation on an increasing scale, until at the end of ten years he had amassed a fortune of £200,000 on the New York Stock Exchange. In 1889 he returned to England, having accomplished the Whittingtonian feat, so applauded by right-thinking people in Victorian times. But Whittaker Wright did not become Lord Mayor of London; he had other ambitions. Very soon he was engaged in immense transactions, which were still further increased by the Westralian gold boom. This enabled him to float the West Australian Exploration and Finance Company and the original Globe—or to give it its full title, the London and Globe Finance Corporation—with a capital of £200,000 each; later he floated the Lake View Consols, Paddington Consols and other concerns, while in 1897 he amalgamated the two original companies into a single concern with a capital of £2,000,000. This concern was the new Globe, and had ramifications in Australia, British Columbia, the Yukon and the Pacific. The extent of its interests can best be gauged by the following list:

Date of floating.	Name.	Capitalisation.
December, 1897	British American . .	£1,500,000
February, 1898	Standard	1,500,000
November, 1899	Le Roi Mines . . .	1,000,000
August, 1899	Caledonian Copper . .	750,000
November, 1899	Nickel Corporation . .	750,000
November, 1900	Baker Street and	
	Waterloo Railway .	2,385,000
November, 1900	Loddon Valley Gold Fields .	750,000

The prestige of W.W., as he came to be known in the City, was enormous. As Sir Edward Parry has said, he was looked upon as a sort of Midas, who had only to touch a scheme to turn it into gold. His shares were taken up with alacrity and his invitations to subscribe responded to with enthusiasm; his actions were watched and his example followed; his advice was besought and his nod attended to. Nor did social eminence lag behind financial prosperity (it rarely does). He had all the trappings of success; a house in Park Lane next to Londonderry House, a marvellous country seat at Lea Park near Godalming, a racing-yacht *Sybarita*, which had defeated the Kaiser's champion *Meteor*. His houses were famous for their Louis XV and Louis XVI furniture, and in the drawing-room at Park Lane there was a replica, made at great expense, of the *Cabinet des Rois* of Louis XV, the original of which is in the Louvre. The house at Lea Park was even more magnificent, and armies of workmen were constantly at work upon it giving expression to his ideas. There were fishing-ponds and a billiard-room under the lake; there was a marble fountain transported from Italy, on which the figure of Neptune was replaced by a mermaid struggling with an octopus, for this improbable combat was apparently more to his taste. But W.W. was not content with transplanting works of art; he usurped the prerogative of the deity and changed the face of nature, transplanting mountains and orchards, if their position did not please him. As for the stables, which were built to hold fifty horses, a contemporary account may be quoted: " The ceilings are of moulded plaster, showing, in fine deep relief, scenes of the chase. Each horse has over his stall a separate picture, and from end to end the complete story of the hunt is depicted. Over one set of stalls harriers are represented and over the other a fox-hunt. Behind the horses the space allowed is very wide and is furnished all along with old oak settees upholstered in leather on which princes might recline to admire the horses or the fittings, the whole of which in the stable are of polished gun-metal. The effect is gorgeous." It must have been.

But uneasy is the head that wears a crown—even if it is only a tinsel one. And in spite of his prestige and his palaces, in spite even of the fact that he had as Chairman of the Globe, Lord Dufferin, ex-Viceroy, ex-Ambassador, ex-Governor-General, W.W.'s position was not spared from attack. Nor indeed, behind the imposing façade, was it impregnable; for the Baker Street and Waterloo Railway project absorbed his ready capital, and he had on that account to borrow for his market operations. Aided by this and the depreciation of values after the Transvaal War, the " bears " attacked with determination, and battle was joined. To counter their activities W.W. determined on a " million syndicate," which was to " bull " Lake Views—or so he alleged, for the members of the syndicate, whom he accused of betraying him by selling below the agreed price, denied that there was any " bull " syndicate, and said that they merely lent money to him against collateral securities. Be that as it may, the great corporation failed. On December 29th, 1900, the Globe failed to meet its obligations at the Stock Exchange settlement; Lake Views fell from 13 to 8½ that day, and a total eclipse followed. The crash was enormous; the Standard and the British America came down with the Globe, involving all sorts of others in their fall, and thirty members of the stock exchange were hammered in a single transaction. Panic, excitement, and indignation swelled into a frenzy; was it possible that so rich and well-thought-of a man could really have had feet of clay? But, if so, there were twenty thousand stockbrokers would know the reason why.

Lord Dufferin and the directors met the shareholders on January 9th, 1901, when Lord Dufferin frankly admitted that he knew little about what was going on, and indeed little about finance at all. The explanation, therefore, was left to W.W., who was in fact the autocrat of the company; but, astute as he was, and practised in the art of conciliating angry shareholders, his words had lost their glamour and he failed to carry the meeting in support of his proposed scheme of reconstruction. A proposal for voluntary liquidation was, therefore, accepted, and for it ultimately a compulsory winding-up was substituted. The long and tedious process of official liquidation, in which Rufus Isaacs appeared and Whittaker Wright was subjected to examination and cross-examination, made it appear not improbable that Whittaker Wright had issued false balance-sheets, and for this the general feeling was that he should be prosecuted. But could a prosecution in law be launched with any reasonable prospects of success? The Attorney-General, Sir Robert Finlay, evidently thought not, for he declined to authorise a prosecution by the Director of Public Prosecutions. This decision aroused much criticism, which found expression in an amendment to the Address, moved in the House of Commons by George Lambert, M.P., on February 19th, 1903, expressing regret that no prosecution had been instituted against the directors of the Globe. In the course of his speech Mr Lambert referred to the " aristocratic directorate of the Globe, and claimed that what is sauce for Jabez Balfour—the middle-class ' nonconformist swindler ' —must be sauce for the Globe." This view won a certain amount of support from the Liberal rank and file, but Liberal lawyers like Henry Duke and Sir Robert Reid, afterwards Lord Chancellor as Lord Loreburn, endorsed Sir Robert Finlay's action, while the Solicitor-General said: " It is said that Mr Whittaker Wright published a false balance-sheet. I believe that he did. I think that it is an admitted fact that this was done; but will anyone get up and say that a man can be prosecuted because he publishes a false balance-sheet? "

The answer was by inference in the negative, but this view of the law was not taken by everybody. It was not taken, for instance, by Mr John Flower and certain other brokers, who had suffered in the crash; they appeared before Mr Justice Buckley, a Chancery judge and a great authority on Company Law, and asked him to sanction a prosecution to be paid for out of the remaining assets of the corporation. In answer to the suit, in which Rufus Isaacs played the virtually impartial and spectatorial rôle of counsel for the Official Receiver, Mr Justice Buckley gave a judgment, sanctioning a prosecution, for, without in any way prejudicing the issue he gave it as his opinion that the facts were such that a prosecution would lie. But the long-awaited trial was to be still further postponed, for Whittaker Wright was a man of decision; he left the country, travelled through France under an assumed name, and reached America. Here he was recognised, and extradition proceedings were started; but technical difficulties arose, owing to W.W.'s residence in the United States, and it was not until August that Mr Flower and his associates triumphantly haled him back to England. Finally the trial came on in January 1904— three years after the crash—and Rufus Isaacs, who had been briefed by the private prosecution to undertake the task from which the Attorney had shrunk, found himself face to face with the ablest financier of the day.

Whittaker Wright was accused, in lay parlance, of being a swindler. But this is scarcely a sufficient key to a case which, as Rufus Isaacs rightly said, was one " of as great complexity as has perhaps ever been presented." There were in point of fact twenty-six counts in the indictment, and when it was suggested that an abstract of them should be put before the jury so that they could find a separate verdict on each count, Mr Justice Bigham remarked: " I might as well give the jury Archbold's Criminal Pleading or the Encyclopaedia Britannica." But if we follow Rufus Isaacs' advice to the jury to " concentrate your attention on the salient points of the case and not allow yourselves to be diverted into the bye-paths of finance," it can be made clear what Whittaker Wright's offence was. He was charged under sections 83 and 84 of the Larceny Act of 1861, and the charges referred to the balance-sheets of 1899 and of 1900, which he was alleged to have published with a knowledge of their falsity and with intent to deceive and defraud the shareholders. What he had done was to deceive the shareholders into the belief that the companies were in a flourishing condition, whereas in reality they were on the verge of collapse, at the same time disembarrassing himself of his own shares—by the end of 1900 he had got rid of all except 2,500 in the Globe. His method was to create bogus assets and, although involving the most intricate manipulations of figures, was in conception simple; it depended on his position as autocrat of so many companies, for all his companies were really just Whittaker Wright. All that he needed to do, therefore, was to make a huge transference of assets from, say, the Standard to the Globe, when the Globe balance-sheet was to be made, and to transfer them back again to the Standard for inclusion in its balance-sheet. Actually, of course, nothing changed hands at all; it was merely W.W. as managing director of one company making adjustments with W.W. as managing director of the other.

It was this charge which Rufus Isaacs had to substantiate in detail when the trial opened before Mr Justice Bigham on January 11th, 1904. The atmosphere was not at all like that of an ordinary criminal trial, for the case was tried, not at the Old Bailey, but in the King's Bench Division in the Law Courts—a circumstance which was to have an amazing and unforeseen result—in order to secure the advantage of a special jury. Consequently Whittaker Wright was spared the indignity of the dock, and sat like an ordinary civil litigant in the well of the Court with his advisers, a massive figure in all the dignity of flowing frock-coat, high collar, and the imperial beard which he had lately grown. Sitting by him were his counsel, Mr Lawson Walton

—who was thus matched with his former pupil—Mr R. D. Muir and Mr Felix Cassel, while Mr Rufus Isaacs had supporting him, Mr Horace Avory, K.C., Mr Guy Stephenson, and Mr G. A. H. Branson, two of whom afterwards became High Court Judges. Despite the obscurities and technicalities of the financial background of the case, the public interest was immense and the Court always crowded, for behind the mass of figures was the sense of drama and the presence of great events.

Rufus Isacs opened the case for the prosecution in a five-hour speech, a lucid, unimpassioned survey, emphasising W.W.'s autocratic control and his divestment of his shares. He pointed out clearly, too, just what items in the two balance-sheets the prosecution challenged. In the 1899 balance-sheet there was the supposed cash balance at the Bank of £534,455, which really represented only the result of a paper transaction, the transference of liability from one company to another; the report, however, had stated, after mentioning the extent of the balance, that " the aim of the directors during the past year has been to consolidate and strengthen the position of the company, and one result of this policy may be seen in the fact that more than the whole amount to the credit of the profit and loss is in cash, a much stronger position than existed last year." This statement, in consideration of the real nature of the " cash balance " was, in Rufus Isaacs' contention, a deliberate attempt to misrepresent the position of the company to its shareholders. With regard to the 1900 balance-sheets, Rufus Isaacs indicated four items, which the prosecution did not accept as being a true account of the position. There was the list of shares put at £2,332,632, os. 1d.—the penny being, as Rufus Isaacs observed, " quite an artistic touch; " then there was the omission from the debit side of the balance-sheet of liabilities amounting to £1,603,000, which had been informally transferred to the Standard and British American Corporation in the way mentioned above. There were in addition an alleged profit of nearly half-a-million, which was obtained by the conversion of certain shares into other shares of a higher value, and an item of £113,671, 9s. 10d. cash in the Bank, which had in reality accrued from loans from the bankers.

On the second day of the trial the evidence for the prosecution began, and continued for five days. It was for the most part intricate stuff and made dull listening. But an acute observer watching Rufus Isaacs conduct his examination of the accounts and officials from the Bankruptcy Department could see those special qualities in him which peculiarly fitted him for such a case; the great financial acumen, which enabled him to follow the most obscure and intricate details with ease, the imperturbability which allowed him to steer his way to his desired end, unruffled through the multitude of suggestions from his own side and the interruptions from the Bench and opposing counsel, which rained upon him during this part of the case, and the economy of energy which enabled him to maintain an undiminished keenness of mind through the duration of an exceptionally wearing case. An advocate less versed in financial affairs could not have found his way with sure enough step through the maze of figures and manipulations; an advocate more temperamental would certainly have given way to irritation. But self-discipline, calmness, and clarity of mind were always foremost in Rufus Isaacs' armoury of qualities; and in cases like the Whittaker Wright case they can succeed where mere eloquence would be helpless.

On the seventh day of the trial, Tuesday of the second week, Whittaker Wright entered the box. He had begun to show signs of strain during the lengthy hearing of the evidence for the prosecution, but the week-end's rest had revived him, and his face had once more the ruddy glow of self-confidence. As Rufus Isaacs watched him, leaning forward with his arms on the box—he had declined the offer of a seat—and answering Lawson Walton's questions with an ease and rapidity which displayed his entire mastery of his subject, he realised that he would be a difficult opponent in cross-examination, for any slips or hesitancy on his part would afford a contemptuous triumph to the infallible W.W. Indeed as question and answer passed between them, W.W. leaning forward almost confidentially and Lawson Walton with his air of quiet, unhurried certainty, it seemed almost as if the old infallibility had never been challenged; for it appeared not like an examination in Court, but like a conversation between two experienced business men in which W.W. was telling Lawson Walton just what had happened, and what stupid misinterpretations had been made by uninformed persons. There was nothing wrong with the 1899 balance-sheet; it was merely that the Globe wanted to convert their assets into cash for the end of the financial year and had done so by payments made by the subsidiary companies in respect of transactions, " not one of which were illegitimate, but happened every fortnight in the City." And as to the omission of the liabilities to stockbrokers amounting to £1,603,000 in the 1900 balance-sheet, that was not to deceive the shareholders; far from it —it was, did they but know it, to save the poor creatures from the " bears " who were trying to wreck the Globe.

It was this atmosphere which Rufus Isaacs had to destroy; the atmosphere of the benevolent autocrat, whose good intentions had been misunderstood by persons not in a position to judge, and whose course of conduct, if not interrupted, would have led to an honourable salvation for all. And this could only be done by a cross-examination, which would leave no doubt of the facts; W.W. must be convicted out of his own mouth. With so formidable an antagonist as Whittaker Wright the task could not but be long and difficult, and the cross-examination, which started as soon as Lawson Walton's examination was concluded on the seventh day of the trial, continued until 3.15 in the afternoon of the ninth day. The struggle was a true Homeric contest; for, though there was no spear save that of interrogation and no shield save that of explanation, there were the endurance, the resource and the determination, which are at once the product and the condition of heroic struggle.

Rufus Isaacs' first questions concerned W.W.'s leaving the country after Lambert's motion in the House of Commons. He then turned to the inter-company payments:

" You received," he said, " all this money as chairman of one company from yourself as chairman of another? "

" I do not like that way of putting it. The money was paid by one company to the other."

" On September 30th," Mr Justice Bigham explained, " you, as the Globe, sold £72,000 of nickel shares to the Standard. Two months afterwards, you, as the Standard, bought back the same shares at £80,000. The effect was that you borrowed £72,000 from the Standard for two months."

W.W. was then questioned as to the balance-sheet and directors' report of 1899, but he remained stubborn. " You will never get me to the crack of doom," he said, " to admit that there is anything the matter with the 1899 balance-sheet." Rufus Isaacs, however, pressed him as to whether he thought the shareholders would be more impressed with the statement that the directors intended to make the company a ten per cent. investment company when they saw that there was a large balance in cash; to which W.W. replied that he was not responsible for what inferences they might draw, and added, " it is the sort of statement ninety-nine chairmen out of a hundred would make at a shareholders' meeting." Next day Rufus Isaacs returned to the attack, and slowly, bit by bit, the financier was forced to admit to having made " slips " on two occasions, when he was anxious to conceal the true state of affairs. It had been a " slip," for instance, when in his letter to Lord Dufferin he had said that the amount of profit shown was after allowing for a deduction of £500,000 from the market value of the shares; he should have said " cost or par value." Similarly it had been a " slip of the tongue " when he had said at the meeting that if the market value was less than the cost, the shares were marked down to market value. At last, stung by the searching questions which were compelling these admissions, W.W. exclaimed in a rare burst of indignation —for his manner in the box was quiet, with never a trace of anger or hostility—that counsel would like him to be chairman, secretary, and everything in the company. " No," answered Rufus Isaacs, amid laughter, " I think you were quite enough."

It was clear as the day wore on that Rufus Isaacs was gaining. Hour after hour the deep guttural Northumbrian burr replied to the melodious voice with the clear ring and faultless intonation; and hour after hour the closely-packed spectators turned from the lean, courteous figure in the front row to the stocky, self-confident figure in the box, not understanding all the figures and details which were the ammunition of this combat, but realising that these two men were gladiators of no mean order, locked, for all the courtesy of combat, in the death-throe of an epic struggle. For five hours Whittaker Wright stood there, facing the calm, relentless, dispassionate interrogation, and then utterly weary he sank into the seat which had been offered him from the start, and remained there, huddled and exhausted. But his brain had lost none of its keenness and the great duel went on; the Whittaker Wrights of the world do not give a walk-over, nor do they ask for quarter.

Rufus Isaacs was asking about the loss of the £750,000 of Lake Views in 1900.

" Did you want to disclose the true state of affairs? "

" Not with regard to every operation of the market."

" Did you wish to keep from the meeting the loss of £750,000 on Lake Views? "

" No, it was well-known."

" There was no reference to that loss at the meeting of 1900? "

" It did appear in the figures given."

But finally Whittaker Wright was forced to admit that the loss was nowhere specifically referred to. And again, after searching questions, he had to admit, though only with considerable hesitation, that there would have been about £1,600,000 assets in December of 1900, which could have made no appearance on September 30th—for W.W. had taken advantage of the fact that in law he could postpone the issue of the balance-sheet from September to December.

The second day had left Rufus Isaacs leading strongly; fortunately, however, on the following day Whittaker Wright showed no signs of the exhaustion which had come upon him towards the end of the day before, while Rufus Isaacs was standing up to his ordeal, which was only less severe than Whittaker Wright's, with the toughness that is in part concealed and in part suggested by the spareness of his frame. But before the contest was resumed there was another thrill, for Mr Justice Bigham did not take his seat until 11.0, and then it was observed that there was a worried expression on his ruddy-cheeked, keen-eyed, normally jovial face. He referred to " abusive anonymous letters " which had been received—it may be remarked parenthetically that the *cause célèbre* seems inseparable from abusive anonymous letters—and then referred to " attempts of a much more serious character in other directions to interfere with the course of justice." But while the crowded Court was wondering to what this might refer, Rufus Isaacs and Whittaker Wright had taken their places in the lists, and were once more the cynosure of all eyes. Once more the attack was pressed home, not savagely or vindictively, but firmly and unwaveringly. Rufus Isaacs was now concentrating on 1900—on the £2,000,000 odd " assets," on the concealment of losses, on the alleged writing down of the shares by £500,000 to allow for depreciation.

" You made a speech at the shareholders' meeting; you knew there were rumours as to the state of the Globe's affairs? "

" No doubt."

" You were anxious to put the best face on affairs you could? "

" No doubt."

" You knew that the important matter to the shareholders was the item of £2,332,000 value of shares held in sundry companies? "

" The state of the company was the important thing."

" The company owed to sundry creditors £570,000? "

" Yes."

" Your assets were about £2,700,000? "

" Yes."

" The largest item in the £2,700,000 was the £2,332,000? "

" Yes."

" It was important to know how much had been written off? "

" Yes."

" You dealt with that in your speech? "

" I answered questions."

" You said over a million sterling had been written off for depreciation; that was untrue."

" I do not admit it; you must take the whole report together."

" You said over a million sterling."

" I should have said ' for loss and depreciation.' "

" Have you any doubt that this statement is absolutely untrue? "

" In its connection it is true. But I ought to have said ' loss and depreciation.' It was an extempore utterance."

" That is, as it stands," concluded Rufus Isaacs with quiet decisiveness, " the statement is untrue? "

The questioning continued:

" Had the company a single Lake View at this time? "

" I think they had forty-eight."

" I was referring to 1900."

" I thought 1899 was referred to. There were none in 1900. This was a loss and I should have said ' loss and depreciation.' "

" You said you had marked them as low as possible. Had you in the list of assets—the £2,332,000—marked them down a penny? "

" I did not take into account the half-million."

" Then you had not marked as low as possible. Would you like to say it was a slip of the tongue? "

" Yes, if you like. I am not an accountant. The half-million was deducted—wiped out. It was no longer a reserve."

"You must get a plain answer to that," put in Mr Justice Bigham, and Rufus Isaacs proceeded:

"You had deducted £500,000 from your list of assets. Had you not put that back?"

"I know that this was no longer reserve; it was, I suppose, put back."

"The effect was to write up the value of the assets?"

"I cannot admit that."

"I must have an answer," said the Judge sternly.

But W.W. was obstinate: "I cannot admit this," was all he replied.

"In 1899," Mr Justice Bigham explained, "you had £500,000 for contingencies. In 1900 this was put to the credit?"

"That is how it would come out at the finish, no doubt." The admission was reluctant.

"Explain the marking down," resumed Rufus Isaacs; "what had you taken off?"

"The half-million."

"You had not marked this off, but put it on." The correction was gentle, but irrefutable.

"You edited the report, put in the 'hear, hears' and so on?"

"Yes, and rightly."

"But the slip of the tongue was left uncorrected," replied Rufus Isaacs, for though the sentence preceding the one which spoke of the "marking off" was corrected, that sentence itself had not been touched.

W.W. said something to the effect that his time being absorbed, somebody else should have seen to it—as it was, he had to do everybody's business in the company. And so the great battle had ended in something very like a rout; the great financier, compelled time and again to make damaging confessions, was forced at last to take refuge behind the defence of the maid-of-all-work—"I had too much to do."

As Whittaker Wright stepped from the box—there had been a brief re-examination by Lawson Walton—the mantle of his fate already seemed to hang upon him; he resumed his place in Court, and listened to Rufus Isaacs' speech, sitting forward with his head in his hands and scarcely exchanging a word with his advisers. At least, however, he had a respite from activity, though not from anxiety. Not so Rufus Isaacs, for like a good general he had to consolidate the advantage which he had gained in his cross-examination, by his final speech, and within a short time of the conclusion of the cross-examination he was again on his feet. He spoke for the rest of that day and the whole of the next (the tenth of the trial) lucidly, effortlessly, without a falter and, as usual—in spite of the intricacy of the case —almost without a note. The speech, coming as it did at the end of a most exacting week, was a triumph of sober achievement; he eschewed rhetoric and invective, and was content to elucidate to the jury what the evidence had shown. For in this type of case it is especially true to say that the jury prefer instruction to edification.

He began his speech by saying that he had nothing to withdraw of what he had said in his opening speech, since there had not been a single statement of fact, as opposed to inference, disproved; indeed Whittaker Wright had convicted himself out of his own mouth, when he admitted in cross-examination that he had published the 1900 balance-sheet in order to conceal from the shareholders the true state of affairs. It was clear that W.W. had set out to commit the offence, for he had been engaged in a heavy gamble in the autumn of 1899, when the Globe lost £750,000 and the Standard £250,000 in Lake Views; by September 30, 1900, there was still a heavy loss, and the accountant had computed that if the balance had been taken on that day on the Globe method, there would have been a loss of £1,600,000, including the reserve of £500,000. Whittaker Wright's problem was how to conceal the loss from the shareholders so as to tide over the bad period and win his encounter with the " bears " of Lake Views. By virtue of his position at the head of so many companies, he had been able so to manipulate the figures as to make it appear that the Globe not only had its capital intact but had made a profit of £463,000 in those bad times; meantime, while he was thus trying to persuade others, by concealing the true position to increase their holdings in Globe, he was himself unloading his own share—in August and September of 1899 he sold 166,000. The ordinary individual would look at the balance-sheet to see the position, and what was the result of that? On December 5th, 1900, the accounts showed assets of £2,700,000. Mr Wright at the meeting said that that was after writing off a million sterling. Could any fact or argument be more eloquent of the true state of things than the fact that within eleven days the company came to grief with creditors for £2,000,000, who got a shilling and might get another sixpence in the pound? Could anything be more pregnant with meaning, and not a penny for the shareholders, let them allow all they pleased for realisation in such circumstances? As to W.W.'s statement that a million sterling had been written off for depreciation, he had had to admit in cross-examination that, so far from this being true, they had actually appreciated their assets, while admittedly no corrections had been made in the report sent out, of those various " slips of the tongue " which had so misrepresented the position. Finally there was the omission of the £1,600,000 from the liabilities of the Globe in the 1900 balance-sheet, which as Whittaker Wright had admitted in cross-examination, was done to conceal the facts. These liabilities had been transferred to the Standard; was this a bona fide transaction, and was the Standard in a position to shoulder this liability? The answer can be supplied in Rufus Isaacs' own words: " The position was that it had £200 in its banks; on December 28th it came to grief, and the shareholders to the extent of its whole capital did not get a penny, while the creditors got sevenpence in the pound. This was the company that was taking over £1,600,000 of liabilities."

Rufus Isaacs had laid a long siege, and as a result the position of the defence had fallen in at every point. After a week of cross-examination and exposition the facts were laid bare, and they were apparently fatal to Whittaker Wright. During the week-end which followed Rufus Isaacs' speech, the country was in a fever of excitement as to the issue of the trial, though by this time an adverse verdict was probable. However, Mr Lawson Walton had still to make his speech for the defence, and it proved to be a great effort. He spoke for five hours, striking a more human note than Rufus Isaacs—as he was entitled to do since he was appearing for the defence—but at the same time not shrinking from the technical issues. He complained that it was a vindictive prosecution and that Whittaker Wright had been singled out of the other directors to be put on his trial alone. There was little evidence, he contended, of anybody having been misled, and indeed Whittaker Wright had been acting in what he conceived to be ultimately the best interests of his shareholders. Lawson Walton made considerable play, too, with the Attorney-General's refusal to sanction a prosecution at the public expense, and concluded his speech with an eloquent appeal: " Every spot," he said, " outside this Court—the whole outside world— has been ringing with the clamour of denunciation against this man on the part of those who have not stopped to hear my speech, who do not trouble to listen to his defence. He has been brought here by a hue and cry, which has had its reflection in the gallery of this Court. I urge you to show the courage of Englishmen, to decide this case not on prejudice. And as you are entitled to bring in a general verdict of Not Guilty, I urge you, if you think right, to return such a verdict, and thus save the defendant from the ruin that an adverse verdict would involve upon him and all concerned with him."

The next day, the twelfth and last of the trial, Mr Justice Bigham summed up. As a luminous exposition of the facts and issues of the case his summing up cannot be too highly praised; it was scrupulously fair, but it left little hope for Whittaker Wright. He at least had no illusion as to his chances, for his bent head and the occasional quick glances which he darted at the jury during the summing up, betokened a hopeless demeanour. Indeed a change seemed to come over his face, even while the Judge was speaking, and those who were curious to see how he took the summing up saw, instead of the firm, ruddy features of W.W., a heavy sagging of grey flesh and puckered eyes, the face of a dying man. " It was as if we saw a man aging before our eyes." And there were those who could not take their eyes off the ghastly and pathetic spectacle; the shadow of his doom lay only too plainly across the great financier.

The jury were absent for only an hour and returned at 2.45, when it was observed that Mr Justice Darling, unrobed, accompanied Mr Justice Bigham to the Bench. Nobody could doubt the verdict, for, considering the course of the case, so short a retirement could mean only one thing; but doubtless there were many in that Court looking anxiously and fearfully at the foreman, in whose hearts hope, irrational as ever, was an unconscionable time in dying. " Guilty; " it was inevitable. But Lawson Walton was on his feet, speaking in mitigation and indicating the possibility of appeal. And then all eyes were turned to Whittaker Wright, as he rose to receive sentence. Would he collapse or would he make a brave front? Did that ghastly pallor mean that his courage had deserted him? But he stood and faced the Judge squarely, and the coat folded about him heightened the impression of a Roman Stoic facing his doom, as he listened to the sentence of the Bench.

" Mr Whittaker Wright, in my opinion the jury could have arrived at no other opinion than that which they expressed in their verdict. I confess that I see nothing that in any way excuses the crime of which you have been found guilty, and I cannot conceive a worse case than yours under these sections of the Act of Parliament which defines your offence. In those circumstances I do not think I have any option except to visit you with the severest punishment which that Act permits, and that is to go to penal servitude for seven years."

It was what Whittaker Wright had expected, for on his blotter were discovered several W's and at the bottom the

Roman numeral VII, with the word " intent " in the middle. And he did not falter as he answered the Judge in a deep, firm voice: " My lord, all I have to say is that I am as innocent as any person in this Court of any intention to deceive or defraud the shareholders. And that is all I have to say." The last words were shouted in vehement defiance. It was his last defence—save one; for the Stoic philosophy allowed one more.

After the sentence Whittaker Wright was taken by the assistant-superintendent of the Courts and a tipstaff to the room which had been set aside for his use during the trial; and there, after locking the door, they left him with Mr Eyre, who had entered into recognisances on his behalf, Mr Morten, the former chief accountant of the Globe, and Mr George Lewis; W.W. seemed composed, though his face still bore the ashen look which had come over it during the summing up, and several times he protested his innocence and his amazement at the verdict. Then, looking round, he said in his slow, deep voice: " I wish to thank you very much for all you have done for me," and added, " everything that could have been done has been done." Mr Eyre then asked if he had not better telephone to Mrs Whittaker Wright, but W.W. waved him back; " No," he said, " there is plenty of time for that. Sit down." He was clearly anxious that all should stay in the room, but moved about restlessly himself, crossing the room and sitting down in the armchair at the far end of it. " Morten," he said, " give me another cigar." Morten gave him a cigar and with it a lighted match, which W.W. raised to his cigar. But instantly he threw it to the ground and his face, which had been pale, went dark; in a moment he had collapsed. They hurried to him, but he spoke no more, and though a doctor was hastily summoned, Whittaker Wright was dead.

He had made a dupe of Fate as easily as of his shareholders; for there was no doubt as to the manner or intention of his death. He had died of suffocation caused by swallowing cyanide of potassium, and the pathologist discovered a place at the back of his tongue where the mucous membrane was more corroded than elsewhere; it was there that W.W. had nursed the little tablet during the day's proceedings, ready to live a free man or to die rather than face the dishonour of confinement.   And so that there might be no mistake he had carried in addition a six-chambered American revolver, fully loaded and cocked, which was discovered when his body was searched after death.   Had he been tried at the Old Bailey search would have been made beforehand so that he would certainly not have been able to carry the revolver, and might possibly have had no opportunity of using the cyanide of potassium; but in the Law Courts, which are normally devoted to civil litigation there is no provision for search, and so Whittaker Wright could take his life unhampered.

The case was a great triumph for Rufus Isaacs, but the occasion was not one for personal triumph; rather there was the dull reaction after an exhausting case, the gladness that it was over, and perhaps the instinctive sorrow at the fate which had overcome a gallant antagonist.   For, however much Whittaker Wright may have deserved his fate, it is impossible to withhold sympathy from him in the encountering of it; the flinging down of greatness is a constant theme of tragedy, and the sense of tragedy is sharpened, if one has oneself been an instrument in bringing about the downfall.   For tragedy, whose appeal is irresistible, takes no heed of elementary ethics; it demands only greatness in its subject, and, despite his ostentation and his crudity, it is impossible to deny a certain greatness to Whittaker Wright. That he was rightly convicted there can be no doubt, for though genius may have its own rules, society, which has no genius—not even financial—must protect itself from their operation.   As in the cases of Oscar Wilde and Roger Casement—the two other, and greater, tragic cases of the last half century—the conviction was undoubtedly right in law, and the convicted as certainly has our sympathy.   But, whereas Wilde left the legacy of his literature and Casement the heritage of faith, Whittaker Wright left nothing; and yet in a sense he had fallen from a higher position, for he had been a dictator in his province, an uncrowned king. And now all his glories, conquests, triumphs, spoils, were shrunk to the measure of death and ignominy.

> " But yesterday the word of Caesar might
>   Have stood against the world ; now lies he there,
>   And none so poor to do him reverence."

None falls so low as the stricken favourite of Fortune. But there were some who did him reverence; for as his coffin was borne on a wet and wintry morning through the lanes of Surrey, the villagers came out and uncovered. They had known him as a man of great wealth, but as a man of generosity, kindliness and humanity; and as such they judged him, for they knew little of Lake Views and Finance Corporations. They were simple folk, and simple folk judge by simple things. And they are not always wrong.

CHAPTER XI

THE READING BYE-ELECTION: IN PARLIAMENT

THE Whittaker Wright case placed Rufus Isaacs at the very pinnacle of the Bar, both in its own estimate and in that of the public. It finally consolidated and secured the great position which the advocacy of the preceding three years had won for him. Indeed, young as he was—he was only forty-three at the time of the Whittaker Wright case—he had risen to be perhaps the leading Common Law advocate in the land; the Victorian giants, Russell and James, practised no longer, Sir Edward Clarke was past his prime, Sir Edward Carson as Solicitor-General was restricted in his activities, and Lawson Walton had never occupied quite the position at the Bar at which his former pupil had already arrived. The chambers in Garden Court were besieged with briefs of every sort, for Rufus Isaacs' was always a comprehensive practice; company cases, libel actions, divorce suits, Trade Union litigation, criminal defences, even Chancery work—he took them all in his stride, often several of them together, for at the Bar he was never a mere specialist. He could turn his hand to anything, and generally excel the people who did only that one thing; consequently his practice was immense, and already greatly more lucrative than the £7,000 a year with which he had quitted the junior Bar. It was in this year, too, that his position at the Bar and his personal popularity in the profession won the pleasantest of all legal recognitions in his election to the Bench of the Middle Temple; he has thus been a Master of the Bench for nearly thirty years, and on his return from India was elected in 1928 Treasurer of the Middle Temple—the highest honour that the Society can bestow on its members.

On January 27th, 1904, the very day after the conviction

155

and death of Whittaker Wright, Rufus Isaacs appeared for the Yorkshire Miners' Federation in a most important case, whose ramifications we shall encounter later. In the Spring he was counsel for the great City firm of Gibbs, Bright and Company in the action known as Lake George Gold Mines *v.* Gibbs, Bright and Company. Actually Lake George Gold Mines was in liquidation, and the action was brought for the benefit of the company which had taken over its rights. The claim for damages was in respect of alleged fraudulent misrepresentation and negligence, for the plaintiffs contended that Gibbs, Bright and Company had fraudulently manipulated the Lake George Companies for the purpose of making gains on the Stock Exchange and not in order to develop the mines for the benefit of the shareholders; and they said that in furtherance of their purpose they had used false reports of the state of the mines, knowing them to be false. In this case Rufus Isaacs again found himself matched against Sir Edward Clarke, while he had with him Charles Gill, K.C., and Charles Matthews; in addition to these two, there was fourth counsel in the person of Douglas Hogg who had just been called to the Bar at the comparatively mature age of thirty-three. The case was soon over, and was extremely satisfactory to Rufus Isaacs. In the course of cross-examination, he succeeded in making it clear that the reports had been made by honest and competent metallurgists, and that there was no intention to defraud; he then addressed the jury, and at the conclusion of his speech, Mr Justice Lawrence ruled that there was no evidence of fraud to go to the jury, since the charges had been disproved out of the mouth of the plaintiffs' own witnesses. Rufus Isaacs then proceeded to deal with the issue of negligence, but before he had finished, the jury decided that that charge too was effectually disproved and intimated that they need hear no more. And so the case ended in complete and speedy victory.

The year contained other notable cases, but the main interest of the later part of 1904 was Rufus Isaacs' entry into Parliament. After the General Election of 1900 he had been perforce comparatively inactive in politics for about two years; but then he became interested in the constituency of Reading, where it was realised that the sitting member, Mr G. W. Palmer, the biscuit manufacturer and a great local figure, was unlikely, owing to increasing deafness, to fight another election. In point of fact Mr Palmer did not wait for the general election, but retired in the summer of 1904, and Rufus Isaacs, who had then been nursing the constituency, whose name he was one day to take as his own, for eighteen months, was adopted as Liberal candidate in his stead. Both Mr Palmer and Mr Keyser, the Tory candidate, were local men of substance, with many interests and activities in Reading, while Rufus Isaacs, of course, was not; he had, on the other hand, the compensating advantage of being a national figure, for, though he was an apprentice in politics, his name was known to all as an advocate, who had been leading counsel in most of the great cases in the preceding lustrum. And, though most constituencies like to be represented in Parliament by local men, they also like the distinction of sending to Parliament a famous figure, whose presence there is desired by the party and valuable in debate.

On general grounds, too, Rufus Isaacs was much more favourably placed than at North Kensington in 1900. For Reading, though it had rather a see-saw record at elections —it had been Conservative in 1885, Liberal in 1892, Conservative again in 1895, and Liberal in 1900—had returned a Liberal at the " Khaki Election," and was therefore hardly likely to reverse the decision four years later in favour of a Government whose sands were running out. The tactical disadvantages of a split party, too, were now to some extent transferred to the Conservative Party, for, while the Liberals had been welded into a certain unity under the leadership of Sir Henry Campbell-Bannerman, the Conservative Party was labouring in the difficult waters of Protection. Mr Chamberlain, who with Midland directness was for a bold policy of Protection was followed by the more ardent members of the party; but Mr Balfour, mindful of the strong

Free Trade element within the party, employed all the resources of a philosophic mind in subtle dialectical evasions of the " plain issue," and could be pushed no further than " reciprocity." The difficulties which this situation presented to a Conservative candidate in a bye-election, who did not happen to possess his leader's talent for combining metaphysical clarity with political obscurity, hardly requires stressing. Mr Keyser, however, did his best, and his election address said: " The question of Fiscal Reform has long had my careful attention, and I am of opinion that the state of Trade in the Empire necessitates a most careful inquiry into the whole matter, and that some measures should be adopted to preserve to this country the industries and manufactures that are now so seriously handicapped by unfair foreign competition."

This exposition of his attitude might pass in certain quarters, but it was hardly likely to survive the criticism of one of the acutest intellects at the Bar; and at the great meeting in the Town Hall, with which he opened his campaign, Rufus Isaacs successfully poured ridicule upon it. " I can't help thinking," he said, " that he must have been reading Mr Balfour's speech at Sheffield and out of the maze of it he must have penned this paragraph: ' The question of Fiscal Reform has long had my careful attention.' Mark that. Mr Keyser is not starting upon his initial study of Fiscal Reform, but it has long had his attention. ' I am of opinion that the state of Trade in the Empire necessitates a most careful inquiry into the whole matter.' One would have imagined that one might have arrived at that conclusion without long and careful consideration." His own attitude was clear and definite. He declared unreservedly for the Liberal programme of Free Trade, taxation of land values, retrenchment, and economy. With regard to the particular storm-centres of the time (outside the fiscal issue) he advocated Army reform to promote efficiency, and attacked the Government's Licensing and Education Bills; his view on education was " in favour of a great and comprehensive system of education, free and controlled by the people, so that the utmost advantages to be derived from study should be brought within reach of the poorest of the community." In respect of the position of the Trade Unions after the Taff Vale judgment—the details and importance of which he had every reason to know—he declared himself " in favour of amending the laws affecting Trade Unions so as to afford adequate protection to the association of working men."

The election, which lasted nine days (including August Bank holiday), was hardly contested, but with an agreeable absence of personalities and hooliganism. Rufus Isaacs had, on various nights, the support of rising young Liberals. There was Mr Herbert Samuel, who made a long speech on a hot night; there was Mr Winston Churchill, who pronounced a paean upon his own consistency, for he had always preached one gospel since the controversy began. " Free Trade," he said, " is not only a British cause, not only an Imperialist cause; it is also a human cause." There was, too, Mr Lloyd George, who spoke in the Town Hall and urged them " not to allow the Tory Ark to rest at Reading." Contemplation of the subsequent careers of these distinguished gentlemen gives point to Rufus Isaacs' remark: " it is quite possible that on some questions we do not agree to the fullest extent—as no body of Liberals possibly can." Rufus Isaacs could not perhaps rival the election eloquence of these notable sponsors, but he made an excellent candidate. He was especially good at meetings, when he was subjected to considerable heckling; he retained his self-possession and said that the warmer the meeting, the better he liked it. This is, of course, a stock remark of Parliamentary candidates in the circumstances; but where Rufus Isaacs differed was that he managed to look as if it was true.

There was great excitement in Reading on the night of the declaration of the poll, and a huge crowd was rewarded at 10.15 by the appearance of a placard, bearing the inscription: " Rufus D. Isaacs, K.C., M.P." So great was the storm of cheering that Rufus Isaacs, who had appeared on the balcony, could not make himself heard, and had to speak

on an improvised platform indoors. Here he spoke frankly
of his position. After referring to the fact that Palmer and
Keyser were both local men, he said: " I came of course as a
stranger. I only wooed you as a politician. I never attempted
to do anything else than to appeal to you as a politician."
This was true in 1904; but time was to make him more than
merely a politician in Reading. The evening ended with
Rufus Isaacs and Mrs Isaacs being dragged round the town
in their carriage; and on arriving at the hotel, they received
another ovation. This time, however, he merely appeared
at the window and said " Bravo, Reading; this is your
victory, not mine," and, with these few words to sustain
them, the crowd remained undispersed till the early hours
of the morning.

The remarks of the *Morning Post*—a hostile paper—on
the election may perhaps be quoted: " Mr Isaacs on the
other hand had all the advantages of platform power, for
no man is more richly gifted in making the worse appear
the better cause, and the arguments for Liberalism have
never been presented more alluringly than during this short
contest."

He had now entered, however, into a longer contest, and
he had a wider platform on which to advance the arguments
for Liberalism. That the occasion presented a considerable
opportunity is undeniable, for Rufus Isaacs entered the
House of Commons at a time when a Conservative Government had been in power for nearly a decade. The Conservative Party, which had been in office since 1895, had in 1900
been re-elected on issues which in 1904 had taken their place
in history, and there were not wanting signs that the
administration was losing not only the confidence of the
electorate but of its own supporters in Parliament. Joseph
Chamberlain had retired from office in order to be more free
to prosecute a vigorous campaign in favour of Protection
in the country, and he had taken with him the driving force
of the party and the loyalty of its most active members. Nor
was he the only critic within the ranks, for the " Young
Tories," headed by Lord Hugh Cecil, had for some time

been vehemently demanding a more spirited policy from the Government, while even those who had no particular sympathy with either Mr Chamberlain or Lord Hugh Cecil, were bewildered by Mr Balfour's subtleties of phraseology and disappointed with his failure to give a clear lead. The Conservatives presented to the country the pathetic spectacle of a great party unable to make up its mind, while Mr Balfour failed to realise that a democratic electorate will not take subtleties in exchange for leadership, but demands from those who aspire to lead a clear enunciation of principle, cost what it may. The Government, disunited and paralysed as it was, with confidence neither in its hold on the country, in the enthusiasm of its followers, nor in the adequacy of its performance, was faced by an opposition to which the experience of adversity and the prospect of office had given new unity and determination.

Such was the situation which presented itself to the new member for Reading, when he took his seat, and that situation is the measure of the opportunity which offered. It is true that he had not wrested a seat from the Government, but proof of the unpopularity of the Government in the country had already been supplied in a succession of such losses. And it were not as if he were a mere local somebody; he was eminent in his profession—and it is a profession peculiarly allied to the House of Commons—and all were familiar with the appearance, the prowess, and the talents of one who was perhaps the leading advocate of his day. Inevitably, therefore, his maiden speech was awaited with the keenest expectation (for contrary to a certain opinion the House does expect great things from prominent lawyers in spite of certain disappointments in very recent years, which will spring at once to the minds of Parliamentarians). It might have been expected that the great advocate, the new member representing the new state of the mind of the country, would hurl himself in a series of philippics at the tottering citadel of Conservative supremacy. He might have anticipated by twelve months, in very different circumstances, the famous maiden speech of F. E. Smith. He might have done; but he did not. In point of fact, his first intervention in the House was a question to the Minister in connection with the refusal of the Local Government Board to sanction a change of dietary in the Reading Vagrancy Board.

It was not exactly that Rufus Isaacs failed in the House of Commons; one does not associate him with failure and he certainly did not fail, in the sense that he failed in a given undertaking, as on the Stock Exchange. One cannot fail in that sense where one does not compete, and Rufus Isaacs could not aspire to be an F. E. Smith in the House of Commons. The qualities and limitations of Rufus Isaacs' parliamentary equipment have been discussed in an earlier chapter, and it is sufficiently clear from these why he made no philippics. One further reason may be added; in Lord Reading's own words, " I was tired out when I got to the House," and the importance of this can scarcely be exaggerated. It is impossible to expect as much from a man who has spent the early morning in the study of his briefs, the whole day in addressing the Courts, and the evening in the strain of attendance in the Chamber with the addition of that exhausting and nerve-wracking purgatory of private members, known as " catching the Speaker's eye," to perform as well when his turn does at last come, as, for instance, a Minister who chooses his time and who has spent the afternoon in being coached in his speech by his secretaries and his department. His preoccupation with the Courts, therefore, and the fact that his style of speaking was more suited to the Courts than to the Commons, prevented Rufus Isaacs from being a " House of Commons man." It did not prevent him from being a useful member; but it did mean that his efforts had to be of a contributory rather than of a vital or dominating nature.

His maiden speech was made in connection with the Aliens' Bill, a Conservative measure for the regulation of the rights of aliens with regard to immigration, naturalisation and so on. Mr Balfour proposed a motion to give definite and restricted times for the discussion of the various stages of the Bill on the ground that only eleven out of the

Session's seventy-three days had been devoted to legislation (that is, as distinct from Supply, the Address, and so on). In his speech on this motion Rufus Isaacs remarked that, whatever charges might be made against the Liberals of obstructing the business of the House, he could not be said to have done so, since he spoke as a " new member who has his lessons to learn, but who has been sitting and learning them now for some time." One lesson seemed not to reflect very much credit on the House, for he said: " Judging from my short experience of the way in which Parliament's affairs are conducted, the House of Commons, as a means of passing legislation, is a very ineffective body indeed." It is an opinion that the years have made more popular. The speech, which was made on July 5th, 1905, won him the congratulations of Mr Balfour, who referred to him as " the honourable and learned gentleman who has a deservedly high reputation in other spheres of activity." Twelve days later, on the Report Stage of the Bill, Rufus Isaacs moved an amendment to a clause of the Bill, affording protection to those seeking the asylum of these shores as a result of persecution on account of their religious opinions; his amendment, which was seconded by Lord Edmond Fitzmaurice, was designed to extend the protection to persecution for political opinions as well. It was opposed, however, by Sir Robert Finlay on behalf of the Government and rejected by 214 votes to 152.

But issues other than the rights of aliens were looming up; and they were to be voted on not by the House of Commons, but by the country. In point of fact the Conservative Government did not wait for the verdict of the electorate, but resigned office in the lifetime of Parliament. Sir Henry Campbell-Bannerman was called upon to form a Government and, as soon as he had completed his task of selecting his administration, he recommended a dissolution. This took place in December, and on New Year's Day of 1906 Rufus Isaacs was once again in Reading Town Hall, but this time as the sitting member, asking for re-election to support the Government.

CHAPTER XII

RUFUS ISAACS' entry into political life did not affect his practice at the Bar, and in 1905 the annual avalanche of briefs was in no way diminished. In the first part of the year especially, he figured in a number of intricate and unusual cases. There was, for instance, a very big commercial case in the Chancery Division, in which the Chinese Minister, Chang, was one of the parties; in this case, in which Rufus Isaacs was led by Mr Hughes, K.C., seven " silks " took part. Another Chancery case in which he figured at about this time was the suit brought against the noted King's Counsel, Fletcher Moulton, by his step-daughters. Then there were the Ogden " Guinea Gold " and the Denaby Colliery cases, both of which involved argument before the House of Lords. So, too, did the Watt case, which was concerned with the matrimonial complications of Hugh Watt, formerly a member of Parliament. For the libel actions in which he appeared . for Colonel Morgan, on the other hand, brief hearings in the court of instance sufficed.

The Ogden Guinea Gold case—or, more properly, the case of Ogden Ltd. *v.* Nelson and Telford—is in some respects unique. It arose out of a great tobacco war, in which the American firm of Ogden's competed desperately against the British Imperial Tobacco Company for control of the British market. They started to try and outbid each other in the inducements which they offered to retailers, and so extravagant did the offers become that Ogden's ultimately promised a bonus distribution of their entire net profits and an additional sum of £200,000 a year for four years. Payment of £50,000 was actually made for the first quarter of 1902, but a pace had been set which could not last. In September, Ogden's sold their business to the Imperial Tobacco Company and in October the firm went into voluntary liquidation, so that the retailers got no more largesse. Thus it was that when Ogden's sued a provincial retailer called Nelson for a sum of £58, he put in a counter-claim for his share of the distribution, and it was held by Lord Alverstone that the offer was bona fide and that, therefore, although there had been no profits for the six months ending September 1902, Nelson was nevertheless entitled to £70 as his share of the £200,000. The decision was contested in the Court of Appeal and in the House of Lords, where Rufus Isaacs, who had not appeared in the hearings in the lower Courts, was briefed; but Lord Alverstone's judgment was upheld and Ogden's remained liable. The not unnatural consequence was that writs poured in upon Ogden's from retail tobacconists all over the country until it was estimated that upwards of £700,000 was claimed in eight hundred cases. It was in these cases that F. E. Smith really established his position at the Bar, for though he was unsuccessful in many of them they gave great play to his forensic talents. Finally in 1906 the agreement between Ogden's and the Imperial Tobacco Company was brought to a successful conclusion, and peace reigned once more in the tobacco industry after a disastrous and expensive war of advertisement.

With the cases—for there were two—arising out of the Denaby coal strike, Rufus Isaacs had a longer and closer connection, and they provide a good illustration of his tactical skill. The strike started at the end of June, 1902, and the two cases of Howden v. Yorkshire Miners' Association and Denaby Collieries v. Yorkshire Miners' Association, in both of which Rufus Isaacs was briefed for the Association, represented the effort of the colliery company to transfer the seat of war from the industrial field to the Courts.

Briefly, the first case was designed to put a stop to the strike and the second to recover damages from the Association for fomenting and supporting it. Of course, in theory the company had nothing to do with Howden's case, for

Howden was himself a member of the Association, who was asking the Court for an injunction to restrain the executive of the Association from paying away in strike pay funds to which he had contributed and on which he had a claim; in fact, he was acting as the nominee of the company, for if the injunction was granted it meant that the strike must end for want of funds to carry it on. The case had been heard on January 15th, 1903, and after two days the jury had given their verdict for Howden. The Association appealed, and the appeal was heard almost immediately; for a favourable decision would be of little use to the company or to Howden if it did not come in time to break the strike. The interest of the Association, however, was that the proceedings should continue long enough for the strike to go on successfully, and to this end Rufus Isaacs had to protract his defence. He based his case in the Court of Appeal on the section of the Trade Union Act of 1871, which forbids the Courts to entertain any legal proceedings, instituted with the object of directly enforcing agreements for the application of funds to provide contributions for members. He claimed that Howden's injunction was a form of directly enforcing an agreement, for what he was really doing by asking for an injunction was to claim that the Asociation should be compelled to retain their funds in order that they might be applied to other objects, *i.e.*, those benefits in which he was himself interested. Montagu Lush, however, for Howden, countered this argument by saying that if this was a " direct " enforcement, it was difficult to see what an " indirect " one would be, for the effect of granting an injunction to Howden to restrain the misapplication of the funds of the Association was not of itself to establish his title to benefit out of these funds. This view carried the day, and the Court of Appeal unanimously found in favour of Howden. But the form of injunction remained to be decided on, and in the consideration of this it was possible to postpone its final coming into operation until March 3rd, when the Association accepted the inevitable and called off the strike.

The case ultimately went for further hearing to the House of Lords, for, though the practical interest had gone, the point of law was important. But in the meantime the other case, in which the Denaby Colliery Company claimed £125,000 damages from the Association in respect of the strike was heard in January 1904, before Mr Justice Lawrence and a special jury, who found for the company, whereat the Association appealed. Rufus Isaacs, however, saw that if the House of Lords judgment in the Howden case confirmed the findings of the lower Courts, it would mean that the payment of strike pay had been held *ultra vires* the Association, and that the acts of the branch officials, who had authorised the strike, were not the acts of the Association, of which Howden was part; from this it followed that the Association, since it could not ratify or support the strike, could not be made liable in its funds for a strike in which, *qua* Association, it had neither part nor responsibility. The colliery company, in its eagerness to break the strike by the injunction, had demonstrated that the Association was not responsible for the strike, and their counsel, who had argued in the Howden case that the acts of the branch officials must not be taken to be the acts of the Association, were now called upon, in order to make the funds of the Association liable, to argue exactly the reverse. The company was trying to penalise sheep and goats alike, the innocent Howden along with the wicked and subversive officials. He applied, therefore, that the hearing of the appeal should wait until after the judgment of the House of Lords in the Howden case; his application was granted, and in April of 1905, the Lords, by a majority of four to two, gave judgment in favour of Howden, thus affirming the decisions of the lower Courts. The Denaby case came on shortly afterwards, and Rufus Isaacs made great play with the inconsistency of the company's position and with the advantageous finding in the Howden case. This time his arguments triumphed and the unanimous decision of the Court of Appeal went in his favour. The company took the case to the Lords, where " the arguments ranged over every point that could be raised by the ingenuity of counsel; they cited many cases, none of which were thought material by the House." Rufus Isaacs' position, therefore, remained unshaken and the Lords unanimously affirmed the decision of the Court of Appeal. The long proceedings, though perhaps wearisome to the layman in their detail, afford a notable example of the value of a sense of strategy in the advocate. Rufus Isaacs had achieved a practical advantage from the Howden case as far as it was possible, and had then used the adverse judgment as the basis of his contention in the Denaby case. He had made up on the roundabouts what he had lost upon the swings; or rather, he had more than made it up. For the chief practical importance to his clients of the Howden case had been the ephemeral one of the duration of the strike, while in the Denaby case he had saved them £125,000, not to mention costs. It takes, therefore, deservedly high place in the long list of Rufus Isaacs' Trade Union cases.

Very different from these protracted proceedings were the two libel actions in which Rufus Isaacs appeared for Colonel Morgan. Colonel Morgan had been Director of Supplies in South Africa, and the cases were a final echo of the allegations of corruption in the Boer War. The libel was alleged in the report of a case in Pretoria, in which a Mr Hunter was the plaintiff; now Hunter had been manager of a farm for supplying the troops in South Africa, which was under the general superintendence of Colonel Morgan, and it had transpired in the case not only that Hunter had made a profit of £1,800 on chaff, which he had bought from the Government for £300, but that one-third of his profit had gone to Colonel Morgan's brother, who had entered into partnership with Hunter after Colonel Morgan's departure from South Africa. The *Central News* account of the proceedings ended with the words: "The Judge after thus reviewing the case, concluded by saying 'Comment is unnecessary'," and the account was duly printed in the *Daily News* on June 4th, 1904, under the heading "War Stores Scandal. A Transvaal Army Deal." There was also a leading article, entitled " Shame and Scandal," which indicted the supposed corruption with true Radical fervour: " Now a sample case," it ran, " has come into the Supreme Civil Court, and the report says a Colonel Morgan (ex-Director of Military Supplies) sold to one Hunter for £300 goods on which the purchaser made a profit of £1,800, one-third of which went to Morgan's brother . . . The story of the sordid corruption grows daily more shameful; the wretched land, now that murder has done its worst, seems delivered over to the kites and vultures."

Colonel Morgan issued a writ for libel, and Rufus Isaacs was briefed to appear for him. After the issue of the writ the *Daily News* inserted an article saying that " the *Central News* is informed that Colonel Morgan has been exonerated from complicity in the so-called Pretoria forage scandal," but the paper was on very weak ground in fighting the case, for not only had Colonel Morgan left South Africa before the sale or before his brother had any connection with Hunter, but the *Central News* statement in regard to the trial hardly expressed the full facts. The Chief Justice of the Transvaal had used the expression " Comment is unnecessary," but in a different context from that implied; for he had said, " I say nothing about Colonel Morgan because he is not before me; I do not know what his account of the case may be . . . but what I do say is this, that there has been shown in this action a transaction by which Government stores had been sold for £300 and they realised £1,800. Comment is unnecessary." The words " comment is unnecessary," that is to say, were used after Colonel Morgan had already been dismissed from consideration, and not, as implied, in reference to his conduct. In the circumstances, the case gave little trouble to Rufus Isaacs, and after his opening of the case and examination of Colonel Morgan, Mr Robson, who represented the *Daily News*, said that his clients accepted Colonel Morgan's straightforward denial of having made the sale, and made sincere expression of regret; further, they were willing to make full indemnity. This latter offer Rufus Isaacs waived on behalf of his client, who,

he said, was satisfied with the complete vindication of his
character and had not brought the action to put money into
his pocket. The *Times* was not quite so easily dealt with,
for Mr Eldon Bankes, who appeared for the paper,
differentiated the case from the *Daily News* case, on the
ground that the *Times* had not seen fit to include any
indignant references to " kites and vultures " or the rest.
The case, therefore, went its course, and Rufus Isaacs cross-
examined Mr Moberley Bell of the *Times,* and examined
General Lyttleton and Sir E. Ward, the Permanent Under-
Secretary to the War Office, who were called for Colonel
Morgan. Ultimately after two and a half hours' consideration, the jury found for Colonel Morgan with £250
damages.

But perhaps the greatest case in which he appeared in
1905 was his defence of Sir Edward Russell; and it is a
case which he looks back upon with especial pride and
pleasure. For, although the case lasted only three days,
it had features in it which differentiated it from the ordinary
run of case; and it was a proud and memorable case for
Rufus Isaacs both because it gave him an opportunity of
excelling in the field of eloquence and because it was his
privilege to defend an illustrious public man from the ignominy of conviction in a criminal case. His client, Sir
Edward Russell (later the first Lord Russell of Liverpool),
was, after a lifetime spent in journalism, the editor of the
Liverpool Daily Post, a Liberal organ, and a much respected
figure—the last person one would have expected to find
indicted on a criminal charge, in fact. But our criminal law
provides remedies not only for offences against the person
and property, but for offences against reputation in addition.
And when one eminent and respected gentleman casts slurs
on the reputation of other eminent and respected gentlemen,
litigation on a large scale almost invariably ensues. It is
ordinarily civil litigation, but libel may involve criminal
prosecution; and if it is a libel of public men in the exercise
of a public duty, then there is an instrument known as
criminal information, which takes the place of an indictment,

and exempts the prosecution from the ordinary preliminaries. It was these circumstances that led up to, and this instrument which secured, the prosecution of Sir Edward Russell.

The prosecutors were eight members of the Licensing Committee of the Liverpool Justices; for it was this worthy body which Sir Edward had failed to treat with proper respect. His criticism was provoked by the operation by the Conservative members of the Liverpool Licensing Committee of the powers given to them and similar bodies by the Licensing Act of 1904. The aim of this Act—which, as we have seen, was the cause of controversy in the political world—was to reduce the number of licenses granted to publicans in cases where there were complaints or where there were too many public houses in a district. Those who did not have their licenses renewed were to receive compensation, and the Act gave power to magistrates to levy compensation on every house in the district which did receive a license; this procedure was based on the assumption that the surviving licenses would benefit by getting a proportion of the trade which had formerly gone to those whose licenses were extinguished under the Act. The consequence of this procedure was that, as compensation had to be paid and as this was the sole method provided for obtaining it, the extent to which existing licenses could be extinguished depended upon the amount of compensation which was levied upon the surviving licenses; and the determination of the rate to be levied lay within the province of the Licensing Justices. It followed, of course, from the working of the system that it was in the interest of the liquor trade to have the compensation levied at the lowest possible rate, for then there was the dual advantage of having to pay less in compensation and having fewer licenses extinguished.

Now in Liverpool the Licensing Committee numbered sixteen, and Sir Edward Russell had proposed in the *Liverpool Post* that the two parties should be equally represented on the Committee with Sir Thomas Hughes, a Conservative, as chairman. This suggestion, however, did not commend itself to the Conservatives, who were in a

majority on the main body of Justices and considered it
their right that their numerical superiority should be pro-
portionately reflected in the Committee; and, in consequence,
the Licensing Committee consisted of ten Conservatives,
including Sir Thomas Hughes, and six Liberals.   On July
12th the Committee met to discuss the rate of compensation,
and the Liberal minority proposed to levy the full rate;
this was opposed, however, by the eight Conservatives, who
proposed half the rate.   Sir Thomas Hughes proposed
three-fifths of the full rate as a compromise, thinking that
this amount was the least that would do; but his motion
was defeated and the Conservative proposal for a half rate
carried.   The next day Sir Edward Russell denounced the
Conservative attitude in his paper, on the ground that they
were not trying to put into effect the reformist purpose of
the Act, which indeed was what was to be expected of the
friends of the liquor trade.   The eight Conservatives concerned interpreted this as being a personal reflection on their
public conduct, and determined—perhaps rather hastily—
on strong action.   Mr F. E. Smith was briefed, and on July
19th moved in the Divisional Court for a rule nisi for a
criminal information for libel against Sir Edward; the rule
was granted and on August 9th was made absolute, after
argument before the Lord Chief Justice.

In Liverpool the sensation was tremendous.   The local
party leaders were facing each other not in the decorous
venue of political controversy, but in the more spirited
arena of the Courts; and that, too, not as parties to civil
litigation, but as prosecutor and accused in a grave criminal
charge.   The case was heard at the Liverpool Assizes in
December of 1905 before Mr Justice Bray, and there was a
strong representation of counsel from the Northern Circuit;
Mr F. E. Smith was led by Mr Taylor, K.C., while for
Russell, Rufus Isaacs led Mr Horridge, K.C., later to be
better known as a High Court Judge, and Mr Hemmerde.
The attention of the country was occupied primarily with
the coming General Election, and the Liverpool trial was
felt to be somewhat of a sideline—or perhaps a rehearsal.

But in Liverpool the trial dwarfed all else; it was the sole subject of conversation, the sole focus of attention. Feeling ran high, too, and excited partisans eagerly debated the merits of the case; the balance of merit perhaps inclined to Sir Edward, but Liverpool has always been a stronghold of Conservatism, and he was wise to have secured the services of so redoubtable a Liberal champion as Rufus Isaacs.

The trial lasted for three exciting days, and was a notable triumph for Rufus Isaacs. Sir Edward Russell had pleaded "not guilty" on the ground that the alleged libel was true and published in the public interest, and that there was no imputation of corrupt or dishonest motives. Thus Rufus Isaacs defined the issue as "substantially a question of whether or not Sir Edward Russell was making a comment which he had a right to make upon a public body." It was, therefore, Rufus Isaacs' honourable task to vindicate the great principle of freedom of speech, for the case was, as he maintained, a "political case and nothing else." But first he had to prove out of the mouths of the hostile witnesses that this was so, and for this purpose the principal witness was Isaac Morris, the Conservative vice-chairman of the committee, a typical, hard-headed, slow-moving, northern business man. In the course of a skilful cross-examination, in which he was quickly out-flanked, Mr Morris was forced to admit that he had insisted on a proportionate, as against an equal, political representation, and that he had then at once gone to the Conservative Club to "invite" men to serve. When there were divisions in the Committee, too, he had to admit that they were on party lines. An important piece of evidence, with which Rufus Isaacs was to make great play in his final speech, came from Sir Charles Petrie, one of the eight plaintiffs, who stated that when he read the article he had not construed it as an imputation of corrupt or dishonest motives.

At the conclusion of the evidence for the prosecution on the second day, Rufus Isaacs opened his case in a speech of an hour and fifty minutes. The speech, spoken in a Court packed with enthralled spectators, is—partly, perhaps, on account of its comparative brevity, but mainly because he had so good a theme—one of his greatest forensic efforts.   His appeal to the principle of free speech was unqualified: " I don't hesitate to say in a public Court that not only was Sir Edward Russell entitled to make the observation contained in this article upon the action of these licensing justices in Liverpool, the predominant political party on this committee, but that he was entitled to comment upon the action of the judge upon the bench, and upon the action of all the magistrates in every court throughout the country.   The days are not far coming in this country when criticism of those holding public positions is to be narrowed down by elaborate technicalities and the microscopic examination of every bit of the phraseology used in this article . . . Fox's Act established this one great principle, the fundamental principle of justice in this country—that the question whether an article is a libel or not is not to be decided by the judge, however strong his views may be, but the question is to be decided and left by him to the consideration and determination of the jury.   This is the law of this free country, and you, gentlemen of the jury, are called upon to administer that law."   His peroration struck the right balance between the personal note and the note of defiance: " You are dealing with a man of Sir Edward Russell's position, known to you as he must be after an honoured life extending over a vast number of years, greater than most of us in this Court have attained to, but I am not going to say one word—I would scorn to say a word, because I know that he would be the last man to wish that I should say a word—that would deal with this case as one of mercy to him.   What he is asking, what he is begging of you to do, is to deal with this case fairly and impartially, whatever your political views may be; deal with him as an honourable citizen, holding the views that he has published bona fide in the criticism, which he was entitled to administer to a public body.   Deal with him as an honourable man, who says that he never intended what it has been alleged against him that he did intend; deal with him as one who has done in this as in everything else that he has done throughout his life, as one who is well known to you as a man only anxious to continue in the sweetening and purifying of the city to which he has the honour to belong, and which has the honour of claiming him as one of the foremost of its citizens."

On the following day, after the evidence of Sir Edward Russell, Rufus Isaacs again addressed the jury. Sir Edward had meanwhile in cross-examination defined his attitude and shown the difference between criticism of a public body and the imputation of personal dishonour. " I will suppose," he said, " that A.B. on that select committee knew C.D., a license-holder, who could in any way profit by his vote. If A.B. gives his vote in reference to the interests of C.D., he is a dastard. But I should say that if A.B. is a member of a large political body, which is in definite and continuous alliance with a certain trade interest, and if, coming to the conclusion with any sort of conscience, they think it is for the public good that the trade should be supported and should have its way, then I don't call that personal dishonour, even if their vote proves to the advantage of that trade." Sir Edward made a very good witness, and when Rufus Isaacs rose to make his final speech, it was with the encouraging knowledge that so far the case had gone without a hitch.

He started his speech by solemnly reminding the jury of their responsibility and their duty " to consider the matter in no narrow or jealous spirit." There were two questions for their consideration; first, whether the article passed the limits of that comment which every man is entitled to make upon the public acts of another, and, secondly, whether the criticism was true in substance and in fact. But in point of fact there should have been no necessity for them to try these issues; for " if that statement which Sir Charles Petrie made in the witness box, and with which the others, who were not called, are said to agree, had been made at an early stage of this case, when these proceedings were initiated, when this great cumbrous machinery of our criminal law was set in motion . . . all this antiquated, obsolete—as many have thought it, at any rate—system of law would never have been requisitioned and put into operation, and you would never have been here to try this case, if only it had been known from the start that Sir Charles Petrie, as a sample of the bulk, thought that this article imputed no corrupt or dishonest motives to the magistrates who were attacked." But as it was, " this farce— I am entitled to call it a farce and I do—this farce is to be gone through of asking you to find that this article does not mean what my friend is saying, and I have to ask you to find that this article means what Sir Charles Petrie, the prosecutor, says."

He urged that as the criminal procedure could only be justified by the imputation of dishonest motives in the discharge of public duty, and, since there was no such imputation in this case, an ordinary civil action should have been brought. " But you could not be right to set this procedure in motion for the trumpery and trivial thing which you are now discussing when you once get rid of the imputation of corruption or dishonest conduct. Why, the question which we are really discussing is whether Sir Edward Russell is to be found guilty . . . because he has ventured to criticise strongly, perhaps exaggeratingly, the conduct of these eight members of the Licensing Committee —public men—in connection with the discharge of their public duty." He then went through the article piecemeal to show that it was in substance an accurate and fair comment. At the end of this analysis the speech took a dramatic and unexpected turn, for Rufus Isaacs interpreted the feelings not of his own client—which is quite a stock concomitant of the eloquent peroration—but of his client's accusers. " That," he said, " is the whole article. When you come to deal with it in the light of the facts which have been disclosed in this Court, don't you think, gentlemen, that the prosecutors are at the present moment feeling very considerable regret that they ever thought fit to bring these proceedings? Don't you think that in their heart of hearts and in their better moments, when political passion or par-

isanship are not in the ascendant, that they will themselves
probably think at this moment—men of honour, all of them
men of position—that they hope that your verdict will be
one of acquittal of the defendant, so that they may not have
upon their minds the burden of responsibility of thinking
that they have brought down a high-minded and honourable
man from the position which he has occupied to the credit
and glory of the city to which he belongs."

These two speeches of Rufus Isaacs won high praise both
from the Bench and from opposing counsel. Mr Taylor,
before going on to criticise the substance of the case, paid
tribute to its presentation in a reference to " two magnificent
speeches . . . brilliant in their language, telling in their
appeal to you, dramatic in their force, touching in their
references to the man whom he was defending," while Mr
Justice Bray, who was a comparatively new judge, said, " I
have never heard, while sitting upon the Bench, two finer
addresses than those which you, gentlemen of the jury,
have been privileged to hear to-day and yesterday." Indeed,
Rufus Isaacs' speeches and conduct of the case had left little
doubt as to the verdict, and it only took the jury eighteen
minutes after the summing up to find Sir Edward Russell
not guilty. The expected verdict was received with
tremendous enthusiasm, and a huge crowd outside the
Court acclaimed Sir Edward in triumph; indeed so popular
was the verdict that we can believe, with Rufus Isaacs, that
the prosecutors themselves were secretly glad of it. Sir
Edward paid a most generous tribute to the talent and
character of Rufus Isaacs, and declared that " one of the
many good results of my prosecution as a criminal is that I
have gained him as a friend." The *Liverpool Post* was
equally appreciative: " And perhaps the greatest result of
all this episode in which we have been concerned will be
that the magnificent championship of Mr Rufus Isaacs,
worthy of Erskine and Lord Russell of Killowen, acknowledged by the very Bench to have conferred distinction on
the Northern Circuit and on the whole Bar, will arouse the
Press to a sense of its rights, the country to a recognition of

the Press's services to right and reform, and juries to a feeling that they must imitate the wisdom, the courage, and the high morals of the jury which acquitted Sir Edward Russell."

But Rufus Isaacs was not himself present to receive the universal applause, as he had had to leave Liverpool before the verdict. For the law and politics are stern taskmasters, who extort the labour of achievement and allow but sparingly indulgence in congratulations or the contemplation of success; and in December of 1905 the finger of politics beckoned Rufus Isaacs to a new struggle.

CHAPTER XIII

THE LIBERAL TRIUMPH OF 1906: THE TRADES DISPUTES BILL

THE election of 1906 is a famous election, for it had more than a passing interest. It was hailed by Liberals at the time as the turn of the tide; Liberalism was restored to power after ten years in the wilderness. But 1906 brought something more than general post in Whitehall; it brought a new vitality to politics and a new bitterness. It brought, too, for the first time the strong influence of organised labour, and, arising in part out of this, a speeding-up of that new process in politics, of which the good side is represented by a desire for social amelioration, and the bad by a reckless irresponsibility in the pursuit of its attainment. That 1906 would bring a Liberal victory was, after a decade of undistinguished Tory Government, inevitable; but that the victory should have been so sweeping a triumph was due to more particular causes. It was due to the fact that the Liberals had a cause, a catchword, and the support of a sectional interest; the cause was Free Trade, the catchword, " Chinese Slavery," and the sectional interest, Trade Unionism. These three together converted Tory defeat into rout and the Liberal victory into a sweeping Pyrrhic triumph, for which the price was ultimately paid in the destruction of the party.

At Reading, Rufus Isaacs fought mainly on the Free Trade issue; he declared that Home Rule was not an issue, and would have nothing to do with the Chinese slavery scare. " It is an impossibility," he said, " to deal with two such questions as Free Trade and Home Rule at one election; " while as for Chinese labour, " it could only be introduced if the majority of the white people of the colony were in favour of it. That was one of the issues upon which

179

we fought the 1904 election and I have always held the
view that the Liberal Government must allow the colonies
to govern themselves, and if they choose to have recourse
to Chinese labour, and think it good for them, they must
decide and deal with it and this country must not interfere."
It was typical of the moderation of his attitude, but in spite
of it—or can it be that it was because of it?—he aroused
great enthusiasm among the electorate. At this election he
had with him not only his wife but their son Gerald too,
now a young Etonian of sixteen, and frequently at the conclusion of meetings delighted supporters would drag them
in triumph in their carriage through the streets. Once
again the contest was spirited, but not quite so free from
personalities, and Rufus Isaacs had to face many attacks on
him for his religion, which were made by irresponsible
opponents—not, of course, by Mr Johnstone, who had
succeeded Mr Keyser as Tory candidate or by any of his
accredited supporters—to which he merely replied, " When
I came to Reading I said, as I say now, that I am a Jew
and proud of it." The result was declared on the night
of Saturday, January 13th, after a fortnight's hard cam-
paigning, and an excited crowd welcomed the re-election of
Rufus Isaacs by 697 votes. " I do feel," he said, " now
that Reading has a second time chosen me as her representative, that you mean me to remain." His prophecy was fully
justified for he was returned at five successive elections—
once unopposed—and was never rejected by the borough.

It was a very different House of Commons to which
Rufus Isaacs returned. Cohorts of Tories had been driven
from the scene, and their place on the Government side was
filled with the solid phalanx of the vast Liberal majority.
Mr Balfour had followed his party into retirement, as a
result of his defeat in Manchester (although a seat was soon
found for him in the City of London), and Sir Henry
Campbell-Bannerman reigned in his stead, with Mr Asquith
as his chief lieutenant; others on the Treasury Bench were
Mr Lloyd George, who was President of the Board of
Trade, Mr John Burns, Home Secretary, Sir Edward Grey,

Foreign Secretary, and in lesser positions " Lulu " Harcourt, Sir William's son, and Mr Winston Churchill. The administration was upheld by vast battalions of Liberals with the support of the solid company of their Irish Nationalist and Labour allies; many of the majority, as in all such Parliaments, had entered the House for the first time, made no mark and never returned. Among these, as among the more permanent Parliamentarians, Rufus Isaacs was popular, and he now had friends in high places such as Lloyd George, Lawson Walton, who had become Attorney-General, and Herbert Samuel, whose Parliamentary zeal and abilities had been rewarded with the office of Under-Secretary at the Home Office. Rufus Isaacs himself, of course, remained a private member, and private members have fewer chances of distinction in support of the Government than in Opposition; Government Whips have a discouraging habit of preferring the votes of private members to their speeches, and the opportunity of delivering philippics is rare indeed. But Rufus Isaacs had not, as we have seen, availed himself of such opportunities, when they lay ready to his hand; nor indeed had his attendance in Parliament been that of the aspiring politician, for his preoccupation with the Bar and a little ill-health at the beginning of 1905 had prevented him from attending more than a hundred divisions out of the three hundred and sixty-four which had been taken between the time of his return for Reading and the 1906 election. He had, therefore, no reason either on public or on personal grounds to regret the changed situation in which he found himself, especially since, however large the majority, there were still subjects in which he was better versed than the bulk of his colleagues.

Chief of these was perhaps the vexed question of the Trade Unions, which occupied a prominent position in the formidable list of projected legislation contained in the King's Speech at the opening of Parliament in 1906. In point of fact, neither the Trade Union Bill nor the other principal measures went quite according to Liberal plan. The reason for this was that behind the impressive façade the Liberal position had weaknesses, which the piled-up radicalism of the House of Commons could neither cure nor altogether conceal; and an understanding of the political history of the next few years depends upon the realisation of the existence and nature of these weaknesses. The difficulties of the Liberal position were two-fold; one of them they were eager to point to in the hopes of being able to gather strength to destroy it, while the other they concealed in so far as they recognised it, because it was organic and went to the roots of Party integrity.

The first obstacle was the House of Lords, which, after having lain dormant through many years of Tory Government, now resurrected its powers and its activity to make a very successful onslaught upon Liberal legislation. The Liberal Education Bill passed its second reading in the House of Lords, but then came in for such drastic revision at their lordships' hands as to be unacceptable to the majority in the Commons when it returned to the Lower House. The Plural Voting Bill was likewise strangled in the Upper House, and the Government deemed it wiser to relegate the discussion of their Licensing Bill to a later date. Thus there was hostility between the Lords and the Commons long before Mr Lloyd George's Budget of 1909, and the origin of the hostility had nothing to do with the finances of the country, which were still controlled by the impeccable Mr Asquith. The Liberals, both in Parliament and in the country, eagerly denounced this obstacle to the declared will of the nation, and in course of time engaged the foe in a long and bitter combat which resulted in the annihilation of the Lords as a political force.

There was one Bill, however, which the Lords had not seen fit to touch, and this was the Trades Disputes Bill, which owed its immunity not so much to the good will of the Lords as to their reluctance to challenge the strength of organised labour. Nevertheless the Trades Disputes Bill did not go entirely according to preconceived plan; and the reason for this must be sought in the second great point of weakness in the great Liberal majority. The House of

Lords was a declared foe, which could be challenged and overthrown; the other weakness was organic, and in the long run proved fatal to the Liberal Party. The truth was that the great Liberal majority was neither compact nor homogeneous. The election showed a return of 513 Ministerialists against an Opposition of 157; the Liberals, however, only numbered 377, the total being made up of eighty-three Irish Nationalists and fifty-three Labour members. Of the Labour members twenty-nine acted as an independent party, while thirty-four were, broadly speaking, identified with the Liberal Party; the Labour Party were thus in the strong strategic position of having a " ginger group " within the party, and a potential cave of Adullam outside it on the Left. Nor were the Liberals themselves a really homogeneous body; for one thing, sectional interests were very strong, there being, for instance, 157 English nonconformists in the House, while a man like Charles Masterman showed that High Church Anglicanism was not incompatible with the finest Liberalism. But differences went deeper than this. The Liberal Party had not in reality been a unity for a very considerable time—even in the days of Gladstone there had been a fundamental cleavage of opinion between Whigs and Radicals; the defence of Free Trade had given the Party a rallying-point and a semblance of unity in 1906, but the unity did not go very deep in the matters of philosophy and political action. Different groups wanted different things, and variously interpreted the creed and policy of Liberalism; but all were Liberals, and consequently an effort was made to satisfy by legislative action as many of the points of view as possible. It was because of this —because lack of basic unity made adjustment and compromise necessary—that the Labour wing was able to exercise so strong an influence; for numerically it was still comparatively insignificant, and its vote was not essential to the Liberal majority. But it was an organised and solid minority, and as such its strength was considerable and its influence often decisive, as in the case of the Trades Disputes Bill. And because the Liberal Party could not effectively control or oppose this force on the Left it finally and inevitably succumbed to it.

Of the four main Government Bills mentioned, Rufus Isaacs played a prominent part only in the Trades Disputes Bill. He had an intimate knowledge of Trade Union law, and had been counsel in the main Trade Union cases of the previous years. He had, as we have seen, appeared almost invariably for the Trade Union, and had on that account the best reason for being aware of the difficulties of their legal position after the Taff Vale judgment. He felt strongly, too, that the pronouncement of that decision—that the funds of Trade Unions were liable in damages for tort —amounted almost to a revolution, since, in view of the long practical immunity, it had become the settled legal conception that they were not so liable. The change, therefore, which was implied in the declaration of the law on this point by the Law Lords in the Taff Vale judgment was, in Rufus Isaacs' opinion, so far-reaching in its social consequences that it must be submitted to the will of the people; it was contrary to both democratic and legal principle that what was in effect a change in the law should be made judicially. The will of the people had been taken and there was no doubt that the result of the 1906 election had been to give the Government a mandate to revise the law in a sense favourable to Trade Unions.

The question then merely was: what form should the revision take? The Royal Commission which had been appointed in consequence of the spate of cases, which had followed the Taff Vale decision, had recommended a measure of protection for Trade Union funds and the relaxation of the law of conspiracy and the law against peaceful picketing in the interests of the Trade Unions. In the matter of the law of conspiracy and peaceful picketing there was general agreement within the Government ranks; and indeed the inconsistency of maintaining a right to strike at all together with the existing law on picketing is clear from Mr Justice Wills' remark in the Taff Vale judgment: " You cannot make a strike effective without doing more than is lawful."

As regards the funds, however, there was not this unanimity. It was clearly wrong that the contributions of the members of a Trade Union, which they had made in the prospect of certain definite and assured benefits, should be at the mercy of the Courts whenever the irresponsible acts of say, a branch official, should give cause of action; and in the opinion of Rufus Isaacs, the best way to safeguard them was to restrict the application of the law of agency in favour of Trade Unions, so that their funds might be protected from the consequences of unauthorised and uncontrolled acts. This was without doubt the best solution of the problem, for it would both protect the Trade Unions from the consequences of unauthorised and irresponsible acts, and at the same time fix their liability for acts which the Union authorised or made its own. It is clear, too, from the biography of Lord Oxford and Lord Haldane's autobiography that this was the course proposed by Mr Asquith and Mr Haldane, who, with Lord Loreburn, the Lord Chancellor, were the two most eminent lawyers in the Cabinet. They pressed this view upon the Cabinet, but there were some to whom it was less attractive than the attitude of the Labour Party who, in the words of Mr Keir Hardie, " claimed in no uncertain voice absolute immunity for Trade Union funds from any claims for damages arising out of trade disputes." Unfortunately neither Rufus Isaacs nor either of the two Law Officers of the Crown, Sir John Lawson Walton and Sir William Robson, were in the Cabinet, and so the legal point of view was under-represented, while the fundamental weakness of the Liberal Party as a whole made it difficult for the lay section to resist the demands of Labour.

In spite of this, however, a Government Bill was framed in accordance with the legal point of view, and was introduced by Lawson Walton on March 28th. The relevant portion ran: " Where a Committee of a Trade Union, constituted as hereinafter mentioned, has been appointed to conduct, on behalf of the Union, a trade dispute, an action whereby it is sought to charge the funds of the Union with damages, in respect of any tortious act committed in contemplation or furtherance of the trade dispute should not lie, unless the act was committed by the Committee or some person acting under their authority:

" Provided that a person shall not be deemed to have acted under the authority of the Committee if the act was an act or one of a class of acts expressly prohibited by a resolution of the Committee, or the Committee by resolution expressly repudiate the act as soon as it is brought to their knowledge." The passage may not be a masterpiece of elegant prose, but it constituted a straightforward piece of legislation which would admirably have combined the protection of Trade Union funds with the safeguarding of society. It was very far from recommending itself, however, to the Labour element and to that large body of Liberals who had committed themselves in their constituencies to the advocacy and support of extreme legislation, and they condemned it in consequence as " incomprehensible." The Labour Party accordingly pressed on with the second reading of their own Bill to give Trade Union funds a complete immunity—it had been introduced originally on February 22nd as a Private Members' Bill, by right of ballot—and Campbell-Bannerman, who was not a lawyer, thought it best in the circumstances to adopt the Labour proposals. He, therefore, advised the House, as Prime Minister, to pass the second reading of the Bill, which they loyally did by a majority of 414 to 66, but not before they had undergone the raking fire of F. E. Smith's sarcasm. " The House, the Party, and the country asked the Government for a lead, and the Government put up the Attorney to say that they were better at following . . . I congratulate the honourable member for Merthyr Tydvil (Keir Hardie) on the captures he has made on the Front Bench. He may say ' The Treasury Bench is my washpot and over the Attorney-General have I cast out my shoe.' "

But, despite the taunts of the Prince Rupert of the Tories, complete immunity had become the policy of the Government, and Asquith, Haldane, Rufus Isaacs and the rest accepted it.   Complete immunity was the will of their party and the decree of their leader; and it may be that the dangers of such a policy did not loom so large as the necessity of bringing in some sort of legislation to rescue the Trade Unions from the admittedly inequitable position in which the Taff Vale judgment had placed them, for it might seem in the conditions of the time as if Campbell-Bannerman spoke truly when he said that there was in the two policies " not a difference of object but of method." And, in addition to this, it was possible for those who believed in the principle of altering the law in favour of the Trade Unions but would have preferred a less drastic measure to do something in Committee to keep the details of the Bill on the right road.   But nevertheless, it was unfortunate that the Liberal Government was compelled to legislate in accordance with the views of the Trade Unions themselves, rather than with those of the lawyers of the party, whose vision was enlarged by the contemplation of the effect of the measure on the community as a whole. The essential defect of the Trades Disputes Act, as finally passed into law, was that at a single bound it placed the Trade Unions outside the ordinary law in respect of civil liability, and gave them a privileged position as against other litigants.   It was this privileged position, this feeling that they were outside, if not above, the ordinary courses of the law— a position and a feeling which they would not have had if Campbell-Bannerman had stood firm, or the rank and file been less deeply committed—which encouraged the Trade Unions to challenge the community in 1926 and to force the issue of the General Strike.

On April 25th, the Solicitor-General, in the absence of Lawson Walton, introduced the new Government measure, which now approximated to Keir Hardie's original Bill. Rufus Isaacs, who in view of his experience was recognised as a leading authority in his party on the subject, was selected to follow the Leader of the Opposition.   " I thought," he said, " as the right honourable gentleman was speaking that he was going to accuse the Government of having unsettled convictions. There is no one in this House who has a right to speak with greater authority on that subject." And he went on to twit Mr Balfour with the indecisiveness of the preceding régime on the subject of Protection. He then gave it as his opinion that the effect of the Bill would not be to multiply the number of strikes; but the main point of his speech was his contention, already referred to, that the opinion of the vast majority of lawyers, who had any connection with Trade Unions—and the unanimous opinion of the Court of Appeal in the Taff Vale case in addition—had been that Trade Unions could not be sued and that the decision of the House of Lords had virtually amounted to a change in the law. Such a change must have the sanction of the people of the country, and the election had proved that there was no such sanction; it was now, therefore, for Parliament to legislate in accordance with the declared will of the people, and to remove them from the unfair position to which the Taff Vale decision had relegated them.

The Committee stage of the Bill occupied a great deal of Rufus Isaacs' parliamentary time that summer—and, indeed, there is more time spent upstairs in Committee and a more effective direction given to legislation there than people sometimes realise. He made contributions on amendments concerning picketing and inducement to breach of contract, while his personal knowledge of the subject was often of service to the Committee. Thus, when Mr F. E. Smith and Sir William Robson entered into argument about the facts of the case of Linaker v. Pilcher, Rufus Isaacs intervened and explained them; for he had been leading counsel in the case in 1901. One of his most valuable interventions in the Committee stage was his opposition to an amendment of Sir Charles Dilke, which would have given the Trade Unions a complete immunity in respect of any unlawful acts which they might commit, in addition to the immunity from the recovery of damages out of their funds, which the Bill had already given. " The result would be that the Trade Unions would be able to commit unlawful acts if they were so minded and no Court would be able to restrain them, although they might have expressed their intention of committing such acts, and mean to carry this intention into effect. I do not for a moment believe that the representatives of the Trade Unions claim any such immunity." His decisive stand carried the day and Sir Charles Dilke withdrew an amendment which would have greatly aggravated the less satisfactory features of the Bill. He spoke again on the Report stage and on the Lord's Amendments, and here again his contributions were luminous and well-informed; and by the time the measure finally became law, it had absorbed a considerable proportion of the Parliamentary efforts of Rufus Isaacs.

CHAPTER XIV

RUFUS ISAACS AND CARSON: THE "GAIETY" GIRL
DIVORCE CASE

IN May of 1907, Rufus Isaacs figured once again as leading counsel in a *cause célèbre* in the Divorce Court. The "Gaiety Girl Divorce Case," as the case of Bryce *v.* Bryce and Pape was popularly known at the time, was less rich in aristocratic names than the Hartopp case, but collected an equally brilliant array of counsel. For besides Rufus Isaacs, there were Sir Edward Carson, Mr Henry Duke, and Mr Barnard, while the case was tried before Mr Justice Bargrave Deane, who had been counsel in the Hartopp case and had since been promoted to the Bench. The fall of the Conservative Government had sent Carson simultaneously into Opposition and private practice, and in both he was supremely effective; and in the greatest cases in which Rufus Isaacs figured in this last period of his career as an advocate, Carson was his antagonist. In the case of Bryce *v.* Bryce and Pape they were in that sort of unofficial alliance which generally exists between counsel for the respondent and counsel for the co-respondent in divorce cases; but generally they were, of course, in conflict. There were the two great newspaper libel actions, Lever *v. The Daily Mail* and Cadbury *v. The Evening Standard;* there was the prosecution of Sievier, and the Archer-Shee case. In all these cases Rufus Isaacs and Carson were matched against each other, and their contests began to assume for the public the measure of excitement afforded by great sporting events. The zest with which their contests were watched was in part due to the supreme position occupied by the pair at the Bar and partly due to the fact that, while they had some qualities of advocacy in common, there was sufficient dissimilarity of equipment and method to point the contest and make interesting comparison. It is an over-simplification of the issue to use analogies like the bludgeon and the rapier, for these obscure the real line of distinction. In that they were both relentless and penetrative in cross-examination, lucid in exposition, and expert in argument, Rufus Isaacs and Carson had equipment not wholly dissimilar; but there were real differences. Carson had a measure of eloquence—though it was not so much the polished, literary eloquence of the scholar as a shrewd, forceful eloquence, reinforced by an enormous physique and an Irish brogue—and a native wit which Rufus Isaacs could not rival; but he, in his turn, had a faculty for the mastering and memorisation of intricate facts and figures, combined with a discretion in handling judge and jury and a tactical brilliance in the conduct of a case, which neither his great rival nor perhaps any other advocate has ever equalled. The difference in equipment reflects a difference in personality. Carson was dominating and masterful, while Rufus Isaacs was suave and courteous. Carson thundered, while Rufus Isaacs coaxed; Carson stormed, while Rufus Isaacs suggested. The keenness apparent in Rufus Isaacs was in Carson cloaked by brusquerie; the force apparent in Carson, was in Rufus Isaacs cloaked by suavity. But, fundamentally, Rufus Isaacs could concede little to Carson in acumen, and his own forcefulness was not so much behind that of Carson. Both had a splendid and comprehensive array of forensic weapons, and both were expert in their use; that alone could have given them their great position. They differed in many things, but both alike had that aggregation of qualities, that makes not the great lawyer or the great orator, but something that partakes of both and is in the legal world perhaps greater than either, the great man of the Courts. The comparison between them is not concerned with excelling; it is a question rather of emphasis.

The " Gaiety Girl Divorce Case " found these two great advocates, who during Carson's term of office had been opposed in the Criminal Courts in such cases as the Doctor Krause prosecution and the Slater Agency case, in as near a forensic alliance as they were ever in. The case got its popular name because Mrs Bryce was Mabel Duncan, the former Gaiety girl. Her parents were people of some social position; indeed her father, who had been at Eton and Cambridge, had been a rich man. Unfortunately, while Mabel was still a girl, her father had disappeared; this might have been forgiven him, but he was inconsiderate enough to leave no money behind, and so Mabel, who was a pretty, talented girl, took to the musical comedy stage. While still only seventeen, she met Francis Bryce, the eldest son of a Devonshire family of good position, who was at that time coaching for the Army. He fell in love with her, and, being a young man of honourable intentions, wanted to marry her. In this he was opposed by his parents, but, being a determined as well as an honourable young man, he threw up his commission in the Army, and went onto the Stock Exchange where, after an initial struggle, he attained a position which justified him in marrying independently of his parents' consent. And married they were on January 14th, 1898, at the Paddington Registry Office. Their courage and independence won its reward, for Francis Bryce's father befriended the young couple and under his benign influence the family duly received Mabel Bryce into its corporate bosom.

Here one could have wished the story to end, with young love installed in Hyde Park Mansions, and accepted in Devonshire. But, unhappily for marital felicity, they attended in the summer of 1905 Commemoration Week in Oxford, where they met Harold Pape, a rich and attractive young man from Christ Church, who promptly—as is often the way of young men with married women slightly older than themselves—fell in love with Mabel Bryce, and decided to see more of her. Consequently the Bryces came to stay at Harold Pape's father's deer-shoot in Scotland, and later, while Bryce was away at work, Mabel would go to race-meetings with Harold Pape, who was himself an accomplished gentleman-rider. In January of 1906, they all went to the County Ball at Exeter, where Harold spent most of the evening with Mabel, while Francis was very attentive to a young lady whose identity was to be hidden from a curious public under the anonymity of " Miss A." and in the Spring the four of them went to stay with Pape's father in Monte Carlo.   Later on, in July, Bryce saw his mother in Paris, who told him that people were talking of a liaison between Mabel and Harold Pape and advised him to see Sir George Lewis.   So, like countless others in similar situation, he consulted Sir George, and then engaged detectives to watch the suspected pair.   On July 21st, when her husband was away, Mabel Bryce went down to stay with her friends Doctor and Mrs Ellison at Windsor; with her went Miss Kindersley, but on their arrival they found the accommodation at the Ellisons' rather limited, and so they went to the White Hart Hotel near-by.   Here Harold Pape had taken the best room, but he gave it up to Mabel, taking a smaller one for himself.   In August Mabel again went to stay with the Ellisons—this time at Bembridge, where they were on holiday—and again Harold Pape stayed in a hotel in the vicinity, the Spithead Hotel.   Again, too, they were shadowed by the detectives, who reported, amongst other things, that one afternoon Harold Pape had been in the house with her, while she changed her dress, at a time when the Ellisons were out.   Finally on August 24th, Bryce discovered amongst his wife's things a bundle of letters from Mr Pape, and he decided to institute proceedings for divorce.   He shut up his house, turned his wife's things out, and refused to see her or hear a word in explanation. Meanwhile his solicitors wrote to Mr Pape saying that " he only trusts that though you have behaved to him in the way that you have, you will at all events adopt the only honourable course towards his wife, when the marriage has been dissolved, particularly in view of the great professions of love which you have made to her."

It turned out, however, that Mabel Bryce wished to remain Mabel Bryce, and Harold Pape to remain a bachelor; they denied the charge of adultery, and Harold Pape in his pleadings added charges of connivance and conduct conducing on the part of Francis Bryce. In the course of the trial, however, the plea of connivance was withdrawn. Mr Bryce, for whom Mr Henry Duke and Mr Barnard appeared, really relied, to establish his case, on the night spent at the White Hart at Windsor, on the episode at Bembridge, on the evidence of William Amos, a former chauffeur of the Bryces, that he had seen Mabel Bryce and Pape " kissing and cuddling like lovers " during the visit to Scotland, and on Pape's letters. The contention was that these letters and their conduct proved the existence of a guilty affection, and the various visits provided opportunities for its indulgence; the two together were sufficient to ask the jury to infer adultery. Rufus Isaacs and Carson, however, maintained that Amos' evidence was imaginative nonsense, and Pape's letters were those of a young man in love, but not of an adulterer, while the episodes at Windsor and at Bembridge could be explained on quite ordinary grounds without reference to adultery. At Windsor, Mabel Bryce had gone to the White Hart merely so as not to inconvenience the Ellisons; if she had wanted to commit adultery, she would have stayed in London, since her husband had been away on a visit to his mother that week-end. As to Bembridge, Pape had made two visits, wiring from London in the interval to ask if it was all right for him to return. The suggestion for the petitioner was that his return had depended on whether Bryce was coming to Bembridge or not; Rufus Isaacs, however, contended that Pape's action in inquiring was merely one of courtesy, arising from a natural desire not to be an infliction on the Ellisons, and in point of fact Mabel Bryce's reply to him that it would be all right for him to return had been despatched before she heard definitely that her husband was not coming.

The issue, therefore, depended to a certain extent on the interpretation of conduct, and the respondent's case was hardly assisted in this respect by the multitude of Harold Pape's love-letters, which were before the Court. Some of these were what he called " riddle letters," that is, written in an elementary code, which consisted of inserting the letters

" ap " into words; thus " yapou sapaid yapou caparaped fapor mape; dapou yapou rapeallapy " meant " you said you cared for me; do you really? " and so on. One letter was headed " Friday night," and read: " I shall not be able to sleep for some time if I go to bed, so I am writing to you even if I don't give you this letter in the morning; it somehow makes me feel happy to write to you. I can't tell you what my feelings are to-night. I only know I love you, I love you, and can't bear to think you are going away from me to-morrow. Daparlaping apone, do you really care for me a little? . . . I do feel I could really love you; you are so like what I always thought a woman ought to be. It is no passing fancy or passion because I am awfully fond of you in every way; you are such a great friend and I love just to talk to you. I feel like a thief in the night—by all the laws of everything, including honour, I ought to have stopped myself caring for you, ought never to have told you that I loved you, or shown it. I have, I think, only one excuse—I love you so much, and because I love you so much I am prepared to give you up entirely if you think it would be better for your happiness, or if you think it dishonourable for us to love each other. I love you so that I could forget everything except that I love you." Another letter said: " I do so wish you were here to-night. I want you awfully. I will try my best to stay in London over Sunday, but I cannot promise unless I get a good opportunity, it would be so foolish . . . I want to be in London with you over Sunday awfully . . . Good-night, my own darling." These are fair specimens of the letters, which were read by Henry Duke on the opening day of the trial. That they were love letters of a fervent sort—at any rate, for a young man who admittedly found writing difficult—is clear; but a careful reading of them will show that there is nothing in them to necessitate an inference of adultery. Indeed there are certain passages such as " you are such a great friend and I love just to talk to you," and " I love you so much that I am prepared to give you up entirely," which suggest an honourable and platonic relationship.

The case was opened by Mr Duke on May 5th, who read the letters at length, and interspersed the narrative with harsh comments on Pape, whom he represented as the worst type of idle and dissolute " man about town." On the second day, he called Bryce, who denied that he had left his wife alone with Pape, or that he had himself been too intimate with " Miss A."; " Miss A." had stayed with them in Cadogan Gardens for a fortnight in June of 1906, and there had been two week-end parties to Sonning, consisting of himself and his wife, Pape and " Miss A." Rufus Isaacs directed his cross-examination of Bryce to his relations with " Miss A." with a view to proving that Mabel Bryce was jealous of " Miss A," and that it was her husband's familiarity with " Miss A." which was the chief source of trouble between them; he was anxious to show, too, that Bryce's desire to be with " Miss A." led him to throw his wife in Pape's company. But Bryce denied this and said that his wife had always given him to understand that she got bored with Harold Pape.

" So that," replied Rufus Isaacs, " was why he was asked so often to meet her! Did you not know that she was fond of his society? "

" No."

" And was out with her late at night in punts on the river? "

" Quite an ordinary thing at Maidenhead."

" I will not discuss the habits of Maidenhead with you," concluded Rufus Isaacs drily.

Bryce also came off badly in his cross-examination with Carson, who questioned him as to the " pairing-off " at Sonning and in cabs and so on, especially as he was one of those irritating people in whom convention has taken such deep root that they describe their conduct by reference to axiomatic general propositions. Thus when Carson suggested that they might all have gone to the theatre together in a four-wheeler, instead of pairing-off, he said in a shocked voice:

" No one ever goes in a four-wheeler to the theatre."

" Oh well," replied Carson, with a deepening of the Irish brogue, " I'm perhaps out of date myself."

Similarly Bryce kept on saying that he had done things " in the ordinary way; " it was " in the ordinary way " that he had gone only a mile in his punt in nine hours, and he had afforded his wife the same protection " as any husband would."

" I hope," observed Carson, " that that will not be taken as dogmatic." Bryce said that he loved his wife at this period, not perhaps as in the first year of his married life, but " in the ordinary way."

" Everything you do seems to be in the ordinary way," said Carson.

" Yes, because all these incidents are all very ordinary one's," replied Bryce; " I followed my mother's advice and went to a solicitor in July."

" You are thirty years of age and she advised you to go to Sir George Lewis—in the ordinary way, and you went— in the ordinary way? " said Carson, and his summary was received in loud laughter.

There followed a sharp exchange between Carson and Duke, for neither had quite the suavity of Rufus Isaacs. Carson had followed up his previous question by asking:

" That was on July 26th? "

" August," corrected Henry Duke; and then, looking at his brief, he added: " No, I see you are right."

" I am glad," replied Carson sarcastically, " that I am right for once."

" It is a phenomenon no doubt," rejoined Henry Duke in the same tone.

" Miss A." succeeded Bryce in the witness-box, and was the object of many curious glances in Court. She was a pretty girl of nineteen, and many speculated as to her identity; but she was a young girl of good family and it would have done her no good to be associated with the case. Consequently all parties agreed to give her the pro- tection of anonymity.

Rufus Isaacs cross-examined her as to the " pairing-off,"

to which she replied that Bryce had shown no more liking for her than for any other friend.

" But we have heard you spent nine hours covering a mile on the river," objected Rufus Isaacs.

" Have you ever been in a punt, Mr Isaacs? " asked the Judge, amid laughter.

" Yes," replied Rufus Isaacs, smiling, " but—"

" Now don't make any confessions," said Duke.

" I am not going to be tempted to do so," he replied, " even by my Lord. I am older."

The witness proved to be " unable to remember " many things, and this gave Carson an opportunity of outflanking her.

" Come now," he said, " can't you remember? Are you clever? "

" No," she replied, " I have a bad memory."

" Then you musn't be offended," said Carson, " If I venture to say I do not agree with you."

The next witness was William Amos, the chauffeur, who said that in August, 1905, he had seen Mabel Bryce and Pape " kissing and cuddling like lovers " on the road near Foich. He was not shocked as he had often seen such things before.

" Where? " asked Carson.

" Everywhere," replied the much-travelled young man; " in England, Ireland, Scotland and Wales."

" Oh please leave Ireland out, Mr Chauffeur," said Carson, and the Court laughed. " Is cuddling and kissing, in your experience, an epidemic all over the United Kingdom? " he continued, and the laughter broke out again.

Amos said that he could not fix the date, but remembered that he had gone out to look for white heather to send away.

" To a lady? " inquired Carson. " Did you get any? Come now, that is an awkward question? "

The chauffeur, however, encouraged by the success which he seemed to be having in the witness-box, was in no mood to be bantered by Carson.

" What business is it of yours? " he retorted pertly.

In a moment he regretted his insolence, for Carson drooped his great height and leant forward with his chin projecting angularly like a danger signal; he fixed Amos with his menacing glare, at which witnesses, counsel, Cabinet Ministers and the Bench itself had learnt to tremble, and addressed him:

" Will you say that again just in the same tone? "

It was a simple question, but Amos crumpled. " I did find some, and sent it away, too," he replied with a mixture of humility and jocular pride, and a very evident desire not to offend his formidable antagonist again.

The cross-examination affords in its details an interesting comparison between Carson's methods and those of Rufus Isaacs. Rufus Isaacs would not have been able to annihilate a hostile or insolent witness with the speed and decisiveness with which Carson dealt with Amos—as indeed no other counsel could have done—for his appearance, though impressive, lacked the formidable quality which is peculiarly Carson's. But, if Rufus Isaacs could not quell opposition so easily, he did not so readily evoke it. He would never, for instance, have addressed a witness as " Mr Chauffeur; " he treated witnesses with invariable respect and, not having Carson's wit, was rarely tempted to make jokes at their expense. Nor would he have had the brush with Henry Duke that Carson had; indeed in the whole course of his long forensic career, I have found not a single instance of his having had a serious clash in Court, either with counsel, witness, or judge. Such a phenomenon was not due to weakness with opposition or subservience to the Bench, any more than the outbursts of Carson and Marshall Hall were due to truculence; indeed a notable instance of the way in which he handled the Bench is provided in his final speech in this very trial. It was due to his own tact, resilience and self-discipline, which prevented him from provoking other people, and to his flair for handling people and situations; for these qualities were as much the hall mark of Rufus Isaacs as that formidable personality was of Edward Carson.

There were several other witnesses before Rufus Isaacs opened the case for the respondent, but only Hoare and Newton, the private detectives, were really important. They gave evidence of watching Mabel Bryce and Pape at Bembridge in August, but Rufus Isaacs' searching cross-examination left their evidence very battered. Hoare said that his note-book did not show how every five minutes of his time was occupied, but it practically showed it.

"If you say it practically does so, that means it really does not?"

"My colleague and I only relieved each other for refreshment, and we did not want much food on a hot day."

"But refreshment on a hot day does not necessarily mean food," said Rufus Isaacs sagely.

Later the witness said:

"On another occasion I saw them walking in Love's End Lane."

"Whom does that refer to?" inquired Rufus Isaacs.

"The respondent, the co-respondent and Mrs Ellison," replied the witness.

"So there were three of them. But do you realise that it is on this sort of evidence that adultery is alleged?"

"Not by me, sir," replied the man apologetically.

When Rufus Isaacs opened his case, he had no more attentive listener than his client, whose eyes filled with tears as she looked pathetically at her husband's stern and unrelenting face. But the unfriendly demeanour of Mr Bryce was hardly likely to affect Rufus Isaacs, who pointed out that not a single witness had been called to show that Mrs Bryce had committed adultery, except perhaps the chauffeur, the value of whose evidence the jury could judge for themselves. The life led by the quartet had been an extraordinary one; that they knew from Bryce's own evidence. But he did not suggest that Bryce had committed adultery with "Miss A." in these circumstances, and so why from the same facts should the jury be asked to infer adultery between Mrs Bryce and Harold Pape. It was, of course, foolish of Mrs Bryce to receive those letters from

" an enamoured and foolish young man; " but what might be a fault was not on that account a crime. She was probably flattered by his attentions and, having the fullest confidence in herself, failed to realise her strict duty to her husband. But, when this grave charge was made against her, she had been denied by her husband even that opportunity of explanation which is afforded to every criminal. And yet what was there to substantiate the charge? Not a single servant had been called to prove adultery, and the detectives' evidence—such as it was, with its contradictions and inadequacies—was in her favour, since they could depose to no single act of familiarity.

After Carson had also addressed the Court, Rufus Isaacs called his client, who entered the box, her white dress accentuating her careworn appearance. She was given a seat in the box, however, and answering Rufus Isaacs' questions clearly and smilingly, made a good impression on the jury. At the end of her examination, she faced her great ordeal with Duke's cross-examination, which lasted for eight hours and contained two thousand three hundred questions. He questioned her closely as to her relations with Pape, her tiffs with him and so on, and often she had to answer " I don't remember," " I dare say," " More or less, I suppose."

" When Mr Pape wrote ' I want you to-night awfully, awfully,' what did you understand? " asked Mr Duke.

" I thought he wished me to be with him."

" But did you not understand by that something improper? " interposed Bargrave Deane.

" No, my lord; he so often put into his letters ' I wish you were here.' "

" But ' to-night ' ? " said the Judge testily. " You are a married woman and understand these things."

" I looked upon the words as a figure of speech," she replied.

Duke asked her what she thought the end of her relationship with Pape would be, and she said that Pape knew that she was jealous of her husband.

" Then in February was the position this—you were jealous upon the supposition that Mr Pape wrote love letters to another lady, and jealous of your husband because he was attracted by ' Miss A.' ? Can you be jealous of two people at once, and does not jealousy arise from love? "

The question perhaps goes rather deep for a question from counsel to witness, but Mrs Bryce, although she had not the illuminating divorce-court experience of the future Lord Merrivale, answered wisely and truly: " That is a matter of disposition. I was very annoyed with my husband and very jealous of him."

This was on the morning of May 16th, her third day in the box, and the strain and exhaustion were clearly telling on her. Shortly before noon she fainted, and was carried out of Court, sobbing unrestrainedly; half an hour later she returned, very pale, to resume cross-examination, but towards the end of the day her voice became very emotional and, leaning back helplessly in the box, she said weakly, " I forget what I'm talking about, I forget what I'm talking about." The Court adjourned, and as Mrs Bryce left the box, she fell fainting into the arms of a friend. Next morning, however, she was bright and well once more, and the cross-examination was concluded. She had not perhaps proved a " good witness," but she had emerged from the box in a very fair position. If a man breaks down in the witness box, his case is almost certainly lost; but this by no means applies in the case of a woman. Indeed it is often the most effective thing she can do, for it shows a proper delicacy of feeling, and makes—or, at any rate, did in the time of exclusively male juries—an immediate appeal to the chivalry of the jury; and if, in addition, she can reappear looking radiant, there is an aesthetic appeal by contrast to reinforce further her position.

It was not to be expected that Harold Pape would make quite such a good impression, but nevertheless his slim, athletic-looking figure and boyish face hardly bespoke the monster of iniquity which Henry Duke had represented him to be. He admitted that he had been in love with Mrs

Bryce, and had tried to hide his affections because he felt it to be dishonourable, but he strenuously denied adultery. But perhaps the greatest assistance to Rufus Isaacs' case came from the Ellisons, for Mrs Ellison described how she had come into Court as a hostile witness, but now that she had heard the evidence, she reverted to her belief in Mrs Bryce's innocence, in which she had only been shaken because, knowing Bryce as an honourable man, she did not suppose that he would bring proceedings against his wife without due cause. She was, however, quite certain that Mrs Bryce had not committed misconduct at Bembridge, and she had come forward as a woman to help another woman, in spite of the efforts that had been made to keep her from the box. There was one more interesting witness for the defence in the person of Sir Alfred Fripp, the famous surgeon, who said that he had attended Harold Pape from November, 1905, to July 26th, 1906, when he underwent an operation for the distressing complaint of haemorrhoids, which had necessitated the wearing of bandages until September 5th. It was, therefore, improbable, though not impossible, for him to have committed adultery on August 21st—the date at which he was alleged to have done so at Bembridge.

It was with the support of all these varied sorts of evidence to assist his interpretation of the conduct of the parties that Rufus Isaacs rose to make his final speech to the jury on May 31st. If his first speech had won the graceful tribute of tears from his fair client, this speech won the still more emphatic, if less graceful, tribute of hysteria. For so great was his eloquence that Mrs Bryce broke down and sobbed like a child, and her frail body swayed helplessly to and fro until it was finally engulfed in a fit of uncontrolled hysteria; indeed, it was not until after lunch that she regained her composure. In the circumstances it was perhaps hardly surprising that Rufus Isaacs started his speech with a reference to the ordeal which his client had undergone in her lengthy cross-examination; but he went on: " I still desire to say nothing which may imperil the chances of a reunion between these parties, for I still hope that that is possible; but I cannot help saying that things might have been different if only Mr Bryce had been guided more by those human instincts of kindness which should be only natural in a husband towards his wife. If only Mr Bryce had not jumped to conclusions, if only he had not rushed off to his solicitors and detectives, if only he had given his wife one chance to explain, as was surely only reasonable, as she was entitled to, then indeed we might have been saved this lengthy trial."

He then proceeded to a consideration of the facts. There were none of those incidents of familiarity, noticed by friends and servants, which were usual in this type of case, always excepting the inaccurate evidence of that " inventive genius," Amos. Two specific charges there were, of adultery at Windsor and at Bembridge. The Windsor charge was absurd, for if Mrs Bryce had wished to commit adultery, she could have done so more easily and unostentatiously by remaining in London, as her husband was away. As to Bembridge, the petitioner's sheet-anchor was the afternoon of August 23rd, when Mrs Bryce and Pape had been alone in the cottage for a time in the absence of the Ellisons and for ten minutes in the drawing-room; but during this time Powell, the maid, and Mrs Fry, the landlady, had been in the house, and most of the time was spent by Mrs Bryce in changing her hat and gown—a most important business, as it was regatta day, the great day, at Bembridge. That was the afternoon, on which the petitioner relied most strongly; and it amounted to no more than that. This was all that Bryce's detectives had been able to discover, and in exchange for it, " whatever the result of this case, Mr Bryce cannot but look back with shame upon his conduct at that time. He did not shrink from causing his wife to be watched at the houses of friends where both he and she were honoured guests." Much of Mrs Bryce's conduct was wrong and unjustifiable. In the matter of the letters for instance; but the letters were no conclusive test of the case, as it was not suggested that adultery was taking place at the time when the letters were passing. Further, though the letters showed that the writer was in love with Mrs Bryce, they also seemed to show that the love was unrequited and the desire unsatisfied. The jury must judge Mrs Bryce's conduct in the light of their knowledge of women. " Many women," he said, " especially young and pretty ones, like the attention of a young man to go about with them and act as their escort; but it would be doing the sex a grave wrong to infer from such attention that a woman has forfeited her right to her good name and her position in the world. Mr Bryce jumped to that conclusion. Why did he not instead make an effort to prevent his wife from going, as he thought she was, to her doom? The only manly thing to have done would have been to ask his wife to drop her friendship with Pape and order Pape out of the house." A notable speech, which had skilfully mingled an exhausting analysis of the facts with the appeal *ad misericordiam*, ended with a plea that Mrs Bryce had already suffered sufficiently for her indiscretion and that it might not yet be too late for a reconciliation between the parties.

Rufus Isaacs' speech, which had occupied nearly five hours on the thirteenth day of the trial, had covered the ground thoroughly and effectively, and Carson, who followed, said that after " the eloquent and exhaustive speech of my friend, Mr Isaacs," he did not intend to rehearse the whole matter. This was a wise decision for the case had already been attractively presented by Rufus Isaacs, who was representing a client who would excite more sympathy in the jury than could Harold Pape. Similarly Carson referred in his speech primarily to the effects which an adverse verdict would have on Mrs Bryce rather than on his own client, since a verdict for her would entail a verdict for him as well. He did not defend Pape's conduct, " but," he said, " all sentiment and decency do not die because a young man of twenty-four has the misfortune to fall in love with a young and pretty married woman." The peroration of his speech was an appeal for Rufus Isaacs' client: " As Mr Pape wrote these letters, so I beg you to look on them as only Mr Pape's acts—acts which he bitterly regrets.

Award him censure for his acts, but do not let these letters weigh in the scales of justice against a woman who was only the recipient of them, and against whom there is not one act or gesture in evidence that she has been other than a faithful wife to him who is now trying to get rid of her."

Carson's speech, which had lasted an hour and three-quarters, was followed by a lengthy reply on the whole case by Henry Duke, in the course of which he said that he had never heard a finer demonstration of the art of the advocate than that given by Rufus Isaacs. The summing up was indeterminate and the jury were absent for nearly an hour and a half. On their return, Mrs Bryce looked anxiously at the foreman, who declared that the jury had found that no adultery had been committed, " though the conduct of the co-respondent, as disclosed in this case, is deserving of the severest censure." There was an outburst of applause in Court, prompted, in the case of the majority, by the verdict rather than by the opinion of Harold Pape's conduct; but the applause was instantly suppressed and all eyes turned on Mrs Bryce. For she had fainted for the third and last time in the trial.

The case is a perfect example of the type of case which should never, in the interests of the parties, have come into Court at all. The private lives of the three were exposed to the full glare of publicity, and survived the exposure no better than would most. This does not mean that these lives were shown to be in any way immoral; it merely means that a jealous husband, employing detectives to track his wife, and a young lover, writing " riddle letters " in a code which would not deceive a child, are scarcely objects to command public respect. And the fifteen days of undesirable publicity were purchased at a cost of £15,000; for the four leading counsel had briefs marked at a hundred and fifty guineas with refreshers of a hundred guineas each a day, while there were in addition the various other sources of expenditure. (Counsel's fees in a *cause célèbre* are normally at a very rough estimate about half the total costs.) But for those whose interest in the case is less personal than that

of the protagonists, there is no need to regret the case, for
it provides, in addition to its intrinsic interest, an interesting
comparison of the methods of Rufus Isaacs and Carson in
handling the same material; for this case, being practically
the only one in which they were engaged in alliance, is in
some respects more instructive than the various cases in which
they appeared in opposition, and were consequently concerned with different interpretations of the facts.   Rufus
Isaacs' speech, too, affords a good instance of his skill in
handling the Bench; he had said to the jury, " you must be
satisfied that adultery has in fact been committed—it is not
enough to be satisfied that there was an opportunity for it;
you must be satisfied that they took the opportunity."   The
ensuing dialogue speaks for itself.

" That is not quite correct.   I shall leave two questions
to the jury—first, was there a guilty willingness, a guilty
desire between these parties, that is between both of them,
and, secondly, was there opportunity?   If these two were
present, the jury may infer that adultery has taken place."

" But the jury must be satisfied that adultery has taken
place."

" No: you go too far.   You suggest that the jury must
find the actual occasion; that is not so."

" I do not suggest that.   I only say that the jury must
be satisfied that adultery has been committed before they
can infer from opportunity and desire that it has."

" You may put two people in bed together; that fact
does not prove adultery, but you may infer it."

" My lord, I only mean that the jury must be satisfied
that adultery has taken place, and that they need not infer
it by reason of desire and opportunity being proved."

Rufus Isaacs then went on to say that the jury must be
satisfied beyond reasonable doubt of the accused persons'
guilt, and that he was very glad to accept that dictum from
the Bench.   Now, in point of fact, he had more or less
re-stated his own original position, but had attributed it to
the judge, whom he had taken good care not to antagonise.
It was in this sort of difficult situation that Rufus Isaacs

excelled. There have been prominent advocates who have
been quick to show their zeal for their clients' interests by
promptly quarrelling with the Bench on such occasions; but
in such situations discretion is generally the better part of
valour, and they might be wiser to imitate the adroit tactical
management of Rufus Isaacs.

CHAPTER XV

THE famous case of Joel and Sievier belongs to the
genre of the Chetwynd-Durham suit and the Hartopp
divorce case, and indeed is one of the last of such
cases; for the leisurely nineteenth century had been
succeeded by a sterner epoch. Nevertheless popular attention was caught by the Sievier case as strongly as it had been
by the Hartopp; nor were there wanting reasons. Both
protagonists were Turf personalities and in one way and
another considerably in the public eye. J. B. Joel, brother
to the famous Solly, was like him a man of great wealth,
who, after making a fortune in South Africa, had established
a racing stable in England; and indeed this case, in which
Mr Joel instituted criminal proceedings against Mr Sievier
for blackmail, was on its personal side the culmination of a
long-standing Turf quarrel between the two. Now the
Turf at that time contained no more interesting devotee
than " Bob " Sievier, as he was called by those who knew him
and thousands of those who did not. In his 'teens he had
served in the Army in the Zulu wars, and had then turned
actor; as a further proof of versatility he afterwards became
an owner and trainer of horses, in which capacity he became
in a comparatively short time one of the most successful
men on the Turf. But it was perhaps as the owner of the
famous filly, Sceptre, which won four out of the five
" classics," and in 1902 won the Derby for her owner that
he was best known, and, as the British public, or at any
rate that not inconsiderable section of it which " follows "
racing, has the pleasing custom of transferring to the owner
of a horse some of that affection naturally felt for an animal
which habitually proves a good investment, he was a popular
man.

Soon after his great triumph in 1902, however, Mr Sievier's luck for a time deserted him. In 1904, he felt constrained to bring an action for slander against Sir James Duke; he had briefed Rufus Isaacs, but he had not been able to appear and the case was lost. This misfortune caused him to give up his stud, and to recoup himself he founded the *Winning Post*, a " spicy " racing weekly, which instantly became very popular. One of the features of this paper was a weekly series entitled " Celebrities in Glass Houses," and on October 15th it was announced that the next subject would be J. B. Joel; on the 22nd, the article appeared. Now there had been for some time a feud between Mr Sievier and Mr Joel, and Mr Sievier's autobiography had contained some very biting references to him; nor was the treatment of Mr Joel in the *Winning Post* of the gentlest. In addition, Mr Sievier had discovered that in 1884 Mr Joel left South Africa in circumstances which it was thought Mr Joel would not be anxious to have made public.

The culmination of the feud was reached in June, 1908, when Mr Joel instituted a prosecution for blackmail. On June 29th Mr Sievier was arrested at a race meeting, and on the next day appeared on preliminary inquiry at Bow Street on the charge of threatening to publish a libel on J. B. Joel to extort £5,000, and of promising to abstain from printing and publishing such matter to extort £5,000. The gravamen of the charge, as outlined in the Police-Court proceedings, was that Sievier had tried to get £5,000 from Joel as the price of his immunity from further attacks upon him in the *Winning Post*, and in particular to prevent the publication of his portrait between that of two murderers. After a hearing of some days, Sievier was committed for trial, and the case was opened at the Old Bailey on Tuesday, July 28th.

The trial attracted enormous public attention, because of the position of both men on the Turf and in the world of sport (indeed, by a curious coincidence their recreational interests are almost identical, according to *Who's Who*, Mr Joel's being " all kinds of sports " while Mr Sievier " hunts, shoots, plays cricket, and indeed all games.") But the public was attracted, too, by the clash of counsel, for once again Rufus Isaacs and Carson were in opposition, Charles Gill, K.C., and Archibald Bodkin, afterwards Public Prosecutor, appearing with Carson, and Montagu Shearman, K.C., and R. D. Muir, who had conducted the Police-Court proceedings, with Isaacs. But the trial had not gone very far before it was seen that this time it was Rufus Isaacs who dominated the Court and riveted the attention of the public; deadly in cross-examination, lucid in exposition and vigorous in his pleading, his conduct of the case was masterly.

What the prosecution had to prove in order to substantiate their allegation of blackmail was that Sievier had used his attacks on Joel as a lever to extort money from him, and that he had pressed Joel to buy him off. The prosecution started with one outside fact apparently in its favour, namely that Joel was a rich man and Sievier at the time was in financial difficulties; but this was a consideration that Isaacs was later to turn dramatically in favour of his client. From the start of the case Isaacs realised exactly where to join issue; if he could show that, so far from Sievier despatching emissaries to Joel to demand money from him, Sievier had made no move to approach him, and had in fact himself been approached by Joel, the presumption against Sievier's having blackmailing intentions was tremendously strong. This was really the central consideration in the case, and never for a moment did Isaacs lose sight of it himself or allow the jury to do so.

The small Court was packed when Carson opened the case for the prosecution. He painted a graphic picture of the misery caused to Joel by the frequent attacks upon him, and his anxiety to get them stopped for his own sake and that of his family. While Joel was in this state of mind, Sievier was in financial difficulties, and the prosecution's allegation was that he took advantage of Joel's misery and distress to extort £5,000 from him. Joel and Sievier had had no direct transactions, and the prosecution's case was that Sievier had used the offices of two mutual friends, Bendon, who was a broker on the Stock Exchange and an owner of race-horses, and one Mills, who was a betting agent. These two who had had a number of interviews at Joel's house to discuss the matter were, in addition to Joel himself, the chief witnesses for the prosecution, and much, therefore, depended on Isaacs' handling of them.

In answer to Carson, Bendon had told how he had tried to borrow £2,000 for Sievier from Solly Joel, and that on his refusal he had applied to J. B. Joel; but Sievier had said that he would only deal with J. B. Joel through Mills. At the start of his cross-examination, Isaacs drew from the witness the admission that he was anxious to oblige the Joels, for whom he did business; and further that it was Mills' influence, and no question of monetary transaction, which had prevailed on Sievier to discontinue the attacks on Solly in the *Winning Post*. And then, leaning forward a little, Isaacs put the question:

" Had you any notion that a trap was being laid for Mr Sievier? " and then the soft voice, hardening in its emphasis, he added slowly " Trap is the word."

" I suspected something at the second interview at Mr Jack Joel's house. I told Mills I thought it a very dirty business."

" When you called it a dirty business you were referring to the trap? "

" Principally."

And then Isaacs asked: " Did you think Mr Solly Joel was more to be trusted? " to which the witness answered that " we knew him better," and the Court laughed at the naïveté of the reply.

It was the next witness, Mills, " who executed bets for Mr Solly Joel, but did not receive any commission, being content to back the same winners," who had been the chief intermediary; but Isaacs' treatment of him was on the same lines. Mills, in his examination-in-chief, told how he first saw Joel, who said that he wanted to settle the matter; this information he passed on to Sievier, who had said that he would do it for £5,000. Joel had offered half, but Sievier had refused, saying that if Joel did not agree he would publish his photograph in the *Winning Post* between those of two murderers. At this Joel had consented to £5,000 on condition that Sievier wrote a letter to be kept by Mills, saying that he would molest him no further.

But witness had substantiated Bendon's statement that his own influence was sufficient to induce Sievier to give up the attacks on Solly; and Isaacs urged the point that a much more powerful influence might well have operated to the same effect in this case.

" Did you say that Mr Joel had told you that Mr Rothschild had said that this matter must stop? "

" Yes."

" Mr Rothschild is a man much respected in racing and other circles and what he said would have great influence with Mr Sievier? "

" Yes."

" And it did have? "

" Yes."

On the next day, Isaacs resumed his cross-examination of the witness.

" You must have been amazed when you heard of Sievier's arrest? "

" I was amazed. I first heard from Chief-Inspector Drew that what had taken place was a criminal offence."

" You realised the part you had played in it? "

" I realised my position was an unpleasant one."

And then he asked the same question as he had already asked, with such effect, of Bendon.

" You thought a trap had been laid for Sievier? "

" Yes."

" Did you think that the person who had got you into it had played you a dirty trick? "

" Yes."

" That was Joel? "

" Yes."

" Do you think Joel played you a dirty trick? "

" Most decidedly."

It will be noticed that this cumulative series of questions, all asked to establish the same point, and pressing it home with tremendous force, was a series of. what are known as " leading questions." This form of questioning, which by the form of the interrogation suggests the answer, would not be valid in examination-in-chief or re-examination; but it is a rule of evidence that it is permissible in cross-examination, where of course, it is unlikely that the witness, being " hostile," will take his evidence from the suggestion of counsel.

By the time Joel took Mills' place in the witness box, the prospects of the prosecution were distinctly less rosy, for Isaacs had handled the two witnesses with skill; he had treated them gently on the whole, but he had elicited the points which he wished to establish, with dramatic directness, and when they left the box they gave the impression of men who had been brought unawares into a transaction which they would never have touched had they known its true character. But it was Isaacs' cross-examination of Joel which was the masterpiece of the trial. Hour after hour the Court watched him, fascinated, as his keen, relentless questions drew from the millionaire the whole shabby story of his desire to prosecute Sievier, his use of Sievier's friend Mills as go-between, and his concealment of Chief-Inspector Drew in the wall behind the curtain during his interview with Mills. Isaacs' dry humour raised a laugh at the start. He had put it to Joel that he wanted to prosecute not to give hush-money, to which Joel replied:

" Yes. There never was sufficient material on which to prosecute."

" Well I am glad to hear you say that," remarked Isaacs. " I rather agree."

But there was not much laughter during that ruthless cross-examination.

" At the first interview with Mills did you ask him to see what Sievier would take? "

" I did not use those words. I asked him to see what he could do. I expected he wanted money."

" Did you then hope to get evidence against him so as to prosecute him? "

" Yes, if the opportunity occurred." And then, conscious that Isaacs was getting the better of him, and anxious to justify himself, he added: " He had been persecuting me for four years."

But Isaacs went on ruthlessly to cross-examine him with regard to his use of Mills.

" Did you know that Mills was a great friend of Sievier, possessing great influence over him? "

" Yes."

" And you used him for that reason? "

" Not intentionally. I did not know how far it would go."

" It would go all the way as far as you were concerned."

" Yes, certainly."

" You were using Mills. Do you consider that was a dishonourable thing to do? "

" It was an unfortunate thing," admitted the witness.

" What! " said Isaacs, his composure for once deserting him, and an unaccustomed note of anger sounding in his voice. " It was a dishonourable thing. Who wrote the telegram," he continued, " ' £5,000 ridiculous after offer to accept £2,000. Would give half ' ? "

" My solicitor."

And then once again that brief, deadly question: " It was a trap? "

The question had already been answered twice by witnesses for the prosecution. This time there was no answer, but only a justification, which was more complete an admission than an answer would have been: " He had threatened to publish my picture."

The Court had been spellbound during this lengthy cross-examination, but the atmosphere changed from one of dramatic intensity to one as near comedy as is possible in a Court of Justice, when Rufus Isaacs put his client, Sievier, in the box, as the sole witness for the defence. His answers to Isaacs' examination-in-chief were, however, important, for he explained how he had told Mills that he would keep Joel's name out of the paper to oblige him, but that he did not want to make any money out of it. He did, however, wish to borrow some; and, after giving him a cheque for £1,000 on the 24th, Mills had surprised and delighted him by telling him that he could lend him £5,000.

Under cross-examination, however, Sievier began to develop theories of his own. Rufus Isaacs, as we have seen, had been careful to make no allegations against Mills and Bendon; he had taken the line that they had been drawn into the business, unaware of Joel's desire to prosecute Sievier. Sievier, however, in cross-examination, now suggested that both Mills and Bendon were committing perjury and were in a conspiracy against him. He must have realised how far this theory differed from Isaacs' interpretation of their actions, and if this was really Sievier's serious opinion at the time, it must have been due to the not unnatural indignation of a man who feels that he has been let down by his friends. His evidence, however, was given in a very cheerful, natural manner, which kept the Court in a good humour. He raised considerable laughter in Court when in answer to Carson's question: " He must be an awful liar? " he said " Either he is or I am! " And again, when Carson said " Mills was pressing money on you and you were trying to resist it? " the Court found Sievier's mock-horrified protest " Oh dear, no. Oh! Lord, no! " quite irresistible.

As Isaacs had called no witnesses to fact for the defence except the prisoner, the right to speak last should normally have been his. But the rule is that documentary evidence is for this purpose the same as spoken evidence, and Isaacs had put in documentary evidence; it was not clear, however, that the evidence which he had put in was such as to be sufficient to deprive him of his right. An argument followed, but in the end Carson chivalrously waived his claim on the ground that if there was any doubt the prisoner should have the benefit of it. At this Sievier thanked him cheerfully from the dock, only to meet with a scowl from Carson and the reply, " I don't want any thanks from you." An appreciation of life's lighter moments was perhaps not foremost in the armoury of gifts of this great fighting advocate.

Carson's speech took full advantage of the new turn to the defence, which Sievier's evidence implied. " The whole case of the last two days," he urged, " has been abandoned at the eleventh hour," and went on to claim that the only defence was perjury on the part of Joel, Bendon and Mills. The speech, which was spoken with considerable power, contained one great phrase, " If you do, this will be a day of Magna Charta for blackmailers," and ended with an appeal to the jury not to let Sievier's popularity affect their verdict or deflect them from their duty.

And then Isaacs rose to make his final address. He had made a great impression with his cross-examination of Joel, but since then the case for the defence had been complicated somewhat by Sievier's quixotic theories, and the jury had heard Carson's oratory. Isaacs first, therefore, replied to Carson's taunt about " eleventh hour " defences; he pointed out that the question of a trap had been raised from the first, and suggested that it had been unfair for Carson to wring from Sievier an answer to the effect that Joel and Mills had conspired against him. He took up, too, Carson's reference to prejudice. " Prejudice! " he exclaimed. " There has been enough prejudice introduced against Mr Sievier in this matter. The fact that he has had to borrow money has been used against him." What, in any case, was the reason for this complicated method of proceeding? Joel could have sought his remedy by action for libel or by prosecution for criminal libel, and to the latter charge the mere truth of the statement complained of would have constituted no defence.

He then came on to the central issue of the case. " It is significant," he said, " that for seven weeks from April 29th Mr Sievier made no single move to extort money. According to Mr Joel himself, everything that Mr Sievier could have said had been said before the alleged threat . . . As to Joel's mind on June 23rd, he knew Sievier was broke, and I put it to you that his thought was, 'Here is my opportunity for getting rid of the man for Heaven knows how long. He is broke, and here comes the opportunity for my money. I must get somebody to help me.' That somebody had been Sievier's friend and the method was as described." And Isaacs' voice took on a note of indignation as he went on, "I make no complaint as to putting a detective in hiding in order to detect a crime which it was known was going to be committed. But in this case the trap was laid to induce a man to commit acts which could be made to look like a crime. That is a dirty, disgusting, disgraceful transaction from which every man's mind will recoil with horror. What was the beginning of the conversation with Mills? Joel said 'Well, what have you done?' Let me draw particular attention to the reply, 'I have done what you want.' . . . The prosecution must prove that the proposal came from the prisoner. I can hardly restrain my feelings in discussing it. The proposal in this case came from Joel, not from the man in the dock."

The voice rose, as he swept on to his peroration: "Imagine a man with the power of money behind him, knowing that another man whom he hated was hard up and broke. Imagine him getting hold of the man's best friend, and most trusted confidant, setting him to work to make him take gold, forcing him to take it, and then arresting him, prosecuting him . . ." And then in a quieter tone, compelling by its contrast, "Sir Edward Carson has eloquently put before you the wrongs of Joel. I am not going to appeal for sympathy for Sievier, or for mercy, but to ask you to weigh the evidence which has been presented to you."

He had finished and, as he sat down, volleys of applause rang out from the whole Court, and could hardly be restrained. When silence was at last obtained, Lord Alverstone, the Lord Chief Justice, began his summing up which proved to be rather long and indecisive. And then the jury retired to consider their verdict. On their return there was a great hush of expectation, and a tenseness of suppressed excitement could be felt all over the Court.   But when the foreman of the jury pronounced " Not guilty," restraint was cast aside and an enormous cheer went up, which was promptly taken up outside and re-echoed by the vast crowd waiting patiently outside the Old Bailey.   Five thousand of them had gathered to welcome the popular hero, who on surveying his supporters must have thought that he was emerging from the frying pan into the fire; he wisely decided to leave by a side door, but there was no escaping the popular approval, and Sievier was driven away through cheering crowds with the delighted coachman pointing to the hero with his whip and shouting " I've got him in here; I've got him in here." When Rufus Isaacs left the Old Bailey he was greeted with round after round of tremendous cheering, a tribute at once to the way in which he had conducted his case and the popular conclusion to which he had brought it.

These scenes of enthusiasm evoked a good deal of hostile comment at the time, and *The Times* in particular devoted a leading article to gloomy prophecies of what such conduct must lead to.   It is certainly true that scenes such as these are unsuitable, possibly at any time, and certainly as a reception of the verdict of a Court of Justice; to Carson particularly, as he left the Old Bailey—he was on the unpopular side this time—the sight must have called up memories of the disgusting frenzy of triumph which followed the downfall of Oscar Wilde.   It is said, too—and truly said—that the case of Joel and Sievier was not of a very elevating nature; but the Courts of Law do not choose, nor do they create, the circumstances which lead people to seek their intervention, and many of the greatest legal battles and the most important judicial decisions have a petty, or even a sordid, background.   And Isaacs himself had no reason to look back on the case with other than a just pride, for it had been the occasion of one of his best speeches to a jury, and one of the most deadly cross-examinations in the history of the Courts.

CHAPTER XVI

COMMERCIAL MAGNATES *v.* PRESS LORDS

THE Sievier case followed the famous libel action of Lever *v. The Daily Mail*, in which Rufus Isaacs and Carson were in opposition. The facts of this case, however, which originated in a great newspaper campaign, left Rufus Isaacs with little chance, save to make the best of a bad job. William Lever, afterwards the first Lord Leverhulme, who had started life as an assistant in his father's grocery store, had later turned his attention to the manufacture of soap, in which he had so prospered that a business which had started as a factory at Warrington, where twenty tons of soap were turned out weekly, had expanded in twenty years into the giant concern at Port Sunlight with a capital of £6,000,000, a weekly productivity of three thousand tons, and a pay-roll of three thousand five hundred employees. In 1906, however, there came a threat in the shape of an increase in the price of the raw materials used in the manufacture of soap; but Mr Lever decided not to offset this by a rise in the price of the finished product. Instead he reduced the weight of the standard sixteen ounce tablet to fifteen ounces and sold it at the same price, giving notice of the change of weight. This did not solve the problem, however, and accordingly Mr Lever hit on the idea of a great soap trust, so as to economise the costs of competition and advertisement. But in this he had reckoned without Lord Northcliffe and *The Daily Mail*, which decided that the creation of a trust was merely intended to run up the prices against the public, who would be deprived of the protection of salutary competition. It would, therefore, be contrary to the public interest to permit the unchallenged existence of the combine, and it would certainly be contrary to the advertising interest; for Lever Bros.

had expended half a million of money in their outlay on Press advertisements, and, as the *Times* remarked in a leading article commenting on the verdict, " the interests of the accuser, too, were against a soap trust, which would tend to diminish the number of advertisements."

The Daily Mail has in its history waged many campaigns; all have been vigorous, and many successful. Whatever its ultimate success, in point of vigour the attack on the soap trust left nothing to be desired. In the autumn months of 1906, article succeeded article in *The Daily Mail* and the *Evening News,* developing one or another of the lines of attack; for the charges were numerous. Lever Brothers had disguised the reduction of weight in the sixteen ounce tablets, so as to deceive the public; they had dismissed a large number of employees in consequence of the amalgamation; they had cornered all the raw materials in the market, so as to be able to control prices; they had used unsavoury fish-oil in the manufacture of soap; they had attempted to bribe the Press, but had had to abandon the effort because patriotic papers like *The Daily Mail* refused to be bribed: such was the burden of the attack, and it was reinforced by headlines such as " Soap Trust Arithmetic; How Fifteen Ounces make a Pound," " Squeezing the Public. Trust Soaps Already Dearer. The Sunlight Sales Falling. How to Fight the Trusts," " Cruel Blow to the Poor," and so on, while cartoons appeared headed " Port Moonshine." The attack got home; Mr Lever was forced to restore the sixteen ounce tablets, and to resume advertising in the Press. The two million preference shares had been reduced in value a pound apiece, and the whole structure of the Company had received a staggering and a damaging blow. In the circumstances only one course was possible, and Mr Lever issued a writ for libel, claiming heavy damages.

There was no doubt that *The Daily Mail* had overreached themselves, and let their zeal outrun their discretion. The only hope for the defence, as Rufus Isaacs saw, was for him, in cross-examination of Mr Lever, to extort sufficient admissions to show that there was a strong basis for *The Daily Mail's* main case, compared with which the exaggerations of the actual presentation of the case were incidental. But when the case came on at the Liverpol Assizes in July, 1907, Carson, in a comprehensive and eloquent opening, put the case for Lever Brothers in a very strong light, and then at once called Mr Lever, who proved as efficient in the witness box as in the conduct of his business.. Rufus Isaacs brought all his powers to bear in cross-examination, but Mr Lever, conscious of the integrity of his motives and his expert knowledge of the whole question at issue, remained unshaken. When the end of the second day of the trial arrived, Rufus Isaacs had made no headway; it was clear to him that the case was hopeless. To continue would only make bad worse and aggravate the damages, especially as Carson, in calling Mr Lever, had challenged Rufus Isaacs to call Lord Northcliffe; and Lord Northcliffe, who, however pure his intentions, had no expert knowledge of the facts, could not hope to survive Carson's cross-examination with the same degree of immunity as Mr Lever had survived Rufus Isaacs'. Rufus Isaacs sized up the situation, and informed his clients as to the position, advising them to make an immediate settlement as the best way of cutting their losses. They agreed to this course of action, and empowered Rufus Isaacs to settle for whatever sum Mr Lever should demand. Now Mr Lever had no intention of taking less than £50,000, but, when Rufus Isaacs met Carson next morning, he offered at first only £10,000; it was not that he expected this sum to satisfy the plaintiff, but a low initial offer was the best method of creating an atmosphere of moderate amounts. The offer was refused by Carson on behalf of his client, and after further negotiation the sum was fixed at £50,000. A juror was accordingly withdrawn and Lever Brothers had won the final round of the long strugle in the short space of two and a half days.

That Rufus Isaacs acted correctly in the interests of justice and wise in the interests of his clients in advising a settlement, is indisputable. In fact, Mr Justice Lawrence went so far as to say, " on the evidence before me it is the right and proper and only honourable course to take." Admittedly the damages were large—they were the largest ever awarded in a libel action to that date—but they were not unduly large in relation to the damage suffered or to the great wealth and position of both parties; and, in comparison with the sums not infrequently awarded in breach of contract cases, £50,000 is by no means an enormous sum. It is quite possible indeed that if Rufus Isaacs had allowed the case to go to the end, the damages would have been higher. *The Daily Mail* at all events had no dissatisfaction with the settlement made on their behalf: " In view," they wrote, " of the unshaken testimony of Mr Lever in the witness box, no other result was possible. The effect of his statements on oath and the impression which they produced upon the Court, left no course open to us but to withdraw the plea of justification which had been entered, and, in expressing our entire approval of the action of our counsel, we do not desire to depart in any particular from the words which he used . . . We fully and frankly adopt every word used by our counsel, both by way of withdrawal and by way of apology, and we have only to add that we are glad to observe that he accepted without question Mr Lever's own estimate of the amount of money which we were to pay as damages."

The year 1908 saw another forensic duel between Rufus Isaacs and Carson of a very different sort; this was the mammoth contest of Wyler *v.* Lewis, perhaps as protracted and difficult a case as has ever been heard in the Courts. Both parties were connected with firms of stockbrokers, and the case arose out of a long struggle for the control of the Nyassa Company which in 1893 had acquired by charter sovereign rights, administrative powers, and a commercial monopoly in Portuguese Nyassaland. Isidore Wyler had originally been approached to finance the company, but Lewis and Marks had tried unsuccessfully to negotiate a purchase of the rights. Then, according to the plaintiff, they entered into a conspiracy to induce the company to repudiate the agreement so that they might themselves acquire control; and ultimately when an agreement was entered into for a form of joint control, they had not intended to carry it out, but had entered it merely so as to be able to oust Wyler from his interest in the company, and by intentionally mismanaging the concern had brought it to voluntary liquidation. Lewis and Marks denied the charges, and claimed that Wyler had never entered into a valid agreement with the original Nyassa Company. Rufus Isaacs led for the plaintiffs and Carson, supported by Mr Montagu Lush, K.C., for the defendants. The trial lasted thirty-three days, Rufus Isaacs' opening speech lasting for two whole days and Isidore Wyler occupying the witness box for eleven, which, as Mr Justice Phillimore remarked " is as long, probably longer, than any witness in any other known case." The jury finally found for the plaintiffs with an award of £64,472 damages; but Carson took the case to the Court of Appeal, where the decision was reversed after an argument extending over eighteen days. Rufus Isaacs' speech on this occasion occupied nine days, which was probably longer than any other speech ever made in the Court of Appeal.

Much shorter and much simpler, and infinitely more dramatic than this commercial marathon was the case of Cadbury v. *The Evening Standard,* the last great action in which Rufus Isaacs and Carson opposed each other in private practice. As in the case of Lever v. *The Daily Mail,* a great commercial firm had been goaded by the incessant attacks of a leading newspaper into adopting the only weapon available against the Press, a libel action in the Courts. But in this case there could be no question of commercial bias on the part of *The Evening Standard,* nor had the facts merely to be stated in full in order to reveal the exaggerations of the charges. Such bias as the *Standard* had was a legitimate political bias, since, as Mr Marjoribanks observed, " beneath the surface the whole ethical foundation of the doctrine of Free Trade was in question." For the Cadbury family, as is well-known, embodied many charac--

teristics; they were manufacturers, newspaper proprietors and politicians. They were philanthropists too, and temperance reformers, Quakers in religion and Radicals in politics. They combined the control of the *Daily News* with the institution and supervision of the model village at Bourneville. Such versatility is highly commendable, but a little dangerous. For instance, the political portion of Cadbury's, as represented in the *Daily News,* had taken a leading part in the agitation against Chinese slavery, which had so materially assisted the Liberal triumph of 1906. But supposing it turned out that the commercial part of Cadbury's was fed by the produce of slave labour; where stood Radicalism then? And supposing it transpired that the trim gardens and pleasant parks of Bourneville were laid with the sweat and the agony of less fortunate employees whose sufferings were the dark secret of distant lands; where was philanthropy then? It was just such a contrast as this that the *Standard* believed itself to have discovered; and, with an animation which was the more lively in view of the approaching General Election, they vociferated the question in a rising crescendo of majestic wrath. Were these things consistent with the philanthropy which had built Bournville, with the Radicalism which had denounced so indignantly the horrors of Chinese slavery?

For, in point of regrettable fact, part of the raw material used by Cadbury's *was* the product of slave labour. This was that portion of it which it was their custom to import from the Portuguese islands of San Thomé and Principe on the West Coast of Africa. Information reached Cadbury's that there was in force here a system of compulsory labour, barely distinguishable from the worst forms of slavery, and the firm felt it to be its duty to make inquiries. Ultimately, in conjunction with the other great cocoa manufacturers, Messrs. Fry and Messrs. Rowntree, they sent out Mr J. Burtt to investigate conditions on the spot, the greater part of the cost of the expedition, which was in the neighbourhood of £4,000, being borne by Cadbury's. Mr Burtt's report was an emphatic endorsement of the view that the labour system in the islands was one of slavery; further, it was slavery of a peculiarly brutal sort—having, in fact, all the attributes which Victorian Radicalism attributed to slavery, and which were perhaps more often found in " free labour." Mr William Cadbury took the report to the Foreign Office, then presided over by Sir Edward Grey, and asked his advice as to whether the report should be published and whether Cadbury's should stop buying their raw material from this tainted source.   Sir Edward answered both questions in the negative; His Majesty's Government was on excellent terms with the Portuguese Government, and diplomatic pressure would be brought to bear on our most ancient and honoured allies, which must not be anticipated by action on the part of private individuals.   This was in October of 1906; but the ways of diplomacy are traditionally slow, and it was January, 1909, before diplomatic intervention was finally judged to have failed. Messrs. Cadbury then stopped buying from the islands, eight years having passed since the suggestion of slavery was first made known to them.   And eight years, measured in the agony of a crucified humanity, is a long time.

In the circumstances the attitude of the *Standard* was not surprising.   Whatever it was that Cadbury's had done had been ineffective, and they had continued to buy the cocoa year after year in full knowledge of the conditions in which it was produced.   And these were the people who in a different capacity had led the campaign against " Chinese Slavery " in 1906!   There had been an election in 1906, and there was another imminent in 1909; so what had been sauce for the Liberal goose could clearly be sauce for the Tory gander.   Consequently the *Standard* referred to Mr William Cadbury's journey of investigation to the islands as a " Quaker filibustering expedition," and in an article of October, 1908, said: " We congratulate Mr Cadbury upon his journey, which does not come too soon . . . One might have supposed that Messrs. Cadbury would themselves long ago have ascertained the conditions and circumstances of those labourers on the West Coast of Africa and the islands adjacent, who provide them with raw material." The article went on to refer to Mr H. W. Nevinson's report—for Mr Nevinson had been commissioned by an American magazine to report on conditions and had painted a most lurid picture of their barbarity—and said: " it is not called slavery—' contract labour ' they name it now—but in most of its essentials it is that monstrous trade in human flesh and blood against which the Quaker and Radical ancestors of Mr Cadbury thundered in the better days of England . . . The so-called contract is a farce . . . There is only one thing more amazing than his statements, and that is the strange tranquillity with which they are received by those virtuous people in England whom they intimately concern."

The attack provoked the only possible reply; the issue of a writ for libel. The case came on for hearing at Birmingham in bitterly cold weather towards the end of November. Public interest in it was naturally enormous, greater even than in the Lever case for, like the trial of Sir Edward Russell, the case seemed in some sort a rehearsal for the General Election. The great Liberal family concern of Cadbury's was matched against one of the foremost of Conservative newspapers, and it was, therefore, politically appropriate that the *Standard* should entrust its fortunes to Sir Edward Carson, and Messrs. Cadbury rely on two Liberal Members of Parliament for whom the future held high office, Rufus Isaacs and John Simon. Carson, however, was supported by counsel whose future lay elsewhere than in politics—Eldon Bankes, a future Judge, who had been with Rufus Isaacs in his first great newspaper libel action of Chamberlain *v. The Star*, and Henry M'Cardie, whose courageous attitude and independence of mind were subsequently to make him outstanding among post-war judges.

Rufus Isaacs, in opening the case for Cadbury's, had many factors in his favour. There was the high reputation and undoubted integrity of his clients; there was the opinion of the Foreign Office, which was to be supported by the

evidence of Sir Edward Grey himself; there were the efforts
which Cadbury's had in fact made, the visits of Mr William
Cadbury and the equipment and despatch of Mr Burtt's
commission. All these points were touched upon and ampli-
fied by Rufus Isaacs, who also contended that the case had
nothing to do with the *Daily News*, with which in fact Mr
William Cadbury had no connection. The issue, as he saw
it, really was whether it was true to say that when the
knowledge of the conditions was brought to his clients, they
made no attempt to ameliorate them, but wilfully shut their
eyes in order to continue in the enjoyment of their profits.
This was not exactly what the *Standard* maintained in their
plea of justification, however; they admitted that efforts
had been made—indeed, in view of the facts, it would have
been difficult not to do so—but suggested that they had been
insincere efforts, undertaken in order to satisfy appearances.
This change in defence gave Rufus Isaacs an advantage of
which he was quick to avail himself, for it added the charge
of hypocrisy to that of indifference. The *Standard*, in effect,
had said: " You have done a great deal, but you are a set
of canting hypocrites; you are liars and frauds who have
been pretending to do things; you have been pretending to
work, to labour, on behalf of those people; you have been
doing it simply in order that you may be able to say so one
day, and to point to what you have done." Such, said Rufus
Isaacs, were the charges which the *Standard* were called
upon to substantiate.

Rufus Isaacs' principal witness was Mr William Cadbury
—one of the five members of the family who were directors
of their firm and plaintiffs in the action—to whom had been
assigned by the firm the task of superintending the investigation of conditions. His evidence, however, was interrupted
by the arrival of Sir Edward Grey, who was at once put
into the box and examined by Rufus Isaacs. He confirmed
the contention of the plaintiffs with regard to the attitude
of the Foreign Office, namely that there should be no publication of the report nor public step taken as a result of it
before it had been laid before the Portuguese Government.

" My recollection," he said, " is quite clear on the point—that a certain situation had arisen, and that the information which Messrs. Cadbury had should not be made public use of at the time. My opinion was that the information should be dealt with first by negotiation with the Portuguese Government before any public step was taken." Mr Cadbury's evidence was then resumed and he told the story of his efforts on behalf of the unfortunate " contract labourers " and of the difficulties which had stood in his way; he had told Sir Edward Grey, too, that if he thought that their buying of the cocoa stood in the way of action, he had only to write to them and they would do what he thought best. That Mr Cadbury was an honourable man, with a genuine horror of the conditions of slave labour was obvious; that he had made considerable efforts to do his duty in ameliorating those conditions was clear from the evidence. And it might have been expected that in his own citadel of Birmingham, where his qualities were best known and respected, his evidence, with the moral backing of his great reputation, would have carried the day. Probably, opposed by any ordinary advocate, his position, if not impregnable, would have been safe enough. But Carson was no ordinary advocate, and he invested his conduct of the cross-examination with the whole force of his tremendous personality. Much of it has already appeared in Mr Marjoribank's book, but it is nevertheless entitled to reproduction here; for, although to get the full effect of it one must see the tall, lean figure, hear the deep, Irish brogue and feel the impact of that towering personality, even the coldness of the printed word cannot rob it of its vigour and effectiveness.

" Is it a fact," asked Carson, " that San Thomé's cocoa has been slave grown to your own knowledge for eight years? "

" As far as the report from Ayola and the island of San Thomé is concerned, I am quite satisfied that slave-grown cocoa describes the condition, generally speaking."

" Would you say it was slavery of a very atrocious character? "

" Generally speaking, as far as the collecting of labour in Ayola goes, that is true."

" The cocoa you were buying was procured by atrocious methods of slavery? "

" Yes."

" Men, women, children taken forcibly away from their homes against their will? "

" Yes."

" Were they marched on the road like cattle? "

" I cannot answer that question. They were marched in forced marches down to the coast."

" Were they labelled when they went on board ship? "

" Yes."

" How far had they to march? "

" Various distances. Some came from more than a thousand miles, some from quite near the coast."

" Never to return again? "

" Never to return."

" From the information which you procured, did they go down in shackles? "

" It is the usual custom, I believe, to shackle them at night on the march."

" Those who could not keep up with the march were murdered? "

" I have seen statements to that effect."

" You do not doubt it? "

" I do not doubt that it has been so in some cases."

Carson passed on to question him about the interview with Sir Edward Grey.

" Did you expect the Foreign Minister was going to keep in his mind what you had said about it, and if he sent you a line you would stop buying cocoa? "

" Yes, I thought he would."

" You never took any pains to put that on paper for him? "

" No."

" How many interviews do you think he would have a day? "

" I don't know."

" You expected him to keep it in mind and drop you a postcard if he wanted you to do anything? "

" Yes. I never had any doubt about the good faith of Sir Edward Grey."

Carson's last two questions were shattering in their directness.

" From 1901 to 1908, when you ceased dealing with the islands, was there anything effective that you did at all in the direction of reforms? "

" I think there was myself. It is perhaps a matter of opinion. I readily admit that my efforts resulted in a great deal less than I should have liked."

" Have you formed any estimate of the number of slaves who lost their lives in preparing your cocoa during those eight years? "

" No, no."

The last answer was half a cry, half a protest, and Mr Cadbury winced visibly as it was put. On the next day, however, Rufus Isaacs' re-examined him with a view to rehabilitating the position. The re-examination was directed to establish three points: that the individual ceasing to buy on the part of Cadbury's would have been useless; that the firm had been advised to give the Portuguese Government time to act; and that it had been actuated throughout by a sincere desire for reform. Rufus Isaacs' last two questions, though not informed by the force of Carson's, effectively concentrated attention on the aspect of the case, favourable to his client.

" Can you tell me," he asked, " during the time when you were carrying on the work for your firm and other firms, looking back upon it now, is there any step which you could has taken which you did not? "

" No, I am sure there is not."

" Whether the Foreign Office succeeded or not was not a matter within your province? "

" No."

Later, Mr George Cadbury, the head of the firm and a

director of the *Daily News*, gave evidence, and in cross-examination admitted to Carson that from 1901 to 1907 there was no mention in the *Daily News* of conditions in San Thomé, which were worse than those in the Transvaal, against which the *Daily News* had waged its campaign. Having secured as much advantage as he had in his cross-examination of the brothers Cadbury, Carson boldly resolved to call no witnesses for the defence. It would have been expected that he would at any rate have called the defendants, who had put in a plea of justification, but Carson decided that his case should consist entirely of his own speech to the jury. In this he was wise, for he had in his cross-examination made the case peculiarly his own; to call his clients would have been to expose them to Rufus Isaacs' cross-examination and thus to give him the chance, which he wanted, of deflecting the case from the plain ethical issue of slavery, to which Carson was so successfully steering it. Carson's speech was a masterpiece of strong, passionate pleading, a speech, as Rufus Isaacs termed it, of " power and scorn and invective." The essence of his speech was simple. Here was slavery of the vilest sort; and Cadbury's had spent £1,300,000 on slave-grown cocoa. What was their explanation? " Oh, we continued this for eight years for humanitarian purposes; we did it very much against our sentiments, in the interests of the people of San Thomé and Principe." Then there was the defence, " if we didn't buy it somebody else would "; what a splendid defence for a receiver of stolen goods! In point of fact, Cadbury's had been spinning the matter out for eight years, and continuing to buy cocoa on the grounds that it was a useful lever in negotiation. And what was the upshot? Nothing had been done till the end, when they announced that " our Mr Cadbury has found things so bad that we must discontinue using all this cocoa and with great regret give up our humanitarian policy and withdraw the lever that has been applied for eight years."

Rufus Isaacs in his reply criticised strongly a case which relied solely on counsel's speech. Why had not the defendants been called?   Why especially had not Mr Nevinson been called although he had been sitting in the front of the Court all the week, passing notes to counsel?   He then detailed the various steps taken by Messrs. Cadbury, in refutation of Carson's contention that nothing had been done save to spin out time. The basic charge was one of hypocrisy. " But is it," he asked, " consistent with the charge of hypocrisy that Mr Cadbury should risk his life and health in a land devastated by pestilence, and then, when he saw for himself that the promised reforms were not being carried out, to cable home to use the last weapon against the planters —namely, 'stop buying'? "   The effort had been made by the defence to represent the matter as one of public interest; but it must not be regarded as that.   The honour of the firm of Cadbury was in question, and that alone was the issue.

The conclusion of Rufus Isaacs' speech was greeted with applause in Court, and the detailed summing up of Mr Justice Pickford turned out to be definitely favourable to the plaintiff's case.   It was no surprise, therefore, when after fifty-five minutes the jury returned to announce a verdict for the plaintiffs, and cheers again broke out in Court, but they stopped abruptly when, in answer to the Judge's question as to the amount of damages, the foreman replied that they had awarded Messrs. Cadbury's a farthing.

The award of the smallest coin of the realm is, of course, contemptuous damages.   The result was, therefore, in a sense a victory for the *Standard;* and it was certainly a personal triumph for the advocacy of Sir Edward Carson. But it is easily possible to exaggerate the extent of the victory, for there is a clear difference between the award of a farthing's damages and a verdict for the defendants.   " The verdict is not, " said the *Times,* " and—the small damages notwithstanding—ought not to be construed as in any way a verdict for the defendants."   Indeed, if the *Standard* did claim it as a victory, it was at best a Pyrrhic one; for the costs, which were heavy, were adjudged to follow the verdict and were awarded against them.   Nevertheless the contemptuous damages undoubtedly betokened a censure of

Messrs. Cadbury, and such a censure was no mean embarrassment to the famous philanthropists. It is in the circumstances impossible not to feel sympathy with them, for they were undoubtedly men of honour, anxious to do their duty. But, as Quakers and Radicals, they had arrogated to themselves an especial prerogative of rectitude, and the grant of the monopoly had been extended to the whole Liberal Party, whose shrill denunciations of the alleged horrors of " Chinese Slavery " were accompanied by an assumption of ethical superiority. This being the case, there was one course and one only which Messrs. Cadbury could have taken wholly consonant with the undiminished maintenance of their reputation; and that was to have shunned the unclean thing from the very moment when its tainted origin was made known to them. They did not do this, and a representative British jury awarded them a farthing's damages. For it is one of the most salutary of the national instincts of the British people that from those who make proclamation of virtue shall virtue be exacted to the last jot and tittle.

This was the last great case in which Rufus Isaacs and Carson were matched in private practice. The following year found them once more opposed in the lists; but by this time Rufus Isaacs carried the colours of His Majesty's Government.

CHAPTER XVII

A POLITICAL CHAPTER: SOLICITOR-GENERAL

WE have seen how the bright hopes of the Liberal majority had been largely involved in shipwreck on the rock of difficulties which in the heady triumph of 1906 they had been unable to anticipate. The anger which this misfortune provoked was as great as the frustration had been unexpected and, as it grew in intensity, it became concentrated on the House of Lords, which had proved so effective a stumbling-block to the passage of the Education Bill and the Plural Voting Bill. The feeling of the Party found concrete expression in the construction by the Cabinet of a scheme of reform for the Upper House in the Summer of 1907, the sense of which was indicated by the Prime Minister in the Resolution, which he proposed in the House of Commons on June 24th. (A House of Commons Resolution, it may parenthetically be mentioned, is a pious expression of intention or opinion, which has no immediate legislative relevance.) The three-day debate on the Resolution provided Rufus Isaacs with the opportunity of making his second big speech in the House in 1907. The first had been made on February 20th in the course of the debate on the Address, when he spoke on the subject of Free Trade; his speech on that occasion, although part of it was devoted to a clever analysis, in the forensic manner, of the Conservative policy on the question, contributed only the stock arguments to the perennial controversy.

The Resolution of June 24th read: " That, in order to give effect to the will of the people as expressed by their elected representatives, it is necessary that the power of the other House to alter or reject Bills passed by this House should be so restricted by law as to secure that within the limits of a single Parliament the final decision of the

Commons shall prevail." The machinery by which it was proposed that this result should be arrived at is interesting as an anticipation of the provisions of the Parliament Act. Thus it was suggested that a Bill, which had been passed three times in the Commons and from which the Lords continued to dissent, should become law; this proposal was ultimately embodied in the Parliament Act, but in the scheme of 1907 not so long a time would have been required to elapse between the first and third passings of the Bill by the Commons as the two years stipulated by the Parliament Act. There was, however, no reference to Money Bills in the 1907 proposals, but there was, on the other hand, a suggestion for a standing conference, appointed in equal numbers by both Houses, which should be held when agreement between the two Houses was impossible. The adoption of this machinery would have brought this country into line in this respect with the Dominions, where joint-sessions or conferences are part of the Constitutional arrangements.

The Resolution gave rise to a three-day all-star debate. On the first day Mr Balfour replied to Sir Henry Campbell-Bannerman, while literature was represented by Mr Hilaire Belloc, and constitutional law by Sir William Anson. On the following day there was aristocracy in the person of Lord Robert Cecil, Labour in the person of Mr Arthur Henderson, and vigorous dialectic in the person of Mr Winston Churchill, who denounced the House of Lords as a " one-sided, hereditary, unpurged, unrepresentative, irresponsible absentee." On the third day, Mr Lloyd George made an impassioned oration, " informing the House," as Mr F. E. Smith said, who followed him, " with eloquence and in tones which quivered with emotion of the suffering of people who are living in slums." (The motion under discussion, it will be remembered, was a constitutional one relative to the powers of the Second Chamber.) Mr F. E. Smith was in his turn followed by Mr John Simon who, with the masterly understatement of a Liberal and a lawyer, described the preceding speech as an " indignant oration." Rufus Isaacs' turn came late on the third day after this attractive display of rhetorical fire-works had exhausted itself. His own speech contained no pyrotechnics, but was for all that competent enough, calm, analytical, and unimpassioned. It provided, too, an instance of his consistent refusal to be rattled by interruption. When talking of the referendum he pointed out that a referendum could not in fact be taken without the introduction of unconnected matters, at which somebody shouted " Chinese labour, for instance." Rufus Isaacs, quite unflustered, adopted the suggestion, saying: " Yes, Chinese labour, if you like. That is a good argument against the referendum."

The Resolution was finally carried by 432 votes to 147. Its terms were a clear declaration of war upon the House of Lords, and from this time onwards it is true to say that domestic politics were dominated by the impending conflict with the Peers. Early in 1908 Campbell-Bannerman died and his loss was a matter of great importance to the Liberal Party; for Campbell-Bannerman, though not possessed of the great ability, the wide culture, or the subtle sensibilities of his successor, was probably more representative of the rank and file of the composite Liberal Party than was Asquith. The more Radical element of the party feared that the installation of Asquith, who had been a Liberal Imperialist, in the Premiership in place of Campbell-Bannerman, who had been a " pro-Boer," would upset the nice adjustment of forces. Especially were they concerned about foreign affairs for Sir Edward Grey belonged to the same group as Mr Asquith and was known to possess his especial confidence and friendship; with such a combination in charge of the direction of foreign policy, what might not be anticipated in the way of imperialism, foreign complications and increased armaments? The fears of the Radicals were unfounded, for, in point of fact, Campbell-Bannerman's death had the reverse effect to what might have been supposed. It is true that, in view of the German naval challenge and militant policy in those years, the foreign policy of the country was probably safer with a man of Asquith's temperament at the head of affairs than it would have been with Campbell-Bannerman; but nevertheless Campbell-Bannerman had been sufficiently impressed with the requirements of the situation to sanction, for instance, the military conversations with France—indeed Mr Churchill states that only the fact that Campbell-Bannerman had given his sanction enabled his successor to prevail on the Liberal Party to accept the policy* In the realm of domestic affairs, on the other hand, Mr Asquith was succeeded at the Exchequer by Mr Lloyd George, who was right in the van-guard of advanced Radicalism; and it was clear that, what with the increased revenue required for social services and for a naval programme to offset the German challenge, the Exchequer was to rank with the Foreign Office as the centre of interest and the point of controversy. Increased revenue would necessitate increased, and possibly revolutionary, taxation; and it was virtually certain that what the Lords might perhaps have granted in face of financial necessity in other circumstances would not be yielded to a Chancellor who had carried on a guerilla warfare of exceptionally violent harangues against the House of Lords.

But this is a slight anticipation. The main interest of the year 1908 in domestic politics was the struggle over the Licensing Bill. This measure, which had been postponed in 1906, was finally introduced by the new Prime Minister himself in April of 1908. The Bill was a controversial measure proposing a considerable reduction of licenses in ratio to population, and the principle, though not the immediate practice, of compensation was to be abandoned. The Bill was strenuously opposed by the Conservative Party, and legal questions arose as to the property of in-vestors; to this aspect of the case Rufus Isaacs addressed himself in the debate on the Second Reading of the Bill in a clear succinct speech which was quite free from the fanati-cism which grips so many people—especially Liberals—in the discussion of " temperance." Rufus Isaacs showed himself to be capable of discussing a temperance measure temperately. " I am not," he said, " a member of any

* *The World Crisis.* Vol. I, p. 34.

temperance party. My views are those of a moderate, average person anxious to consider this Bill upon its merits." Whatever its merits may have been, however, they were not apparent to the Conservative majority in the House of Lords, and in November the Bill was rejected by the Upper House by the emphatic majority of 272 to 96. The Liberal Party interpreted this action as a definite challenge, and in December of 1908 the Prime Minister gave the signal for battle; " I invite," he said, " the Liberal Party to-night to treat the veto of the House of Lords as the dominating issue in politics—the dominating issue, because in the long run it overshadows and absorbs every other."

This is not the place to attempt to tell the story of the conflict between Lords and Commons in 1909-10. Suffice it to say that the famous Lloyd George Budget of 1909— the " People's Budget " as it was called in certain circles— which was designed to raise fourteen million pounds of additional revenue by means of increased income-tax, super-tax and taxation of land values, was bitterly opposed by the Conservative Party and ultimately shared the fate of the Licensing Bill in an even more decisive rejection by the Lords. But, whereas the Lords were clearly within their rights in rejecting an ordinary piece of legislation, finance was thought—at any rate in Liberal circles—to be the ex-clusive province of the Commons; and certainly there was nothing in the nature of a recent precedent to give authority to their action. But from a strictly constitutional stand-point the Lords were acting with undoubted propriety; and it may be added that such invasions of their rights as that which Mr Gladstone perpetrated in 1861, when he intro-duced the system of " tacking," *i.e.*, bringing in controversial points under cover of a comprehensive Budget, affords at once reason and excuse for such drastic action. Be that as it may, the Lords considered it their duty in the discharge of the responsibility, attaching to them under the Constitu-tion, to reject the Budget; the Liberal majoriy in the Commons deemed the rejection to be an obstruction of the will of the people, as expressed in their elected representatives. The situation had clearly reached an impasse, and Mr Asquith dissolved Parliament, in the hope of obtaining from the country a mandate for action.

The General Election of January, 1910, provided Rufus Isaacs with his third contest at Reading; but it was the first of the three in which the Liberal fortunes had not been on the ascendant. The Election, however, was fought not so much on the four years record in office of the Liberal Party as on the specific issues of the Budget of 1909 and the House of Lords. Rufus Isaacs put these two issues in the forefront of the campaign at Reading, which he carried on with the vigour which had marked his other contests. This time he had the active speaking support of his son Gerald; and a new Conservative opponent in the person of Major Renton, a former Liberal M.P. for Gainsborough, who was a recent convert to Conservatism. He was, as one would expect, moderate in the expression of his criticism of the House of Lords; indeed his statement that he would infinitely prefer to do away with the House of Lords and have an elective second chamber instead would probably find an echo in the Conservative Party to-day. (Not, it may parenthetically be added, a very substantial echo, for though the Conservative Party is not now convinced of the necessary efficacy of personal heredity, it sees that a second elective chamber would merely be a burdensome reduplication of the House of Commons.) In the course of the election he went to speak for Mr Lloyd George, who made a return visit to Reading, while among others who spoke for Rufus Isaacs was a promising young Oxford undergraduate, called Philip Guedalla. Mr Lloyd George's speech was interrupted at the word " robber " by the apparition of two dishevelled suffragettes, who had been hidden under the platform for seventeen hours and then emerged dustily, shouting " you are a robber because you take away the women's money and don't give them the vote." This unseemly attack upon the great democratic leader was very properly resented, and the two young women, in the full happiness of martyrdom, were forcibly ejected by the stewards. A rather grimmer note of humour was struck by another passage in his speech, in which he derided the Conservative agitation for a strong navy. "During last year," he said, "they were clamouring for a bigger and more expensive fleet. There was a great national crisis; they said the security of our shores was in danger. The Germans might come any day." The enunciation of this last absurdity of Tory anticipation won its reward in loud laughter; it was the rich careless laughter of happy people, dwelling by the volcano. It is pleasant to hear, but it echoes mockingly down the corridors of time.

In the result Rufus Isaacs was duly re-elected, though by a decreased majority, and he returned to the new Parliament as a private member once more. But Mr Lloyd George's prophecy that he would see Rufus Isaacs by his side in the next ministry was soon to be fulfilled, in effect if not quite literally, for in March 1910, Sir Samuel Evans, who had become Solicitor-General when on Lawson Walton's death in 1908 Sir William Robson had succeeded to the Attorneyship, was created President of the Probate, Divorce, and Admiralty Division in succession to Sir John Bigham. The office of Solicitor-General, therefore, stood vacant. There could be no doubt as to who was the fitting successor. Rufus Isaacs' yearly earnings at the Bar had by this time reached the monumental figure of £30,000, and he had shown that there was no kind of case which exceeded his capacity; his practice was at once lucrative and varied, versatile and comprehensive, and together with Carson he stood unquestionably at the head of the profession. It is true that he had made no great Parliamentary reputation, but his interventions had been competent enough, and the qualities required in a law officer of the Crown are not precisely identical with the more truly Parliamentary gifts which go to the making of effective private members' debating speeches. The offer, therefore, was duly made to Rufus Isaacs, and, despite the fact that office would entail abandonment of his enormous private practice and a considerable sacrifice of income, was promptly accepted.

It was at this time necessary, under a Statute passed in the reign of Queen Anne, for private members who were appointed to the Ministry in the course of Parliament to present themselves to their constituents for re-election. (The necessity has since been obviated by an Act of 1925.) The Conservative Central Office and Chief Whip were anxious to fight the seat; but the course of events had clearly indicated that there would be another General Election within a short time, and the local association was not anxious to have three contested elections within a few months. Besides, Rufus Isaacs was popular in Reading, and the honour done to the town by his appointment to office was appreciated irrespective of political differences. Consequently it was decided not to contest Rufus Isaacs' return. The news of the decision reached him as he was just concluding a speech in St. John's Hall, Reading, and he at once said: " I accept the decision in the same spirit in which it has been arrived at by the Conservative Party, and as in no sense a Party triumph. If it is, as I expect, that the Conservatives have arrived at the conclusion that they do not desire to contest the seat in view of the honour conferred upon the gentleman who was the member for Reading, then I say that I appreciate much the courtesy and the graciousness of that decision. I trust there will be found no one in the constituency who would in the slightest degree attempt to make any party capital out of it."

It was a graceful acknowledgment of a graceful action.

Sir Rufus Isaacs, therefore—for he had received the honour of knighthood—returned to Parliament without opposition, to take up his seat on the Front Bench and the discharge of the ministerial duties to which he had sacrificed his private practice at the Bar after over twenty years of almost unchequered success.

CHAPTER XVIII

THE ARCHER-SHEE CONTROVERSY

RUFUS ISAACS' tenure of the Solicitor-Generalship was to be short indeed, though its brevity was not due, as might at one time have been expected, to the early fall of the Liberal Government. On the contrary, Rufus Isaacs was not destined to resume private practice, for the vacation of his office was a result of his promotion to the Attorneyship in the following October. But the short period when he was Solicitor brought the last and not the least famous of his duels with Carson; this was the case of the Osborne cadet, George Archer-Shee.

It is not my intention to narrate the circumstances of this famous episode, but merely to make a few comments on it; the long, chivalrous struggle of Sir Edward Carson on behalf of his boy client has already been vividly described by Mr Marjoribanks, and it is only necessary to state here that George Archer-Shee was a cadet at Osborne, who was expelled from the College on the grounds that he had stolen and cashed a postal-order belonging to his friend, Terence Bach; the boy strenuously denied the charge, but on the evidence of the postmistress who had cashed the postal-order, and of Mr Gurrin, the handwriting expert who declared the forged signature to be in the writing of George Archer-Shee, the Admiralty decided that he was guilty and dismissed him. The Archer-Shee family, however, were convinced of the boy's innocence and enlisted the powerful services of Carson, who threw himself into the cause with a whole-hearted vigour that was characteristic of his energy and devotion, and pressed the Admiralty to grant a judicial inquiry. All that the Admiralty would do, however, was to have an investigation by Mr George Elliott, K.C., and an inquiry by the Judge-Advocate of the Fleet, Mr Acland,

K.C., at neither of which George Archer-Shee was allowed professional representation; the result, therefore, in these circumstances was not unnaturally that the Admiralty found no reason to alter their decision. Carson, therefore, decided to seek the intervention of the Courts; but herein lay a very serious difficulty.

It is, of course, well known that the Crown in litigation occupies a peculiar and favoured position; that is to say, it is not liable in tort, and though it has a liability in contract by the procedure known as Petition of Right (which, it may be noted, is at any rate in theory granted as a matter of grace and not of right), this method leaves it with its prerogatives in pleading and practice. However, a liability in contract does exist, and perhaps the advisers of George Archer-Shee might proceed by this method, on the ground that the boy's dismissal was a breach of the contract between the Crown and the parents for the education of the boy at Osborne. But here there was a serious difficulty, for it has been clear law ever since the decisions of Dunn v. The Queen and Mitchell v. The Queen in 1896 that appointments in the service of the Crown are determinable at the pleasure of the Crown and that a petition of right will not lie for breach of such contract; for, as Lord Esher said in the latter case: " The law is as clear as it can be, and it has been laid down over and over again as the rule on this subject that all engagements between those in the military service of the Crown and the Crown are voluntary only on the part of the Crown, and give no occasion for an action in respect of any alleged contract." There could, therefore be no question of the Crown being made liable for an alleged breach of contract in severing Archer-Shee's connection with Osborne; for, young as he was, the contract was the same as that subsisting between the Crown and any professional soldier or sailor. But his position was peculiarly unfortunate, because, although he shared to the full the contractual disadvantage, his status as a cadet did not entitle him to the compensating privilege of being able to demand trial by Court-Martial. There was thus no remedy within the boy' power, except what the Admiralty had chosen to give; and this Carson rightly felt was not enough.

So ultimately when after two years—during which time George Archer-Shee had returned to his old school, Stonyhurst—the case came on in Court, it was a petition of right for breach of contract which was pleaded; and in answer to this, as Carson very well knew, the Crown had only to plead that a petition of right would not lie in such a case, and his case was gone. But, wrote Mr Marjoribanks, " it seemed impossible that the Crown could object in any formal way to the trying of the facts of the case before a jury. The Crown surely would not dare to condemn a helpless and perhaps innocent child to lifelong ignominy by sheltering behind the prerogative claim of the Crown to immunity. Yet this is precisely the plea which Sir Rufus Isaacs was instructed to raise." When the case came on before Mr Justice Ridley, Rufus Isaacs did in fact raise the technical plea of privilege, and insisted that he was entitled to judgment. Readers of Mr Marjoribanks' book will remember how Carson then stalked indignantly out of the Court, and succeeded in having the case heard by the Court of Appeal only six days later; how, though Rufus Isaacs still relied on the privilege of the Crown, Carson carried the day with the three Lord Justices of Appeal, who decided that the facts should be heard; and how, after a trial of tense excitement, Rufus Isaacs finally withdrew on behalf of the Admiralty and declared that they entirely acknowledged George Archer-Shee's innocence. Ultimately—though not for a longer period than was creditable to our public departments— £7,120 was paid to Mr Archer-Shee by the Treasury in settlement of costs and compensation.

That money could not fully compensate for the pain and suffering caused to the family of an innocent boy, wrongfully convicted, and for the setback to his career, is clearly demonstrable. Nothing can, or should, obliterate the fact that the whole affair was tragically unfortunate and it becomes all the more regrettable in view of the attitude of the Admiralty. For in two major points I regard the conduct of the Admiralty as being open to the severest criticism. Their failure to communicate with the boy's parents, while the matter was being investigated, seems quite indefensible in view of the serious nature of the charge; and it is almost as regrettable that the Department did not see fit to allow Archer-Shee professional representation in the inquiry held before the Judge-Advocate of the Fleet. It is true, as was pointed out at the time, that the other party, which was the Crown, was not represented either. But the position of the Crown and that of a young boy, though each may be equally parties to a case, cannot really be compared; especially as the boy was on trial, whereas the Crown, of course, was not. And although, since the Crown was not technically " heard " at the inquiry, the maxim *audi alteram partem* would not apply, the whole proceedings were a violation of the fundamental and equally respectable maxim, which forbids that anybody should be condemned unheard.

And what of Rufus Isaacs' reliance upon the privileged immunity of the Crown, when the case was heard? Mr Marjoribanks condemned his action strongly; but in his indignation at the clumsy injustice of the Admiralty and the unfair advantage attaching to the Crown, he perhaps looked too much at one aspect of the question. For a Law Officer of the Crown had duties other than to individuals. Mr Marjoribanks is right, of course, in the contention that the interests of justice come first; but the difficulty is to determine what in any given case are the interests of justice, for it is clear that if individuals are allowed to judge the question for themselves, society is liable to revert into the primitive system of barbarism, from which the institution and enforced observance of laws originally rescued it. If the law decrees immunity or privilege for the Crown in certain cases, it must be because it is considered that the cause of justice and the interest of the community are best served by such privilege. Privilege is an instrument not only laid ready to hand for a law officer in these cases; he is already armed with it, and must actually divest himself of it, if he does not intend to use it. As Rufus Isaacs himself said, " what I say is that it is not for me as law officer to make the law, but it is for me to administer it, and I have to deal with the law as I find it, and the books are full, as every lawyer knows, of decisions that there is no such right of action, and that the Court cannot even discuss such an action if it is brought before it." He was the guardian of the rights of the Crown; but, of course, it would have been possible to waive privilege. Should he have done so on this occasion? " This is," he said, " just one of those matters in respect of which a law officer has no right to waive the privileges of the Crown, *i.e.*, the rights of the public, and he must not waive them. If those rights have to be abolished, it is entirely a matter for Parliament, and once Parliament has done it, anyone can bring such an action." But since he was armed, on behalf of the Crown, with the weapon of privilege, Rufus Isaacs felt that he ought not lightly to cast it aside. " I have found, on studying the cases of waiving of privileges by law officers, that they are very jealous indeed of waiving privileges, and I have been unable to find a single precedent in which there has been a waiver of the Crown Prerogative, allowing such a case to be brought. I should have been only too glad if I could have said, as law officer, ' Try the case.' What objection could I have to trying the case? My difficulty was this. I stepped into the matter when the record was already completed, when the plea of the demurrer was already on the pleas, and there was that plea on the very threshold of the case which had to be dealt with, and I should have been wanting in my duty if I had said, ' This is an unpleasant matter for me to have to argue. I do not care to have to take this point in a case where a boy is trying to vindicate himself; therefore I will waive the right of the Crown, and will allow the case to be tried.' "

It is clear, therefore, that the matter was hardly as simple as Mr Marjoribanks would lead us to believe. On the one hand there was this boy, not yet known to be innocent—in fact adjudged guilty—but who might turn out to be innocent; on the other hand there was the position of the Crown, which could not lightly be sacrificed by an abandonment of its privileges in a manner that might establish precedent. For Carson, though his task was one of enormous difficulty which would have transcended the powers of any other man, the course was clear; he had only to think of his duty to his client. For the Solicitor-General the issue was more complex. If he did not waive the privilege, then the unfortunate boy's last chance of vindicating his good name was gone; but on the other hand, he saw grave objections to the course. Rufus Isaacs decided to use the " demurrer "—*i.e.*, to say that the other side had no case in law—which had been entered on the pleadings; and, having so decided, he insisted on it in the Court of instance, and was only prevailed upon to abandon it at the expressed and unanimous desire of the Judges in the Court of Appeal. (It is worth noting that the demurrer was never overruled in the Court of Appeal; nor could it have been, for it was undoubtedly sound in law, and the Crown to-day could successfully adopt just the same tactics if similar circumstances arose.)

There had perhaps never been a harder case than that of poor George Archer-Shee, whose position as apprentice sailor deprived him of every form of legal redress, and it is well known that hard cases make bad law. Rufus Isaacs was undoubtedly acting with legal propriety in taking the attitude which he did. Nevertheless one can only be glad, in view of circumstances, that Carson was able virtually to compel a trial of the facts; for that and that alone could establish the innocence of George Archer-Shee. One is forced, therefore, to consider whether it would not have been better for Rufus Isaacs to have waived privilege at once, and submitted to argument on the facts. This was, as we have seen, neither as easy nor as obvious a course of action as has been suggested; but nevertheless there were several factors in the case which made it the desirable course. In the first place there was the anomaly of Archer-Shee's status. Had he been a fully-fledged naval officer, he could have demanded a court-martial; and the impossibility of obtaining a remedy in the civil courts would not have precluded him from the opportunity of vindicating his character. He was, however, only a cadet, and the position was so unusual as to be virtually unprovided for; consequently a law officer of the Crown could adopt a fairly wide latitude of discretion. There was all the more excuse, if not necessity, for it, on account of the conduct of the Admiralty in having refused representation to Archer-Shee at any inquiry; for if the mistake of the Admiralty was not rectified by generosity on the part of another Government department, Archer-Shee would have been condemned unheard. In these circumstances, it seems to me that Rufus Isaacs would have done well to waive at once the privilege, whatever the force of precedent—which is not, in such a matter, binding in any case—and to allow a hearing on the facts. For the fact that the demurrer was entered on the pleadings did not compel him to argue it; counsel may not argue points that are not in the pleadings, but he is not bound against his better judgment to argue everything that the pleadings contain. And, with regard to this, a law officer of the Crown is in a special position, for he is not, like ordinary counsel, concerned merely with the legal or technical issue. He is, in addition, a member of the Government, who must advise on the aspect of the policy; that is to say, if for example a prosecution for sedition is mooted, he does not merely inform the Government as to whether it is sound in law, but gives his opinion of its desirability with regard to public policy in addition. And, as a matter of public policy, it was clearly inexpedient—to put it no higher—to put up the bulwark of Crown prerogative against the hearing of Archer-Shee's case. For the lay public, which knows little of prerogative —and dislikes that little—is deeply and instinctively convinced that the right of a fair hearing for all must be at the root of the sound and equitable administration of the law; and to such a hearing George Archer-Shee's anomalous status did not entitle him. He got his hearing in the end, but it is a pity that he did not receive it through the voluntary action of the Crown. For, though there is no fundamental law in this country, to which a citizen can appeal against the operation of the ordinary laws, it is fundamental to the nature of a free state that nobody should be put outside the law and denied even the opportunity of satisfaction from it. Such, at least, is the sense of public opinion; and in such a question it is entitled to respect.

CHAPTER XIX

SIR RUFUS ISAACS did not long remain Solicitor-General after the Archer-Shee case, for in October, 1910, Sir William Robson was appointed a Lord of Appeal; and so, shortly before his fiftieth birthday, Rufus Isaacs became Attorney-General and titular leader of his profession. It may be observed that in his case, judged by the previous extent and position of his private practice, the title had a stronger savour of reality than is sometimes the case. His place as Solicitor-General was taken by John Simon, then only in his fortieth year; and together they made one of the youngest and most effective of Governmental legal teams in recent years.

The new change in status did not, of course, necessitate a bye-election, as the original appointment to office had done. But before very long he was faced with the challenge of another General Election. An early General Election had, as we have seen, been anticipated in March, when it had been decided not to oppose Rufus Isaacs at Reading; for King Edward took the view that a second reference to the electorate was necessary before the Government could be considered to have a mandate for applying compulsion to the Lords. And, indeed, even the most hardened Liberal partisan could hardly consider the shrunken majority of January, 1910—filled out, too, such as it was, with the solid block of the Irish Party—as an enthusiastic invitation to proceed with the work of drastic reform. The King's death in May, however, altered the situation, for clearly it was undesirable to inaugurate the new reign by a bitter political controversy, especially as the Crown Prerogative was likely to be appealed to. The device of the Constitutional Conference was, therefore, hit upon; this was an effort to reach agreement by way of a compromise to be worked out between representative leaders of the two parties. A species of truce, therefore, subsisted between the two parties during the Summer; but, like most truces, it was an uneasy period more in the nature of a preparation for the inevitable war than the prelude to permanent peace. The truce was, however, duly observed during the period of the Conference, and the reforms, proposed by the Conservatives, were discussed; the proposals were in themselves a considerable contribution to the solution of the lasting difficulty of an appropriate balance between the two Chambers, restricting, as they did, the power of the House of Lords over finance, but not leaving it stripped of all effective share in ordinary legislation, while constitutional legislation was to be left to the final arbitrament of a referendum of the whole people. Difficulties of definition arose, however, and the chances of reaching agreement were not increased by the existence in the Liberal Party of a strong body of feeling, which was considerably more interested in crippling the power of the Lords than in arriving at a balanced adjustment of the relation between the two Houses, and this had its counterpart in that section of Conservative opinion which preferred a retention of the status quo to any reform of the Lords.

In these circumstances it is surprising neither that the Conference broke down without achieving result, nor that its breakdown was hailed with something very like relief by politically-minded people. It happened that the news arrived in Reading during a meeting of the Women's Liberal Association. A telegram, announcing the breakdown, was handed to Rufus Isaacs during his speech; he read it out, and the news was received with loud and prolonged applause. " For my part," said Rufus Isaacs, " I believe I speak your views when I say this: ' that we are glad our tongues are now loosened,' " and accuracy of his assumption was promptly provided by the renewed applause which greeted the statement of this belief. The collapse of the attempt to arrive at a negotiated agreement, however, meant that the contending forces would once more go into action; and Mr Asquith advised a dissolution of Parliament and an appeal

to the electorate.   Before he did so, however, he obtained
an assurance that he might " understand that in the event
of the policy of the Government being approved by an
adequate majority in the new House of Commons, His
Majesty will be ready to exercise his constitutional powers
(which may involve the prerogative of creating Peers) if
needed to secure that effect shall be given to the decision
of the country."   This meant that, if the country this time
so far endorsed the Liberal policy as to give the party an
" adequate majority "—the precise interpretation of this
phrase was not supplied—then the resistance of the Peers
could be overborne.   In other words, the struggle was to
be decisive; naturally, therefore, it was fought primarily on
the great issue and with great energy and determination on
both sides.

The House of Lords had, in point of fact, before the
election put forward a scheme of reform of their own, on
the lines of the Conservative recommendations at the Constitutional Conference.   This the Liberals were quick to
stigmatise as a death-bed repentance, and Rufus Isaacs at
Reading described it as the sort of repentance felt by the
criminal when the policeman's hand is on his collar.   This
was the third time in twelve months that he had sought
election at Reading, but on this occasion he was able to
spend less time in the constituency than he had at previous
elections, for he was now a person of political importance,
whose services as a speaker were in demand elsewhere.   He
was able, however, to make a fair number of speeches—in
the course of one of which he said, " Don't be afraid of the
cry of Single Chamber government and hasty legislation.
We have always had Single Chamber government when the
Tory Party was in power "—in Reading, where the Conservative cause was being vigorously championed by a new
Conservative candidate in the person of Captain Leslie
Wilson.   (In all his elections at Reading, Rufus Isaacs was
never opposed by the same opponent twice.)   But Rufus
Isaacs was compensated for his periodical absences in other
constituencies by importing Mr Asquith and Sir John Simon

to speak at Reading, which was favoured during the last week of the election, as Mr Balfour spoke for Captain Wilson. On December 3rd, Rufus Isaacs was declared re-elected; but his majority had shrunk to ninety-nine and, though great enthusiasm was manifested in the constituency, there was a certain disappointment on both sides. This feeling indeed was to a certain extent general as a result of the whole election, though Liberal disappointment was considerably less than it had been in the preceding January, for although the position was almost precisely the same, it was now felt that the country's verdict was unmistakeable. Actually the Election resulted in the return of 272 Liberals, who wanted to curtail the powers of the Lords; 271 Conservatives, who were opposed to such action; 42 Labour members, who were returned primarily as Trade Union representatives but who also strongly desired a diminution, if not total abrogation of the powers of the Lords; and 84 Nationalists, who were willing to have or to do anything provided that it got them nearer to the goal of Home Rule. The Government could, therefore, in a critical division, count on a majority of about 130; and with this " adequate majority " Mr Asquith advanced into action.

The Parliament Bill was promptly introduced into the new House of Commons and came up for discussion on its Second Reading at the end of February, 1911. Of course, its passage through the Commons was now a certainty, and the critical struggle was reserved for the Lords. The story of the struggle is now a matter of History, and it would be hardly in place to recapitulate it here. Detailed accounts of it are to be found in the biographies of those prominently concerned in it, and to these the reader is recommended. There are two main points of controversy connected with the passage of the Parliament Bill. The first is: were the Conservative peers other than the " Diehards," right in refusing to reject the Bill and to challenge the creation of peers? The two points of view on this question are well put in the " Life of Lord Lansdowne," who advised acquiescence by the Conservative peers, and in the " Life of Lord Halsbury," who led the party of resistance. The other, and prior issue, is as to whether Mr Asquith was justified in getting from His Majesty the assurance that he would in certain circumstances use his prerogative of creating peers, without advising him as to the possibility of an alternative Government. There is a very able defence of his action in the Biography by Mr Spender and Mr Cyril Asquith, and a brilliant indictment of it in Sir John Marriot's "Second Chambers."

Rufus Isaacs spoke on the third day of the debate on the Second Reading, when he had the honour of following Sir William Anson, the distinguished constitutional historian. In his speech he defended the Government from the charge of having no mandate for carrying through such radical reforms; "the only mandate to which I, at any rate, would subscribe, apart from supporting the general policy of the Government, is that kind of mandate which is a negative mandate. We have never." he went on, "drawn any distinction between constitutional changes by Act of Parliament and any other. The equally ultimate authority, I will ask the House to remember, with our Constitution is a newly elected House of Commons. That is the greatest authority that is known in the Constitution." The repudiation of the validity of any mandate save a negative one, and of any distinction between constitutional changes and any other, is an accurate description of the constitutional practice of the country. With the last-quoted sentence, however, he is on considerably less safe ground. It may be true in practice now; but then, as Mr Baldwin said, we can never dogmatise as to what is constitutional practice, though we can define fairly accurately what it has been at any given time. What is certain, however, is that the House of Commons *per se*—at any rate before the Parliament Act—has no authority in our Constitution; it is the King-in-Parliament, which alone has authority, and, though this in practice may now approximate closely to the House of Commons, it is largely as a result of the Parliament Act and not a condition precedent of its passage.

But the views of Liberals, and indeed of the Commons generally, had ceased relatively to be of much importance. The Bill inevitably passed its Second Reading in the Commons, and on May 15th its Third Reading, on which Rufus Isaacs did not speak, was carried by a similar majority. A fortnight later the Lords passed the Second Reading of the Bill without a division, reserving the struggle for the single throw of the Third Reading; but the Second Reading was not carried before a brilliant and mordant attack on the Bill had been delivered by the former Liberal leader, Lord Rosebery. The Lords then proposed amendments to the Commons, which included provision for referenda to be taken on such questions as were certified by a joint committee to be of sufficient public importance. The proposals, however, did not commend themselves to the Liberal Party, and Mr Asquith wrote to Mr Balfour on July 20th, telling him that he would ask the House to reject the Lords' emendations and, if necessity arose, would advise the King to create new peers. Four days later the question of the amendments came before the House of Commons, but feeling had by this time reached such a pitch that Mr Asquith, on rising to address the House, was shouted down by the Conservatives, headed by Mr F. E. Smith and Lord Hugh Cecil, and subsequently Mr F. E. Smith was in his turn refused a hearing; finally, after one of the most astounding sessions in its history, the House adjourned " in view of grave disorder." Ultimately, after Mr Balfour had moved a vote of censure to the effect that the advice given to His Majesty, whereby the pledge to create new peers was obtained, was " a gross violation of constitutional liberty," the Commons rejected the Lords' amendments, and on August 9th the Parliament Bill came before the Lords for its Third Reading. After a two days' debate of considerable distinction and a tensity of feeling perhaps unparalleled in Parliamentary history, the motion for surrender was carried by seventeen votes, thirty-seven Conservative peers voting with the Government. The surrender involved the exclusion of the House of Lords from the realm of finance and the substitution of a two years' suspensory veto for the right of absolute veto, which had previously been theirs. It meant, in fact, subject to the unredeemed promise in the preamble to the Act " to substitute for the House of Lords, as it at present exists, a Second Chamber constituted on a popular instead of a hereditary basis," the extinction of the power of the House of Lords and the virtual establishment of a unicameral legislature. It was a significant, if perhaps tactless, action on the part of the victors to carry a motion in the House of Commons for the payment of members, on the very day on which the Lords acknowledged defeat.

The despatch of the Parliament Bill in the Commons left the Government free for the consideration of other measures. Of these the chief were the National Insurance Bill and Home Rule; in both the Attorney-General took a part, though not a leading one. The National Insurance Bill was introduced, and to some extent inspired by Mr Lloyd George. The measure, providing as it did for compulsory contributory insurance, marks what is practically a social revolution, and it is safe to say that no legislative measure has affected more vitally and more profoundly the lives of the great mass of the people. The Bill was read a second time in the House of Commons without a division—there were not wanting those who said that the Conservatives failed to oppose it merely because they did not understand it— and, though there was a certain amount of opposition, especially from the medical profession, much praise has been lavished on it both at the time and subsequently. The scheme did undoubted good in extending the principle of insurance, and has to some extent obviated the hardship which comes in the train of industrial depression; for, before the Act came into operation, it was estimated that only 1,400,000 people were insured against unemployment, that is, about half of the number of people actually unemployed at the time of writing. The Act is most open to criticism on account of its compulsory element, and for a brilliantly unorthodox attack upon it the reader is recommended to

Mr William Saunderson's " Statecraft," where the suggestion is made that the Act is a first step to nationalisation of
labour.   The Bill's Second Reading was introduced on
May 24th by Mr Buxton, President of the Board of Trade,
and Rufus Isaacs made a long speech, giving a general
outline of the Bill and comparing it with the German
insurance structure.   The speech contained a graceful
reference to the helpful attitude of all parties in the House:
" I cannot help thinking," he said, " that the speeches on
both sides of the House during the course of this debate
have shown the House of Commons at its best, from one
aspect."

The Irish question was not one with which Rufus Isaacs
was closely identified. His race, as we have seen, was an obstacle against that temperamental absorption in the issues,
which overtook many political leaders of the day. He did not
feel with the same passionate intensity on the subject as
did, from their different points of view, Carson and
Redmond.   Indeed it may fairly be doubted whether by
1911 the Liberal Party was imbued with a particularly
passionate desire for Home Rule; there must have been
springing up in some quarters a feeling scarcely acknowledged but comprehensible, that the whole matter was a
great nuisance.   Mr Austen Chamberlain indeed referred
in the House of Commons to the absence in Ministers, in
discussions on this question, " of that note of deep-toned
conviction which rang in every utterance of Mr Gladstone."
But then Mr Gladstone had believed that it had been God's
intention that Ireland should have Home Rule and that he
was to be the humble instrument of its attainment; and it
was a little difficult perhaps for the Liberal Party to entertain such exalted sentiments on the subject, when they were
well aware that, independently of divine intention, the
Irish Party was going to insist on their instrumentality in
the attainment of Home Rule.

The approach of the Liberal Party, therefore—and that
of Rufus Isaacs amongst them—to the question was more
mundane.   He took the view that, if the majority of the

Irish people wanted self-government they should have it. But there were clearly difficulties and dangers in such a project, and, therefore, it must be local self-government with the retention of safeguards; and he stressed especially the necessity of the retention of the supremacy of the Imperial Parliament and of the power of the Judicial Committee of the Privy Council to decide whether or not Bills introduced into the Irish Parliament were *ultra vires*. Within these limits he advocated self-government, which he favoured also on the practical and utilitarian grounds that devolution would give the Imperial Parliament more time for the discussion of matters of importance, and at the same time leave the Irish time for a fuller discussion of matters of purely Irish concern.   The possibility of Civil War was a thing to be strongly deprecated, and he criticised the attitude of the Unionist leaders on this ground.   Of Bonar Law he asked: " Does he mean to encourage Civil War?   Let me add that it is no use riding off by not dealing with the question.   You cannot do that in a matter of this character; you are either for the Crown or against it." His speech on the Second Reading of the Government of Ireland Bill epitomised his attitude to Irish settlement: " It can be obtained; it can undoubtedly be obtained if only you are a little more generous, a little less suspicious, and a little more trustful.   Then the Irish people can live with the Irish in an Ireland governed according to Irish ideas . . . If only all will bear in mind a saying of Mr Gladstone, given with all his unmatched and unrivalled experience, ' Suspicion is the besetting sin of politicians, and trust is often the truest wisdom,' we shall not be long before we arrive at a settlement."   Brave words!   But the settlement was to be postponed until long after Rufus Isaacs had been translated—temporarily—from the field of politics; nor did events even come to their crisis in the short remainder of his period in the House of Commons.   As it turned out, his next and most famous connection with Ireland was to be the occasion of his presiding over the trial of one whose love for Ireland led him into treason to the Empire.

CHAPTER XX

THE HONOUR OF THE KING

ALTHOUGH Sir Rufus Isaacs' Parliamentary position was, of course, considerably enhanced by office, he was not yet a member of the Cabinet; and it is probably true to say that a law officer, if he is not at the same time a Cabinet Minister, is more concerned with the legal aspect of his duties than with the direction of policy. The number of Crown cases in which a law officer appears, is generally large and of mixed interests; and Rufus Isaacs was especially fortunate in having, in his period as Attorney, several cases which from their various points of view were not a whit less interesting than the greatest of his cases in private practice. One of the earliest of them, which was tried just after the reassembly of the new Parliament of 1911, had a quality, unusual in Crown cases; that is, it nearly concerned the wearer of the Crown. This was the prosecution of the Republican agitator, Mylius, for a criminal libel upon the King.

Rumour is a thing as elusive as it is persistent; it can be traced to no source, tied down to no authority, fastened on no person. When the subject of the rumour is a person highly placed, every element of the rumour is magnified; its range is more extensive, its basis more fragile, its origin more obscure. And in proportion as such rumour is baseless and anonymous, it is likely to travel and to increase. It was a rumour of this sort, inexplicable but malignant, cruel but persistent, which attacked in 1910 no less a person than the Sovereign himself; and, paradoxically enough, there is probably nobody more defenceless in face of rumour than a ruling monarch. In this instance, the rumour was more than ordinarily cruel, for it attacked his domestic life; it

260

was said—nobody knew by whom or for what reason or from what beginnings—that Queen Mary was not the King's lawful wife. He had, they said, contracted a morganatic marriage previous to his marriage to her, and his royal marriage was, therefore, invalid. It may fairly be doubted whether anyone believed so mischievous and fantastic a tale; but, believing it or not, there were many who listened attentively and repeated it assiduously. And so, like the prairie fire, starting, it seemed from nowhere, the story had soon reached giant and dangerous proportions.

At last the story was repeated in a form direct, challenging, and offensive; and at once the challenge was taken up. The challenger was an obscure but obstinate young Republican, called Mylius, whose political beliefs had become somewhat of an obsession; to him the story was not merely an opportunity for idle gossip. It was rather a stick with which to beat the monarchy, the more effective because it was aimed at the person of the monarch rather than the principle of monarchy. And people on the whole, as Mr Mylius realised, are more eager to listen to the slander of persons than to the criticism of systems. His task was the easier since he occupied the proud, though strictly honorary, position of London distributor and correspondent of a Republican journal, printed in Paris and known as the *Liberator*. To this paper, therefore, he contributed the information of the alleged bigamy of the King. He did not first make any attempt to verify the accuracy of his information, a course which would seem to have been dictated both by prudence and honesty. But then to people with an *idée fixe* an ounce of suspicion, which supports, generally carries more weight than a pound of fact which refutes.

The *Liberator* made the most of its scoop, and the November issue contained a lengthy diatribe: " During the year 1890 in the island of Malta," it ran, " the man who is now King of England was united in lawful, holy wedlock with the daughter of Sir Michael Culme-Seymour, an Admiral of the British Navy. Of this marriage offspring were born . . . In order to obtain the woman of Royal blood for his pretended wife, George Frederick foully abandoned his true wife, the daughter of Sir Michael Culme-Seymour, of the British Navy, and entered into sham and shameful marriage with the daughter of the Duke of Teck in 1893. The said George Frederick, not having obtained any divorce from his first wife, who, by the common law of England and by the law of the Christian Church remained, and if she still lives remains, his true wife, committed the crime of bigamy, and he committed it with the aid and complicity of the prelates of the Anglican Church. This is the sickening and disgusting crime which has been committed by the English Church which has married one man to two women. Our very Christian King has a plurality of wives, just like any Mohammedan Sultan, and they are sanctified by the English Church. The daughter of Sir Michael Culme-Seymour, if she still lives, is by the unchangeable law of the Christian Church, as well as by the common law of England, the rightful Queen of England, and her children are the only rightful heirs to the English throne." This lengthy indictment was followed up more crisply the following month with the remark: " The *Daily News* of London informs us that the King plans to visit India with his wife. Would the newspaper kindly tell us which wife? "

The story, thus confidently related, contained not a shred of truth. Practically the only true statement in the whole rigmarole was to the effect that Admiral Culme-Seymour had a daughter—he in fact had two—who had been to Malta. But beyond this the story was almost impudently innocent of fact. The King had not been in Malta after the year 1888 until some years after his marriage to the Queen, and he had certainly not been there in 1890. As to the Admiral's two daughters, the younger of whom had died unmarried in 1895 while the elder had become at the time of the trial Mrs Napier, they had not gone to Malta until the late Autumn of 1895, that is to say, some months after the King's marriage to the Queen. Nor had they, while in Malta, even met the King. The younger, in fact, had never met him to talk to in her life; while Mrs Napier, about whom the charge was made, met him twice only before she sailed for Malta. The first meeting occurred when she was eight years old, while the second took place at a reception in February, 1893, where she did not even get an opportunity to speak to him. It was on this slender basis that the *Liberator* had built its crazy structure of slanderous allegation; but the people responsible for its publication had a disregard for the facts as airy as their inattention to verification was complete. For there had appeared in *Reynolds' Newspaper* of October 30th, 1910, a copy of a letter from Sir Arthur Bigge (subsequently Lord Stamfordham), the King's private secretary, referring to certain statements in the *Brisbane Telegraph* and denying on his authority the existence of any morganatic marriage. Mylius had enclosed a cutting of this to James, the editor of the *Liberator,* in Paris, who replied: " I do not attach much credence to the statement made by Bigge and published in *Reynolds'*. If there was no marriage, why do not these people explain why for years everyone has passed the word around that there was a marriage? We must run this matter down and get at the truth." Later he wrote another letter, explaining his rather curious method of attaining this praiseworthy object: " In writing the bigamy article I decided to publish the facts at once without waiting for further verification. The best and quickest way to get at the truth is to begin to agitate the matter. If we have not stated the facts correctly, we will hear what the other side has to say."

What " the other side " had to say was a criminal prosecution. It was quite clear to the legal advisers of the Crown that the case called for the action of the criminal law, and the question only remained: what form of criminal procedure would be resorted to? The question did not arise on account of any difficulty which the Crown felt itself to be in on the score of making out its case, but it came rather from the fact that alternative courses presented themselves. For it was clear, in view of the statements printed in the *Liberator,* that a prosecution for seditious libel would lie.

But in this case the defendant could not legally enter a plea of justification, whereas in a case of criminal libel he could avail himself of this defence.   That is to say, if he was charged with criminal libel merely, Mylius could gain the verdict by proving that his allegations were true and published in the public interest; but if the charge was seditious libel, then the question of the truth or falsity of his allegations would not be material.   It was clearly desirable in this case that the facts should be tried; for, if Mylius was unable to enter the plea of justification and raise the issue of the truth of the facts which he alleged, then it would always be open to people to suggest afterwards that, though his words were seditious and therefore criminal, they were nevertheless true. The Crown decided, therefore, in order to prevent this, to prosecute him for criminal libel, thus affording him the opportunity of establishing the truth of what he had said. The method adopted was that of a criminal information which is, in the case of misdemeanours, an alternative to the ordinary procedure by indictment, from which it differs by being tried in the civil court and not requiring the preliminaries of trial by magistrate and presentment by grand jury, which must precede the trial of a prisoner indicted in the usual way.   The procedure is important because it provided Mylius with his one real line of defence.

As the prosecution was by criminal information it was at the Law Courts and not at the Old Bailey that the trial took place.   The excitement of the public was naturally intense, and great crowds gathered outside the Court early in the morning; for the word had gone round that the King himself would give evidence. The Court itself was thronged with those privileged people who were able to secure admission.   The Judges' Gallery was full of ladies, Lady Darling being prominent among them, while others sat among the witnesses.   Rufus Isaacs sat in counsels' seat, supported by the Solicitor-General, Sir John Simon, Mr Muir and Mr Rowlatt, and in front of counsel sat the Home Secretary, Mr Winston Churchill.   Mylius appeared in person and sat at the solicitors' table between two officers in mufti, a diminutive figure with square, flabby face and obstinate nose, poring over his papers or gazing with an air of unconcern around the Court.

There was a strained attention on all sides when the Attorney-General rose to open the case for the Crown. " I am very anxious," he said, " that you should understand from the outset that in these proceedings in this prosecution no complaint has been lodged because of the Republican sentiments and views which this gentleman and those associated with him in this leaflet may choose to advocate. A man is free in this country to advocate political opinions, even to raise the question of the proper form of government for this country. He is probably freer in this country than in any country in the world to publish his views and to circulate them; and so long as he keeps within the law, which is framed on very broad and generous lines, no complaint is made against him, however much you and I may differ from every sentiment which is expressed in the paper. But I want you quite clearly to appreciate that this prosecution is not in respect of any observations of that character which may have been made in this leaflet." He then went through the facts of the case and after about ten minutes the strained attention of the Court relaxed, when it was seen on what a foundation of sand the defendant's case was built. Since he had pleaded justification the onus of the proof, as Rufus Isaacs pointed out, was on the defendant; but they did not intend to wait for that, and would call witnesses of their own in refutation. Would the King be one of them? " The Solicitor-General and I, after careful consideration, have come to the conclusion that His Majesty has not the right to vindicate his character on oath—an advantage possessed by all his subjects. This is not a private privilege which the Sovereign can waive at pleasure, but it is an absolute incapacity attached to the Sovereign by the Constitution for reasons of public policy. There is, in fact, no precedent for the reigning monarch giving evidence in the Courts, and the reason is obvious. It is not, of course, a personal disability, for King Edward VII, as Prince of Wales, gave evidence in the Tranby Croft case; it is due to the fact that the Courts are the King's Courts, and clearly a man cannot be subpoenaed to give evidence in his own Courts. So Mylius did not have his desire gratified of cross-examining his Sovereign in the witness box. But he did not on that account suffer any injustice, for the Lord Chief Justice had already decided that Mylius had no facts which the King could prove. Nor, happily, did the King suffer from his disability, for his personal evidence was not necessary to a complete refutation of Mylius' charges.

The case against Mylius was that he had circulated the libel with a full knowledge of its contents, that he had taken part in writing the article or in supplying the information on which it was based, and that he was aware that they had failed to get any information of the sort which would have been required to support the story. He must have been aware that the object of the libel was to destroy the respect felt for the Sovereign by his subjects. And in order to do this, the rumour, which had been set at rest by Sir Arthur Bigge's statement, had been deliberately revived and circulated with an indifference to the facts clearly demonstrated by James' letters to Mylius. Rufus Isaacs concluded an unanswerable case with a peroration not unworthy of the occasion: " It is not for the Monarchy that the protection of this Court has been sought by means of this case. The Monarchy in this country rests upon foundations more secure than any that could be undermined by the attacks of James or the defendant Mylius. But the protection is sought for the King as a man, for the King as a husband, for the King as a father. Your protection is sought for the honour of the King. In submitting this case to you, I do not ask you to deal with it any other way than you would the most ordinary case, as between one citizen and another. The same rules of evidence and the same considerations must apply. You have to determine this case, and you will determine it, of course, upon the evidence that will be laid before you. You will judge it fairly and impartially. You will, I am sure, consider everything that can possibly be said or may be urged either as defence or in any other way by the defendant. But you will also, I know, bear in mind this; that the King is none the less entitled to the verdict of a jury and to protection in an English Court of Justice in any attack made upon his honour because he happens to be the King of England."

The Crown witnesses were then called, including Sir Michael Culme-Seymour, his sons, his daughter Mrs Napier, Sir Arthur Bigge, and the Crown-Advocate of Malta. The effect of their evidence was to demonstrate the utter impossibility of the allegation; and Mylius did not avail himself of the opportunity of cross-examining any one of the witnesses. Consequently the case for the Crown was concluded by lunch time. After lunch Mylius, being asked if he wished to call evidence, said that he preferred to address the Court first on a point of law. The point which he raised arose from the procedure by criminal information, and was in purpose another effort to get the King into Court in person. For there are two forms of criminal information; an information *ex officio* filed by the Attorney-General, and an information by the Master of the Crown Office, filed by him at the instance of a private individual. In the second form of procedure, the individual instigating the prosecution must swear affidavits and himself appear in Court; the first is more in the nature of a public prosecution, and is generally used in cases of gross misdemeanour of a political character. It was this latter form of information which was filed against Mylius, and consequently he had no right to demand the appearance of the King in person; he protested, therefore, that as he was not being prosecuted for seditious libel and as the Attorney-General had stated that it was not a political case, he should have been proceeded against by the other form of criminal information, which would have entitled him to demand that the prosecutor should swear affidavits and appear personally in Court. The Lord Chief Justice, however, overruled his contention, reminding him that he had no power to subpoena the King, and that he had already found in Chambers that the prisoner had no facts which the

King could prove. Whereupon Mylius, perhaps wisely, refused to proceed further with his case.

" You said you wished to call evidence," Lord Alverstone reminded him.

" That is my evidence, my Lord."

" Do you wish to say anything more, Mr Mylius? "

" No, my Lord. I rest my case there, as I have been denied the constitutional right of a fair trial."

Lord Alverstone then proceeded to sum up and referred to Mylius' contention. " As a matter of fact," he said, " the evidence that could be obtained in such affidavits is before you to-day in the fullest measure. But that is not the ground upon which I declined to accede to Mr Mylius' application. I tell you . . . it is the right of the Attorney-General in any matter of libel or public wrong which he thinks of sufficient importance to justify a criminal information, it is his right and in one sense his duty, to file a criminal information." He then summed up on the main part of the case; but the evidence was quite clear in itself, and without leaving the box, the jury found a verdict of guilty. Lord Alverstone then turned to the prisoner, who was now standing.

" Mr Mylius," he said, " you have no right to say anything to me, but if you have anything to say before I pass sentence upon you, I will hear you; but you must direct it solely to that."

" My Lord," replied Mylius, stubborn to the end, " I have made my protest, and I have nothing more to say."

Sentence was duly passed upon him of twelve months' imprisonment, and the Court thought all was over. But Rufus Isaacs rose, and it was seen that he held a piece of paper in his hand. The crowd was silent again in expectation, as he began to speak.

" Now that sentence has been passed in this case, there is a matter to which I should like to refer, and which I did not think your Lordship would have thought it right for me to mention until after the verdict and sentence had been passed. I hold in my hands at this moment a document, under the hand of His Majesty the King, from which with your Lordship's permission I will read." He raised the paper and continued. " I am authorised by His Majesty to state publicly that he was never married except to the Queen, and that he never went through any ceremony of marriage except with the Queen. And further that His Majesty would have attended to give evidence to this effect had he not received advice from the Law Officers of the Crown that it would be unconstitutional for him to do so. That statement, my Lord, is signed by the King himself."

A murmur of approval greeted the conclusion of his statement, and the Mylius trial was over in less than a single day. So fizzled out one of the most impudent and fantastic attempts to discredit the Monarchy, that imagination can visualise. But Mylius, in his stubborn stupidity, had in one way been the instrument of good; for his trial enabled a base rumour to be finally scotched, which had been calculated to cast a cloud over the fair name of the British Sovereign.

CHAPTER XXI

VERY different from the quick despatch of the Mylius case was the protracted struggle of the Seddons' trial. This case—perhaps the most celebrated of poison trials—was the only murder trial in which Rufus Isaacs ever appeared, and in it he played the rôle of prosecuting counsel. His talents indeed were not those of a defending counsel in a murder trial; he had not that gorgeousness of eloquence nor that subtle sense of infusing his own personality into the case which are the marks of the great criminal advocate. These were the qualities preeminently of Marshall Hall, who was chosen as his antagonist in this trial. Never perhaps has there been a sharper contrast of methods and personalities. Both men were handsome; but Rufus Isaacs had the aquiline features of his race, and Marshall Hall had the broad flat features of the Anglo-Saxon. Both men were persuasive; but Rufus Isaacs' was the persuasiveness of accumulated argument, Marshall Hall's of tempestuous oratory. Both were men of vigour; but Rufus Isaacs' vigour was cloaked and conserved by his quietness of manner, Marshall Hall's accentuated and exhausted by the nervous tension of his disposition. Marshall Hall took by storm, while Rufus Isaacs laid siege; Marshall Hall was a crusader, Rufus Isaacs was a tactician; Marshall Hall was a Rupert, Rufus Isaacs was a Cunctator.

The man who was responsible for bringing about the clash of these two personalities was himself a personality of no small interest. Frederick Henry Seddon was at first glance one of those unattractive, worthy people, who are moderately successful in worthy, but unexciting, professions. He was, in point of fact, an insurance superintendent of middle age, who had progressed steadily up the ladder of prosperity, acquiring in the ascent a wife, Margaret, an attractive mild-eyed creature, a daughter, Maggie, and a fourteen-roomed house in Tollington Street, situated in one of those London suburbs which generally seem to acquire notoriety through the medium of an occasional murder trial, but do in fact regularly exist in discreet and unadvertised respectability.   But in spite of Tollington Street and the fourteen rooms, the life of the little household can hardly have been one of enthusiastic and uninterrupted felicity.   It was rumoured of Seddon that he had a way with the ladies, and no doubt if his tastes lay in this direction, he would have found means of gratifying them.   But, however this may be, he had other faults, even more destructive of connubial happiness.   He was hard, avaricious, mean, tyrannical and unsympathetic; and he appeared to glory in these qualities, thinking them to be a proof of additional cleverness in himself.   Marshall Hall in an adroit understatement, said of him: " he is a northcountryman, a thorough man of business and not a man of sentiment."   A more detailed, if less sympathetic, account describes him as " a shrewd, acute, keen person . . . a man full of cunning and craft, actuated by greed and covetousness."   But perhaps the best insight of what life must have been like in the household was revealed unconsciously by Mrs Seddon in her evidence, when she said, " he never used to take any notice when I said anything to him; he always had other things to think of."

Poor Margaret Seddon had other things to think of too, for, in spite of his accumulating prosperity, Seddon thought it desirable to keep only a general servant, and thus much of the work of the household devolved upon Mrs Seddon and her daughter, Maggie. In spite of this, however, Seddon increased his household by taking in a lodger, one Miss Barrow, a woman of forty-nine, possessed of some modest means and a querulous temper, which had caused her to quarrel with her cousins the Vonderahes, with whom she had previously lodged not far from Tollington Park.   Her advent to 63 Tollington Park made an increase of two in the house, for she brought with her a small orphan boy, called Ernie Grant, who appeared to be the only human thing for which this miserly and rather disreputable woman seemed to entertain any affection. She paid Seddon 12/6 a week for her lodging, with an additional 7/- to Maggie for attending her. This was but a modest outlay for a woman of her means, for she was the owner of the lease of the Buck's Head public house and the barber's shop next door, in addition to £1,600 of 3½ per cent. India Stock. This property, however, did not remain long in her hands after she took up her abode with Seddon, who soon obtained a considerable empire over her mind, and induced her to conclude a transaction with him, by which she made an assignment of her property to him on condition that he paid her an annuity of some £155. This he duly paid in monthly instalments in gold; and Miss Barrow's stock of gold was later considerably augmented when, in a scare as to the solvency of savings-banks, she withdrew her deposit of £216 from the Finsbury and City of London Savings Bank, and had it paid to her in gold.

There was, therefore, at any rate the presumption that there was a good deal of gold in the house at the beginning of September, 1911, when, after about fourteen months' residence with the Seddons, Miss Barrow was taken ill. It was a distressing illness involving sickness and diarrhoea, but Miss Barrow had at least the advantages of the medical skill of Dr Sworn and the devoted nursing of Mrs Seddon. But, in spite of this, there was no noticeable improvement in Miss Barrow's condition and, what with the heat and the offensive nature of her symptons Miss Barrow's room must have been a far from pleasant place; this, however, it may be observed, did not prevent her from having Ernie Grant to sleep in her bed. On September 10th a letter arrived from Seddon's sister, Mrs Longley, asking if she and her niece might stay at Tollington Park. Seddon wrote back to say that he was not too conveniently placed for receiving visitors, but that they might come if they cared to take pot-luck; accordingly on the 11th the Longleys arrived. But by this time Miss Barrow was worse, and by the evening of the 13th she was suffering great pain. Mr Seddon had gone out to the theatre and returned at about 11.30, rather put out by a dispute with the box-office clerk, to hear that in his absence the wretched Miss Barrow had crawled out of bed in agony, wailing " I am dying." He then went up to see her more than once, and found her each time in dreadful pain. At last she crawled out of bed and held herself on the ground in her agony, and Ernie Grant called out " Chickie "—for this was his nickname for her—" is out of bed." The Seddons came up and sent the terrified boy to his own room, while Mrs Seddon sat down by Miss Barrow's bed and Seddon took up his position outside on the landing. And so they stayed through the night, Mrs Seddon by the bed and Seddon reading and smoking on the landing, with the bedroom door open. Miss Barrow then fell into a heavy sleep for a time, snoring heavily, and the dawn broke to find her still alive. But shortly after six in the morning the breathing became more violent, and she was found to be dead.

Seddon, immediately after seeing the doctor, character-istically though scarcely creditably, set to work on a thorough search of the house to see what cash he could discover; but, in spite of the presumption that Miss Barrow must have collected a good stock of gold in the house, Seddon found— or so he said—only about £10. He decided, therefore, that what with medical bills and other expenses, it would only be possible to give the dead woman a public funeral in a common grave. It might have been supposed that, as Miss Barrow had the right of burial in a family vault, Seddon would have at once informed her relatives, the Vonderahes, who might perhaps have desired to make good the necessary expense; but Miss Barrow and he himself had been on bad terms with the Vonderahes, and he did not send round to acquaint them, although they lived but a very short distance away. He did, however, as he alleged, write a letter to inform them, and he was certainly able to produce a carbon copy of it to reinforce his statement; but the Vonderahes never received any such letter. Consequently Seddon set about the preparations for a funeral himself. He had received on the morning of Miss Barrow's death a certificate of death from Dr Sworn to the effect that she had died of epidemic diarrhoea, which that obliging practitioner had sent without the formality of a further visit. The actual business of the funeral arrangements gave Seddon a chance to show that his business acumen was by no means affected in moments of stress, for by a friendly agreement with the undertaker he received a commission of 12/6 for introducing the business to him. The body was removed from the house, after Mrs Seddon had pressed her lips to the dead woman's forehead in last salute; and on the Saturday following her death Miss Barrow was buried at Finchley.

In spite of the miscarriage of Seddon's letter and his reluctance to have personal relations with them, the Vonderahes soon discovered their cousin's death. They called, therefore, to see Seddon, who was not very informative, taking his stand upon the ground that, as they were not the next of kin, he was under no obligation to make full disclosure. They did find out, however, that she had surrendered her property to Seddon in exchange for an annuity, that she had made a will with Seddon's assistance scarcely three days before her death, and that only £10 had been discovered in the house. These facts were enough to make them suspicious, and other facts were revealed which seemed to lend corroboration. The upshot was that on November 15th the body was exhumed, and examined by Dr (now Sir Bernard) Spilsbury and Dr (later Sir William) Willcox. On November 29th, in a further examination by Dr Willcox, after the inquest had been adjourned, he came to the conclusion that there had been more than two grains of arsenic in the body at time of death, which pointed to death from acute arsenical poisoning as a result of a fatal dose taken less than three days before death. This was followed on December 4th by the arrest of Seddon.

" Absurd," he said, when they came to arrest him. " What a terrible charge, wilful murder! It is the first of our family that has ever been accused of such a crime." The remark was quaint, but showed that he retained his instinct for respectability even in moments of crisis, and his practical nature was not far behind for he added, " Are you going to arrest my wife as well? Have they found arsenic in the body? She has not done this herself. It was not carbolic acid, was it, as there was some in her room, and Sanitas is not poison, is it? "

Two days later there occurred an incident which was to be of considerable importance in the trial. Maggie Seddon was sent by her father's solicitor to a chemist in Tollington Park to buy some fly-papers. Now the theory of the prosecution was that Miss Barrow had been poisoned by an arsenical solution extracted from fly-papers, and Seddon's solicitor wanted the fly-papers for the purpose of analysis. But the chemist, a Mr Price, refused to serve her, as he did not wish to be mixed up in the case; later when the police examined her, Maggie Seddon said that she had not been to Price's shop to buy fly-papers. This was untrue, although it was true that she had not succeeded in buying any. Now her visit to Price's shop, or indeed her denial of it, were not matters in themselves of very great importance to the trial; but what was of importance was another visit to a chemist which Maggie was supposed to have made. This was the visit to Thorley's shop on August 26th, when she was alleged to have bought the fly-papers which were used for the poisoning of Miss Barrow. Maggie denied this visit, but the force of her denial was weakened by her untrue denial of her visit to Price's shop. The visit to Thorley's shop, however, was not strongly supported by evidence, for Thorley—who had previously seen Maggie Seddon twice at his house, for she knew his daughter—had only identified Maggie as the girl who had bought the fly-papers, from a crowd of twenty women, of whom only two were girls with their hair down their backs, after he had seen a picture of her in the papers in connection with the case. The whole business

of the visit to Thorley's shop rested too much on probabilities
and was perhaps the weakest and most unsatisfactory link
in the long chain of evidence which the prosecution succeeded
in forging.

But this is to anticipate. The inquest was resumed on
December 14th, and the jury brought in a verdict of wilful
murder by some person or persons unknown. Over Christ-
mas and the New Year the magisterial hearing took place
and on January 15th Mrs Seddon was arrested too. On
February 2nd, 1912, they were both committed for trial,
and just over a month later the Seddons took their place in
the dock at the Old Bailey to answer the charge of murder.
It was no ordinary murder, if murder it was; it was no
sudden killing in a violent affray, no *crime passionel*, no
sex-starved killing by some deranged, unhappy creature. It
was a murder, if murder it was, planned by an able man for
the sake of gain; a murder, prompted by no gust of passion,
but dictated by the balancing of certain gain against
improbable detection. It was a murder, if murder it was,
that was different; and it was because of its emotional
coldness, because of the absence of those evidences of lack
of self-control, because it did not provide those elements
which usually grip the public interest, that popular attention
was fascinated by it, as by some repulsive, but strangely
hypnotic reptile. There were other things, too, besides the
nature of Seddon and the character with which he invested
proceedings, to arrest the attention of the public. There
were mysteries to be explained, and difficult points at issue,
which ensured a good fight on the facts; and there were the
combatants, too, who could make a good fight of it—the
Attorney-General, whose first murder trial it was, but who
brought with him the great reputation which his private
practice had conferred upon him, supported by that expert
team of Treasury counsel, Messrs. Muir, Rowlatt, and
Travers Humphreys, and opposed by Marshall Hall, rich
in experience of criminal trials and the most eloquent
advocate of his day. Mrs Seddon was independently represented by Mr (now Sir) Gervais Rentoul, but the young

counsel wisely allowed Marshall Hall to encroach a good deal upon his territory.

The hearing began with Rufus Isaacs' opening speech, a succinct outline of the facts, which occupied two hours. The Court was crowded to hear him and remained so during the rather dreary evidence of Miss Barrow's financial relations with the Seddons. On the fourth day of the trial, however, public interest quickened, and in the afternoon so great was the throng of junior members of the Bar that many of them sat on the floor. The occasion was the cross-examination of Dr Willcox by Marshall Hall, which furnished one of the most acute and penetrative cross-examinations of expert witness ever heard in the Courts; but then Marshall Hall had the advantage, not shared by many counsel, of being himself something of an expert on scientific questions. The cross-examination was of first importance because it raised a question prior to that of Seddon's guilt or innocence; it raised the question—was there a murder at all? For Marshall Hall's theory was that death had taken place not, as the prosecution maintained, from acute arsenical poisoning, but from chronic arsenical poisoning plus epidemic diarrhoea; the difference, of course, is that whereas in acute arsenical poisoning the fatal dose must have been taken shortly before death, chronic arsenical poisoning may be merely the aggravating and decisive factor, working on some other main cause—in this case the epidemic diarrhoea. It followed, therefore, that if Marshall Hall's theory could be established, the case against Seddon collapsed. He did, in fact, come within an ace of establishing it. Dr Willcox had used the Marsh test to decide upon the amount of arsenic in the body at time of death; for, it being impossible to weigh the entire amount of arsenic in the body, it is necessary to extract a specimen from the viscera and weigh that, then multiply it by the multiplying factor indicated by the Marsh test, which could be as much as two thousand. That is to say, the slightest inaccuracy or uncertainty of calculation would be magnified enormously in the final result. Now Dr Willcox had estimated a quantity of 2.01

grains of arsenic in the body at time of death, and this, as he told the Attorney-General in his examination-in-chief, was in his view part of a dose of five grains; and two grains is a fatal dose. The first part of Marshall Hall's cross-examination of Dr Willcox, therefore, really amounted to an emphasising of the minuteness of accuracy, necessary to such tests, especially when the multiplying factor is large. " There is not," he said, " sufficient evidence for you to say that those quantities are based upon a sufficiently accurate basis to enable you to rely on them absolutely." He then proceeded to ask him with careful unconcern as to the disposition of the arsenic in the hair. The importance of this was that if the amount in the " distal " (*i.e.*, further) ends was large, relatively to the amount in the " proximal " ends, that is the ends nearest the roots, it would mean that the arsenic had been taken over a period, and that death was due to chronic, and not acute, arsenical poisoning. Marshall Hall was able to gain from Dr Willcox the admission that the distal ends of the hair did in fact contain such large quantities of arsenic, relative to the proximal ends, as to suggest that arsenic had been taken over a period.

This result was a triumph for Marshall Hall, but not the complete triumph which it would have been if he could have convinced Dr Willcox himself. Dr Willcox, however, was not convinced, and, feeling certain that there must be an alternative and correct interpretation, he sought for it in his mind and hit upon it during the actual course of the cross-examination. It was just before proceedings drew to a close on the fourth day when, in answer to a question of counsel's as to the metabolic changes in the hair, he quietly interposed: " There is one point which I have not mentioned, which I ought to mention here, which rather affects these results, and that is that when I took the hair for analysis it was at the second examination, and the hair had been lying in the coffin and it was more or less soaked in the juice of the body." This theory, if true, smashed the whole structure of Marshall Hall's careful edifice, and he strove hard against it; but Dr Willcox was certain that he was right this time, and the simple expedient of taking somebody else's hair and soaking it in the liquid in which Miss Barrow had rested afforded ocular demonstration that the effect was the same. Thus the explanation was much simpler than Marshall Hall had imagined and by its very simplicity it carried conviction all the more readily to the jury; but he had come very near to winning the case for his client in the first round.

Marshall Hall had failed to prove that the mode of death was such as could not have been murder; and the remaining question was the more personal one—did Seddon commit murder? The onus of proof was, of course, on the prosecution, and at the end of the evidence for the prosecution Marshall Hall submitted that there was no case to go to the jury; and, although Mr Justice Bucknill ruled that there was, the case for the prosecution was by no means cast-iron. The chief difficulty was that it rested entirely upon circumstantial evidence; nobody had seen Seddon administer poison, nobody could even suggest any particular occasion when he had actually done so. In point of fact, of course, it was unlikely that there could be; but nevertheless juries are notoriously and rightly, reluctant to convict of murder on circumstantial evidence alone. The defence, therefore, was on tolerably strong ground, and Marshall Hall, in his short opening speech went so far as to urge that the commission of the crime showed a knowledge of poisons that could not be attributed to Seddon. Besides, if he was so hardened and so expert as an acceptance of the prosecution's view would make him out to be, then would he not certainly have completed the business by getting a second certificate from the doctor and having the body cremated? Then there was Thorley's identification of Maggie Seddon, which Marshall Hall urged was inadequate, and other points of criticism, which taken together would afford serious obstacles in the way of the prosecution. In the circumstances, Marshall Hall was not anxious to put Seddon into the box, for this would give the Attorney a chance to cross-examine him; and Marshall Hall realised that Seddon was one of those men whose intellectual arrogance too often leads them to commit themselves. There was nothing about him either that would make a favourable impression on the jury; his coldness, his calculation, his hardness, his very ability—or, at any rate, the way in which it was bent to subserve his avarice—all the things which he considered to be marks of his especial distinction, were to the jury, viewed against the background of Death, nauseous and repellent. But Seddon had neither misgiving nor reticence; he would show how clever he was and defy the Attorney-General in a dialectical duel with any weapons of which he should choose to avail himself. Now Marshall Hall, as we have seen in an earlier connection, was very sensitive on the question of putting his clients into the witness box on criminal charges; he would advise and warn, but he would not try to compel. Advice and warning were likely to have but little effect on Seddon's buoyancy and he duly entered the box, which he was to occupy for over eleven hours.

He had already stamped his personality on the case and on the Court, and there were great queues outside the Court to see him in the box. His demeanour during his four hour examination—during part of which Marshall Hall sat, owing to the strain and fatigue which the case was imposing on him—was easy and confident; the examination-in-chief was entirely successful, for Seddon's conceit was not of the affected character of a previous client of Marshall Hall's, Robert Wood, whose examination-in-chief, Mr Marjoribanks informs us, Marshall Hall found more difficult than any cross-examination. The examination lasted from the Friday afternoon into the Saturday morning and, as soon as it was concluded, the Attorney rose to cross-examine. The Court was still with the nervous silence of expectation, as for a moment the eyes of the two antagonists rested on each other, like two wrestlers manoeuvring for the first throw; but Seddon, though he knew that the lithe figure and aquiline features confronting him represented the hero of a hundred cross-examinations and the conqueror of Whittaker Wright, remained serene and unperturbed. It was a great moment in his life; let the Attorney-General do his worst.

The first question was asked, almost a formal one:

" Miss Barrow lived with you from July 26th, 1910, to September 14th, 1911? "

" Yes."

And then the second question, just as softly, just as simply:

" Did you like her? "

It was the cleverest question conceivable in the circumstances, and the one that Seddon least expected. He had come into the box prepared to defend and to explain, to answer logically and arithmetically, and here right at the beginning was a question which could not be so answered. Rufus Isaacs had torn down the protective palisade of figures, behind which Seddon, the business man, proposed to shelter; he would return to deal with these aspects, but first the jury must see Seddon, the man. And the simple question " did you like her? " was one that baffled Seddon, the astute man of affairs.

" Did I like her? " he repeated.

" Yes, that is the question."

Seddon paused and then replied: " She was not a woman that you could be in love with, but I deeply sympathised with her."

In point of fact, Seddon's coldness was strongly brought out in cross-examination, and told against him with the jury. Thus when later in the cross-examination Rufus Isaacs asked him, in reference to the doctor not having seen the dead woman, whether he did not want for his own satisfaction to make sure that the woman was dead, he answered: " I had no desire. I had no idea at all in the matter."

The cross-examination was lengthy, six hours in all, and traversed in detail the whole range and complexity of the case. It dealt, for instance, with Miss Barrow's money affairs and her attachment to the boy, Ernie Grant.

" But she certainly had some desire to leave property to the boy, had she not? "

" She was satisfied that the boy had a good home with me," was the stubborn answer.

There was, too, the question of the annuity which had been very profitable to Seddon, and for which he had given no security; there was the will of September 11th which he had drawn up in his own handwriting; there was the mis-leading letter to the Vonderahes on September 14th—" I must also inform you that she made a will on the 11th instant, leaving all she died possessed of to Hilda and Ernie Grant."

" You meant that as the formal document from you as executor of the estate . . . and if they had not suspected you that would have been the end of the thing? "

" I don't see that."

" Not even now? "

" I do now."

" That letter is not a very frank statement, is it? "

" That is the view you have taken of it and I have agreed."

" I understand you agree with that? "

" Well, I could have put more in the letter evidently."

" It would have taken less words to have said that you had sold her the annuity and had got the property? "

" But what difference did that make? "

" Don't argue with me," said Rufus Isaacs sternly; for witnesses are in the unfortunate position of having to speak when they are spoken to and not ask questions.

" And then did you say this," asked the Attorney (referring to Seddon's interview with Vonderahe). " I had nothing to do with it? "

" No, I did not; because he would find me out in a lie, would he not? "

" But you see it takes a great many inquiries to find out some lies," was the suave but ominous response.

Seddon was straitly cross-examined, too, about his conduct on that last night.

" Why did you want to stay up outside the door when your wife was dozing and the patient was sleeping peacefully? "

" Because my sleep was broken."

" Was it not because you were afraid the end was coming and you didn't want your wife to be alone? "

" Certainly not. My sleep was broken, being up the best part of the night off and on, backwards and forwards."

" There was the question, too, of Miss Barrow's money; what had become of that? Now we will take off the £10 that you paid her on September 2nd, and that will leave £402 in gold, according to the evidence which we have got? "

" Yes."

" Traced to her in eight months, to the end of August, 1911? "

" Yes."

" Now, of that £402, as I understand your statement, when you came to look for the money on the morning of her death, you found threepence in copper in her purse? "

" Yes."

" And that is all? "

" Yes."

" Did you make any inquiry about the money? "

" I hadn't any idea regarding it."

" Then does that mean you made no inquiry? "

During the whole long cross-examination Seddon remained calm and collected, parrying the thrusts of his expert opponent. Only twice in the entire six hours did he show any trace of feeling. Once was in reference to the suggestion that his assistants saw him counting Miss Barrow's gold in his office.

" The prosecution are suggesting that I am dealing with the deceased woman's gold; that I should bring it down from the top of the house to the bottom into the office in the presence of my assistants and count it up? Is it feasible? "

" I do not want to argue with you, but you know that sometimes people do very foolish things? "

" Well, I am not a degenerate. That would make it out that I was a greedy, inhuman monster."

" What? "

" That I am a greedy, inhuman monster, or something

with a very degenerate mind, to commit a vile crime such as the prosecution suggest, and then bringing the dead woman's money down and counting it in the presence of my two assistants, and flouting it like that. The suggestion is scandalous."

The outburst would probably have done Seddon good with the jury, for it showed that he was not the heartless, passionless automaton that his general demeanour would suggest. But he undid the good effect by adding in his usual tone, and with an almost defiant sneer: " I would have all day to count the money."

The second occasion on which Seddon's feelings broke through the icy detachment of his demeanour, showed him in a more human light than at any other time in the whole course of the trial. Rufus Isaacs was reading to him the statement of the police-officer as to his conduct on arrest.

" And then," he said, " it goes on, ' Are you going to arrest my wife as well? ' "

" No, not then. I said ' Can you not take me home and let my wife and family know that I am arrested? ' He said ' You need not worry about that, you will see your wife at the station; I am coming back for her.' I said ' Are you going to arrest her as well? ' That, I swear before God, is the words that took place, and I have been waiting for the opportunity to get into this box for to relate the true words that were spoken on this occasion."

" All the statements that you are making are statements before God."

" Yes, sir, I recognise that. I want to emphasise that, because I do not look upon it as material—it does not make me innocent or guilty, but I want the truth and I was very much upset at the North London Police Court when the evidence was given. . . ."

" I will read you the statement and you can tell me——"

But Seddon broke in with vehemence: " There is nothing hurt me more than that since my arrest."

" Listen to the question," said the Attorney. But the tide of Seddon's indignation, once unloosed, was not easily to be dammed. " Do you think," he broke in again, " that a man with five children would want to see his wife arrested, and a baby ill which had been to the doctor that day? "

" It is not suggested that you wanted to see your wife arrested," interposed Sir Rufus.

" Yes, it is suggested. ' Are you going to arrest my wife too? ' That was my greatest concern. It has been the greatest trial of my life since she has been arrested, and we have neglected the five children."

The unfeigned indignation of Seddon, as a family man, undoubtedly did much more to help him with the jury than all the acumen on which he so prided himself. These two episodes were unique, isolated moments of passion in his great and unvarying imperturbability. In the course of cross-examination, Rufus Isaacs had steadily gained, and had pierced his flank in many places. It was not the devastating business that the cross-examination of Whittaker Wright had been, for Seddon had not been annihilated. Since the evidence was entirely circumstantial, the cross-examination could hardly have the quality of sharp finality. Rufus Isaacs had bent his efforts to establishing the existence of motive and of opportunity, and of showing from the evidence of subsequent conduct that Seddon had yielded to temptation and availed himself of the opportunity. And so successful had he been that, when Seddon left the box, the shadow of the gallows had crept appreciably nearer than when he had entered it in the jaunty confidence of three days ago.

Seddon was succeeded in the box by his wife, who made a very different impression. For whereas Seddon's whole demeanour had been one of challenge, Mrs Seddon's constituted an appeal to the sympathy of the jury. He had been strong, reserved, arrogant and unemotional; but she, with her nervous habit of smiling, her low voice—which was so difficult to hear that the Judge had to move his chair nearer and then repeat her answers to the Court—her pretty, refined, rather faded appearance, had a general air of pathos which could not but appeal. She broke down when questioned about Miss Barrow's death by Mr Rentoul, and exclaimed to Rufus Isaacs with the frenzied intensity of the weak: " She was not dying, certainly. I never wish anybody dead. I thought too much of Miss Barrow. I waited hand and foot on her. I did all I possibly could to get her better." It was clear that the jury would differentiate between her and her husband, not so much because of anything she had said—for in her evidence she had to admit to several dishonesties—but because it was quite clear that neither in desire nor in the strength of execution was she a murderess. Whatever she might have done had been done as the merest accessory; the eye, the hand, the brain, and the will were her husband's.

The evidence for the defence closed on the ninth day of the trial, and daily public interest was growing keener and more excited. The Court had been especially crowded during the Seddons' evidence, and many women were in Court to hear Mrs Seddon. At the conclusion of the evidence came what, from the spectatorial point of view at any rate, was likely to be the most enthralling portion of the trial—Marshall Hall's final speech for Seddon.

His speech was worthy of himself and of the occasion; it was a magnificent plea to the jury not to " sweep these two people off their feet by the waves of prejudice, and then drown them in the backwash of suspicion." " If you are against these people," he said, " and if you think the evidence is against them, I do not say for one moment there is not sufficient evidence of opportunity, and sufficient evidence of motive; " but of real proof there was none. All Seddon's actions could be, and had been, explained by reference to ordinary commonplace consideration of business and domestic life. And yet the prosecution was insisting on an explanation, which demanded all sorts of assumptions; it demanded the assumption of an expert knowledge of arsenic on the part of Seddon, " and yet . . . you have got to assume that, having made this extract of arsenic for the purpose of poisoning this woman, he never discovered the one thing which is the characteristic of arsenic, which can be found in

any book dealing with arsenic, that it has a preservative effect upon the body, and therefore from that point of view, and from the prisoner's point of view, it is one of the most dangerous poisons that can be used. You have got to assume that he was entirely ignorant of that, or you must assume this, that he could have been such a madman as not to take advantage of the opportunity of cremating her, which would destroy all traces of the crime . . . All these assumptions are to be drawn against these two people because of two things. First of all, because the male prisoner benefits by the death of the deceased in that the annuity ceases, and secondly, there is the suggestion—and here I submit that there is no evidence at all worthy of your consideration—that Miss Barrow was in possession of a large sum of money at the time of her death, and that they murdered her in order to obtain it . . . Gentlemen, eight assumptions have to be made against these two people. Am I not justified in saying that every one of them is a violent assumption? "
It was a convincing and comprehensive speech, not shirking the issue of fact on any point, and studded with passages of great eloquence. After four hours' close development of the argument he expanded into a magnificent and moving peroration: " Gentlemen," he said, " I often think, when I look at the great figure of Justice which towers over all our judicial proceedings, when I see the blind figure holding the scales—I often think that possibly the bandage over the eyes of Justice has a two-fold meaning. Not only is it there so that the course of Justice should not be warped by prejudice or undue influence one way or the other; but sometimes I think it is put there so that those who gaze should not see the look of infinite pity which is in the eyes of Justice behind that bandage, the look of infinite mercy which must always temper justice in a just man. Gentlemen, in that hand of Justice are held two scales, and you are the people to watch and decide, as the inanimate hand of Justice holds those scales aloft—it is you who decide what is the result of the weighing . . . Gentlemen, the great scientists who have been here have told us much of the manuals of

science, and of the deductions that can be made from science.
There is one thing the scientists have never yet been able
to find, never yet been able to discover with all their research
and all their study, and that is, how to replace the little
vital spark that we call life. Upon your verdict here
depends, so far as I am concerned, the life of this man. If
your verdict is against him, that vital spark will be extinguished, and no science known to the world can ever replace
it."

Marshall Hall sat down at 3.10 on the afternoon of the
ninth day of the trial; Gervais Rentoul, for Mrs Seddon,
wisely relied mainly on the great effort of Marshall Hall's
speech and himself made only a short appeal, stressing the
emotional aspect. He finished at 3.45 and it was Rufus
Isaacs' turn to wind up for the Crown. He was thus
separated from Marshall Hall's great effort by only half
an hour, but wisely made no attempt to recapture, or to
challenge, the atmosphere of it. It would not, of course,
have been proper for him to do so, for prosecuting counsel
may not plead with the whole-hearted ardour which had
informed Marshall Hall's speech. But in any case he would
not have done so; for, as we have seen, he fought with
different weapons. In his own sphere, of great eloquence
and passionate appeal, Marshall Hall was supreme; but it
was not the province of Rufus Isaacs. In fact in his opening,
Rufus Isaacs seemed almost to exaggerate the difference,
for his manner was quiet, even for him, and he hesitated for
his words. But, as he proceeded, it was seen how entirely
he had the case in hand; and steadily, surely, almost
inexorably, he forged that " chain of gossamer links joined
together with immense ingenuity," which hanged Seddon
in the end.

There were two main questions for the Court to consider:
first, whether Miss Barrow died of acute arsenical poisoning,
and, secondly, if so, whether Seddon had administered it.
On the first point, in view of the evidence of Dr Willcox
and Dr Spilsbury there could not be much doubt; indeed,
Dr Rosenheim, the defence's expert witness, had not been

called " for the simple reason that he could not contradict anything that Dr Willcox and Dr Spilsbury had said." The Attorney-General then turned to the second and main issue; was Seddon guilty of murder? And here, there being, as we have seen, no direct evidence, he relied on establishing bit by bit and with gathering force, the evidence of motive, opportunity, and subsequent conduct. Motive? There was the reversion of Miss Barrow's property, which had been made over to him in exchange for an annuity, without a single scrap of writing. " I am going to suggest to you," said Rufus Isaacs, " of course for your consideration, that she had no notion during the whole of this time that she was parting with her property, with her gold, or with her notes, and had never intended to get rid of gold or notes in the ordinary course of things . . . that she meant to retain it for her boy, whom, in the maternal instinct, no doubt, of the spinster heart, she was cherishing, and to whom she had become devoted." But, in point of fact, poor Ernie Grant did not benefit greatly by Miss Barrow's death; it was Seddon who benefited by her death, and the circumstances of it connected him with it. The prosecution's case was that she had been poisoned by a solution from arsenical fly-papers, administered by Seddon, and that the fly-papers had been purchased by Maggie Seddon on behalf of her father for that purpose on August 26th. The defence contested this purchase, and claimed that Thorley's identification of Maggie Seddon was not to be relied upon; but if he was right, and she did make the purchase, then " all the views put forward by the defence break down and the case for the defence crumbles away because no attempted explanation has been given as to why it was that those fly-papers should have been asked for on August 26th." And why should Thorley have made an inaccurate identification? He had no interest in the case except to keep out of it; and he remembered the sale specifically because she had asked for four packets, and he had only been able to give her one as that was all he had in stock. If this was the true explanation, it fitted in very well with the dates, for Miss Barrow had fallen ill on Sep-

tember 1st.   But the story of the defence was that Mrs
Seddon had bought arsenical fly-papers on September 4th
or 5th (*i.e.*, some days after Miss Barrow fell ill), and that
these four fly-papers had been put into four separate saucers,
from which they were changed into one soup-plate on the
12th; the suggestion implied was that, after the fly-papers
were put into the soup-plate, Miss Barrow, in her raging
thirst, had got out of bed and drunk the water on top of
the fly-papers.   But " during the whole of this case so far,
what seems to have been forgotten is that there is plenty
of water in her room.   No one has suggested that she had
not any water in her room."   Indeed, according to the
evidence, there were two jugs on the washstand with water
in them, a water-bottle, a soda-syphon, and also brandy.
Besides, as to the fly-papers, who were the people who
would have seen them if they were there?   There was
Ernie Grant, Dr Sworn, Chater the servant; and none of
them had.   Against this improbable story was to be set the
version of the prosecution.   If the arsenical fly-papers were
introduced into the house at the end of August, then it was
much easier to understand why Miss Barrow was taken ill
at the beginning of September.   For, of course, Seddon
would know that the fly-papers were poisonous, and it would
be the easiest thing in the world for him to administer it
with Valentine's meat-juice or brandy.   This done, he knew
on the night of death that the end was near, and, therefore,
he waited up because he could not leave his wife alone to
see it; perhaps, indeed, she would not stay alone to see it.

Rufus Isaacs then passed on to the question of subsequent
conduct, and here again, he contended, the evidence was
convincing.   He had called in a doctor, it was true; but if
he had not, there would have to have been an inquest, which
would have been a much more serious thing for him.   As
for Marshall Hall's suggestion that if Seddon really had
committed murder he would certainly have had the body
cremated, " that is the kind of argument you hear in every
criminal case that ever comes before a Court.   If every
criminal knew, when he was committing the crime, of all the

various steps that he might take in order to prevent the detection of the crime . . . no doubt there would be a great many more undetected crimes than at present." His refusal to give information to the only relatives, of whom he had knowledge, the Vonderahes, was clearly suspicious. He said that he had written a letter to them, informing them of Miss Barrow's death and of her will, but they had not received the letter nor had anybody seen it, although he was ready armed with a carbon copy of it to substantiate his allegation. Yet, when the Vonderahes called in person, he flatly refused to give them information, which was clear evidence that he did not want the truth to be known. And so, hour after hour, cold, logical, precise, the Attorney-General's speech, unadorned by eloquence and undegraded by passion, swept on to its majestic conclusion: " All I ask you is, when you have made up your minds, not to shrink from the conclusions to which you think you are forced by the evidence that has been given. If you are satisfied, say so, whatever the consequences. If you are not satisfied, do not hesitate to acquit either the one or both. Give effect to the results of your deliberations and the conclusions you come to, and, if you have done that, you will have done your duty, and justice, I am satisfied, will have been done."

Rufus Isaacs' speech finished on the tenth day of the trial, and Mr Justice Bucknill started his summing up. If Rufus Isaacs' cross-examination and speech had made Seddon's conviction probable, the summing up made it virtually certain. Unfortunately the summing up was the summing up of an old judge, exhausted and upset by the lengthy trial. One cannot help feeling sorry for Mr Justice Bucknill, whose feelings about the trial were expressed in his own remark to the jury: " I am sure there must be men in your body who would have given anything not to have been in this case. I can only tell you, as far as I am concerned, I have the same feelings." But nevertheless it was unfortunate that the jury in so complicated a case did not receive a more adequate direction. In point of fact, Mr Justice Bucknill's summing up lasted only two hours and " left an impression

as strongly against Seddon as it did in favour of his wife."
Indeed he virtually directed an acquittal of Mrs Seddon,
when he said to the jury: " You have seen this woman.
Do you think she is lying? Well, if she was lying she was
lying very cleverly. If you think she was telling the truth
with regard to what took place on the night of the 13th to
the 14th, and with regard to the last illness, I should not be
astonished if you found her not guilty." Towards Seddon,
however, his attitude was very different, and unfortunately
he twice made use of the expression " do not be prejudiced
too much," once in reference to his not sending for the doctor
on the night of Miss Barrow's final agony, and secondly,
in reference to his funeral arrangements. Now there should
be no suggestion of the jury being prejudiced at all in legal
proceedings; no doubt there are occasions when this is a
legal fiction, but at any rate it should be maintained from
the Bench. It is clearly unfortunate that the jury should
get the idea, sanctioned from the highest quarter, that prejudice on their part is inevitable or even possible.

The jury retired at 3.58 on the afternoon of Thursday,
March 14th, and were absent an hour. When they filed
back into Court, the stream of chatter was frozen into
anxious silence. Everybody looked at the foreman's face
to try and read his secret of life and death. The Deputy-
Clerk of the Court addressed him.

" Do you find Frederick Henry Seddon guilty or not
guilty of wilful murder? "

" Guilty," came the reply.

Every gaze turned to Seddon, but he moved not a muscle;
he remained aloof, unconcerned. But the Deputy-Clerk
was again addressing the foreman, and, as if fascinated, the
eyes swung back again.

" Do you find Margaret Ann Seddon guilty or not guilty
of wilful murder? "

" Not guilty," came the reply.

At once Seddon turned to his wife in the dock, and kissed
her. As the Court watched this last salute, it was as if
they were spectators of some ghastly tableau between life

and death. The awed silence was broken by a moan from Mrs Seddon.

"Tell her she is discharged," said the Judge. And Mrs Seddon, sobbing uncontrolledly, was half led, half lifted out of the dock by the wardresses. She resisted, as much as her feeble strength would allow, flinging her arms out towards her husband and giving a terrible cry. But Seddon had paid his tribute to emotion, and was once more the practical man of affairs; he waved her back and though hearing her cries, which growing ever fainter, still harrowed every other person in the Court, he paid no heed. For he was anxious to make his statement.

His statement made in a firm voice, was clear, concise and well-reasoned, a remarkable performance for a man who had just been found guilty of murder. It ended with the words "anything more I might have to say I do not suppose will be of any account, but still, if it is the last words I speak, I am not guilty of the crime for which I stand committed." The Judge then assumed the black cap, but his voice trembled as he addressed Seddon; and his distress had been increased by Seddon's Masonic oath, "I declare by the Great Architect of the Universe that I am not guilty, my Lord," for Mr Justice Bucknill was a leading Freemason. He nerved himself to his task, however, and said, in faltering tones: "This murder has been described by yourself in the box as one which, if made out against you, was a barbarous one—a murder of design, a cruel murder. It is not for me to harrow your feelings."

"It does not affect me," said Seddon in a steady voice. "I have a clear conscience."

"Try to make peace with your Maker," urged the Judge.

"I am at peace," came the reply.

As the Judge proceeded to sentence, ending with the exhortation "and may the Lord have mercy on your soul," he was seen to be in tears. But Seddon merely watched him with slightly raised eyebrows and an expression of supercilious astonishment. As the Judge wiped his eyes he gave a final faint shrug of his shoulders, and made for the stairs to leave the dock, undirected and unassisted. One cannot withhold admiration from the hard man, whose indifference to the misfortunes of others is equalled by an imperviousness to his own.

Seddon's advisers took the case to the Court of Criminal Appeal, where it was heard by Mr Justice Darling, Mr Justice Channel, and Mr Justice Coleridge on the first two days of April. Marshall Hall, who never liked appearing in a Court of Appeal, argued skilfully and vehemently, but the Court dismissed the appeal without even calling upon the Attorney-General. So Seddon had to die.

Was the awful crime, of which he was accused and for which he had to pay so heavy a penalty, brought home to him beyond the possibility of reasonable doubt? He had had a fair trial, and had been found guilty by a representative jury of his countrymen; but such verdicts have been wrong before now. At the time there was a strong enough feeling that his guilt had not been established, for three hundred thousand people—and it must be remembered that Seddon was not an attractive or sympathetic character—to sign the petition for his reprieve. He was condemned on a combination of scientific and circumstantial evidence, which did not greatly commend itself to the plain man. It is true that the prosecution had forged so long a chain of suspicious circumstances that it is almost impossible that it could be linked together by anything but the supposition of murder. But it is just possible that alternative explanations were the correct ones. It is just possible, for instance, that the fly-papers had been in the room, although nobody had noticed them, and that Miss Barrow, in her agony, had drunk the solution from the soup-plate; it is just possible that Miss Barrow had previously disposed of the gold and that Ernie Grant was wrong in his recollection of seeing her count it in August, 1911; it is just possible that Seddon's letter to the Vonderahes was lost in the post, and that his taciturnity to them derived from a dislike of them rather than from a desire to conceal the facts. It is just possible, in short, that Seddon, though grasping and avaricious, was not a murderer. It was not likely; but the possibility, combined with such things as the unsatisfactory circumstances connected with Thorley's identification of Maggie Seddon, makes us appreciate Mr Filson Young's comment that " the moment was excruciating for any one who, if not assured of Seddon's innocence, was certainly not assured that his guilt had been satisfactorily proved, and there was more than one such person in the Court."

It was suggested at the time that the prosecution, whose attitude in a capital case should be almost judicial, pressed too hard upon the prisoner, and the Attorney-General's speech has been described as a " hanging speech." It is, of course, true that this was Rufus Isaacs' first, and only, murder case, and that he was not familiar with the atmosphere of murder trials. It is also true that his cold, impersonal attitude was not likely to inspire the jury with much sympathy for the prisoner; but then this is perhaps scarcely part of the duty of prosecuting counsel. If the prosecution do press unduly hard, it is the duty of the Judge to restore the balance; unfortunately, in this case, as we have seen, the summing up was not very satisfactory. In point of fact, Mr Justice Bucknill said that " the Attorney-General has conducted this case with remarkable fairness," and Marshall Hall paid high tribute to it. " The nature of the prosecution," he said, " is always more deadly when it is conducted with the fairness with which this case has been conducted by the learned Attorney-General, and I hope it will be a model to those who practise in these Courts of the way in which prosecutions should be conducted by the Crown."

As for Mrs Seddon, that weak, well-meaning, baffled creature, her troubles did not end with her acquittal. She tried to collect funds in Hyde Park to help her husband's petition, but a hostile demonstration forced her to retire. Her neighbours, with a singular contempt for the finding of the Court, insisted that she was a murderess, and, in order to silence this unfriendly gossip, she signed a " confession " which appeared in the *Weekly Dispatch*, to the effect that she had seen her husband give poison to Miss Barrow and had been terrorised by him into silence. Under the influence of *John Bull*, however, Mrs Seddon retracted her " confession " and said it was untrue. Having got affairs into this muddle she conceived a happy and feminine solution of her difficulties by marrying again and going abroad. I trust that in a new world she found happiness in her new life.

The petition for Seddon's reprieve failed, and his execution was fixed for April 18th. He was bitterly disappointed at the failure of his final hope, but he remained stoical to the end, maintaining his innocence at the last. But public interest, which had followed closely the trial of this strange, striking personality, so narrow in his strength, so unattractive in his ability, was diverted from his death. For the shadow of the gallows, which overtook him, was lost in the greater shadow of unexampled catastrophe.

CHAPTER XXII

THE TITANIC DISASTER

IT is in a way curious that the *Titanic* disaster, separated as it is from us by the long agony of the War, should abide so vividly in the memory. It might have been thought that senses, blunted by the long accumulation of accustomed horror, would have reacted but dully to the memory of an earlier and less lasting calvary. But it has not been so; rather it has proved that people, looking back for some harbinger of the great disaster which was to engulf their lives, found it in the wreck of the *Titanic*. They did not find it in the Irish troubles, for they were too " political "; but the seas which engulfed the *Titanic* swept away ordinary people in the quiet pursuance of their avocations. There, but for the grace of God, went lords and ladies, the butcher, the baker, the candlestick maker, just and unjust, sinners and saints; it was potent because it might have happened to anybody. People at that time—or, at least, certain classes of them—were living in a state of unparalleled security; it may be that they were confounding comfort with civilisation, and it may be that it was a dull and soulless security. But, whatever it was, people, ignorant or careless of the signs that high politics provided, felt that it would last for ever. They were wrong, and their first suspicion that they were wrong came with the *Titanic* disaster; irrationally, perhaps, but intuitively and irresistibly, they felt in it a shock that undermined the basis of the cushioned security in which they lived; as it turned out, it was to be swept away for ever. For, as the crash of the *Titanic* echoed and re-echoed, it was as if, in spirit, one heard the first rumblings of the prelude to Armageddon.

The *Titanic* disaster, great in its magnitude, was infinitely greater in surprise. For the *Titanic*, built in homage to the

pre-War twin ideals of comfort and security was itself the
best embodiment of those ideas.   There had lately been a
competition for the speed record of the North Atlantic
route; it had passed from the White Star *Teutonic* to the
Cunard's *Campania,* from the *Campania* to the Hamburg-
Amerika *Deutschland* and thence back again to the *Maure-
tania* and the *Lusitania.*   But such competition was indulged
in only at a price, for a speed of twenty-seven knots costs
roughly five times as much as a speed of twenty-one knots;
nor is the price paid only in money, for great speed entails
a vibration which is detrimental to comfort.   Besides, what
is speed after all?   It may be essential to the arriviste, but
there are things more important to a generation which has
arrived.   The White Star line, therefore, decided to build
a ship designed, not to compete in speed, but to surpass in
safety and luxury; the *Titanic* would carry business men like
gentlemen.   And indeed her size and appointments were
such as to impress even the most hard-headed captains of
commerce.   The *Titanic* was a ship of 45,000 tons, half as
big again as the 30,000 ton Cunarders.   She had watertight
doors which could be closed in half-a-minute from the
bridge; automatic fire-alarms; the most powerful wireless
installations afloat; double bottoms; fifteen watertight compartments, of which any two could be smashed without
endangering the safety of the ship.   She carried fourteen
ordinary lifeboats, four collapsibles, and two emergency sea-
boats, a provision more than half as great again as that
required by the Board of Trade regulations (but it may here
be remarked that the Board of Trade, with that complacency
which is so pleasing a feature of our Government departments, had framed its regulations to apply to ships of ten
thousand tons, and had not since seen fit to revise them).

But if the *Titanic's* structure, engines and safeguards were
an object of wondering remark to those who could appreciate
such things, her appointments and fittings were a source of
delight to the most uninitiate.   There were gymnasiums for
the athletic, lounges for the lazy, shops for the trivially
acquisitive and dining-rooms for all; and all was done on a

lavish scale, which took by storm the imagination of a generation, as yet untrained by Hollywood and Messrs. Lyons to the customary inspection of rococo magnificence. She carried, too, on her maiden voyage a cargo of great names to people her apartments. There was Bruce Ismay, managing-director of the White Star Line; there was finance in the person of Benjamin Guggenheim, and rich philanthropy in Isidor Straus; there was Major Butt, A.D.C. and adviser of the President of the United States, and W. T. Stead, famous Radical journalist; there was Charles Hayes, President of the Grand Trunk Railway of Canada, and Colonel Astor, one of New York's social luminaries, Sir Cosmo Duff-Gordon and his wife and many more. In all there were 322 first-class passengers and 277 second-class. And in addition to these, the *Titanic* carried 709 third-class passengers, many of whom were emigrants, bearing with them the stock of their small possessions. Not for them the luxurious appointments of the first-class deck; but they carried aboard with them the frail and priceless cargo of hope. And so it was in high spirit and brave array that the *Titanic* moved slowly from Southampton harbour at noon on Wednesday, the 10th of April, 1912.

For four days the *Titanic* steamed smoothly and steadily across the ocean. All went according to programme and a keener edge was given to the passengers' enjoyment by the knowledge that they were assisting at so auspicious a maiden voyage. On the Sunday warnings were received from the *Baltic*, *Touraine*, *Caronia* and other ships that ice was prevalent. But this was neither unusual nor unduly alarming, for at this time of the year, when a rather more southerly course was taken on account of the danger of ice (since the loss of the *Titanic* it has been pushed farther south), ice was to be expected; no large ship, however, had ever been lost by collision with ice, though slight fractures had been sustained, and no captain ever thought it necessary to slow down in clear weather on account of reports of ice. And the *Titanic* was no ordinary ship. Had it not bulkheads and watertight compartments? And was it not in the trusty charge of Captain Smith, the doyen of the White Star Line? No, the *Titanic* was no ordinary ship; she was, in the expressed opinion of one of the passengers, as " unsinkable as a railway station." Little things like ice were of no concern to the passengers; they were matters for the crew. The passengers had few cares and no fears. Eating, drinking, talking, playing, dancing; the time passed merrily in an atmosphere of gay good fellowship. It was almost as if they had said, " Let us eat, drink and be merry, for to-morrow we die." But no one had any thoughts of death; that was a thing out of place and far away from the *Titanic* as it glided on its smooth progress through the calm Atlantic waters. Here was life and laughter and love and human pleasure, untroubled and unthinking. And above, the inscrutable destiny of Providence brooded over the serene vulgarity of man.

Darkness fell on that Sunday evening in April with the *Titanic* still maintaining its pace of 21½ knots, and headed for the ice zone. Orders had been given to the officers of the watch and to the look-out men in the crow's nest to keep a sharp look-out for ice; but the conditions were such as must have seemed ideal to the amateur. There was no wind, no swell, no moon, a state of unbroken calm. This was, however, " an extraordinary combination of circumstances which you would not meet again in a hundred years," and it meant that the detection of icebergs would be extremely difficult, as there would be no breaking of the surf to reveal their presence. One of the two look-out men afterwards said that he discerned a slight haze ahead about half-an-hour before the collision; but, as this apparition was totally unsubstantiated, it is probable that it was invented to offset any suggestion of negligence on his part, and it seems certain that the night was perfectly clear. At any rate the thought of disaster was absent from every mind—Captain Smith had in fact retired to bed—when one of the look-out men, shortly after 11.30, telephoned to the bridge to say that he had sighted an obstruction straight ahead. Mr Murdoch, the first officer, was on watch, and acted with great promptitude; he had the helm starboarded so as to swing the bow of the ship to port, put the engines full speed astern, and closed the watertight doors. But events moved too quickly for him, and just over a minute after the warning had been given the *Titanic* struck the iceberg a glancing blow. There was a slight, a very slight, concussion; and that was all that was felt. But, straight and swift as forked lightning, the blow ripped open the hull and the thin, deadly gash tore through 250 feet of the *Titanic's* side.

The slight shock that was felt caused very little anxiety. Many were now asleep, and of these few were awakened; those who were playing cards paused, and went on with the game; some came up on deck, saw that all was as usual, and retired again; the look-out men remarked that it had been a narrow shave; and the junior wireless-operator, coming on duty at midnight, was aware of nothing but the stopping of the ship. This indeed was the one thing that puzzled people; why should the ship stop in mid-ocean? But there was no noticeable list on her, and no signs of damage and distress; it was not thus that accidents happened at sea. Besides the *Titanic* was unsinkable, and the night was cold; so, quickly and happily confident, they retired again. But they were wrong; the gash had opened five of the fifteen watertight compartments, and the ship was doomed. So much at any rate was clear to Mr Andrewes, a representative of the firm which had built the *Titanic*, who examined her immediately after the accident. He saw that the five pierced compartments must gradually but inevitably fill, and that in so doing they would bring the tops of the bulkheads, which protected the remaining two-thirds of the ship, below the level of the sea and consequently of the water in the flooded compartments; thus, even if the bulkheads held, the water would come in over the tops of them, and it would be only a question of time before the rest of the ship was swamped.

Discussion was hastily held on the bridge, which was joined by Mr Ismay, as to what was to be done, and it was decided to gets the boats out at once and to try and get into touch with other ships by wireless. The first part of the policy was not, however, as easy to put into effect as it sounds. The view often held of the *Titanic* disaster, that there was an instant scramble for the boats, is very wide of the mark; in point of fact, the difficulty at first was not to restrain people from the boats, but to induce them to enter them. For people were asked to abandon the apparent security of the ship, which was standing upright in calm water, for a perilous descent, seventy feet sheer down the side of the cliff into the icy water. Even on the deck it was by now bitterly cold, and many people, especially third-class passengers—to whom, in the case of the emigrants at any rate, descent in the boats would mean the abandonment of all their possessions—came up on deck, found how cold it was and how steady the ship was, and promptly retired again. In addition to this, the stewards, in accordance with the usual practice adopted in order to avoid the risk of panic, insisted that it was a merely precautionary measure. One cannot help challenging the wisdom of such a policy; it would seem better to trust people's responsible instincts and tell them the true state of affairs, than to treat them as children and minimise the gravity of the situation. Be that as it may, the policy was justified in that the loading and lowering of the boats was attended by very little panic; but, on the other hand, most of the boats were lowered containing considerably less than their full complement of passengers. This was due partly to the combination of the above circumstances, and partly to the fear of some of the officers that the boats, in being lowered, would not be able to stand the weight of a full complement; in point of fact, the fear seems to have been without foundation, for one of the boats was successfully lowered with a cargo of seventy persons. The loading and lowering of the boats went forward without panic, and even gracefully and gallantly; for the gentlemen doffed hats and handed the ladies into the boats, just as if they were handing them into their carriages after a reception. It was not till the last boats were being lowered that an attempt to rush them was made by some steerage passengers, who were promptly and vigorously beaten back. That was all the panic there was, and when the last boats put out, seven hundred people had been carried from the ship. The capacity of the boats was 1178, and there were 2206 people on board.

The passengers who were taken off in the boats were singularly fortunate, for not a single boat came to grief in the perilous descent, and of the seven hundred people all survived their exposure, except one solitary man, who perished of cold. This happy result was due to the courage and resolution of Captain Rostrom of the *Carpathia* and his crew. The *Carpathia* was a Cunarder of 13,000 tons, which was at the time travelling from west to east—that is, in the opposite direction to the *Titanic*. It so happened that, when she was at a distance of 58 miles from the *Titanic*, her wireless operator returned to his instrument for the purpose of informing the *Titanic* that a batch of messages for her passengers were waiting to be sent from Cape Race. Instead, however, of executing this simple task, he himself received the message, dramatic in its awesome simplicity: " We have struck a berg and are sinking." He lost no time in telling Captain Rostrom, who was himself in bed at the time, and Captain Rostrom in his turn acted with admirable decision. The nominal maximum speed of the *Carpathia* was fourteen knots; but this was a matter of life and death, and Captain Rostrom ordered a speed of seventeen and a half knots. And so, with her captain and all his officers on the look-out, and her boats swung out in readiness for instant lowering, the *Carpathia* sped through the ice-ridden waters to the rescue. There was another ship, too, the *Californian*, which saw the lights of a ship and saw rockets go up; but, unfortunately, her captain did not consider that the situation called for action, and the *Californian* did not go to the rescue. She was much nearer to the *Titanic* than was the *Carpathia*, and what the result of her action might have been to the people on the *Titanic* we shall presently see.

Meanwhile on the *Titanic* the atmosphere was changing and intensifying. The ship was sinking; the boats were gone; they were cut off. That was the stark reality, and they were left to ponder it. Brave men, human men, doomed to slow destruction, and denied the last privilege of effort on their own behalf. Do what they would, they could do nothing to save themselves or each other; they were left to the contemplation of a cruel and inescapable fate, which rose up before them with the insistence of a nightmare. In those dreadful circumstances, which none who has not partaken in may presume to judge, anything might have been expected and forgiven. Some panic there was undoubtedly; but there was, too, calmness, consideration, humour, and great courage. The crew went about their tasks, undeterred by the certainty of annihilation; the stokers kept at work, waist-high in water until nearly two o'clock to keep the lights and pumps going; stewards ransacked the flooded cabins, looking for passengers or their abandoned babies; the post-office clerks dragged up the sacks of mail from the depths of the ship; the band gallantly continued playing dance-music, until the deeper strains of " Nearer, my God, to Thee " carried to all the message that the end was at hand at last. But they may perhaps be envied these opportunities, which evoked their heroism; they at least could put these practical tasks between them and their thoughts of death. But, for the passengers, there was so little that they could do; nothing, save to wait. There were those who resolved to die as they had lived; and the music of laughter, harsh but brave, mingled with the rattle of dice and the shuffle of cards. There were those who resolved to die more intensively than they had lived; and there came the clamour of rich orgies, which prudence had forbidden in life. There were those who resolved to make peace with their Maker while they were yet in the way with Him; and the air was shot with their piteous cries and self-abasement. There were those who resolved to help each other; and old men philosophised in large chairs, and young lovers murmured tenderly in corners. It was a supreme moment of revelation, when human emotions and human instincts rose, straight as a rocket, from the bounds of their restraints; in that moment the people on the *Titanic* stood their test.

But the end was near. Endeavour had exhausted its
utility. " Men," said Captain Smith, " you have done your
duty, your full duty. You can do no more. It's every man
for himself now." Every man for himself; every man
against the most fearful odds. The end came rapidly at last.
The ship, steady so long, began to heel over. " Deck after
deck submerged. There was no lurching or grinding or
crunching. The *Titanic* simply settled." The strains of
hymn and prayer ascended the lonely air, uniting all in one
last sacrament. And then came the end. " It was all over
in an instant. The *Titanic's* stern rose completely out of the
water and went up thirty, forty, sixty feet in the air. Then
with her body slanting at an angle of forty-five degrees,
slowly the *Titanic* slipped out of sight." Many died as she
went down. Mrs Isidore Straus, who had refused to be
parted from her husband in order to enter a boat, saying,
" I'll stay where you are. We've lived for forty years
together, and will not part now in old age," died in her
husband's arms. Others threw themselves into the icy water,
in which there was no survival. Nor could they enter the
boats, for these last boats were full, and further cargo would
mean destruction. " Then there fell on our ears," said Mr
Beesley, one of the survivors who was in a boat, " the most
appalling noise that human being ever heard—the cries of
hundreds of our fellow-beings, struggling in the icy waters,
crying for help with a cry that we knew could not be
answered." The cries soon died away, for soon there were
none to utter them.

And Dawn broke on that Monday morning, hard and
clear over the wreckage of human lives, and saluted the
unexampled fortitude of Man.

Slowly and inaccurately the news of disaster trickled
through. Something had happened to the *Titanic;* it had
been damaged, though not sunk; her passengers had been
safely taken off by other ships; there was no loss of life.
But gradually reports came in from the various ships on the
ocean, denying with disheartening unanimity that they had
any of the *Titanic's* passengers on board; and then, while

the *Carpathia* was still struggling back through adverse weather to New York, a realisation of what had happened began to dawn. The incredible had happened; the unsinkable *Titanic* had gone down on her maiden voyage, with enormous loss of life. The news sent a thrill of horror through two continents, as yet unused to horror; and horror was quickly reinforced by anger. There were those who thought that the disaster was a visitation from God; but they were in a minority. To most one thing only was clear. They had been told that the *Titanic* was unsinkable and she had sunk; someone had blundered. There must be justice, vengeance, sacrifice to placate the gods. And there arose the deep, full-throated bay for blood.

The search for potential victims did not have to extend very far, for they were marked out by the course of events. Mr Bruce Ismay had survived; then he must have conspired to sink the ship, and then used his authority to secure his own escape at the cost of the death of others. Sir Cosmo and Lady Duff-Gordon had been rowed away in a boat, which had not its full complement on board; they had clearly bribed the crew to abandon others to their fate so as not to encumber the boat. Captain Smith was among the dead; that meant that he had committed suicide to escape the consequences of his criminal negligence. Such, and many more, were the stories which were actively circulated on both sides of the Atlantic during those anxious days. Queues formed in Southampton in the hope of news of absent loved ones; and the White Star offices in New York had to be afforded police protection. The American Government acted with prompt, if misdirected, vigour; before the *Carpathia* had reached New York, they had set up a Senatorial Commission of Inquiry. Consequently, when the *Carpathia* at last drew into New York on the evening of April 18th, bearing her tragic cargo, all of whom had been subjected to terrible shock and exposure in the boats, and many of whom had lost their husbands or families on the ship, she was at once besieged by eager senators with subpoenas and the whole paraphernalia of the law. The

Senatorial Inquiry, it may be stated at once, had no claims
to be taken seriously.   It had no assessors, no experts, no
officers of the United States Navy; its moving spirit was one
Senator Smith, a busybody politician, who was so laughably
ignorant of naval matters that he solemnly asked the
Titanic's second-officer whether, when the crash took place,
steps were taken to get the passengers into the watertight
compartments.   It was fittingly described by the American
Merchant Marine Association as a " farcical inquiry," and
aroused much criticism both in the American newspapers and
among individual citizens.   In point of fact, the Commission
had no real jurisdiction, as the *Titanic*, having flown the
British flag and having been lost on the High Seas, was
answerable only to the British Courts.   But so long as the
Commission kept the witnesses detained in Washington, the
Board of Trade Inquiry, which was to be convened in
London, had to be delayed.

But there was undoubtedly urgent need for an authoritative inquiry in England, for there were many points at
issue.   It was decided, therefore, to allow representation of
interested parties, though naturally an effort was made to
keep this within reasonable limit.   Sir Rufus Isaacs, as
Attorney-General, appeared for the Board of Trade, and
with him were the Solicitor-General, Sir John Simon, Mr
Butler Aspinall, K.C., the famous Admiralty lawyer, Mr
S. A. T. Rowlatt, and Mr Raymond Asquith, the then
Prime Minister's eldest son.   Sir Robert Finlay led for the
White Star, and Mr Hamar Greenwood, M.P., (later Lord
Greenwood) for the Canadian Pacific Railway.   The Duff-
Gordons were represented by Mr Henry Duke and Mr
Vaughan Williams, and Mr Clement Edwards, M.P., ap-
peared for the Dockers' Union.   The Inquiry was presided
over by Lord Mersey, who had lately resigned from the
Presidency of the Probate, Divorce and Admiralty Division
and who had years before been Judge in the Whittaker
Wright case.   The scope of the Inquiry was wide.   In
essence, its purpose was to find out the cause of the disaster
and to discover the best and most practical precautions to

guard against its recurrence. The first of these objects involved, inevitably if not explicitly, the question of the supply of life-boats; of Captain Smith's negligence; of Mr Bruce Ismay's actions; of the conduct of the Duff-Gordons; whether the *Californian* had done its full duty, after sighting the rockets and distress signals; and the vexed question of whether the third-class passengers had been sacrificed to their economic superiors (for the Labour press and politicians had discovered in the disparity between the percentages of third-class and higher-class passengers saved another instance of unfair class-distinction), and many more. The issues, therefore, were complex and varied; nor was the position of the Board of Trade itself above criticism. The *Titanic* had conformed, had more than conformed, to the requirements of the Board of Trade regulations, and the *Titanic* had met with swift and overwhelming disaster; was it then the Board of Trade regulations which were at fault? In this connection, the details of the *Titanic's* lifeboat equipment are of interest; there were fourteen large boats, capable of carrying sixty-five persons each, two emergency boats capable of carrying forty each, and four collapsible boats with a capacity of forty-seven. Thus the boats were capable of taking 1178 persons on board, and the fact that only 711 were saved might be attributed to mismanagement on board the *Titanic*. But since there were 2201 people on board, the lifeboats could clearly not, in any event, have carried them all away; and in this respect the Board of Trade regulations could be attacked for not insisting on an adequate number of boats. (It may here perhaps be mentioned that 62 per cent. of the first-class passengers, 41 per cent. of the second-class, 25 per cent. of the third, and 24 per cent. of the crew were saved; 19 per cent. of the men on board were saved, 77 per cent. of the women, and 49 per cent of the children.)

Rufus Isaacs, therefore, had to thread his way through a labyrinth of issues; but it was the sort of case eminently suited to his talents. His detachment, his incisiveness, his admirably ordered mind all united to give him a clear view of the questions and of the conduct of the Inquiry. His task was really dual: he was professionally appearing for the Board of Trade, but also, as a member of the Government and leader of the legal profession, he was peculiarly concerned to get at the facts of the situation and to assist the formation of a Report, whose recommendations would be a real safeguard against the likelihood of a repetition of the disaster. He opened the Inquiry, whose first sessions were held in the Drill Hall of the London Scottish at Buckingham Gate, with a long speech, stressing the Government's desire for a full enquiry and its willingness to adopt any suggestions of the Court. He then sketched the questions for the Court under twenty-six heads, of which the first five were concerned with the details of the *Titanic's* equipment and its adequacy, numbers six to twelve with the precautions against ice, and the remainder with the facts connected with the collision and the recommendations of the Court. The Inquiry lasted in all for over thirty sessions, and, in view of the great difficulty in arriving at the true facts, the multiplicity of interests demanding representation and the amount of prejudice existing in the public mind, it may be considered as a tribute to those conducting the Inquiry that it lasted no longer and strayed no more widely than it did. Much of the evidence, however, would necessarily be very dreary in repetition, consisting as it did in piecemeal contributions to the account of the disaster, which are invaluable in enabling us to reconstruct the circumstances, but of little value or interest in themselves.

There were, however, specific questions to which it was right to get an answer, and which public opinion demanded should be answered. Chief among these was the great question: was the loss of the *Titanic* due to exceptional circumstances, which could not reasonably have been foreseen, or was it the result of human interference or human inaction? There was a certain amount of disagreement as to the conditions actually existing. Thus Reginald Lee, one of the look-out men, said in his evidence on the fourth day of the Inquiry, that there was a haze; this, however, was denied by the other look-out man, Frederick Fleet, and

Lord Mersey declared that he did not believe Lee on this point. But, in point of fact, there was no need to invent a haze, for the conditions, as we have seen, were certainly exceptional. The point really was, therefore, were the conditions in themselves sufficient to account for the accident, or was it due to a neglect of safety, as some suggested, in the pursuit of the speed record for the *Titanic's* maiden voyage? Strength was added to this view by the fact that one of the ice-warnings, received by the *Titanic*, had been handed by the captain to Mr Bruce Ismay, who had kept it until the evening and then given it back without comment; this, it was suggested, was an attempt to use his position as Managing Director of the Company to influence Captain Smith to maintain undiminished the speed of the ship in spite of the danger of ice. He was closely cross-examined by Rufus Isaacs as to this action, and he maintained in answer that he had not thought the note of particular importance, nor had he seen any particular reason for slowing down, especially as the *Titanic* was not at the time going at full speed. Mr Ismay had not, in fact, the reputation for interfering with the captains of White Star ships in the discharge of their functions, and it was inherently improbable that the *Titanic*, which had been built for safety and luxury rather than for great speed, should be attempting to defeat the records of ships better equipped in that respect that herself. Further, if she had slowed down in consequence of the ice, she would have been virtually establishing a precedent for a ship of her class in those waters, for all the captains of ships, who gave evidence at the Inquiry, unanimously stated that it was not their practice to slacken their speed on account of ice.

Second to the question of the responsibility for the crash was the further point: did the boats carry away as many people as was reasonably possible, or were they prevented from taking their full complement by human intervention and, possibly, even human selfishness? This question crystallised into the controversy about the conduct of Sir Cosmo and Lady Duff-Gordon. They had left the ship in emergency lifeboat number one, which with a potential capacity of forty people had actually taken only twelve, of whom five were passengers and seven members of the crew. Sir Cosmo had given each member of the crew who had been in the boat a present of £5, and the allegation was made that this was a bribe, given to induce them not to turn back and pick up as many people as they could, when the ship had gone down. Sir Cosmo's version of the affair was that the £5 was given to the men because they had lost all their kit in the wreck, and that it was not given to them until they were on the *Carpathia*. The only real backing for the allegations against the Duff-Gordons was the evidence of Charles Hendrickson, one of the seamen on the lifeboat; he asserted that he had wanted to go back, but that Duff-Gordon had dissuaded him and he had given way. But even he said that the £5 was given on board the *Carpathia* and that nothing was said or done in reference to the matter until they were picked up; and his evidence on the other point was contradicted by another sailor, George Symons, who was cross-examined at length by Rufus Isaacs on these points. He said, in answer, that he had not been told not to go back by the Duff-Gordons, and that he had not received his present from Sir Cosmo until a day or two before the *Carpathia* reached New York; he also said that the Chief Officer, Mr Murdoch, had ordered their lifeboat to be lowered as it was, as there was nobody else about at the time. Sir Cosmo himself gave evidence, and was cross-examined at length by Rufus Isaacs. It must have been very distressing to have to cross-examine Mr Ismay and Sir Cosmo Duff-Gordon, who, in addition to the horrors of the actual disaster, had been pursued for weeks by the full violence of a prejudiced and uninformed public clamour. But in their own interests it was desirable, to enable them to vindicate themselves, especially in the case of the Duff-Gordons, who were represented by extremely able counsel; for if they had not been cross-examined, it would have been open to people to say that the facts had not really been gone into. What was made abundantly clear by the Inquiry is this: the Duff-Gordons had refused to go in several previous boats; the boat, in which they actually went, was properly authorised to go (we have already seen that there was not the clamorous eagerness to get into the boats, which popular imagination believes); Lady Duff-Gordon was sick and helpless practically all the time; the promise of the £5 was not made at a time when it could affect the action of the men. It seems, therefore, in the highest degree improbable that Hendrickson's story about being dissuaded from turning back has any truth; and to me it certainly seems the most natural thing in the world that a man of means, hearing that his fellow victims of disaster had suffered in a further degree by losing their kit, should make them a present to enable them to replace it.

A third question, whether more of the people on the *Titanic* could have been saved by outside assistance, concerns primarily the conduct of the *Californian*. The *Carpathia*, which had been 58 miles from the *Titanic*, had succeeded in picking up all the boats; the *Californian*, which had been lying stopped only about a quarter of the distance away, had not rescued anybody. Was this the best she could have done? In point of fact, many of the people on the *Titanic* saw the lights on the *Californian*, or what was presumably the *Californian*—and the Courts subsequently held that it was; in any case, the *Californian* was clearly near enough to have come up and rendered assistance, if it had been realised that assistance was needed. And there had not been wanting signs that assistance was required, for, from the *Californian*, rockets were seen going up and the lights of a vessel lying to the South were sighted. Now at the Inquiry it was maintained by some of the witnesses from the crew of the *Californian* that the lights they had seen were not those of the *Titanic*, and that they had not realised that the rockets were distress signals. But these arguments did not impress the Court very strongly, for there was no other ship in the vicinity, which could very well have been mistaken for the *Titanic*; besides there was no entry in the logbook, as would be expected, to record the sight of the rockets.

The *Californian* could not very well be blamed for failing to get the wireless distress message since, like the *Carpathia*, she had only one wireless operator and he had retired to bed; it will be remembered that the operator on the *Carpathia* had only returned to his instrument by chance. But on the other points the witnesses did not do very well on cross-examination, and Lord Mersey said to the second-officer in the course of his examination: " You do not make a very good impression on me at present. Did you know they were distress signals? " " No, sir," he replied; he then had to admit that in his training he had been taught to regard what he had seen that night as distress signals.

When the Report was issued on July 30th, after the Court had had thirty-seven sittings and examined ninety-seven witnesses, it was severely critical of the action, or inaction, of the *Californian*. " The ship seen by the *Californian* was the *Titanic*," the Report decided: " She was within ten miles and had she pushed her way through the ice as she might have done without any serious risk, she might have saved many if not all of the lives that were lost. Masters," it concluded ominously, " should be reminded that it is a misdemeanour not to go to the rescue of vessels in distress at sea." This was a decisive estimate and the whole Report was clear-cut in its conclusions: " The Court having carefully enquired into the circumstances of the above-mentioned shipping casualty finds . . . that the loss of the said ship was due to collision with an iceberg, brought about by the excessive speed at which the ship was being navigated." But it was not the fault of Captain Smith, who was specifically exculpated; he might have reduced speed or turned South, but he in fact followed what was the usual practice. " He made a mistake, a very grievous mistake, but one in which, in face of past experience negligence could not be said to have any part." Similarly there was no truth in the allegations against the Duff-Gordons and Mr Ismay, although it had been improper for Captain Smith to hand the ice-warning from the *Baltic* to Mr Ismay, and improper for Mr Ismay to keep it until 7.15 that evening; but this, the Court decided, had not in any way influenced Captain Smith's behaviour. Captain Smith must have known the danger of ice, but it had always been the practice of ships to maintain speed when near the ice, and hitherto they had done so without disaster. The Court found, too, that the third-class passengers had not been unfairly treated as regards accommodation in the boats; they had, in fact, been reluctant to leave the ship.

As for the Board of Trade, it was blamed for not having brought its regulations up to date since 1894, though it was decided that no blame attached to the officials for having passed the *Titanic* as fit, which seems fair enough. For practical effect the recommendations, as distinct from the findings of the Court, were not of startling value. They suggested an international conference (it may have sounded less inevitable then); and, in fact, as a result of the *Titanic* disaster, the North Atlantic route for that period of the year was pushed further South and a special patrol is now maintained by the United States Government to inform ships of the presence of icebergs, the expense being shared by the principal countries using the North Atlantic. But, generally speaking, the *Titanic* disaster was not a good basis for the consideration of protective safeguards and reforms, for it was in every way exceptional. Thus the *Titanic* was sunk only because it struck the iceberg a slanting blow, which ripped open five watertight compartments; had it struck head-on, about a hundred feet of her hull would have been smashed in, entailing the death of everybody in the stokers' quarters, but the ship would have remained afloat. Thus, paradoxically, if no attempt had been made to avoid the iceberg, and if the apparent damage had been far greater, the resulting disaster would have been infinitely less. Again the experience of the *Titanic* led to a great increase in the number of boats carried; and, undoubtedly, a larger supply of boats on the *Titanic* would have been invaluable, if the passengers could have been induced to get into them. But it may fairly be doubted how efficacious they would prove in the normal accident at sea. For the lifeboats were only lowered successfully from the *Titanic* because of the exceptional circumstance that the collision took place in very calm water. In the majority of cases this would not be so, and a dual difficulty arises; it is extremely unlikely that all the boats lowered over the side of a ship with a heavy list on it will successfully reach the water, and it is equally unlikely that all of those which do reach the water will survive in a rough sea.

On the whole, however, the Inquiry and the Report were a source of credit to the people concerned; for, though the recommendations were not startlingly original, the finding on the facts of the disaster was, as far as can be seen, accurate in spite of all the difficulties of conflicting accounts, and certainly just, in face of much blind prejudice. But the ultimate significance of the *Titanic* disaster lies not in the details of its happening so much as in the fact of its having happened. For even the least imaginative felt it as a shock to a sense of security, which derived from the consciousness of material prosperity. And to many the shock came as a challenge whether a civilisation, based so largely on wealth and size, could be a satisfactory and lasting fabric. But this is a consideration which was perhaps outside the scope of the Board of Trade Inquiry.

CHAPTER XXIII

SUFFRAGETTES AND TRADE UNIONS

THE Board of Trade Inquiry did not monopolise the Attorney-General's attention during its protracted session, for he had an extremely capable team of counsel with him. He was able, therefore, to lead for the Crown in the famous suffragette prosecution, which took place in May of this year.

The suffragette agitation in the years before the War attracted perhaps more public attention than any other political issue except the Irish question. The question of female suffrage was not " practical politics " in the sense that it was espoused by either of the great political parties, but it had the compensatory advantage of a powerful and determined organisation behind it. This was the Women's Social and Political Union, which had been founded by ardent spirits in 1903, and had gone from strength to strength; it was estimated that in six years it had held a hundred thousand meetings in various parts of the country, and it had filled the Albert Hall thirteen times. This concentrated constitutional pressure, however, failed to achieve any result save to annoy (and this it did in considerable measure); so the suffragist movement resorted to forms of petty violence, such as window-breaking, by way of intimidation. In this they were encouraged by their leaders, who were intelligent, cultured people, to whom violence would be naturally distasteful, but to whom it seemed the only effective method of impressing the merits of their case. They were not, however, successful in convincing the Government of the merits of their case, but they did succeed in inspiring in their followers a degree of enthusiasm for the methods which were advocated; and in consequence the Government felt it to be necessary to prosecute Mr and Mrs Pethick-

Lawrence and Mrs Pankhurst for conspiracy to incite members of the Women's Social and Political Union to commit damage.

The trial was of first importance, and all the defendants were people of very considerable ability and standing. Mrs Pankhurst was leader of the Suffragette movement, Mrs Pethick-Lawrence had a great reputation as a social worker, and Mr Pethick-Lawrence, who was a Fellow of Trinity, Cambridge, was to become Financial Secretary to the Treasury in the Labour Administration. Mr Pethick-Lawrence and Mrs Pankhurst elected to conduct their own defence, while Mrs Pethick-Lawrence was represented by Mr " Tim " Healy. In view of the importance of the case, Rufus Isaacs himself came down to prosecute. The trial, which was held before Mr Justice Coleridge at the Old Bailey, lasted for six days, but the Crown's case, which Rufus Isaacs presented clearly but with moderation, was not difficult to make out; for there was clear evidence in pamphlets and so on that acts of petty violence had been advocated, and there was evidence, too, that damage had in fact been committed. Nor was the line of defence adopted a denial of the facts. Their defence consisted rather in " confession and avoidance; " that is to say, they attributed the blame for whatever violence had been committed to the violent and repressive speeches of members of the Government, and reinforced their argument by pointing to the unrebuked violence of F. E. Smith and the Ulster politicians. The whole defence indeed was conducted on somewhat political lines and, after witnesses, including Dame Ethel Smyth and Miss Eva Moore, had been called for the defence, Mr Pethick-Lawrence, Mrs Pankhurst, and Mr Healy all made speeches of considerable eloquence, stressing the political aspects of the issue. Rufus Isaacs then made a moderate and judicial speech, in winding up for the Crown, which was frequently interrupted by Mrs Pankhurst. Thus, when Rufus Isaacs, with the *Titanic* in mind, pointed out that women had certain compensatory advantages for the lack of political rights, for example the doctrine of " women

and children first," Mrs Pankhurst interjected with perhaps
more force than point: "What about women on the
streets?" The question went unanswered, and after
twenty-five minutes' consideration the jury found all three
defendants guilty with a recommendation to clemency in
view of the "undoubtedly pure motives underlying the
agitation." All three asked to be treated as first-class mis-
demeanants, but Mr Justice Coleridge pointed out that this
would enable them to carry on, whilst in prison, the
activities, which they had made no attempt to disown and
no promise to discontinue. They were, therefore, sentenced
to nine months' imprisonment in the second division, a
verdict which was greeted with some hissing in Court and
cries of "Shame;" but as the maximum punishment for
their offences was two years with hard labour, it cannot be
said that the sentence was unduly harsh. As for Rufus
Isaacs' conduct of the case, it was suitably restrained and
moderate, and we may accept the estimate of the *Times*:
"the Attorney-General did not press the case against the
defendants, far less seek to aggravate their crime."

On June 10th there occurred a change in ministerial
office. Lord Loreburn, who had been Lord Chancellor
since the Liberals took office in 1906, resigned on the
grounds of ill-health, and was succeeded by Lord Haldane,
the Secretary of State for War; the vacancy at the War
Office being filled by Colonel Seely. Two days later
institutional history was made, and for the first time the
Attorney-General received a seat in the Cabinet. To be the
first Attorney-General to sit in the Cabinet was, of course,
a great honour for Rufus Isaacs, and, after referring to the
"unprecedented step," the *Times* remarked that the Government did not intend it to be regarded by the Bar as a
precedent, "and that it is a personal distinction conferred
on Sir Rufus Isaacs for his special services. But it is not
difficult," the article continued, "to discover another
possible factor. The Attorney-General might naturally be
considered to have the first claim to the Lord Chancellorship
when it fell vacant, yet, for obvious reasons, Lord Haldane

has succeeded in this office. The distinction now conferred on Sir Rufus Isaacs might, therefore, be regarded in the nature of a solatium." Be that as it may, he was now in the Cabinet and brought into a closer contact with the great problems of the day. As it happened, his tenure of Cabinet rank was not to be a long one, and he had been translated from the political sphere before the Irish question reached its long and frantic crisis and before the Liberal Cabinet was faced with its great decision in August 1914. But great issues there undoubtedly were. The constitutional question was temporarily settled; but Home Rule remained, and was joined by Welsh Disestablishment. These questions, however, national and to some extent religious, were for the orators and the firebrands; Rufus Isaacs was more intimately concerned with the Trade Union Bill, of which he was in charge. For had not the *Times* spoken of his " invaluable help in many directions and not least in regard to the labour troubles! "

The Trade Union Bill, the second reading of which Rufus Isaacs introduced on August 6th, was virtually the same as a measure which he had introduced in the previous year and which had not then been proceeded with. The Bill was prompted primarily by dissatisfaction, especially among Labour members, with the decision in the Osborne case, which held that forced levies, imposed by Trade Unions on their members for political purposes, were *ultra vires* and void. The point brings us back to the perennially vexed question of the rights of the individual against the rights of a society. But the Labour Party which was, of course, in very close alliance with official Trade Unionism, had no doubts as to how the question should be answered; they wanted legislation which would reverse the effect of the Osborne judgment. But the Liberal Government showed itself capable of seeing the matter in a broader light, and the Bill that was brought forward was not a simple affirmation of the rights of Trade Unions to impose political levies on its members. " There are three principles," as Rufus Isaacs said in his speech on the third reading, " underlying the construction of the Bill. The first is that all trade unions shall be free, if the majority wish, to collect funds for political purposes. The second is that members shall be free to express their views by ballot properly taken for that purpose, and the third is that those who object shall be free to obtain exemption from their obligation to contribute to political funds." Rufus Isaacs, therefore, in moving the second reading, stated his opinion that trade unions should be allowed to extend their activities from the industrial to the political sphere. But the Bill, which he was introducing, would only sanction political funds if the rules of the union were approved by the Registrar of Friendly Societies; and they would not be so approved unless the Registrar was satisfied that the application of funds to political objects was authorised by a resolution taken at a bona fide ballot; that members might exempt themselves from subscribing to the fund; and that such as exempted themselves did not suffer in the matter of benefits.

Rufus Isaacs introduced the measure in a conciliatory speech, but its rejection was moved by the Conservatives on the ground that it was unfair to individual Trade Unionists, who did not happen to be in sympathy with the political aims of the Labour Party, and that the interference in politics of organised corporations would be a source of corruption. The motion for rejection, however, was defeated by a hundred votes and the Bill proceeded to Committee, where in the words of Rufus Isaacs, " we had fourteen days of very strenuous work, sitting till close upon four o'clock on all days except the first two in order to get the Bill through . . . I think I should not be exaggerating if I said the Bill had a very stormy and protracted passage through Committee. There were certain adverse winds blowing, not always from the same quarter. There were cross-currents, and the Government had very often a somewhat difficult course to steer owing to the pressure on one side and pressure on the other; but I am glad to say . . . we managed to get it, if not to harbour, at least within sight of harbour, and when we came down to this House on the Report stage we certainly found much quieter and smoother waters." At any rate he got it near enough to harbour, for Mr Bonar Law, on behalf of the Conservative Party, said that his objections to the Bill had been modified by amendments in Committee and in the Report stage, and that he would not therefore oppose the third reading. Rufus Isaacs wound up for the Government in an explanatory speech, in which he welcomed the Conservative decision and defended the Trade Unions from the criticism that they had not been able to do anything to improve labour conditions.

The Bill, which became law on March 7th, 1913, had much to recommend it. If a body of men, organised primarily for industrial purpose, desires to extend the use of the organisation to political purposes, it is a legitimate, if not necessarily a laudable desire; and the Trade Union Act of 1913 sanctioned and facilitated the attainment of this desire, without making compulsory the adherence of individual objectors to the will of the majority. But where the Act would seem to have been mistaken was in instituting the system known as contracting-out; that is to say, it enacted that there was a presumption in favour of the political levy, if decided upon, in the case of individual members, unless they notified otherwise. Now to presume that every person who joins a body for industrial and insurance purposes, should want it to become a political organisation in addition, at an increased cost to himself is illogical; and it is still further illogical to suppose that every such person should necessarily favour the politics of the Socialist Party. But this was virtually the assumption made by the system of contracting-out. It is clearly more logical that those who wish to extend the activities of an organisation into a direction in which it was not the primary intention to go, should have the onus of signifying their intention (not always a popular thing in a community governed by majority decisions). Such at any rate was the view taken by the Conservative Government after the General Strike, and the Act of 1927, while retaining the right to a political fund, substituted a system of " contracting-in " for those who wished to subscribe to it.

Towards the end of 1912 Rufus Isaacs as Attorney-General appeared in the very unusual case which is known as Bowles *v.* The Bank of England.   Mr Gibson Bowles was a Conservative Member of Parliament, a man of independence and of spirit; and so, when the Bank on July 1st, 1912, deducted from the £900 dividend due on his £65,500 Irish Land Stock, a sum of £52, 10s. 8d. by way of income tax, he challenged their right to do so.   And, strangely enough, their right was not as incontestable as admirers of that august institution would suppose.   The income tax of 1s. 2d. in the pound had been imposed, it is true, by the Budget in the ordinary way; that is to say, the Committee of Ways and Means of the House of Commons had passed a resolution approving of the imposition of the income tax for the financial year commencing April 6th, 1912, and this decision had been adopted by the House of Commons as a whole on June 24th, 1912.   On this authority the Bank, as was their custom, deducted the amount of income tax by way of taxation at source.   But, though it was their custom and though the country's finances depended upon the regular collection of taxation, the deduction had in fact no justification in law.   For income tax is not a permanent tax; it lapses at the end of each year, and is reimposed, with a possible variation in rate, by statute.   But taxation can only be by Act of Parliament, and a resolution of " that part of Parliament, which is called the House of Commons " is clearly not an Act of Parliament.   Therefore, when income tax lapsed at the end of the financial year and had been reimposed only by resolution of the House of Commons, the imposition was not valid, and the action of the Bank in deducting the amount was illegal.   So argued Mr Gibson Bowles; and it was in vain that the Bank pleaded that " ever since the imposition of the income tax by the Income Tax Act, 1842, the defendants have always been accustomed to treat such resolutions . . . as sufficient authority to deduct income tax in respect of interest on Government stocks becoming payable after the passage of such resolution . . . before the passing of the Act of Parliament carrying out such resolutions." It was in vain, too, that Rufus Isaacs, on behalf of the Crown and the Commissioners of Inland Revenue, argued that income tax was in substance a permanent tax, and the practice was one of great practical convenience. Mr Gibson Bowles appealed robustly to Magna Carta and to the Bill of Rights, challenging the Attorney-General to show any authority to suggest that the power of taxation is to be found anywhere except in Act of Parliament. Magna Carta and the Bill of Rights carried the day, and Mr Justice Parker delivered judgment in favour of Mr Gibson Bowles. The Bank, as its counsel Mr Romer, K.C., said, had been placed " in the awkward position of being sued by Mr Bowles if it deducts the tax, and of being sued by the Inland Revenue if it does not! " The Government might have been placed in a very awkward position, too, and for a moment the whole financial structure of the country quivered under Mr Bowles' gay assault. But Parliament hastened to the rescue, and the Provisional Collection of Taxes Act was passed to empower the raising of taxation by the authority of a resolution of the House of Commons alone. And so nowadays, Magna Carta and the Bill of Rights would not avail the reluctant income tax payer as they did in the case of the stout Mr Bowles.

CHAPTER XXIV

THE MARCONI " SCANDAL "

THE last period of Rufus Isaacs' Attorneyship was overcast by the dull clouds of suspicion which gathered over him and finally burst into a storm which bade fair to shatter his whole public career. The occasion was the famous Marconi " scandal," which came to be the subject of the bitterest political controversy of the time and the merits of which are still not infrequently matter of discussion to-day. The charges levelled at this period are fortunately charges which are rarely even whispered in public life; briefly, they were that Ministers had used their position to favour a private concern in securing a Government contract, because the Managing Director of the company was the brother of a Minister, and that they had used information, gained by them during the negotiations in their capacity as members of the Government, to obtain shares at a low price and to make great profits on them, by selling them at a much higher price, when the acceptance of the tenders was made known. The company in question was the Marconi Company, and its Managing Director was Godfrey Isaacs, Rufus' younger brother.

The Marconi Company had been formed to exploit the possibilities of wireless telegraphy, which at that period was passing from its infancy to a very promising adolescence; and the name of Marconi was acquiring a fame which had been stimulated in England by his appearance as a witness before the *Titanic* Commission while the disaster itself had emphasised the necessity for a more efficient system of wireless communication. In point of fact there was a British Marconi Company and an American Marconi Company, the British Company having a large holding in the American Company, though the American had none in the British.

In March of 1910 the British Company applied to the Colonial Office to put up wireless stations in various parts of the British Empire, the aim being to link up the Empire with a vast chain of wireless communication. The request was referred by the Colonial Office to the Cable Landing Rights Committee, an inter-departmental body within whose province the matter was deemed to lie. This Committee reported on May 19, 1911, that it was best that such telegraphic stations should be owned by the State, but recommended that negotiations should be entered into with the Marconi Company, which had already worked wireless telegraphy with commercial success. The report was in its turn submitted to the Committee of Imperial Defence, who appointed a sub-committee of nine members to go fully into the matter and on June 1st the sub-committee recommended that a chain of wireless stations should be formed between the United Kingdom, India, and Australia, and that negotiations should be entered into with the Marconi Company. Finally a meeting of the Imperial Conference unanimously resolved on the motion of the Prime Minister of New Zealand that an attempt should be made to bind the various parts of the Empire together by a chain of wireless telegraphic communication.

Fortified by this encouraging accumulation of assent, Mr Herbert Samuel, the Postmaster-General, set about trying to give effect to these recommendations. A committee was set up in August, 1911, with himself as chairman and the High Commissioners of New Zealand, Australia and South Africa included in the membership, and it was resolved that negotiations should be entered into. On February 13th, 1912, the Marconi Company sent in its tender, which was accepted by the Government on March 7th, and on July 19th a formal contract was concluded. But, of course, such a contract requires the ratification of Parliament, and it came before the House of Commons for consideration on August 7th. Here, however, and in the country and the Press as well, there was determined opposition to the terms of the contract, on the ground that they were much too favourable to the company, and in consequence further discussion of the matter was postponed until the Autumn session.   But during the recess ugly rumours sprang up, to the effect that Herbert Samuel had clearly been persuaded by Rufus Isaacs to make a bargain on behalf of the State, advantageous to the company with which Godfrey Isaacs was connected, while Rufus Isaacs and other Ministers had taken advantage of the enormous rise in Marconi shares (they rose from £2 in August, 1911, to over £4 in March, 1912, when the acceptance of the tender was known, and to over £9 by the end of April) to make a vast profit; these rumours were repeated, and grew in the swift, effective anonymity of their kind.   For the most part the charges were whispered and insinuated, but some journals, in particular Mr Cecil Chesterton's *Eye-Witness*, stated them bluntly, and one paragraph read: " Isaacs' brother is chairman of the Marconi Company.   It has, therefore, been secretly arranged between Isaacs and Samuel that the British people shall give the Marconi Company a very large sum of money through the agency of the said Samuel and for the benefit of the said Isaacs." This was plain speaking indeed, and Mr Samuel was concerned as to whether he should take legal action, and consulted Rufus Isaacs on the point, who referred the matter to the Prime Minister.   Asquith wrote back:

> My dear Rufus,
>
> I return the enclosed.   I have read carefully this scurrilous rubbish, and I am clearly of opinion that you should take no notice of it.   Samuel gives some excellent reasons in his letter. I suspect the *Eye-Witness* has a very meagre circulation.   I notice only one page of advertisements and that occupied by books of Belloc's publishers.   Prosecution would secure it notoriety, which might yield subscribers.   We have broken weather, and but for Winston there would be nothing in the newspapers.
>
> Yours always,
>
> H. H. ASQUITH.

And so no legal redress was sought.   But gossip and

rumour went sedulously forward, and Rufus Isaacs gave the House of Commons a vivid picture of his own feelings at that time: "When I returned from abroad," he said, "I found that these charges were being made—whispered from house to house, spoken in the Lobbies, stated in cowardly fashion in magazines to the extent that as I walked across the Lobbies or in the streets or to the Courts, I could feel the pointing of the finger as I passed."

Such indeed was the range and violence of the allegations that the Government felt it better in October to move in Parliament for the appointment of a Committee of inquiry rather than to seek at once Parliamentary ratification for the contract. In the debate on the appointment of the select committee, Rufus Isaacs and Mr Lloyd George, whose name rumour had coupled with his in the transaction, both denied that they had any interest, direct or indirect in the British Marconi Company. If this were so, it seemed as if both the charges must collapse; for the charge of corruptly favouring a private company, which was aimed primarily at Mr Samuel as the allocator of the contract, could not stand in the face of the fact that two committees, with which Mr Samuel had no connection, had recommended negotiations before the matter had come under his official cognisance. And if Rufus Isaacs and Mr Lloyd George had no connection with the company, then the other charge must be equally baseless. Consequently, when the Committee started its investigations, it seemed reasonably probable that the rumour, like so many other rumours, would be found to be not only untrue, but without any sort of justification which might reasonably excuse it.

So it might have seemed; and, as the months went by, the Select Committee appeared to be in no hurry to call the Attorney-General or the Chancellor of the Exchequer before them as witnesses. But then something happened, which altered the complexion of events. On February 14th, 1913, *Le Matin* published, under the title "*un scandale financier en Angleterre*," a repetition of the allegations against the Ministers. Four days later they published a full apology, stating that the official documents did not at all bear out the rumours, and regretting any injury that might possibly have been caused " *à trois hommes dont l'honorabilité ne saurait être mise en doute.*" Nevertheless Rufus Isaacs and Herbert Samuel resolved to bring a libel action and the case was heard on March 19th before Mr Justice Darling. The defendants put in an expression of regret and full apology, but nevertheless a very strong team of advocates, headed by Sir Edward Carson and F. E. Smith, was briefed for the plaintiffs. Now Carson and F. E. Smith were, of course, the foremost Conservative gladiators of the day, and it was widely felt in Conservative circles that they should not have accepted the brief, since it would debar them from expressing an opinion if the matter came up in Parliament. Indeed the criticism was so widespread as to be endorsed in a leading article in the *Times* in June, to which F. E. Smith replied in a characteristic letter: " I will content myself," he wrote, " with saying that I have spent twenty years of my life in strenuous contention on behalf of the Conservative Party. But I have not surrendered to that or any other party, and I never will, my independence of judgment in matters of professional propriety." Be the rights of this question as they may, Carson and F. E. Smith conducted the case, and Rufus Isaacs gave evidence, in the course of which he referred to his purchase of shares in the American Marconi Company.

The result of the case had, of course, never been in doubt. But what attracted attention was not the result, but this new element which had suddenly been introduced. What were these American shares? And why had nobody heard of them before? At once tongues were wagging fiercely as ever to provide explanations, generally uncharitable; and the Liberal Party, which had hoped that the end of the whole business was in sight, felt that the hunt was up once more. At any rate it was now obvious that Rufus Isaacs and Lloyd George must be called by the Committee at once, and called upon they were to give their own explanation and subject themselves to examination.

Now, what in fact was the explanation of the American shares? There was, as we have seen, an American Marconi Company, as distinct from the British Marconi Company, which had no shares in the British Company which had made the contract with the Government. Mr Godfrey Isaacs had made himself responsible for placing 500,000 and suggested to his brothers Rufus and Harry that they should take some, explaining to them that the Company's transactions were limited to the United States and that it had no interest in the British Company's contract with the British Government. Rufus Isaacs decided not to take up any shares, although his brother Harry took 50,000. This was on April 9th, 1912; on April 17th, 1912, he bought 10,000 shares from Harry Isaacs at the market price of £2, having previously satisfied himself by inquiry that the company had no interest in the agreement made with the British Government. On the same day he informed Mr Lloyd George, the Chancellor of the Exchequer, and the Master of Elibank, the Liberal Chief Whip, of his purchase, and they bought one thousand shares each from him at the same price, payment not being required on the spot. The investment at first looked like being an extremely profitable one, for the shares rose in price and Rufus Isaacs sold 3570 shares at an average of £3, 6s. 6d. a share; thus on this transaction he was left with a profit of £4,730. Later, however, the shares depreciated and at the time of his giving evidence before the Committee (March 25th) they stood at one to one and one-sixteenth; therefore on the 6430 shares which he had left (including the two thousand passed on to Mr Lloyd George and the Master of Elibank, who had not as yet paid for theirs) he had a loss of £6430. Setting against this his previous profit, he had lost £1600 in all, of which his two colleagues owed him a tenth each, that is £320. Therefore Rufus Isaacs' personal loss was about £1280.

Rufus Isaacs stated these facts with great frankness, when he appeared before the Committee on March 25. He occupied the witness-chair for two days and a half, and had the experience, which must be unique for an Attorney-

General with the great reputation for cross-examination
enjoyed by Rufus Isaacs, of himself undergoing strenuous
and skilful cross-examination; but he did not flinch from
the ordeal, and showed himself as capable in his unaccustomed rôle as in the more usual rôle of counsel. It was
unfortunate, therefore, that the committee was not better
adapted to its task. It should have been some form of
judicial committee, which could have approached its task
in the spirit of a competent legal tribunal; instead of this,
however, the committee was a Parliamentary committee,
exactly reflecting the existing state of parties in the House
of Commons. In the circumstances, and in view of the
bitterness of party faction at the time and the extent to
which the findings of the committee might influence party
fortunes, it was perhaps inevitable that, while all were
anxious for the truth, some of the Conservatives should be
disposed to find that the truth was not a pretty thing, while
some of the Liberals were convinced that the action of their
leaders could not but have been above reproach. However
this may be, Rufus Isaacs did undergo a tolerably searching
cross-examination at the hands of Lord Robert Cecil, Mr
Amery, and Mr Faber, the banker. The laymen were
perhaps somewhat outclassed, but the exchanges between
Lord Robert Cecil and Sir Rufus Isaacs were worthy of the
Courts at their best; and there is this virtue in cross-
examination, whatever may be its immediate effect on the
examinee, that it does enable him to give his own explanation
—if it stands the test—in the most convincing way.

Rufus Isaacs told the Committee the story of his acquisition of the American shares, and said that he had enjoyed no
undue advantage in the purchase. He was asked whether
the public could have bought the shares at £2 on April
17th, and he said: " I really do not understand why not.
There were £1,400,000 going to be issued. There were
dealings in America, people were buying and selling, and
that was what constituted the market price. I had no full
inside knowledge: I had no more inside knowledge than any
person who might have any of the 1,400,000 shares. The

only extra knowledge I had was that my brother was telling me his views of the prospects which I relied upon." There were, it is true, no formal dealings in American Marconi shares on the London Stock Exchange before April 19th, but there were, he claimed, dealings in them, both on the Stock Exchange and on the street, for several days before April 17th when he had made his purchase from his brother. As to his "reticence" about his American shares in the debate in the House of Commons on the appointment of the select committee, he had not then referred to them because he felt it to be irrelevant to the issues, which up till that time had been raised; it was a question which he considered to belong much more properly to the Committee, before which he had expected to be summoned to give evidence almost immediately. When he found that he was not so summoned, he had taken the first opportunity in the *Le Matin* case to make reference to the matter.

The hearing was enlivened with several sharp passages, and Sir Rufus showed signs of considerable feeling on more than one occasion. On the second day he made a spirited reference to the objects of Lord Robert Cecil's examination: "If any member of the Committee," he said, "is imputing to me anything which affects my personal honour and integrity, then I demand that it should be put into perfectly plain language (Lord Robert Cecil: "Certainly"); I demand also, as I am entitled to demand, that the charge should be formulated. I have raised no question and have submitted myself to the fullest examination and cross-examination without objection. I raise none now, but I do think I am entitled to have at any rate the kind of justice which is meted out to the commonest criminal—namely, that you tell him what the charge is." Later in his answers to Mr Amery's questions he again showed some heat, and his emphatic declaration won applause from the public: "Is there any man," he asked passionately, "who read these articles who would not have thought that what was meant to be conveyed was that we had all been guilty of corruption?"

" Or impropriety," interjected Mr Macmaster.

" No, Mr Macmaster," he replied. " Don't let us get off into that. Let me finish what I have got to say. I will not be stopped. I am being charged with something, and all I mean to say in regard to it is, I ask you, Sir, and I ask the Committee that we cannot have a confusion between a charge of corruption and a charge of impropriety. One concerns the honour, the other concerns the judgment of a man."

" There is no dispute about that," said Lord Robert Cecil. " We are not trying journalists."

" Are you trying me? "

" No, we are inquiring into the facts."

The chairman, Sir Albert Spicer, presented his draft report on May 28th; but before this the prosecution of Mr Cecil Chesterton for criminal libel on Mr Godfrey Isaacs had been begun. Sir Edward Carson and Mr F. E. Smith appeared for the prosecution, but Mr Chesterton would have been convicted, even if faced with less able counsel; for, instead of confining himself to a temperate criticism of the points on which he might justly have commented, he made reckless allegations of corruption and showed a surprising ignorance of the law of libel. He was in consequence convicted after a trial, in which Rufus Isaacs had given evidence in addition to his brother and Mr Herbert Samuel. Mr G. K. Chesterton was a witness to character on behalf of his brother, and stated to the Court that he envied his brother the dignity of his present position.

But considerably more real interest attached to the finding of the Committee, for it had been fairly obvious to everybody that Mr Chesterton's sweeping allegations could never stand the test of inquiry. But what of the Committee's authoritative finding on the whole issue? The Committee was not able to find unanimity although they were all agreed in acquitting the Ministers concerned of all charge of corruption. On May 28th Sir Albert Spicer presented his draft report as chairman; on June 2nd Lord Robert Cecil and Mr Falconer, a Liberal member of the Committee, presented alternative reports. The Committee considered the chairman's report, but on the whole the majority preferred Mr Falconer's report, very large portions of which they substituted for the chairman's report, and the Majority Report, when it was published on June 13th, proved to be highly favourable to the Ministers. It found that there was no foundation for any charge made against Ministers in respect of the negotiation of the contract or of dealings in the shares of the English company; further the people who made the charges had no reason to believe that they were true, and were guilty of a " slander of a particularly vile character, which could not be too strongly condemned." As to the purchase of American shares, the Report found that the Ministers bona fide believed, and had reason to believe, that the American company had no interest in the agreement between the British company and the British Government; and " on the whole matters relating to the conduct of Ministers which have come before the Committee, the Committee finds that all the Ministers concerned have acted throughout in the sincere belief that there was nothing in their action which would in any way conflict with their duty as Ministers of the Crown."

The Report was widely criticised as being a " whitewashing " report; and there was, in fact, virtually no criticism of ministerial action in the whole Report, whose severity was reserved for those who had dared to comment on the affair. As such the Report did not commend itself to the good sense of the public who, although approving the finding of no corruption, felt that there should be some censure of the Ministers, whose indiscretion had inevitably given colour to darker suspicions. Such, too, was the feeling of a large number of the Committee, and the Report was only adopted by eight votes to six. The Conservatives identified themselves with Lord Robert Cecil's Minority Report, which was nearer to the Chairman's report; and both Sir Albert's (who was, of course, himself a Liberal) and Lord Robert's were nearer to the facts than the Majority Report. Both reports agreed with the Majority Report in vindicating the Ministers from a charge of corruption; and Lord Robert's Report, which was the most hostile, categorically stated that no Minister had been influenced in the discharge of his public duties by any interest in the Marconi undertaking, or had used official information for investment or speculation. In respect of the American shares, too, the Chairman's Report found that Sir Rufus had acted in perfectly good faith, believing that the American Company was not in any way connected with the solvency, success or contracts of the English Company; but, added Sir Albert, " Sir Rufus Isaacs would, in the judgment of your Committee, have been well advised if, when invited by Mr Harry Isaacs to acquire these rights he had adhered to the resolution formed by him when Mr Godfrey Isaacs made a similar proposal, and had nothing to with it." Also " if on the occasion of the debate in the House of Commons on October 11th, 1912, it had occurred to the Ministers whose conduct had been impugned to make a statement of facts as disclosed in the action of *Le Matin*, such a statement would in the judgment of your Committee, and as subsequent events have proved, have tended to avert misunderstanding and to lessen, in considerable measure, the labours of your Committee." This mild rebuke was sharply emphasised by Lord Robert Cecil's Report, which found that Sir Rufus had committed a grave " impropriety " by making an advantageous purchase of shares by means of information not available to the public at a time when the contract, though ratified by the Government, had not obtained the sanction of Parliament. The Report was also of opinion that the American Marconi Company was materially interested, although indirectly, in the conclusion of an agreement between the English Marconi Company and the British Government, and, therefore, it was " highly inadvisable for Ministers to take shares in the American Marconi Company, while the agreement was still pending." When once shares had been taken, however, it had been the duty of Ministers to disclose the transaction to the House of Commons in the debate in October, 1912; and " we regard that reticence as a grave error of judgment and as wanting in frankness and respect for the House of Commons."

The Reports were published on June 13th; but unfortunately the matter could not end there. It was clear that the Ministers had not been guilty of corruption; that was no longer in dispute. But it was felt that the Majority Report had not faced up to the issues; and, in point of fact, its signatories had rendered no service to Sir Rufus Isaacs and Mr Lloyd George, for their Report was of necessity for the most part disregarded, whereas a unanimous finding, though it would have been sterner than the Majority Report, might have put an end to the matter. But, as it was, Mr Cave (who was later, as Viscount Cave, to become Lord Chancellor) put down on behalf of the Opposition an official motion of censure upon the Ministers concerned. To Rufus Isaacs and to Mr Lloyd George the occasion was momentous; their very continuance in public life was in peril, and it looked as if the slow accumulation of past achievement and the towering edifice of future aspiration might equally come crashing to the ground. At no period since he had been hammered on the Stock Exchange had the tide of Rufus Isaacs' fortunes ebbed so far. But that youthful disaster had not been irrevocable; this time, if he lost, he lost for ever. And there were not wanting Liberals who urged upon the Prime Minister the advisability of sacrificing the men upon whom suspicion had fallen in such a way as to damage the credit and fortunes of the Party. But Mr Asquith was a loyal colleague, and although in the words of his biographer, " he certainly thought that they had themselves very largely to thank for the suspicion that they had incurred on this occasion, having satisfied himself that there was no corrupt act or intention, he came to the conclusion that the only penalty which he had it in his power to inflict would be out of all proportion to the offending."

Nevertheless, though Mr Asquith refused to cashier his colleagues, the passage of the vote of censure would equally be fatal to the continuance of the two parties concerned in public life. (The Master of Elibank, it may be mentioned, had been called away by business commitments to some inaccessible spot in Mexico.) The House and galleries, therefore, were crowded—and it was a House which had not been above howling " sticky fingers " at Rufus Isaacs and Mr Lloyd George—and the atmosphere taut with excitement, when Mr Cave rose to move his vote of censure. His speech, which was one of studied moderation, was listened to attentively by the House, and not least by Rufus Isaacs on the Treasury Bench and Mr Lloyd George, who sat next to Mr Asquith with arms folded and head thrown back; for Mr Lloyd George belongs to the school of thought which believes that the best defence is defiance. After the speeches of Mr Cave and his seconder, Rufus Isaacs, who had risen so often to cross-examine or to prosecute, rose to speak in his own defence. For a few moments he stood at the box, gripping it with both hands and waiting while the deep, continuous cheers rolled across the Liberal benches; he looked grey and overwrought as he stood there, but in that great moment he faced his judges—for so virtually they were—and did not falter. And then he began to speak, not angrily, nor blusteringly, nor pleadingly; but resolutely, lucidly, and at time with great feeling. Taken merely as a speech, it is probably the best Parliamentary effort that Rufus Isaacs ever made, and it certainly made a profound impression; a contemporary newspaper spoke of it as a " speech the manliness of which deeply impressed his audience." In his speech he gave a long account of his purchase of the shares, emphasising the fact that he had not wished to conceal his transactions from the House in the debate in October; he had expected to be called very early before the Committee, and when that did not happen, he took the first opportunity of revealing the matter in the *Le Matin* action. As to the manner of the purchase, " what I ask the House to accept is that I was receiving no favour from my brother Godfrey, that I accepted no favour, that the offer he made me I refused, and. therefore, from that moment all relations between him and me came to an end."

Nor would he plead for mercy or indulgence: " I do not

ask," he said, " the House or any member of it, to judge
this transaction of mine by any lower standard than has been
applied by the House of Commons at any time—aye, and
I go further, and say that I do not ask this House to judge
my conduct by any lower standard than has been imposed by
the Liberal Party as applicable to Ministers and that is the
higher test." He then proceeded to lay down rules of
behaviour: that no Minister should use any information
obtained as a Minister to further private interests; that
Ministers should be guided solely by public interest and
should not use their influence to obtain contracts with
Government departments for their relatives or friends; that
no Minister should place himself in a position which might
reasonably expose him, in the opinion of fair-minded men,
to suspicion of corruption, even though his conscience is clear.
In regard to this last, and important, point, he said: " In my
view no one can protect himself against the suspicion of the
evilly-disposed. . . It never occurred to me during the whole
course of those transactions that any human being could
suspect me of corruption because I purchased American
Marconi shares some six weeks after the announcement was
made of the acceptance of the tender of the British Marconi
Company by the British Government; if I had had all the
facts present to my mind at the time I entered into that
transaction, if I had known then all that I know now, if all
had been disclosed to me which subsequent events have
revealed, if I had realised that men could be so suspicious
of any action of mine, if I had thought that such misrepresentation could possibly exist, I state quite plainly that I
would not have entered into this transaction. I need scarcely
tell the House that I have given this matter very careful
consideration before I made this statement, and I say
solemnly and sincerely it was a mistake to purchase those
shares."

Thus Rufus Isaacs had coupled with his explanation a
confession that he had been in error; and the confession was
echoed by Mr Lloyd George, for all that he began to speak
in a belligerent tone. This rather took the wind out of the

sails of their critics, for it is poor fun belabouring people to try and make them regret an action which they have already said that they do regret. It seemed not improbable, therefore, when Rufus Isaacs and Mr Lloyd George left the Chamber amid loud cheers from their supporters at the end of Mr Lloyd George's speech (for they could not stay in the Chamber while their conduct was being debated by their equals) that the motion would be withdrawn. But the debate was continued and after Lord Robert Cecil had claimed that Sir Rufus and Mr Lloyd George took too personal a view of the matter, Mr Buckmaster, subsequently to become a Liberal Lord Chancellor, brought forward an amendment to the effect that " this House after hearing the statements of the Attorney-General and the Chancellor of the Exchequer . . . accepts those statements and deems it right to put on record their reprobation of the false charges of the gravest description brought against Ministers which have proved to be wholly without foundation." Mr Buckmaster made a very graceful reference to the Attorney-General: " He is by his official position," he said, " the head of our profession. It is a profession where competition is pitiless and fierce, a profession where few men win and many fail, and . . . the success of no man can be attained without the closest and most searching investigation of character and honour, and yet no one will dispute that the Attorney-General in gaining the position he has gained has won not merely admiration but esteem, honour, and affection from the men whom he has out-stripped and out-distanced in the race."

Nevertheless, it was felt that the amendment, like the Majority Report, was one-sided, for it contained no references to expressions of regret on the part of the Ministers concerned; and after sagacious and generous speeches by Mr Balfour and Mr Asquith, who said—and one can readily believe him—that he had rarely risen to address the House with a greater reluctance, the temper of the debate went up, and Mr Buckmaster withdrew his amendment in the hope that Sir Ryland Adkins' amendment would obtain the unanimous approval which his own had clearly failed to compass. Sir Ryland's amendment ran: " That this House, after hearing ... accepts their expressions of regret that such purchases were made, and that they were not mentioned in the debate on October 11th last, acquits them of acting otherwise than in good faith, and reprobates the charges of corruption brought against Ministers, which have been proved to be wholly false." It might have been hoped that the House would have been able to adopt this unanimously, but it did not meet with the approval of the Opposition, on whose behalf Mr Bonar Law, in a speech in which he spoke of " feet of clay," proposed an alternative amendment, which agreed in its attitude to the charges of corruption but expressed the regret of the House instead of accepting the Ministers' expression of regret. It may seem a small distinction at this distance of time, but one can, of course, see Mr Bonar Law's point; he felt that the circumstances demanded an opinion of the House, rather than a merely passive attitude of acceptance. His amendment did not, of course, commend itself to the majority of the House, and ultimately Sir Ryland Adkins' amendment was carried by 346 to 268, a vote reflecting the strength of the parties in the House.

Such was the unsatisfactory termination of an unsatisfactory episode. At this distance of time, the best comment would seem to be that such disturbances of the even tenor of our public life are rare indeed. There is little in the episode on which any of the parties can congratulate themselves. Sir Rufus and Mr Lloyd George were unanimously, and very properly, acquitted of the charge of corruption, which had been flung at them without any sifting of the evidence or any real foundation; but their purchase of the American shares and their failure to refer to it in the original debate were astounding errors of judgment in men whose judgment is not often at fault. Since the purchase had been made, it would have been much better to disclose it, even if it was not strictly relevant to the subject under discussion; for neglect to do so meant that the Committee had to proceed through many sessions in ignorance of some of the main facts of the case. Disclosure in October would have been the wisest course after the purchase had been made; but it never should have been made. Rufus Isaacs satisfied himself by inquiry that the American Marconi Company had no interest in the British Company's agreement with the British Government, and there is no reason to suppose—indeed, nobody suggested—that he was not sincerely convinced that this was the case. But as a Minister of the Crown and brother to the Managing Director, he was in a position of great delicacy and it behoved him to be especially careful to avoid even the appearance of improper conduct; for, though the American Company had no shares in the British Company, the British Company had shares in the American, and some of the Directors were the same. It would be very difficult, therefore, to be entirely certain that no advantage could possibly accrue to the American Company through the agreement, even though it were not a party to it; and indeed Lord Robert Cecil's Minority Report found that the American Company was materially, though indirectly, interested in the conclusion of the agreement. Be that as it may, however—and Sir Rufus Isaacs and Mr Lloyd George were naturally absolutely convinced that there was no such interest—the action was in the highest degree unwise; and nobody, not even the protagonists themselves, was really concerned to defend its wisdom. Mr Asquith, as we have seen, certainly thought that they had themselves very largely to thank for the suspicion that they had incurred on this occasion, and that is an opinion which would be very generally echoed. In the circumstances one's sympathy perhaps goes less to them than to the Prime Minister, their colleagues and the Liberal Party, who were all to a greater or lesser extent involved in the consequences of their action; and indeed the Liberal Party was further embarrassed by the action of the Master of Elibank in purchasing three thousand American Marconi shares for the Party funds. But although Rufus Isaacs and Mr Lloyd George escaped a vote of censure and were not driven from public life—

although there was undoubtedly a large number of people
who would not have been sorry to see the last of Mr Lloyd
George in public affairs—it must not be thought that they
did not suffer. What they did suffer in those months of
suspicion and recrimination is known only to themselves;
expiation they did make, but it is an expiation which is not
susceptible of measurement or analysis.

Circumstances, however, of a very different sort were soon
to remove Rufus Isaacs from the political sphere. In
October of 1913 Lord Alverstone, who had been Lord Chief
Justice since 1900 and whose retirement had been rumoured
several times, announced his resignation; and the office, in
accordance with custom, was offered to the Attorney-General.
Acceptance meant, of course, or appeared to mean, a sever-
ance with politics; but Rufus Isaacs had not even entered the
House of Commons until he was considerably past forty, and
had not become an assiduous Parliamentarian until he
became a Law Officer of the Crown. His life had been
spent primarily in the law and his great triumphs had been
won there; politics, too, can hardly have seemed very sweet
during the preceding twelve months. The office of Lord
Chief Justice is non-political; but it is a position of great
distinction and responsibility. The Lord Chancellor, it is
true, is at the apex of the legal hierarchy; but he is a
politician, whose tenure of office is bounded by the fortunes
of the party to which he belongs. The Lord Chief Justice,
on the other hand, is permanent and independent of party,
and it is he who to the general public is the embodiment of
the majesty and stability of the law; for he is the
spokesman of the Judges, the chief criminal Judge in the
country, and head of the Common Law courts. It was
perhaps unfortunate that his appointment should come when
the Marconi controversy was so fresh in mind, for there
were not wanting those who criticised it on these grounds,
and, in the words of the *Times*, "it can only be regarded
as a great misfortune that an absorbing controversy should
have brought hesitation and discord into what would otherwise have been a unanimous chorus of approval."

On Tuesday, October 21st, Lord Reading—for so Rufus Isaacs had become—was sworn in as Lord Chief Justice. The scene lacked nothing in impressive grandeur. Nearly all the Judges of the High Court were present, and countless eminent King's Counsel, headed by Sir John Simon, the new Attorney; among them, too, was Sir Edward Clarke, with whom in the heyday of his power Rufus Isaacs had crossed swords. The Lord Chief Justice himself, wearing the crimson robe and gold chain of his office, and flanked by the Lord Chancellor and the Master of the Rolls in their robes of black and gold, took the oath in a very distinct voice, in which a trace of nervousness could perhaps be detected. Only one incident marred the splendid propriety of the occasion. After the oath had been taken, the Lord Chancellor, according to custom, welcomed the new Lord Chief Justice in a speech; he then proceeded to a eulogy of Lord Alverstone, the retiring Lord Chief Justice, which he spoke with considerable emotion. It was all the more shocking, therefore, to those present to hear a barrister, one Mr Hales, exclaim in a loud voice, just as Lord Haldane was drawing to a close, " Speak for yourself, Lord Haldane." Mr Hales was at once hustled out of Court by indignant barristers. But he afterwards took occasion to make it known that he had intended no disrespect to Lord Alverstone; he was hard of hearing and had thought that Lord Haldane was referring to the new Lord Chief Justice.

The Marconi episode died hard, if haltingly.

CHAPTER XXV

WARTIME LORD CHIEF JUSTICE

LORD READING'S tenure of the office of Lord Chief Justice was to last over seven years, and was then to be terminated not, as is usual, by death or honoured retirement into leisure, but by the translation to a new and active sphere. But this was not the only respect in which his period of office was unusual; for a great part of it coincided with the duration of the War, which had as revolutionary an effect upon the traditional concept of the Lord Chief Justice's duties as it had upon so many of the apparently deep-rooted ideas of the time. It must have seemed, when Lord Reading assumed office in October of 1913, that he must contemplate a career of long and unbroken service on the Bench; and to a man in the early fifties, accustomed to the hard struggles and immense rewards of the Bar and to the continual thrust and parry of Party politics, the prospect could hardly appear unduly exciting. *Sed dis aliter visum;* for within less than twelve months of his appointment, Europe was at war. And the War, which was to shake to its foundations the whole structure of society and rip into fragments the destinies of peoples, carried its imperious arbitrament to the destiny of the new Lord Chief Justice.

The War evoked in Lord Reading his talent for negotiation and diplomacy, which had hitherto found expression in the narrower field of Party politics and the consulting-chamber. The talent was found to be in him, and as the War proceeded was called upon in ever-increasing measure. Consequently from 1915 onwards the law and diplomacy ran parallel in his life until, with his appointment as Viceroy in January, 1921, he abandoned active connection with the profession after a period of over thirty years. It may be said at once that the situation of a Lord Chief Justice, who

343

is an international and diplomatic figure, would be impossible except in obedience to the exigencies of war; for the office entails definite legal duties, which must in the course of things suffer if the holder of the office is distracted by the performance of other, and possibly incompatible duties. Indeed, as it was, the frequent absences of the Lord Chief Justice from Court, and sometimes from the country, was adversely commented on in some quarters, for tradition dies hard, even in time of war. But it was a thing for which the Coalition Government had little respect, and it needed the Lord Chief Justice for other duties; consequently, as time went on, Lord Reading was requisitioned more and more for other tasks, until his appointment as High Commissioner and Special Envoy to the United States in 1917 caused a virtual suspension of his discharge of the duties of his legal office.

Almost from the beginning of the War, Lord Reading's financial knowledge was drawn upon by the Government, and it was he who advised the Government guarantee to the great accepting houses; this was an action which involved Government backing for enormous transactions and, in giving the advice that he did, Lord Reading showed that he had early grasped the revolution that the conditions of war was to bring in methods of finance. Towards the end of 1915 he was President of the Anglo-French Mission, which went to the United States in order to raise a loan of £100,000,000, which was to be spent by England and France in America on the purchase of war material. The Mission was successful in its object, and in America Reading scored a distinct personal success, which helped to indicate him for his subsequent appointment in the United States and facilitated his success in its conduct; the pages of Colonel House's volumes bear testimony to the good impression made by Lord Reading and to the measure of success which he secured. But Lord Reading's exploits in America, which won for him his elevation to a viscounty in July, 1916, are outside the scope of this book; and here it is more in point to recall that, in spite of his other activities, he did in the earlier years of the War perform a considerable measure of judicial work of interest and value.

One especially important branch of the law brought to the front by the War was that which relates to aliens, and Lord Reading was called upon to try several cases, which turned on the rights and liabilities of aliens in time of war. The most important of these was the celebrated case of Porter *v.* Freudenberg, in which the appeal was heard by the entire Court of Appeal; that is to say, by all seven judges who nominally compose that Court instead of by the minimum of three, which is in point of fact the normal quota. The case was the result of an action by Porter to recover from Freudenberg the rent due under a lease for the premises in which Freudenberg had carried on business before the War; the War, however, made Freudenberg an alien enemy, and at the time of the trial he was resident in Berlin. Now in time of peace aliens have, with a trifling exception, the same capacity in regard to contracts as a natural-born British subject; but in time of war they may not enter into contracts with British subjects, and contracts made before the war which involve intercourse between the parties or are in any way contrary to public policy are dissolved by the outbreak of war. The case of Porter *v.* Freudenberg, however, raised the further points of the rights and liabilities of alien enemies in the British Courts with respect to contracts that exist before war time. That is to say, in Lord Reading's words, " first, the capacity of alien enemies to sue in the King's Courts; secondly, their liability to be sued; thirdly, their capacity to appeal to the Appellate Courts, and generally their right to appear and be heard in the King's Courts." The finding of the Court on these important issues can best be given in the words of the judgment in which Lord Reading expressed the unanimous opinion of the Court of Appeal: " An alien enemy's right to sue," he said, " or to proceed either by himself or by any other person on his behalf, in the King's Court, is suspended during the progress of hostilities, and until after peace is declared . . . The rule of law suspending

the alien enemy's right of action is based on public policy,
but no considerations of public policy are apparent which
would justify preventing the enforcement by a British or
neutral subject of a right against the enemy. The effect of
this would be to convert that which during war is a disability,
imposed upon the alien enemy because of his hostile
character, into a relief to him during war from the discharge
of his liabilities to British subjects . . . Once this conclusion
is reached that the alien enemy can be sued, if follows that
he can appear and be heard in his defence and may take all
such steps as may be necessary for the proper presentment
of his defence. To deny him that right would be to deny
him justice and would be quite contrary to the basic principles guiding the King's Courts in the administration of
justice."   An only less important judgment was that
delivered in the following year, July of 1916, by Lord
Reading in the Court of Appeal in the case of Halsey v.
Lowenfeld, in which the defendant, whom the War had also
made an alien enemy, was sued for the rent due on the
Prince of Wales Theatre. The question was whether an
alien enemy can be sued during the war in respect of a
covenant made before the war, and the decision of the Court
of Appeal was that a covenant is not extinguished or suspended by the outbreak of war, and the alien enemy may
be sued for the rent accruing during the war.

But the most interesting case of this sort which Lord
Reading was called upon to try, was concerned not with
aliens but with naturalised British subjects of very considerable eminence. Sir Ernest Cassel and Sir Edgar Speyer
were well-known Edwardian figures in the realms of finance
and Society. Both were by birth German Jews, Cassel
having been born in Cologne and Speyer in Frankfort, but
both settled in London and became naturalised British
subjects. Sir Ernest Cassel had enormous banking interests
and numbered among his achievements the founding of the
Agricultural Bank of Egypt and the construction of the
Central London Railway. But he was best known to the
public as a man of vast wealth, great hospitality and con-

siderable philanthropy who had, amongst other munificent gifts, endowed the King Edward VII Sanitorium for Tuberculosis at Midhurst, and whose entertainment was lavish in the extreme at a time when the standards of entertainment were high indeed.   Frequently among his guests was King Edward himself, whose great friend he was, and it was by the proud though unofficial title of " the King's friend " that Sir Ernest Cassel, financier, philanthropist, and racing-man was chiefly known.   Sir Edgar Speyer was like Sir Ernest Cassel in that he was a financier of German origin, but, beyond that, the fact of their being joined in this case has led to a closer association of them in the public mind than the circumstances perhaps warranted.   Speyer was born at Frankfort in 1862, and was thus considerably younger than Cassel; like him, however, he became a naturalised British subject and settled in London, where he was a director of the firm of Speyer Bros., and took the chief part in financing the Metropolitan District Railway and the " tube " trains.   In politics he was an energetic adherent of the Liberal party, and in philanthropy his activities were wide and generous.   But it was perhaps in the sphere of music that London at any rate had most cause to be grateful to him, for in his capacity as Chairman of the Queen's Hall Orchestra his enthusiasm and his wealth enabled him to do a great deal.

The eve of the War, therefore, found the two men leading active, spacious, envied lives in all the various spheres to which wealth, ability or charm had given them entry.   It must have seemed that this was the unalterable order of their existence, and they would tread it unchallenged till the end.   Then came the War, and with it suspicion, mistrust and imaginings, sometimes in moments of alarm deepening into something very like popular hysteria.   For all these feelings Speyer and Cassel were an obvious target; were they not of German birth and had they not vast financial resources and social connections?   Then they clearly had the will to be pro-German, and the means to be dangerously so; so the rumour spread, and at such times rumour spreads

fast and far. To try and stamp it out, to reveal and pro-
claim its lack of foundation was of no avail; rumour, like
the guillotine, is no respecter of persons, and inexorably it
struck down those favourites of fortune, Sir Ernest Cassel
and Sir Edgar Speyer. In the case of Speyer there were
rather more facts on which to base such charges than there
were in Cassel's case, for Speyer's firm had interests in
Germany and his brother in America was notoriously anti-
British. In addition he had a house at Overstrand on the
North Sea, which it was alleged, with a happy disregard for
the fact that he had had it long before the War, he used ·
for signalling and espionage purposes. But even without
any of these circumstances, he would probably not have
escaped the shrill accusations which the temper of the times
was so quick to engender; and, even though there were a
great number of people who refused to listen to the malicious
stories which were so assiduously propagated, things got to
such a pitch that Speyer felt constrained to write to the
Prime Minister in May, 1915, saying, " I consider it due
to my honour as a loyal British subject, and my personal
dignity as a man, to retire from all my public positions. I
therefore ask you to accept my resignation as a Privy
Councillor and to revoke my baronetcy." To this letter
Asquith replied: " I have known you long and well enough
to estimate at their true value these baseless and malignant
imputations upon your loyalty to the British Crown. The
King is not prepared to take any step such as you suggest
in regard to the marks of distinction which you have received
in recognition of public services and philanthropic munifi-
cence."

The answer was worthy of a King and his Prime Minister,
who were able to transcend the clamour of the vulgar. But
Sir Edgar, who for a Privy Councillor must have been
very ignorant of constitutional usage, had asked for the
impossible; for membership of the Privy Council may not
be resigned nor baronetcies revoked. Nevertheless Sir
Edgar was not alone in thinking that he should not continue
in the Privy Council; there were those who thought that

legally he was disqualified by the fact of his alien birth. Prominent among these was Sir George Makgill, a Scottish baronet of old family, who was primarily known, in so far as he was known at all, as the author of stories dealing with colonial life; but late in 1915 he emerged in a new sphere of activity by bringing an action to make Sir Edgar Speyer and Sir Ernest Cassel show by what authority they claimed to be members of the Privy Council. The point was, as developed before Lord Reading and Mr Justice Avory and Mr Justice Lush in the King's Bench Division, that Sir Edgar Speyer and Sir Ernest Cassel, not having been born of British parents or within the United Kingdom or its dominions, were on that account legally debarred from the right to be members of the Privy Council. Now it was indisputably true that such circumstances would in an earlier period of the country's history have prevented Speyer and Cassel from serving on the Privy Council. Thus the Act of Settlement in 1700 had enacted that " no person born out of the kingdoms of England, Scotland, or Ireland, or the dominions thereunto belonging (although he be naturalised or made a denizen, except such as are born of English parents) shall be capable to be of the Privy Council or a member of either House of Parliament or to enjoy any office or place of trust, either civil or military . . . " and the Act of 1844, known as Hutt's Act, though it improved the position of alien-borns, specifically maintained their exclusion from Parliament and the Privy Council. On the other side, however, it was contended that more recent legislation had altered the position, and had made naturalised aliens competent to serve even in these high places.

Before the case could be argued, Sir Frederick Smith, who had become Attorney-General in the Coalition Government and who appeared with Sir George Cave and Mr Branson for the Clerk of the Privy Council, entered a plea that the Court had no jurisdiction in the matter on the ground that, if there was a wrong, it was a usurpation of rights by the Crown, whereas the remedy was provided for usurpation against the Crown of its prerogatives; further no judgment in favour of Sir George Makgill could be enforced, as it would be an order upon the Crown. To this high doctrine Lord Reading did not assent, saying that the remedy was open to a private individual if there had been a usurpation of an office of a public nature. In regard to the other objection, he disagreed that a judgment of ouster, pronounced by the Court would be an order on the King. In any case, " This," he said, " is the King's Court; we sit here to administer justice and to interpret the law of the realm in the King's name. It is respectful and proper to assume that once the law is declared by a competent judicial authority it will be followed by the Crown."

The preliminary objection having fallen to the ground, the main issue was argued. But the case for the defence was argued only on behalf of Sir Ernest Cassel; for Mr Roskill, K.C., who appeared for Sir Edgar Speyer, announced that Speyer was not willing to have the case argued, as he had offered to resign membership of the Privy Council and felt that it would be inconsistent to assert a claim to an honour which he had offered to resign. Sir Ernest Cassel was represented by Sir Robert Finlay, K.C., who led Mr Leslie Scott, K.C., and Mr Henry McCardie, while Mr Powell, K.C., appeared for Sir George Makgill. Mr Powell's case briefly was that, although the British Nationality and Status of Aliens Act of 1914 enacted that naturalised persons " subject to the provisions of this Act. be entitled to all political and other rights, powers and privileges and . . . have to all intents and purposes the status of a natural-born British subject," another paragraph of the Act said that " Section III of the Act of Settlement (which disqualifies naturalised aliens from holding certain offices) shall have effect as if the words " naturalised or " were omitted therefrom." Now, in Mr Powell's contention if that section of the Act of Settlement, which has already been quoted, is read with the omission of the words in question, it means that the disabilities against alien-borns are maintained. The counsel for Sir Ernest Cassel put forward the view that, as the Act of 1914 was intended to improve the position of naturalised persons, it could hardly have been the intention of its framers to revive their disabilities and to undo the effects of all the intervening legislation by a chance paragraph.   Lord Reading, in giving judgment, reviewed the legislation on the subject of aliens and found for Speyer and Cassel.   The Act of 1870 had repealed the Act of 1844, and " the two limitations preserved by the repealed Act of 1844 (*i.e.*, the disqualification from being a member of Parliament or the Privy Council) disappeared in the Act of 1870, and the language of this Act is inconsistent with their continued existence.   Therefore," he continued, " the conclusion is irresistible that the statute of 1870 by implication repealed such of the limitations originally imposed by the Act of Settlement as were preserved by the Act of 1844.   Therefore, the respondents, having been naturalised under the Act of 1870 were capable of being Privy Councillors when they were respectively appointed."   But Mr Powell's argument had been that, whatever their position before it, they had ceased to be capable of being Privy Councillors after the Act of 1914. Here again Lord Reading did not agree: " This statute," he observed, " repealed the Act of 1870, and, it is to be observed, does not re-enact the one qualification in the Act of 1870 as to the status of a naturalised subject.   The Act of 1914 was intended to extend and not to curtail the rights of naturalised subjects and aliens . . . It is to my mind obvious that these words were inserted because of the powers given to the Secretary of State to revoke a certificate.   In any event I think section 38, sub-section 2, of the Interpretations Act, 1889, (which says that where an Act repeals an existing enactment, it shall not, unless a contrary intention appears, revise anything not in force at the time of repeal, or affect the rights and privileges accruing under the Act, which is repealed) is fatal to Mr Powell's argument."

The other two judges were of the same opinion, and so the judgment for Speyer and Cassel was unanimous; the judgment for Speyer was appealed against, but the decision was affirmed by the Court of Appeal in July, 1916.   The story, however, does not end altogether happily. Sir Ernest Cassel made no attempt to retain his previous position, but retired with dignity to Bournemouth, where he lived in virtual seclusion until the end; a man of fundamentally simple tastes—despite his lavish entertainment of others—and little interest in the arts, he developed an unexciting routine, which terminated only with death. Sir Edgar Speyer's story is even sadder. He left England and went to America, where, perhaps maddened by what he felt to be the injustice of the treatment which he had received or perhaps responding to the call of race, he became strongly pro-German. In consequence his certificate of naturalisation was revoked in 1921 by the Committee, statutorily set up, which considered his case in secret; and so Sir Edgar Speyer concluded his life, no longer an Englishman even in name. It is impossible not to feel sympathy for the two men, who, like Timon of Athens, must have felt that there were many to applaud them in prosperity, but few to console them in adversity. But they had built in great measure on the foundation of the approval of the least stable element in the community; and he who builds on sand must fear the tempest.

The sadness of their story, however, is eclipsed by the great tragedy of one who was a citizen of the Empire by birth and honoured in his service to it, but was seduced by his own idealism into committing the greatest and most dramatic of war-time treasons.

CHAPTER XXVI

TREASON AND DEATH OF ROGER CASEMENT

IN the *Times* of Saturday, April 22nd, 1916, there appeared a small paragraph under the heading: "Arms in a Boat: Reported Discovery on the Irish Coast." It ran: —

"News reached Tralee last night that a collapsible boat containing a large quantity of arms and ammunition was seized about 4 o'clock yesterday morning at Currahane Strand by the Ardfert police.

"A stranger of unknown nationality was arrested in the vicinity, and is detained in custody. Where the boat came from or for whom the arms were intended is at present unknown."

This bald statement was the first intimation that the strangest episode of the War had reached its dénouement; it was soon to conclude in the greatest treason trial in the history of the country. The scene changes swiftly from the remote, desolate Irish coast to the unpretentious court at Bow Street, where so many strange tales have been unfolded; but it may fairly be doubted whether any drama of the Courts has been as thrilling, or has been played on so vast a stage, as that in which Sir Roger Casement appeared before Lord Reading to answer the gravest charge known to our Criminal Law.

When Sir Roger Casement retired from the consular service in 1912, at the age of forty-eight, he had a record of peculiar distinction, which had won him a pension—not, it is true, a very substantial one—and the honours of knighthood and the C.M.G. Nor were his services of the conventional, rather plodding order, which so often win similar honours for public servants. It could not be said of Roger Casement that he had been honoured merely because he had avoided making mistakes; the quality of his services had been of no such negative order.   On the contrary his honours were bestowed for actions which scarcely needed the mark of official approval to win for them the applause not only of this country, but of civilised and humane people the world over.   For it was Roger Casement who by his tireless investigations and intrepid energy had exposed first in the Congo, and then in the Putumayo, the abominations to which natives were exposed in the exploitation of natural resources. The horror caused by his revelations was intense, and his name became something to be reckoned with in the Chancelleries of Europe, and an object of veneration in the houses of the people; for gratitude is always felt for those who arouse the national conscience by the exposure of conditions which are sufficiently remote.   And so Casement in 1912 was known as a loyal and devoted servant of the British Empire; but he was recognised above all as a servant of humanity who by his own fearless enthusiasm in investigating in the swamps of Central Africa and South America had placed a moral compulsion on the nations to come to the aid of those least able to help themselves.

The task had only been accomplished at a price.   At the age of forty-eight he was retired, with a small pension and no prospects.   His health was shattered, and a lifetime spent in strange—and often barbarous—places had given him no niche in society; circumstances, and his own shyness, had prevented him, in spite of his gift of quick sympathy and his romanticism, from gathering many friends.   He was lonely, unmarried, poor, broken in health; what could the future hold for him?   But he was an idealist, a romanticist, a quixotic knight-errant, who had spent the best years of his life in the service of poor, ill-treated creatures, who can hardly have known that he was come to help them; and it is the nature of such men to conjure up from the depths of drabness adventures undreamed of and unapproved by their more sedate and level-headed fellow-beings.   And it was to Ireland that he returned.   Ireland, always the happy hunting-ground of unpractical politicians.   And Casement at forty-eight, with no political experience, was the very type and symbol of the romantic theorist in politics; but he had to pay for his theories and his inexperience more dearly than is the rule with politicians.

Casement was—rather unexpectedly—an Ulsterman and a Protestant (although his mother had been born a Catholic). But his sympathies had always been with the aspirations of Irish nationalism, and on a previous visit to Ireland nothing had given him more pleasure than the company of the young zealots for Irish independence.

By 1912, however, the scene was changed. Redmond was using the Irish vote, which since the elections of 1910 held the balance between the English parties, to try and force Asquith to put Home Rule on the Statute Book. This, according to opinion at the time, would have meant the compulsory inclusion of Ulster in a unit, to the creation of which it was implacably opposed; and this the Orangemen and English Unionists like Carson and F. E. Smith were determined to resist with all their strength. Ireland had virtually become two hostile camps, and Casement, though an Ulsterman, threw himself from the first with enthusiasm on to the Fenian side. His reputation, his talents, his energy and his time were henceforth devoted to the cause of Irish independence. He gave, in fact, all he had, with a selfless devotion characteristic of him; but he could never be a great revolutionary leader. However, as Shaw said subsequently, " a nation which could not produce a Garibaldi had to be content with Casements."

Casement himself would not have made the comparison with Garibaldi. He was shy in manner, fumbling as an orator, unused to public life; nor was he one of those hysterical patriots whose exhibitions makes them rehearse their speeches in the dock, long before there is any question of their being put into a position to make them. He was, in fact, without the obvious qualities of leadership, and had only some of the elements of martyrdom. And so, when young enthusiasts suggested that he should place himself in a position of leadership, he gently discountenanced their project; was he not old in years and young in experience of the affairs they would have him lead? But that they should look to him could surprise nobody; for it was the involuntary tribute paid to that selfless enthusiasm and singleness of purpose which he had displayed in the Congo and the Putumayo, and which he had now transferred to the service, as he thought, of his native land.

But in his very qualities was the measure of his inadequacy for the new sphere into which he had plunged his energies; for singleness of vision, which may serve the cause of humanity when directed towards the exposure of cruelties, which have only to be known to be abhorred, is at best a doubtful guide through the subtler problems of national relationships. But it has been the misfortune of Ireland to exact too strong a devotion from her sons, a romantic, fierce devotion which forbids compromise and the humdrum arrangements which are the core of political wisdom; they would serve her better perhaps, if they loved her less. Some no doubt would say that this is as true of Carson as of Casement; for Carson, a Southern Irishman of Italian extraction, felt the same blind, absorbed devotion to the cause of Ulster as Casement, Protestant and Ulsterman, gave to the cause of Irish nationalism. Carson, when he became a Unionist, ceased to be a Constitutionalist; for he became willing to put the attainment of one single issue above the maintenance in all its integrity of that Constitution which ordinarily has first claim upon the Conservative. And Casement, in his zeal for national independence, forgot that even Mazzini would allow the claim to nationhood only when a whole community felt itself to be a nation; and Ulster had no such feeling. Ireland, therefore, would perhaps have been better and happier without its Carsons and its Casements. But History would have been the poorer and the roll of high-minded idealists the shorter, for their absence.

It was to a great extent Carson who formed Casement's opinions on practical questions in Ireland. It was Carson's organisation of the Ulster volunteers which convinced him of the necessity of raising the Irish volunteers to offset them, and Casement's gun-running at Howth was preceded and provoked by the Ulster gun-running at Larne. He himself realised that Carson had put the Irish question on a new footing, and he was glad of it; what was the good of placing your reliance, as Redmond did, on the Home Rule Bill when your opponents openly appealed to the sterner arbitrament of the sword? Casement's method of showing his awareness of his debt to Carson in this respect is typical of his lack of political flair. The method was the simple one of calling for three cheers for Carson at the conclusion of the meeting held to launch the Irish Volunteer movement at Cork; the result of this unexpected request was not unnaturally to rouse the audience to a pitch of fury, which found practical expression in the hurling of all available furniture at Casement and Professor McNeill, who retired in confusion and academic astonishment at this evidence of lack of perception on the part of the masses. In thus expecting an excited political gathering at once to realise the subtle reason for calling for three cheers for an implacable and detested opponent, Casement showed the child-like impracticability which we see again in his suggestion to Redmond that General Kelly-Kenny, who had lost the use of both legs, was the right man as General to rally the enthusiasm of the Irish Volunteers.

But his impulsiveness and his enthusiasm had a more romantic and attractive side, as, for instance, when he wrote early in 1914:

" I've a good mind to write to Carson to-night, and ask him to come to Cork with me!

" My God—I wonder what would happen if he said ' Yes.' Would you all rise to the occasion—or would you tear us limb from limb? What you say about him being King of Ireland—I've said it too—if he would only rise to the height of a supreme occasion. He could save Ireland and make Ireland. But it is a dream to think of him doing it—if he really loved Ireland, as I do, he'd come. Shall I ask him? I don't know him at all, and I've blackguarded him openly in the Holy of Holies (county Antrim), but he knows I am honest, and sincere, and fearless—qualities he himself, I think, possesses. I like him far better than these craven, scheming, plotting Englishmen, whose one aim is to see how *little* freedom they can give Ireland and call it by another name."

The man who wrote that letter might not be a leader of men in the sense in which Lenin or even Lloyd George is a leader of men. But he was a dreamer of dreams that could fascinate, chivalrous and impulsive, full of that dangerous attraction which rallies men to lost causes and leads forlorn hopes. Given that he had abilities and that circumstances favoured him, such a man could be a dangerous as he could surely be a malignant, foe to the greatest of nations.

And Roger Casement, though in some matters almost a child, had in a wider sphere that all too rare quality of being able to recognise the real issues and features in any situation, stripped of all irrelevant considerations, and to prescribe for them accordingly; a quality shared, incidentally, in pre-eminent degree by two great figures in his trial, Lord Reading and the late Lord Birkenhead. His scheme for Ireland was in its essence quite simple. " It is not possible for Ireland," he wrote after his trial, " without effecting foreign help, to cut the connection." Ireland, in fact, so his argument ran, is a small country; England is a great and powerful one. Therefore, Ireland alone cannot exact independence from England. But the very fact that England is a great and powerful country is all the more reason why other nations should have an interest in the independence of Ireland, and it is in enlisting their sympathy and help, or that of some of them, that Ireland's best hopes lie. His view is expressed in a sentence from a remarkable article which he wrote anonymously for the *Irish Review* shortly before the War, entitled " Ireland, Germany, and the Next War." " Ireland," he wrote, " is primarily a European island inhabited by a European people who are not English, and who have for centuries appealed to Europe and the world to aid them in ceasing to be politically controlled by England." Casement was himself about to make one more such appeal; but it was to be no ordinary appeal, for the Power to whom he directed it was engaged in a struggle with Great Britain, which by its very magnitude had swept aside domestic friction and had caught up Ulstermen and Southerners alike into the common ranks of resistance.

The War had been expected by Casement; in the article referred to, he had suggested that German government in Ireland would be better than British, even if Germany did not—as he believed it almost inevitably would—give Ireland her independence. But he did not expect it until 1915. And so it was to the United States that he sailed in the summer of 1914, partly to establish contact with the Irish-American Fenians and partly to gain the ear of Bernstorff, the German Ambassador in the United States, for his schemes of Irish-German co-operation.

Thus it was that Casement was on neutral soil on the outbreak of War. As he was to say later, " it upset my calculations no less than Mr Birrell's." A few more months of agitation in Ireland, perhaps the beginnings of civil conflict, and who could tell whether Irish loyalty to the Empire would stand the strain? Casement, at any rate, thought not. But that bullet at Sarajevo and that scrap of paper had shown no respect to the nice calculations he had made. Great Britain and Germany were at war in August, 1914, and he, powerless in a foreign land, could only share with the detested House of Commons a breathless speculation as to what Redmond would say; would Ireland place the sword, which she had been ready to unsheath to extort her independence, at the service of those from whom she had claimed it? Or would Ireland have no blood to give to any land, to any cause but that of Ireland? They had not long to wait, and Redmond's words showed that Casement was in a sad minority; the cause of the Empire, it was decided, was the cause of Ireland, and Redmond promised " that the democracy of Ireland will turn with the utmost anxiety and sympathy to this country in every trial, and every danger that may overtake it." From this time Casement played a lone hand; he continued to serve what he conceived to be the interests of Ireland, but he served them under no authority but his own.

To Casement the War must have seemed a bitter mockery of all his hopes, his efforts and his faith. He had wished Ireland to take arms for independence; and Ireland was in arms, as he believed, for the continuance of servitude. He had tried to persuade Ireland to look upon Germany as an ally against England; and at Mons, the Munsters, the Inniskillings, the Irish Guards and many more were, side by side with the English forces, helping to stem the flood of German invasion, irrupting into Belgium. Belgium! They had actually gone to war for the sake of Belgium, his old foes in the days of the Congo.

But if all the world had changed and played him false, he would remain constant to his ideas and his beliefs; he would continue to fight for the nationhood and independence of Ireland by the methods which he had advocated. He came to his decision with little or no serious thought on the difficulties and drawbacks of his expedition; he held no mandate save his own impulse, and no passport save Bernstorff's recommendation and his own enthusiasm. He was going, this strange man, weary a little but full of hope, with that childish, courageous impetuosity, which was peculiarly his own. And so, while Redmond recruited for the British Army, and Irish soldiers struggled on at Mons, Sir Roger Casement, knighted and broken in the service of the British Empire, started out, escorted by a Norwegian sailor as servant and armed with an American passport, on that strange mission, which was aimed to bring destruction on the British Empire, but led him to his own.

It was impossible for him to go to Germany direct, and so he was travelling on a Norwegian ship, the *Oskar II*. But the voyage was not uneventful, for the ship was detained for search by H.M.S. *Hibernian*, one of the " eight battleships or cruisers out looking for us," as Casement said. It was six Germans, however, whom the British ship took as prisoners, and the tall " American " and his Norwegian servant were allowed to continue their journey unobstructed. This escape allowed Casement to get safely to Norway, but it was by no means the end of his adventures, for the British Legation seized on his servant, Adler Christiansen, and after subjecting him to inquiries about his master, informed him, in his own words, that " if someone knocked him on the head they would get well paid for it."

The events of the next few days read like an extract from a spy story. Casement was watched by detectives, who were anxious to secure him for the British Legation before he could get the German Legation to obtain his permission to go to Berlin. He sent Christiansen post haste, therefore, to the German Legation, urging him at all costs to evade the embarrassing attentions of the British Legation's detectives. This he succeeded in doing, and arrived by circuitous route at the German Legation, where he was rewarded by an appointment for Casement for seven o'clock. Once again, however, the problem was to shake off the pursuing detectives. But Casement was resourceful, and managed to slip out of his taxi as it was rounding a corner, leaving Christiansen to continue the journey alone as a decoy.

At the German Consulate, Casement was told that they had telegraphed to the Foreign Office and must await instructions. He returned to his hotel, where his spirits were not raised by the gloomy accounts and prophecies of Christiansen, who seems to have shared the fat boy's predilection for " making his flesh creep." That night, however, he received a message from the German Legation telling him to wait in his hotel, till permission came to him to go to Berlin; he had not slept when it arrived at about seven o'clock next morning.

It might have been expected that he could now proceed quietly to Germany, but Norway had more thrills to provide. For that morning Christiansen was taken again to the British Legation, where he was offered a reward to co-operate against Casement. Casement's indignation was unbounded, and he hatched a counterplot by which Christiansen was to pretend to the British Minister that he had succumbed to the temptation of the reward, and would travel with Casement to Germany in order to keep the Minister posted in his movements and activities with a view to his capture. In view of the young man's character, Casement's plot showed that naïveté of mind which was so strong in him. But the arrangement was concluded, and the strange pair—accompanied now by a German, Richard Meyer—set off on the last stage of their precarious journey.

In Germany they were frankly puzzled by Sir Roger Casement. What sort of a man was it who came over, old in the service of the British Empire and unable to speak a word of German, with this strange offer of seducing the loyalty of Irish prisoners of war? Was he a spy? Or a madman? Or could perhaps his plan offer some hope of success? · After all, feeling in Ireland had been roused to a fever heat only a few months before, and it was not perhaps too much to hope that Casement's state of mind was representative of that of his countrymen. " An active cause " Casement had asked for; that meant a declaration of German sympathy with Irish national aspirations. " Given that, I had little or no doubt " wrote Casement, " that scores, perhaps hundreds, of the Irish prisoners would follow me." At any rate, the German Government decided that the prospects were sufficiently good to warrant them taking up the idea. And the prospects of success must have been remote indeed for them to have left untried a project which, if successful, promised so rich a reward. For if all went well, and German troops and an Irish Brigade landed in Ireland and met with a friendly reception, what could not be hoped from this blow in Britain's most vulnerable spot, shaking her and challenging her in the very heart of the Empire?

Consequently a statement was issued authorised by the Imperial Chancellor giving a " categoric assurance that the German Government desires only the welfare of the Irish people, their country, and their institutions . . . their national prosperity and national freedom." This was followed up by the collection of all the Irish prisoners of war in Germany preparatory to despatching them to the special camp at Limburg, where Casement was to recruit them for the Irish Brigade.

What were his chances of success? One thing is plain; he had not to deal with Fenians or politically-minded Irish separatists. On the contrary, the men who were prisoners in those early months were for the most part professional soldiers or reservists, men who had gone to France with the first Expeditionary Force in August, men who had sustained that first great shock at Mons, and had helped by their valour to stiffen the resistance of the whole country to the might of the Central Powers. These were not men whose allegiance was lightly given, or could be lightly revoked; they were "Romans that have spoke the word, and will not palter." It is true that the reward for the blood and the dirt, the valour and the steadiness of Mons was the slaughter of comrades, the long retreat, and now the barbarity, the discomfort, and the hopelessness of a prison camp. But these were not things to conciliate; they could only either crush or nerve the sinews of a splendid loyalty. If Casement came among them he would find the pride of tradition and allegiance and the reluctance of brave men to accept favours of the enemy a strong answer even to the hopes of quitting the living death of a prison camp.

An augury as to which way the struggle would be decided was not long in appearing. On December 1st a communication was received by the prison authorities at Sennelager; it was signed by Irish non-commissioned officers, who desired that it should be forwarded to the Kaiser. It ran: —

SIR,

On behalf of the Irish Catholics now prisoners of war in the camp under your command, we, the undersigned, desire to testify to His Majesty the German Emperor our thanks for his consideration of our situation.

We fully appreciate the kindness extended in (1) grouping us together under one roof; (2) assuring us of better food;

(3) decreasing the amount of fatigue work to be performed; but we regret we must beseech His Imperial Majesty to withdraw these concessions unless they are shared by the remainder of the prisoners, as, in addition to being Irish Catholics, we have the honour to be British soldiers.

Thanking you in anticipation of this appeal reaching His Majesty the Emperor through the German authorities,

We are, Sir,

Yours respectfully,
etc.

The letter is a model of firmness united to dignity and restraint, and its very absence of heroics must have impressed on Casement the character of the men with whom he had to deal and the difficulty of his task; at the same time it must have shown him how well worth winning they were, could he but succeed. Consequently it was after considerable preparation, and not without anxiety and trepidation, that Casement went to open his campaign amongst the prisoners at Limburg—not indeed those who had written the memorial to the Kaiser, for they had not arrived, but others who were already there and whose spirit might be gauged from that of their comrades.

The interest in the camp had been considerable at the announcement of the address by a " distinguished Irish gentleman; " and indeed what announcement could fail to provoke excited comment in the cramped, monotonous routine of prison life? But it was only the sergeants and corporals who were summoned to attend and who gazed with curiousity on the tall, black-bearded man with his faraway, romantic air, looking so little like a politician. Nor was his oratory that of the practised politician; his sincerity was patent, but his speech was halting and his manner nervous. But the gist of what he had to say was obvious; he was pro-German, he was trying to persuade them that Germany was engaged in a war of self-defence and that they, as Irishmen, had no duty towards England and could freely accept the co-operation of Germany.

The pamphlets which he distributed and the proclamation,

which was posted in the Camp, made his meaning clear beyond all doubt. The proclamation announced the formation of an Irish Brigade, which was to be clothed, fed, and armed by the German Government, with a view to securing Irish independence of Great Britain. The Brigade were to wear a special Irish uniform and were to be the guests of the German Government, which guaranteed in addition at the end of the War to send to America such members of the Brigade as wished to go.

The offer was plain. The " distinguished Irish gentleman " seemed to be sincere in his affection of Ireland. But he was clearly a traitor—perhaps in the pay of the German Government—who was trying to tempt them by release, by the hospitality of the German Government, by specious words, to betray their allegiance, to be false to their King and the causes for which they had taken up arms. When this was realised in the camp, feeling hardened against the man, who spoke to them in their own language, but came under German escort to tempt them in the duress of captivity. One or two had announced their intention of joining the Brigade, but the treatment which they received from the majority was not of a kind to encourage imitators, and the adherents of the " bloody Fenian," as Casement was irreverently termed, were met with a strong counter-propaganda. Casement had produced no effect save that of irritation, and from his first entry into the camp the shadow of failure had never lifted from his enterprise.

He concluded, nevertheless, his " treaty " with Zimmermann, the German Under-Secretary for Foreign Affairs. Its main provisions, besides the promise of arms and equipment were that " the object of the Irish Brigade shall be to fight solely the cause of Ireland, and under no circumstances shall it be employed or directed to any German end "; and Article 6, which ran: " In the event of a German naval victory affording the means of reaching the coast of Ireland, the Imperial German Government pledges itself to dispatch the Irish Brigade and a supporting force of German officers and men in German transports with the necessary naval protection to effect a landing on the Irish coast." Article 7 went on to provide that, if the German navy should be unable to open a sea-route to Ireland, the Irish Brigade should be used as Casement should approve; *e.g.* " in this event it might be possible to employ the Irish Brigade in Egypt to help the Egyptian people to recover their freedom by driving the British out of Egypt." The provisions of this treaty have a great importance in view of the defence raised subsequently at the trial.

With this arrangement made, Casement returned to Limburg to recruit forces to enable him to put the project into operation. But by this time apathy and curiosity had both succumbed to hostility, for his mission was understood now, and his appeal was interrupted by shouts and booing. One man actually tried to strike him; this was prevented, but Casement was put to it to keep the prisoners at bay. The men, whom he had hoped to enlist and to lead in the service of his cherished idea, were actually driving him from the camp. He bowed to the inevitable, and retired. For a few more days he pottered round the camp, a melancholy, drooping figure, broken, hopeless, and disillusioned; and then he returned to Berlin. Casement had failed; not thus are men rallied to desperate causes.

To the sadness of failure was soon added the knowledge that he was suspected and unwanted. He busied himself with his vendetta against the British Minister in Norway; and could never understand that to the Germans, or indeed to any detached and rational person, it seemed the most natural thing in the world that a British Minister would do all in his power to stop the passage of a British subject into enemy country, where he was avowedly going with treasonable intentions. Nor could he understand that to the Germans the scruples, which prevented him from carrying out such practical employment as was suggested, must appear evidence of lack of sincerity; they began to say he was a spy or a madman. There were not wanting whispers either, swelling at times to something more than whispers, that he was something else besides; for his servant, who had taken to a most ostentatious style of dress and to painting his face, was soon well known to the Berlin police. And what could a respectable man want with such a servant?

In face of such rumours and distresses, Casement withdrew for a time to Munich; but as month after month passed by and no end to the War came in sight, he knew that fresh effort would be expected on his part. So he returned to Limburg, reinforced this time by Father Nicholson, an American Catholic, and an enthusiastic Fenian. But the prisoners resented a political padre and would have none of him, while their animus against Casement had grown all the greater because they suspected that the reduction of their rations was due to him. So there was nothing for it but to take the fifty or so men who had enlisted in the Irish Brigade back to Berlin. Fifty men, jeered at and hissed as they left the camp by about 2500 who remained loyal; such was the sum of Casement's success and the measure of his failure.

They returned, however, in May, the Irish Brigaders wearing their new Irish uniforms, and once again set themselves to the task of propaganda. But by this time the feeling against the traitors was intense, and found frequent expression in booing and attempts at rough treatment, which could hardly be restrained. It was obvious that no more recruits could be expected, and yet what was the good of fifty? They were too small to constitute a fighting force, and yet when they were left amongst the prisoners—even non-British ones—their especially favourable treatment was a constant provocation to the others. So they were transferred to Zossen, and an ex-soldier called Monteith arrived to drill them, in order to fit them for active service in Ireland should the occasion arise. But to Casement it must have seemed that the chance would never come, and he had even entered into negotiations for the transfer of the fifty men for service in Syria, when suddenly news came that revolutionised the situation. The great Irish rising of 1916 was timed to break out on Easter Sunday; surely here was the chance at last? Casement was galvanised into activity, and the slow tempo of events quickened into breathless action.

The scene changes to the windswept Kerry coast near Tralee Bay, on whose inhospitable shores a few Irish peasants and fisher folk lived simple lives, scarce affected by the giant conflict which filled all Europe. One of these simple folk, a farmer called John M'Carthy, rose early at two o'clock on that Good Friday morning to say his prayers at the holy well, and as he returned along the deserted shore after his pious errand, he was astonished to find a boat. He tried to move it, but it was too heavy, and so he sent his little boy to get his neighbour, Pat Driscoll, to help him to move it. Pat came and together they moved the boat as much as they could. And then M'Carthy found a dagger in the boat, and traced the footprints of three men, going some twenty or thirty yards in the direction of his house. On returning to the boat, he found his little daughter, aged eight, playing with some revolvers. These also he took possession of, and carried all his findings to the police station at Ardfert. This was the discovery of arms reported in the *Times*, and " the stranger of unknown nationality " was Sir Roger Casement.

At about 4.30 that same morning a servant girl, Mary Gorman, saw three strangers, one a tall, black-bearded man. She gave them only the amount of attention that strangers always provoke in quiet places, and resumed her work. But the men were already proving of more interest to Sergeant Hearn, chief constable at Ardfert, who had by now received the information of M'Carthy's strange discovery. Could it be that the Kerry coast was the chosen spot for a descent on Ireland? Well, they should not thrust at the Empire through Tralee Bay, for, in the words of the *Times* special correspondent in an article on the " Coming of Casement " in the issue of May 1st, 1916, " the sergeant, true to the fine tradition of the Royal Irish, promptly rose to the occasion. Himself and three constables constituted the garrison of what had become for the moment an outpost of Empire." The sergeant went down with M'Carthy to the boat, and there a search revealed a handbag containing ammunition and some lifebelts. The gallant sergeant then returned to the police station and gathered reinforcements in the shape of Constable Riley and their carbines.

They came up with their man at M'Kenna's Fort, a circular Irish ruin with a trench round it; it was now 1.20 in the afternoon. The sergeant asked him his business, and the man replied by a question: " By what authority do you ask me the question, and am I bound to answer you? " The sergeant told him that he was so bound, and that if he did not answer, he would arrest him under the Defence of the Realm Regulations. The man then said that he was Richard Morton, of Denham, Bucks, " the author of a Life of St. Brendan." By a strange irony, the name was that of the man in whose house at Denham Casement had stayed after the exhaustion of the Putumayo inquiries, and it was there that he had received the intimation that the honour of knighthood was to be his. The two policemen took him to the police station to charge him. As he left the fort with them, he contrived to drop a piece of paper; it was his code. But the luck which had been once his had not accompanied him on this venture, for it was picked up by a small boy and given to the police, to be used as a damning piece of evidence against him at his trial.

But this was not the sum of the excitement on the Kerry coast that day; nor was M'Carthy the only man to make an interesting discovery. For on the night of Thursday, the 20th, a labourer, called Hussey, sighted a red light flashing out at sea. Next day at about six in the evening H.M.S. *Bluebell* was patrolling off the coast—for there were rumours of a hostile attempt—when she sighted a vessel some ninety miles from the southern coast. The vessel was impeccably painted in the Norwegian colours, but the *Bluebell* was suspicious and signalled her. The answer came back that she was bound for Genoa from Bergen, but this failed to satisfy the *Bluebell*, and the captain signalled that the *Aud*—for this was the name which the Norwegian vessel gave—must follow the *Bluebell* to harbour. The *Bluebell* accordingly moved off ahead, but the *Aud* remained motionless, until a shot was fired across her bows. This decided her to follow quietly, and all night the *Bluebell* steamed south-east in the direction of Queenstown, closely attended by the now amenable *Aud*. Next morning, however, her docility was seen to have been assumed for a purpose. For, to continue the story in Lord Reading's words when summing-up in the trial, " when she was within three and a half miles of Queenstown she seemed to stop her engines, and then a cloud of white smoke appeared; two boats were lowered; flags of truce were carried in these boats; in these boats were twenty German bluejackets and three officers, two of them being identified as German naval officers; and they were taken on board the *Bluebell* as prisoners of war. Within a very few minutes, some ten minutes, of the cloud of white smoke being seen, the *Aud* blows up." Not thus easily, however, were the British to be baffled. Divers were sent down, and Dempsey said that he found " rifles and thousands of other cartridges there."

There was no doubt now that a German attempt to land arms and ammunition in Ireland had been narrowly foiled. And when on the Sunday the Dublin insurrection broke out, the significance of events became clear. If the attempt had succeeded on a bigger scale and had linked up with the insurrection, the issue might have been one of incalculable danger to the Empire and terror to loyal subjects in Ireland; it would in fact have been the consummation of that project for which Casement had schemed so long and so ardently. But he himself was a prisoner under arrest, making the last journey from Tralee to London. On the way they told him that a motor car containing two young Sinn Feiners had taken the wrong turning and plunged into Lake Curragh, where the two men had been drowned. Casement, supposing no doubt that they were Menteith and Bailey, burst into tears and, still sobbing, said: " I am very sorry about those two lads. It was on my account they came. They were two good Irishmen. I know that water well." And then he seemed to grow more cheerful, and asked his escort: " Do you think I shall get a bed? " He had not had a night's sleep for twelve nights. He was to sleep soon in the Tower of London, where so many romantics and so many traitors had lodged before him.

From the Tower Casement was taken to Bow Street Police Station to be charged with Bailey. Pointing to Bailey he said: " That man is innocent. I think the indictment is wrongly drawn against him. Is it within my power to provide defence for this man? I wish him in every way to be as well defended as myself, and if he has no means to obtain his defence I am prepared to obtain it for him." Casement showed that loyalty and consideration for his confederates which in his life was all too seldom returned.

The magisterial proceedings were held at Bow Street on May 15th, 16th, 17th, and on the 17th Casement was committed for trial. On the 25th the indictment was presented to the Grand Jury, who found a true bill against him. It is interesting to note that it was the first indictment for treason drawn up according to the formula prescribed by the Indictments Act of 1915. Formerly indictments for treason always used to contain a reference to the seduction of the traitor by the devil, but with the passing of that worthy from contemporary thought, if not altogether from contemporary conversation, the reference was no doubt thought to be unnecessary.

The trial of Roger Casement for high treason is remarkable in many ways. It is remarkable not only because it was the climax of a strange and thrilling adventure, not only because in the trial itself drama and deep technical argument were so adroitly intermixed, not only because of the compelling interest of the personalities involved. It is remarkable for a reason prior to all these; it is remarkable that such a trial was held at all. In June of 1916 the War seemed endless; hope of immediate victory had succumbed in face of the dreadful reality of the " war of attrition." The Battle of Jutland had perhaps saved this country from invasion, but reports of defeat had shaken faith in our sea-power; in France the Germans still hurled themselves at Verdun, and the British prepared their great counter-offensive on the Somme. In the East the Russians were gaining ground in their tremendous June offensive; in the South, the Italians were pushing forward to the capture of Gorizia. Nearer home the savage fighting in the Dublin streets was still a very recent memory. It was a time of great endeavour and fearful sacrifice. Human life had lost its sanctity when Death was so insistent all around. And yet it was against this dark background of bloodshed, privation and heroic misery that for four days in the High Court the greatest legal luminaries of the land argued the question of Casement's guilt and the interpretation of the Statute of Treasons of 1351. History can show no finer example of the meaning of the rule of law in this country, and can adduce no greater testimony to the unswerving fairness of our Courts. It was indeed, in the words of Serjeant Sullivan, Casement's leading counsel, " a matter of congratulation that such a trial as this at such a time is taking place here in the capital city of your nation in open Court according to the ordinary process of law regulating the lives of the civil subjects of His Majesty."

Casement was charged under the Statute of Treasons, 1351, with " adhering to the King's enemies elsewhere than in the King's realm, to wit in the Empire of Germany." For a conviction of treason in this country, the prosecution must prove at least one overt act, testified to by two witnesses, or two overt acts of the same treason, testified to by one witness each. Against Casement six overt acts were charged, the first five of which related to the Irish Brigade incident, while the sixth was that of the landing in Ireland of April 21st. There was a time when a man thus charged with the gravest of crimes had to rely solely on his native wit for his defence; but the Treason Act of 1695 inaugurated a more merciful state of affairs by directing that the accused should not only have a copy of the indictment and a list of the jurors, but that two counsel should be assigned to him in addition. Thus Casement had the benefit of expert defence in the persons of Serjeant Sullivan, of the Irish Bar, Mr (now Sir Thomas) Artemus Jones, and Professor J. H.

Morgan, the expert on constitutional law: it would appear from this that Casement had three counsel instead of the statutory two, but Professor Morgan addressed the Court in the status of what is known as "amicus curiae," thereby complying with the Act. At all events, Casement was defended by a very strong team, and that in such a charge is only as it should be. But at the time, not unnaturally perhaps, in view of the stress and agony which people were living through in those terrible days, there was a feeling that too much consideration was being given to Casement. This feeling was referred to by Lord Reading in his summing-up, when he took occasion to put the matter in its true light: "There are some persons," he said, "who, perhaps a little thoughtlessly, are inclined to rebel against the notion that a member of the English Bar, or members of it, should be found to defend a prisoner on a charge of treason against the British State. I need not tell you, I am sure, gentlemen, that if anyone has those thoughts in his mind he has but a poor conception of the high obligation and responsibility of the Bar of England. It is the proud privilege of the Bar of England that it is ready to come into Court and to defend a person accused, however grave the charge may be."

Within the Court, when the King's Coroner read over the charges, was a clash of personalities of no mean order. Sir Roger Casement himself in the dock, tall, black-bearded, remote, with his romantic air of sad abstraction, as if "he had taken the sorrows of the world on his shoulders"; not the distress this of a cornered criminal, but the proud melancholy of great and lonely failure. What more striking contrast could there be to the heavily-powerful, clean-cut features of his accuser, once "Galloper Smith," and now Sir Frederick Smith, K.C., Attorney-General? It may be that another in his place, remembering the fierceness of his own partisanship, in those Irish days, would have felt his position at being called upon to prosecute his old opponent with that restraint, almost amounting to impartiality, which is traditionally associated with the Crown in criminal prosecutions; but it was not in the nature of the future Lord Birkenhead,

splendidly equipped with the arrogance arising from the
consciousness of his intellectual mastery, to entertain doubts.
It is not by doubting that glittering prizes are won, and the
Attorney-General, unhampered by doubts as he was unmoved by pity, was prepared to discharge his task with the
superb address which was always his to command.

On both sides was a strong array of talent. For the
Attorney-General had with him his Solicitor-General, Sir
George Cave, later to succeed him as Lord Chancellor, Mr
Archibald Bodkin, afterwards Public Prosecutor, Mr Travers
Humphreys, and Mr Branson; now Judges of the High
Court; while for Casement Mr Artemus Jones and Professor
Morgan, who has a sharp incisiveness of manner which is
more legal than academic, supported the bearded Irish figure
of Serjeant Sullivan. And over them all, supported on the
Bench by Mr Justice Avory and Mr Justice Horridge, pre-
sided the Lord Chief Justice, handsome and composed, the
very embodiment of the cool impartiality of the Law.

The Attorney-General's opening speech outlined the story
of the events of Casement's honourable career in the consular
service, his visit to Germany and attempt to form the Irish
Brigade, and his landing in Ireland. The speech is famous
as a masterpiece of concise and powerful exposition, and the
effect on the jury was considerable when the Attorney sat
down after his concluding sentences: " The prisoner,
blinded by a hatred to this country as malignant in quality
as it was sudden in origin, has played a desperate hazard.
He has played it and he has lost it. To-day the forfeit is
claimed."

The prosecution then called its witnesses, who were for
the most part Irish soldiers who had been prisoners of war
at Limburg—many of whom had been exchanged, thereby
showing the opinion of the Germans as to Casement's
chances of success, and their indifference to his fate—and
peasants from Curraghane like McCarthy and Mary
Gorman. They were excited at being in London and in the
centre of such great events, so far removed from the even
tenor of their daily lives; and the rich Irish brogue of the

witnesses, as they answered the questions counsel put to them, sounded strangely in the Court.

Their evidence was completed on the second day, and the case for the prosecution was concluded. The case for the prosecution was that Casement by his efforts to seduce the allegiance of the Irish prisoners at Limburg and by his descent on the Irish coast had committed acts of assistance to the King's enemies in time of war. Most of the facts were admitted, and substantiated with a considerable degree of unanimity by a number of witnesses. What defence could Serjeant Sullivan raise against this array of fact?

Before Casement had pleaded Serjeant Sullivan had moved to quash the indictment. A motion to quash the indictment is brought by the defence in a criminal action, when it is contended that the indictment reveals no offence known to the law. Lord Reading had then decided, however, that it would be more convenient to take the motion on the conclusion of the case for the prosecution and, with the consent of the Attorney-General and Serjeant Sullivan, this was the course decided on. It was, therefore, to urge the quashing of the indictment, that is to say, to plead that the actions of his client did not constitute the offence of treason, that Serjeant Sullivan rose.

There followed a long technical discussion on the correct interpretation of the Statute of Treasons of 1351. It may seem strange to some that, at a time of great stress and great provocation, the question of the guilt of a man, whom most thought to have been taken in manifest treason, should be decided on a Statute written in Norman French, and enacted over five hundred years before. But the law has its own methods, and it may fairly be supposed that the discussion and decision in the Casement trial have fixed the law on the point beyond dispute.

Serjeant Sullivan's point, briefly, was that the Statute did not recognise as treason acts that were committed outside the realm. This he suggested was the reasonable interpretation of the words: " If a man do levy war against our lord the King in his realm, or be adherent to the King's enemies in his realm giving them aid and comfort in the realm or elsewhere." He asked the judges to read the Statute as if they were interpreting it for the first time, disregarding both the decision in the case of Colonel Lynch, which he suggested was based on the wrong decision in Vaughan's case, and also the opinions of Coke, Hale, and Hawkins; and he maintained that if the statute were read, as if for the first time, it would yield the meaning on which he relied.

This was bold doctrine, for the opinions of men like Coke and Hale, who are among the most celebrated judges in English history, even though extra-judicial, are, if not binding, at any rate very strong persuasive authority. The Attorney-General, however, did not rely solely on persuasive authority to refute the Serjeant's case. He produced various cases, in which he claimed that the point was decided in his favour; that is to say, that the statute should be read, " if a man do levy war against our lord the King in his realm or be adherent to the King's enemies in his realm (giving to them aid and comfort in the realm) or elsewhere." This reading would have the same effect as that suggested by Lord Reading, which was that " elsewhere " could govern both " adhering " and " giving aid and comfort; " both that is to say, allowed the act of adhering to be either at home or abroad. This, as the Attorney-General pointed out, was historically the Common Law view and obviously the commonsense view, since traitorous acts were more likely to be committed outside the realm than within it.

Lord Reading, in his judgment on this highly technical argument, brushed aside Sullivan's contention that the opinions of the great masters of the Common Law should be disregarded. " But if the words of the statute are not clear," he said, " and if it be possible to construe the statute in two different ways, then the comments of great lawyers, masters of the common law, during the last three or four centuries, cannot be allowed to pass by this Court without the greatest regard and consideration." The Statute of Henry VIII, too, was in agreement with these opinions, for it "shows plainly that the offence existed. From that time the statute has regulated the trial of offences committed without the realm." In the trial of Lynch, too, in 1903, when the same defence was raised, although the Court gave no judgment, the then Lord Chief Justice proceeded to sum up and directed the jury as if it was an offence. Finally there was the case of William Cundell, in 1802—one of the cases cited by the Attorney-General—who was executed for adhering to the King's enemies outside the realm. This was an exact and unassailable precedent; what was lawful for Cundell was lawful for Casement. For these reasons Lord Reading ended his exhaustive analysis with the conclusion, which was supported by his brother judges, that " the offence if proved in fact, has been committed in law."

The technical objection, therefore, which all three counsel for the defence had laboured to substantiate, had broken down, and Casement's best chance was gone; for now the case would have to be tried on the facts, and these looked black against him. But before the case entered on its last phase Casement made a statement. It turned out to be a categorical denial of the imputation that he had received German gold or secured the reduction of the rations of the recalcitrant Irish prisoners of war. But the words were spoken with a conciseness and dignity which could not fail to impress, as he said in his slow, soft voice, " I trust, gentlemen of the jury, I have made that statement clearly and emphatically enough for all men, even my most bitter enemies, to comprehend that a man who in the newspapers is said to be just another Irish traitor, may be a gentleman."

Sullivan did not propose to call witnesses, and therefore the last stage of the trial, that of the concluding speeches, had been reached. Normally, as he had not called witnesses nor put in documents in evidence, Sullivan would have had the right to the last word. But there is an old practice by which in cases where the Attorney-General appears he always has the privilege of reply—a privilege which was waived by Sir William Jowitt as Attorney-General in 1929.

Consequently it was Sullivan who now rose to make his speech for the prisoner.

Faced with his formidable task, Serjeant Sullivan showed both ingenuity and courage. The defence that he proceeded to put forward was that Casement's propaganda at Limburg was only a legitimate pursual of his work for the Irish Volunteers before the War; he was asking the prisoners to join an Irish Brigade, which would have for its purpose the defence of Southern Ireland against the Ulster Volunteers when the war was over. This was clearly a very different thing from aiding Germany in a war against Great Britain, which was the substance of the charge against him. The evidence supported this presentment of the case in so far as the vast mass of it agreed that the Irish Brigade was to be used only in Ireland and for Ireland. Against this evidence was only that of one prisoner, John Neill, whom Sullivan had had no difficulty in shaking in cross-examination, and who had had to confess that he " disremembered " dates, numbers and other important facts. As for the charge of setting forth as a member of a warlike and hostile expedition, the ship had after all been found ninety miles from Tralee, and the importation of arms should in any case be treated only as an offence against D.O.R.A.

The defence was plausible, for undoubtedly Ireland had been like an armed camp before the outbreak of war; Sir Roger Casement had been known to be very active in the organisation of the Irish Volunteers, and if he had been carrying on that work without reference to the War, but with a view only to the situation that would arise at the end of it, it would be impossible to convict him of treason. Serjeant Sullivan had stated his case with great vigour and eloquence until on the Wednesday afternoon—the third day of the trial—there came a dramatic interruption. He had been speaking of events immediately preceding the War, and had said " The matters that I have spoken of had occurred since Sir Roger Casement left the Consular Service." He was seen to falter, and then repeated himself, " As I say, those matters had occurred since Sir Roger

Casement left the Consular Service." There was a pause, and the Court was conscious of that uncomfortable sensation which greets a hiatus where none should be. The silence was broken by Serjeant Sullivan. "I regret, my lord, to say that I have completely broken down." He sank into his seat, and sat quite still, resting his head in his hands, while Lord Reading sympathetically announced the adjournment till the following day.

The next day Mr Artemus Jones carried on for Serjeant Sullivan; but, before breaking down, Sullivan had made a courageous and eloquent defence of Irish sentiment. "Sir Roger Casement," he said, "was not in the service of England. Sir Roger Casement was in the service of the United Kingdom . . . In Ireland you have not only a separate people, you have a seperate country. An Irishman's loyalty is to Ireland, and it would be a very sorry day for the Empire when loyalty to one's own native land should be deemed to be treason in a sister country. There is no English authority in Ireland . . . we are your fellow citizens but by no means your inferiors or your slaves." It was a brave man who on the morrow of the Dublin insurrection could speak those words to an English jury; but bravery is a quality that an English jury respects.

The weak point in Sullivan's case was that it depended on showing that Casement did not intend that the Irish Brigade should take any action until the conclusion of the War. But this is exactly what the evidence could not be made to show. The evidence proved that Casement's design was a landing in Ireland after a German naval victory had made such a landing possible; but this, as the Attorney-General was quick to point out, was clearly not necessarily the same thing as the end of the War. And what would Germany's interest be in helping Ireland at the end of the War? "I am unaware," said the Attorney-General, "of anything in the history of the German nation during this war which would lead me to accept with enthusiasm the suggestion that they would be prepared to offer unlimited hospitality to a number of Irish soldiers in order that when the war was over they would be able to write a new page in the purely domestic history of their country."

It is the duty of the judge in summing up to state the law to the jury, to point out to them the issues in the case, to rehearse the facts as brought out by the evidence, and to comment for their direction on the strength and weakness of the evidence that they have heard. It is a task which demands the analysis and exposition of an acute and penetrative mind; it is a task, too, of superlative importance more especially in a state trial for treason, where popular prejudice and political passion may all too easily operate against the prisoner. Lord Reading, therefore, started his summing up by warning the jury to banish political considerations from their minds. "For myself," he said, "I always feel anxiety in a Court of Justice when there is any possibility of the introduction of political passion. Justice is ever in jeopardy when passion is aroused." The Courts of this country have been on the whole singularly free from this malignant influence; but how salutary the warning was may be seen from a study of the trials of less fortunate nations.

Lord Reading then proceeded to epitomise the two points of view: "The defence says that Sir Roger Casement only asked persons, these soldiers, to become members of the Irish Brigade for the purpose of assisting to resist the Ulster Volunteers after the war had concluded . . . The Crown says to you that that is not the true effect; that every fact that you examine points to the contrary; and that what was intended was that at the first sea victory Irish soldiers should be landed, and that the Irish Brigade should then be introduced into Ireland." These were the alternative interpretations of Casement's actions, and the point for the jury to consider was: "Were the acts done such as would strengthen the German Emperor or such as would weaken His Majesty the King?" If so, he was guilty of the offence of treason; and it was not necessary that he should have intended his acts to have that effect, for it is an old legal maxim that a man is presumed to intend the natural consequences of his acts. If Casement acted in such a way as must necessarily redound to the advantage of Germany and to the detriment of the country to which he owed allegiance, then for the purposes of the law he had committed treason.

And then step by step the Lord Chief Justice took the jury through the evidence, his calm serene voice contrasting effectively alike with the passionate appeal of the Serjeant and the heavy, tight-lipped enunciation of the Attorney-General. He was scrupulously fair to Casement, but under his impartial exposition it became increasingly clear how heavy was the evidence against him. The evidence was almost unanimous that the landing in Ireland was only to wait for a German naval victory; and indeed what possible interest could Germany have in Ireland after the War? As to the last charge, why had Casement arrived as he did, and why was he carrying the code, which he had dropped on his arrest? Taken in conjunction with the capture of the *Aud*, the case was indeed black against Casement, for the jury, as Lord Reading said, " will probably ask themselves, was it a pure coincidence that that vessel happened to be there so soon after the prisoner Casement and another man had been seen in Ireland with all the attendant circumstances . . . which you have heard stated in evidence."

The summing up concluded with a solemn warning to the jury that, if there was any reasonable doubt, it was their duty to find for the prisoner; but if not, " it is your duty to return a verdict to that effect, and to take no regard to the consequences which must follow." The jury retired at 2.53 p.m. and at 3.50 on the afternoon of Thursday, June 29th, Sir Roger Casement was found guilty of high treason. But before he was sentenced to death he had an opportunity, in accordance with practice, to " say for himself why the Court should not pass sentence and judgment upon him." He availed himself of this opportunity by reading a speech which he had prepared in anticipation of the verdict, three weeks previously. The speech contained a protest against the jurisdiction of the English Courts and the antiquity of the statute under which he was convicted. Neither of these arguments had any foundation in law, and they were followed by an eloquent defence of his conduct on a political basis. Lord Reading has been criticised for allowing this speech to be made; but such criticism seems to ignore both the humanity which would not condemn a man unheard and the wisdom which shows that the decisions of the law are not afraid of being measured in public opinion against the eloquence of the law-breaker.

Casement, who had faltered at the start of his speech— he had never been a practised speaker—did in fact rise to heights of eloquence as he proceeded. " Self-government," he declared, " is our right, a thing born in us at birth; a thing no more to be doled out to us or withheld from us by another people than the right to life itself—than the right to feel the sun, or smell the flowers, or to love our kind." He flung a last challenge, too, to the Attorney-General, one time " Galloper " Smith: " The difference between us was that the Unionist champions chose a path they felt would lead to the woolsack; while I went a road I knew must lead to the dock. And the event proves we were both right . . . And so, I am prouder to stand here to-day in the traitor's dock to answer this impeachment than to fill the place of my right honourable accuser." These are perhaps the words of a fanatic; but they are the words of a brave and steadfast man.

Then once more the calm, steadfast voice of the Lord Chief Justice held the Court, this time to perform the grimmest task that can fall to the lot of a human being; but, even as the judges assumed the black cap and Lord Reading passed the awful sentence, " you shall be hanged by the neck until you be dead," Casement's face was seen to wear an expression of amusement. Perhaps this was for the benefit of the spectators, for all eyes were on him now; or perhaps it was just relief that all was over, or even— who knows?—a sign of triumph. For had he not declared his pride at standing in the dock? At any rate, a contemporary account records its " irresistible " impression that as he disappeared from sight under sentence of death he was still untouched by contrition and was less harrowed by emotion than those, who had gazed upon him, had been moved by the scene in which they had played a part."

Casement was taken back to prison, and there, helped by the Catholic chaplain, he attained a contentment which had been denied to his feverish activities. The case was heard on appeal and argued with considerable skill by Serjeant Sullivan; inevitably, however, it was lost. And on the 3rd of August, at eight in the morning, Casement—Sir Roger no longer—was hanged at Pentonville.

Casement died at peace, but he left controversy behind him. In the interval between his sentence and his execution, several petitions for his reprieve were put in and obtained a distinguished list of signatures. The general line of argument was one of expediency, that his execution, so long after the crushing of the Irish insurrection, would be interpreted as a vindictive act and would have a bad effect on Anglo-Irish relations; this was supported by an additional claim that Casement had become unbalanced by his labours in the unhealthy climate of the Congo and the Putumayo. The Crown prerogative of mercy could, of course, have been legitimately exercised on this, as on other, occasions. But neither of these two reasons for its exercise seem particularly strong. It is difficult to imagine how any but the most prejudiced person could interpret as an act of vengeance the execution of a man who had conspired against the State in the hour of its peril and who had nevertheless been tried with scrupulous fairness and defended with great skill and distinction; nor can his execution be viewed as an act of particular barbarity, when it is remembered that his actions had been calculated to bring to Ireland too the welter of bloodshed with which Europe was already surfeited.

But there are many who are not content with urging that Casement should have been reprieved. They claim that he was "entitled" to be treated as a prisoner of war, who was captured in an act of warfare. Thus Clement Shorter, who in 1922 published privately twenty-five copies of Bernard Shaw's "Discarded Defence of Roger Casement," writes: "That Casement should have been treated as a prisoner of war I hold to be indisputable. The recent recognition of Ireland's rights as a Free State makes that plea doubly justified." What possible connection the creation of the Irish Free State in 1922 has with the conviction of Casement in 1916 it is difficult to imagine; as well suggest that the Germans would not have been justified in executing traitors in Alsace in 1916 because in 1919 it passed to the French!

Mr Shaw takes the same line and in his "Defence" suggests that that was the plea which Casement should have advanced at the trial. "I saw," he writes, "that if he left himself in the hands of the lawyers, they would make a mess of it; and they *did*." In point of fact, they were far from making a mess of it. Casement's best chance undoubtedly lay in a technical objection, and the defence strove to establish it with great industry and ingenuity; when that failed his counsel put the "Irish" point of view with eloquence and courage. But Mr Shaw would have waived all this, and relied solely on a defence which had no possible foundation in law. He would have had Casement say to the jury: "The Lord Chief Justice will presently tell you . . . he will tell you as he must that legally I am a traitor. But history will not on that account absolve you from the most sacred duty of a jury; the duty of standing on the side of right, truth and justice between all honest laymen and that part of the law that was made against their own consent to destroy them." Unfortunately, the "sacred duty" of the jury is a much less grandiloquent thing than Mr Shaw seems to imagine; it consists in finding on the facts in a given case and bringing in a verdict in accordance with the law and with their finding of the facts. And this is precisely what the jury in the Casement trial, assisted by Lord Reading, did. If Mr Shaw's view of the duty of a jury were to become current, then every verdict might depend on the political and sociological idiosyncrasies of an individual grocer; and that is a chaos from which even Mr Shaw's independent mentality might recoil.

But apart from the legal aspect, the Shorter-Shaw view,

if it may be so termed, is absurd. For briefly what they say is this: " The act of treason is often committed by high-minded and brave men, who, in the event of success—especially if their treason takes the form of trying to win independence for a small community from a big—are usually treated like heroes. It is, therefore, clearly wrong to treat such romantic acts as vulgar crime, and such heroic individuals as common criminals. To applaud Garibaldi and to execute Casement is sheer hypocrisy." But this argument really misses the whole point. Garibaldi was applauded in England because he was not a rebel against England; he was a rebel against Austria, and nobody would have suggested that Austria would not have been right in executing him, if the chance had arisen. Indeed England applauded Garibaldi partly because of the risk he ran of being executed by the Austrians. If, on the other hand, the traitor is always to be excused punishment because of his bravery in risking it, then he need no longer even be a brave man. If there is no danger, there is no bravery; if there is no bravery, there is no need for applause. You cannot at the same time hold people up as heroes and demand that they be allowed the privileged treatment of " heads I win, tails you lose."

If Casement had been treated as a spy or a prisoner of war, it would—as Mr Shaw recognises—have implied a recognition of Ireland as a nation at war. Ireland was at war, but it was at war side by side with England, as fellow peoples of the British Empire. But, apart from this, no action implying Irish independent sovereignty when none such in fact existed, could possibly have been contemplated. A great nation does not grant independence as a side wind; nor should it give it in obedience to a threat of arms. It should give it, if give it it does, as a free gift; but until that time sedition and treason should be treated as the crimes which in law they are. Casement, therefore, was properly tried, and rightly executed. And those who would have had him treated otherwise miss the proper significance of the Casement trial, which is that it demonstrated once again that the act of treason is not incompatible with courage and high qualities, and that neither the stress of war nor the violence of popular prejudice can shake for a moment the full operation of the law and the fair administration of justice in this country.

CHAPTER XXVII

CONCLUSION AND ESTIMATE

THE Casement case was the greatest and most dramatic of the trials presided over by Lord Reading as Lord Chief Justice. It was, however, by no means the last, although circumstances made his tenure of office less active judicially than is customary. For in 1917 he was appointed Special Envoy to the United States, which was by that time an ally in the prosecution of the War, and he continued there as High Commissioner until the end of the War. He returned to England in August of 1918, and before he was due to return to America the Armistice had been signed. This, of course, changed the complexion of events entirely. The appointment of so high a legal officer as High Commissioner had been justified only by the great emergency of War; and even so there had been those who were critical of the Lord Chief Justice's absenteeism. Consequently, when the War was over, it was to be expected that Lord Reading would resume the duties of his legal office. His return to America, therefore, which did not take place till February, 1919, was only for a short stay, in order to arrange for a final departure; and by the Spring he was back again in London to preside once more in the Lord Chief Justice's Court. He was by this time nearing his sixtieth birthday, and it might well have seemed that the Bench would claim him for the rest of his active life. But once again the imperious finger of Destiny beckoned him from his apparent course; beckoned him this time to the responsibility, the gorgeousness and the complexity of viceregal office.

His appointment as Viceroy was made in January, 1921; but before this he had sat in a considerable number of cases as Lord Chief Justice. The most interesting of these was

387

the case famous in criminal law, of Rex v. Beard. Beard had suffocated and killed a girl, while raping her; he was intoxicated at the time, and, although intoxication is ordinarily no defence for a criminal act, it can be a defence to those particular crimes, for the commission of which a special intent is necessary. Now murder falls into this category, for it consists, in Lord Chief Justice Coke's famous definition, in " unlawfully killing a reasonable creature, in being and under the King's peace, with malice aforethought express or implied, the death following within a year and a day." The question, therefore, was: had Beard by killing the girl committed murder? Or did his state of intoxication preclude the forming of the intention or " malice aforethought? " That was the issue, which Lord Reading had to determine. A recent case, Rex v. Meade, had decided that, where the evidence shows that the killer is too drunk to form the intention, the killing is not murder, but manslaughter; Lord Reading followed this case, and reduced the finding of the Court of Instance from murder to manslaughter. The case was further argued in the House of Lords, and in a notable judgment Lord Birkenhead, then Lord Chancellor, reversed Lord Reading's decision. He did this on the grounds that although Beard was too drunk to form the intent to kill, he had not been too drunk to form the intent to commit rape; and since rape is a felony, and since killing in the course of committing a felony is in law murder, Beard was guilty of murder. A curious feature of the case was that Lord Reading sat both in the Court of Criminal Appeal and in the House of Lords. It might have been expected, therefore, that he would have criticised Lord Birkenhead's judgment, and defended the one which he had himself given in the lower Court; but, in point of fact, on the conclusion of Lord Birkenhead's judgment, he merely said, " My Lords, I agree with my noble and learned friend on the Woolsack and have nothing to add." He had the unusual experience, therefore, of acquiescing completely in the reversal of his own judgment.

His American and other preoccupations did not prevent

Lord Reading from presiding over many interesting cases and delivering a number of valuable judgments, notable among them in addition to those already referred to, his judgment in Rex v. Christie, which decided certain points of first importance in connection with the admissibility of evidence. Nor was it his absence and other duties which prevented him from being a great Lord Chief Justice; in point of fact, he was not a great judge, but there is reason to suppose that he would not have been one in any case. He was a good judge, and a learned lawyer; but he was not in the class of Cockburn or Campbell. He had neither the monumental legal erudition nor the literary ability to make judgments of the very first rank. Of course, in being rather less good on the Bench than he had been in practice in the Courts, Lord Reading was not widely different from the mass of very successful advocates, who became judges; there are, however, notable exceptions to this rule such as Lord Russell of Killowen and Lord Birkenhead. But to have expected Lord Reading to have been as successful on the Bench as Rufus Isaacs had been in the Courts would perhaps have been over-exacting.

Lord Reading's activities in America encroached upon his legal duties; his appointment as Viceroy of India severed finally his active connection with the legal profession. With America and India this volume is not concerned; nor has the time in any case arrived to attempt an exact estimate of his services in these directions; and if this is true of war time negotiations it is especially true of the Viceroyalty, for all that has happened in India since the War is a matter of acute and urgent controversy. To see these things truly one must stand further off; they must be allowed time to unfold themselves before the broader background of History. Nor would it be possible, or becoming, to attempt, in Lord Reading's lifetime, an intimate picture of his domestic life. But it is otherwise with his legal career; concluded now some twelve years since, it occupied over thirty years of the prime of a vigorous manhood. The events and importance of that career fall more easily into focus. It is not premature to attempt an exact account and final estimate of that; to provide it has been the purpose of this volume.

Rufus Isaacs' legal career was as varied as it was successful. Pursuit of it has taken us into the intricacies of commerce and the secrets of domesticity, into the councils of crooks and the scheming of traitors. It has reflected for us the ordinary and the exceptional, the lives of the individual and the interests of the nation. We have followed it into sombre Trade Union disputes and into the sprightlier, if more evanescent, bickerings of the Turf. Indeed no department of life is too remote or too lofty to engage the attention of a great legal career. And a great legal career Rufus Isaacs' undoubtedly was; in range and extent it outstripped nearly all rivals. Its greatness was wider than Marshall Hall's, stronger than Lawson Walton's, based on a firmer foundation than Sir Edward Clarke's. Even F. E. Smith, so greatly his superior in the House of Commons, never attained quite his position at the Bar. Of his contemporaries only Carson challenges comparison; these two, since Lord Russell of Killowen, reign supreme.

The greatness of his legal career Rufus Isaacs was unable to transfer to the political field. He was not a House of Commons man, and the reasons for his comparative failure in Parliament have already appeared. Fundamentally, it was a question of temperament. He was not a leader, and therefore could only be an executant statesman; the inspiration had to come from elsewhere. It is thus not surprising that his later appointments flow from his success at the Bar. He was made a Law Officer of the Crown not so much in recognition of his political services as because he was in fact the leader of his profession; and it was that appointment which gave him his chance of distinction outside the purely legal and personal sphere of private practice. It is not too much to say, therefore, that the superstructure of his later career was broadbased on the great position which he had won in the Courts.

In writing of Rufus Isaacs' legal career, one is not writing merely a social document, nor merely the history of romantic achievement; it is as if one were composing at the same time a recipe for success. The success is undoubted; but how was it achieved? We have seen something of the armoury of his equipment, of its strength and its limitations. He had not the dominating personality of a Carson, the soaring eloquence of a Marshall Hall, the profound learning of a Sumner, nor the masterly invective of an F. E. Smith. What then was his secret? He had all the quieter attributes of success. Learned in law, quick and resourceful in argument, penetrative in cross-examination, he had the indispensable adjuncts of forensic success. In addition he was possessed of a memory quite out of the ordinary and a capacity to unravel and elucidate the intricate mysteries of figures, which was unrivalled; in cases like the Whittaker Wright case he was in a class by himself. To these qualities he added a strength, supple and resilient rather than forceful and asser- tive, and an unvarying self-discipline. This self-discipline has been of enormous service to him, for it enabled him to husband his resources, and at the same time diminished the call upon them; there have been numerous instances in this volume to show how his tactics on occasion differed from those that would have been employed by less restrained advocates. With Rufus Isaacs it was in the Courts as in his conduct of life: he did not challenge; he charmed. And, as a result, opposition did not yield—it did not have to; it simply dissolved.

It would not perhaps be true to say that Rufus Isaacs' mental attributes amounted to the possession of a first-class mind. Brought up outside the academic tradition, his stock of learning is slender compared—to cite politicians only— with Lord Balfour's, Lord Haldane's, or Lord Oxford's. More important than that, however, he has not their interest in thought for its own sake; his mind has not busied itself, like theirs, with abstract issues. A man may have a genius for the mechanism of politics or the mechanisms of science; but unless he can apply it philosophically, he has not a first- rate mind. Rufus Isaacs had a genius for the Courts, perhaps a comprehensive genius for affairs; where the end was clear, his mind was adept at devising the means. In application he has combined the readiness and versatility of the terrier with the tenacity of the mastiff. Success has come his way in full measure; it has come inevitably, for his talents were superbly fashioned for its attainment. Whatsoever his hand has found to do, he has done with all his might; such, in epitome, is the career of Rufus Isaacs.

For over seventy years he has been embarked on the voyage of life. In that time he has charted many seas and put in at many harbours. He has sailed placidly in calm seas and weathered high storms. Always he has shown adroit navigation, afraid neither to tack nor to go straight on. He has won the reward of his perseverance, his skill, and his enterprise in the richness of the cargoes that he has borne back, and the splendid variety of the voyages that he has made. He is riding still* the high seas of great affairs, and his sails are still set gallantly to the wind. In the nature of things it cannot be very long before he puts in at his ultimate port; but it would be a rash man who would say what new voyage he may not make and what new harbours he may touch, before he puts in at last for ever.

* May, 1933.

INDEX